To look upon a mummy is to come face to face with our past. This book presents the story of mummification as a practice worldwide. Mummies have been found on every continent, some deliberately preserved as with the ancient Egyptians using a variety of complex techniques, others accidentally by dry baking heat, intense cold and ice, or by tanning in peat bogs. By examining these preserved humans, we can get profound insights into the lives, health, culture and deaths of individuals and populations long gone. The first edition of this book was acclaimed as a classic. This readable new edition builds on these foundations, investigating the fantastic new findings in South America, Europe and the Far East. It will be a 'must-have' volume for anyone working in paleopathology and a fascinating read for all those interested in anthropology, archaeology, and the history of medicine.

Mummies,
Disease &
Ancient Cultures

Mummies,
Disease &
Ancient Cultures

SECOND EDITION

EDITED BY
AIDAN COCKBURN,
EVE COCKBURN
AND THEODORE A. REYMAN

CAMBRIDGE
UNIVERSITY PRESS

393

PUBLISHED BY THE PRESS SYNDICATE OF THE UNIVERSITY OF CAMBRIDGE
The Pitt Building, Trumpington Street, Cambridge CB2 1RP, United Kingdom

CAMBRIDGE UNIVERSITY PRESS
The Edinburgh Building, Cambridge CB2 2RU, United Kingdom
40 West 20th Street, New York, NY 10011-4211, USA
10 Stamford Road, Oakleigh, Melbourne 3166, Australia

First published 1980
Abridged paperback edition 1983
Reprinted 1984, 1985, 1988, 1992
Second edition published 1998

Printed in the United Kingdom at the University Press, Cambridge

Typeset in Quadraat 11/14 pt   [SE]

A catalogue record for this book is available from the British Library

Library of Congress Cataloguing in Publication data

Mummies, disease, and ancient cultures / edited by Aidan, Eve
  Cockburn, and Theodore A. Reyman.
      p.   cm.
    Includes Index.
    ISBN 0 521 58060 9 (hardback).
    ISBN 0 521 58954 1 (paperback)
    1. Mummies.   2. Paleopathology.   I. Cockburn, Aidan.
  II. Cockburn, Eve.   III. Reyman, Theodore A. (Theodore Allen), 1931–.
  GN293.M85   1998
616′.00932–dc21   97-26894 CIP

ISBN 0 521 58060 9 hardback
ISBN 0 521 58954 1 paperback

To Aidan, who started it all

Contents

Contents

Contributors

Bernardo T. Arriaza, Department of Anthropology and Ethnic Studies, University of Nevada, Las Vegas, USA and Universidad de Tarapacá, Arica, Chile.

Antonio Ascenzi, Professor Emeritus, Department of Experimental Medicine and Pathology, 'La Sapienza' University, Rome, Italy.

Robin A. Barraco, formerly Department of Physiology, Wayne State University School of Medicine, Detroit, Michigan, USA (died 1996).

Paolo Bianco, Department of Experimental Medicine, University of L'Aquila, L'Aquila, Italy.

Angela Calder, O'Malley, Canberra, ACT, Australia.

Felipe Cárdenas-Arroyo, Departamento de Antropología, Universidad de Los Andes, Santafé de Bogotá, Colombia.

Aidan Cockburn, formerly President, Paleopathology Association, Detroit, Michigan, USA (died 1981).

Eve Cockburn, Paleopathology Association, Detroit, Michigan, USA.

Mahmoud Y. El-Najjar, Institute of Archaeology and Anthropology, Yarmouk University, Irbid, Jordan.

Christian Fischer, Director, Silkeborg Museum, Silkeborg, Denmark.

Gino Fornaciari, Department of Oncology, Paleopathology Laboratory, University of Pisa, Italy.

James E. Harris, formerly Department of Orthodontics, University of Michigan, Ann Arbor, Michigan, USA (retired).

Gerald D. Hart, formerly Toronto East General Hospital, Toronto, Ontario, Canada (retired).

J. P. Hart Hansen, Department of Pathology, Gentofte Hospital, University of Copenhagen, Denmark.

Brian K. Ingalls, Northville, Michigan, USA.

Ekkehard Kleiss, Professor Emeritus, Department of Embryology, Universidad de los Andes, Mérida, Venezuela.

Peter K. Lewin, Hospital for Sick Children, Toronto, Ontario, Canada.

Nicholas B. Millet, Curator, Egyptian Department, Royal Ontario Museum, Toronto, Ontario, Canada.

Iwataro Morimoto, The Japanese Red Cross College of Nursing, Tokyo, Japan.

Thomas M. J. Mulinski, Chicago, Illinois, USA.

Henrik Nielsen, Department of Medical Biochemistry and Genetics, The Panum Institute, University of Copenhagen, Denmark.

Derek N. H. Notman, Department of Radiology, HealthSystem Minnesota, Minneapolis, Minnesota, USA.

Tamotsu Ogata, formerly Department of Anatomy, Niigata University School of Medicine, Niigata, Japan (died 1980).

William H. Peck, Curator of Ancient Art, Detroit Institute of Arts, Detroit, Michigan, USA.

Peng Long-xiang, Electron Microscopy Laboratory, Hunan Medical University, Changsha, Hunan, People's Republic of China.

Paul V. Ponitz, formerly Department of Orthodontics, University of Michigan, Ann Arbor, Michigan, USA (died 1995).

Graeme L. Pretty, Department of Anatomical Sciences, University of Adelaide Medical School, Adelaide, Australia.

Karl J. Reinhard, Department of Anthropology, University of Nebraska – Lincoln, Lincoln, Nebraska, USA.

Theodore A. Reyman, formerly Department of Pathology, Mount Carmel Mercy Hospital, Detroit, Michigan, USA (retired).

Contributors

Conrado Rodríguez Martín, Instituto Canario de Paleopatología y Bioantropología, Santa Cruz de Tenerife, Islas Canarias, Spain.

Kiyohiko Sakurai, School of Graduate Studies, Showa Women's University, Taishido, Shibuya, Tokyo, Japan.

A. T. Sandison, formerly Department of Pathology, Western Infirmary, Glasgow, Scotland (died 1982).

Edmund Tapp, Centre for Forensic and Paleopathology, Chorley, Lancashire, England.

Ingolf Thuesen, The Carsten Niebuhr Institute of Near Eastern Studies, University of Copenhagen, Denmark.

John W. Verano, Department of Anthropology, Tulane University, New Orleans, Louisiana, USA.

James M. Vreeland, Jr, Arequipa, Peru, formerly Department of Anthropology, University of Texas, Austin, Texas, USA.

Tony Waldron, Institute of Archaeology, University College London, England.

Wu Zhong-bi, Department of Ultrastructural Pathology, Tongji Medical University, Wuhan, Hubei, People's Republic of China.

Michael R. Zimmerman, The University of Pennsylvania, Philadelphia, Pennsylvania, USA.

Aidan Cockburn
30 May 1912 – 19 September 1981

Scholar, scientist, physician, administrator, wit, raconteur; these words, among many others, describe Aidan Cockburn. His contributions as an epidemiologist, specialist on the evolution and history of disease, and on paleopathology established him as an authority on these and other subjects long before his death in 1981. In a sense, however, words cannot capture the essence of the man. Aidan was a man of catholic interests and knowledge. He lived and worked in many countries of the world. (When I first met him his cat had travelled far more extensively than I – a fact that he found most amusing.) The world view that arose from his global work and travel experience gave him a special perspective on many of the problems regarding the evolution of disease. He was the first to introduce me to the obvious but often overlooked concept that evolutionary processes would generally lead to the attenuation of virulence in bacterial disease organisms; the organism that kills its host usually dies as well, thus natural selection will favor the disease organism that does not kill its host. This concept is crucial to an understanding of the history of disease and to the interpretation of paleopathological specimens.

Aidan's influence on the development of paleopathology has been enormous. With Eve Cockburn, he founded the Paleopathology Association in 1973. This international and interdisciplinary organization today has a membership of more than 500. Although his great interest was in the general area of paleopathology, he became best known for his specific interest in the study of mummies. Despite this emphasis he gave enthusiastic support to all research on paleopathology. His interest in and support of the study of mummy tissues stimulated a whole new range of studies, many of which involve the latest technology and methodology in science and medicine.

Mankind may never completely eradicate infectious disease but certainly the perspectives provided or stimulated by Aidan will do much to illuminate those factors that affect human health and provide the time perspective needed to continue the quest to minimize the effects of disease on human life.   DONALD ORTNER, SEPTEMBER 1982

AIDAN COCKBURN

Preface to the first edition

Why mummies? That is the question we are often asked. How did an other-wise respectable physician and a senior member of the University of Oxford, whose field is modern language and literature, find themselves regarded as 'the mummy experts'?

The story begins in Aidan's early medical years. He is cursed with the 'satiable curiosity of the elephant's child and always wants to know 'why?'. Why are diseases the way they are? Were they always like this? Where did they come from? Under the influence of the nineteenth-century ideas of Darwin and Huxley, he worked out a series of theories that would explain how disease organisms evolved, how they changed during the different epochs of the development of human society, and how the interaction of these two streams of evolution resulted in our current infectious disease patterns. Eve, with her nonscientific background, found herself looking at these ideas with the cold and critical eye of an outsider, then helping with the sorting and organizing of theories – and so a partnership was born.

After Aidan's first two books on the evolution of infectious diseases (1963 and 1967), there was a hiatus of several years. Then came two casual conversa-tions, which led to the present line of research and the present book. At a meeting of the American Association of Physical Anthropologists in Boston in 1971, Lucile St. Hoyme of the Smithsonian Institution remarked: 'Aidan, why don't you apply for a grant from the Smithsonian to study in some area where you could find facts to back up your theories? We have local currency funds available in at least seventeen countries'. She listed them, and the obvious one that would provide a fertile field for research was Egypt. Aidan applied for and received a grant to go to Egypt on a reconnaissance trip to investigate the pos-sibility of organizing a project for the autopsy of large numbers of mummies, thus obtaining facts to back up his, until then, largely speculative ideas.

Then came casual conversation number two. Eve was talking to William H. Peck, Curator of Ancient Art at the Detroit Institute of Arts, about the projected trip. Bill asked whether Aidan had ever autopsied or in any way examined a mummy before, and when the answer was no, he suggested that Aidan might like to practice on one of those in storage in the institute's basement. The story of this first, primitive autopsy has already been fully described (*Smithsonian*, November 1973); its importance lies in the idea of examining mummies in American museums rather than those in Egypt.

While in Egypt, Aidan met David O'Connor, who became a major contributor to the final program. At the Pennsylvania University Museum, where he was Egyptian curator, there were several mummies, and David invited Aidan to examine these if he needed to. The first autopsy (PUM I), conducted in Philadelphia at the university, was an unmitigated disaster. No one really knew what to do, and readers of this book will find only passing reference to the project – but it *was* a valuable learning experience. The media had been invited and turned up in full force, so the examination became a three-ring circus, with photographers and cameramen taking over the autopsy room; at one stage there was even a class of visiting third-graders, complete with teachers, wandering through and getting underfoot. Not an atmosphere conducive to serious scientific work!

However, three more mummies were provided by David and successfully autopsied in Detroit, with conditions strictly controlled. The Smithsonian Institution, the Detroit Institute of Arts, and Wayne State University School of Medicine collaborated in the sponsorship of these studies. The first study, of PUM II, became the basis of the Paleopathology Association. Papers presented at the symposium held in conjunction with the autopsy, which had been given the somewhat fanciful name of 'Death and Disease in Ancient Egypt', were printed with a covering letter of information under the grandiose title, *Paleopathology Newsletter*, Number 1. At that time, it really was debatable whether there would ever be an issue number two! However, the publication found an immediate audience, and so the Paleopathology Association was born. There are no association dues, no formal organization, no by-laws. The *Newsletter* is now a viable entity, with more than 300 subscribers in 25 countries, and it is from these that contributors to the present book are drawn. During the past 5 years, a great deal of major scientific work has been performed, all on a strictly voluntary basis. People work because they are interested, consumed by that same 'satiable curiosity that started Aidan off in the first place. We are grateful for what their enthusiasm and energy has produced – and we hope readers of this book will feel the same.

EVE COCKBURN, SEPTEMBER 1978

Preface to the second edition

In the twenty years since Aidan and I first started working on *Mummies, Disease and Ancient Cultures*, the pace of discovery and change has been remarkable. We started from the 1971-75 series of autopsies carried out by our little group on Egyptian mummies, then decided to be adventurous by adding Peruvian. As we continued working, we were surprised to realise how ubiquitous the practice was, and so we continued to add new reports as we went along. Although we were not aware of it at the time, most of the types of mummification described in the first edition had actually appeared in Pettigrew's pioneering 1834 book – as we were humbled to discover some time later.

What a huge change occurred during the next few years! When Cambridge University Press decided in 1995 that it was time for an update, Theodore Reyman (my new co-editor) and I found ourselves suffering from an *embarras de richesses*. Some of the chapters needed very little revision. As far as ancient Egypt is concerned, the facts about mummification practices have been well documented for many years, and so chapter 1 stays virtually untouched. There have been some interesting discoveries about diseases there in ancient times, but A. T. Sandison's classic account (chapter 2) needed no serious change, just updating with additional material. Chapter 3 on dentistry and dental practices reflects the author's ongoing research during the past twenty years, told from today's vantage point, and the four elaborate case reports describing the autopsies of Egyptian mummies carried out by the founders of the Paleopathology Association and their colleagues (chapters 4, 5, and 6) have been condensed to some extent. This was done by eliminating details that do not need to be explained to today's audience; many of the techniques, brand new in mummy studies at that time, are now standard practice in the examination of ancient bodies.

With the existing chapters on mummies of the Americas and mummies of the world, several needed to have only small amounts of information added to bring them up to date, but in other instances, we were overwhelmed. Given the constraints of keeping the most important parts of the original book (and staying within manageable size), it proved impossible to include all the new material we would have liked. For example, in chapter 14 we have included a full description of only one kind of Chinese mummy, although there are others. In chapter 12, we have omitted the extremely interesting religious mummies of Italy, choosing instead to concentrate on the remarkable series of investigations carried out by Gino Fornaciari and his team on members of the Italian aristocracy, mummified by a method that seems to have been unique to that part of the world. (Anyone who has seen the three and a half hour uncut version of *The Leopard* will remember the scene where the Duke looks into the gentlemen's retiring room at the ball, an event at which he is constantly reminded of his own mortality; the collection of chamber pots that adorn the floor would have been a chilling reminder of his future fate.) As Christopher Parish so presciently said, when asked whether he was in favor of bringing out a second edition, 'the subject really deserves a brand new book'.

One major change that has occurred, a change detrimental to paleopathological studies of any human remains, is the drive for 'repatriation', i.e., the return of bodies kept in anthropology collections to their descendants for reburial, plus a refusal to allow any examination by scientific methods. There is no doubt whatsoever that in the past human remains from indigenous peoples were carelessly handled without regard to the sensitivities of their descendants, but now serious researchers are paying the price. It is no use, as the Paleopathology Association found out, to list all the great advantages that will accrue from the study of ancient human remains; in many parts of the world, the native peoples have been too deeply hurt by past lack of respect for their feelings to believe they have any duty to give up the bodies of their ancestors in order to achieve hypothetical medical advances in the future. Countries that have suffered from this drive towards repatriation include the United States, Israel, and particularly Australia. It proved impossible, for example, to get permission to reprint the figures that showed actual aboriginal bodies in the chapter on Australian mummies, and the authors of the chapters on mummies from the southern United States and Alaska voluntarily withdrew their photographs of human bodies, in deference to the sensibilities of the descendants concerned.

On the other hand, in other parts of the world that have remained unhindered by such restraints, mummy research has proliferated. In the first edition, Guanche mummies appeared as a less than two page mention, cobbled together from papers published by Ernest Hooton and Don

Brothwell. From that tiny beginning, which led me to visit the Museo Antropológico y Etnográfico in 1985 while on holiday in the Canary Islands, there developed a major research program (the Cronos Project). This in turn sparked the formation of a World Committee on Mummy Studies, the first World Congress on Mummy Studies in 1992 in the Canaries, the second World Congress on Mummy Studies in 1995 in Cartagena, Colombia, and the Third, now scheduled for 1998 in Arica, Chile. The wealth of new material and new research discovered through these international meetings truly boggles the mind. All these programs have benefited from the tremendous advances in technology that have developed during the past 20 years. We need mention only the magic words aDNA (ancient DNA), CT (computed tomography) scanning, paleonutrition studies, and trace element analysis to give an idea of the vistas that are opening up in this discipline. These advanced investigative techniques will be dealt with in greater depth in chapter 16.

Finally, I must acknowledge the huge debt I owe to Theodore Reyman, my co-editor, without whose willingness to take on the job I would never have considered agreeing to this second edition. We are deeply grateful to our authors, many of them Paleopathology Association members, who have shown tremendous enthusiasm for the project. I have also received generous help and co-operation from many other members, but in particular, I must mention Patrick Horne, who made excellent suggestions in the early planning stages and was a valuable resource for references, especially in dealing with South American subjects. Arthur Aufderheide was unfailingly courteous and helpful when phoned about a looming crisis – even during the time that he himself was struggling to meet a deadline for his own Cambridge University Press book. I could always rely on finding Donald Ortner at his desk by 7 am, ready to field my phone calls, Charles Merbs was a great consultant on numerous details that escaped me, and Keith Manchester joined in the review and discussion of the original outline. Takao Suzuki helped immeasurably, first in re-establishing contact with Kiyohiko Sakurai, whose original chapter on Japanese mummies (chapter 14) needed no change, then by finding the right person to write an addendum. We are deeply grateful to Kenneth Werner, commissioning editor for the first edition, who offered invaluable advice based on his past experience, but with an outsider's impartiality.

I would also like to acknowledge two people who were not able to participate. It was with great regret that we accepted Graeme Pretty's forced withdrawal due to serious health problems. His knowledge and understanding of mummification among the aboriginal peoples of Australia and Melanesia is unsurpassed and irreplaceable, and even without an update, his original chapter, co-authored with Angela Calder, is fascinating. We were also sorry that Svante Pääbo was unable to discuss his seminal work on aDNA in mummies, though delighted to know that (to quote) 'the first edition of your book was a great inspiration to me when I started my own work'. Let us hope that this second edition can be as stimulating.

EVE COCKBURN, MARCH 1997

REFERENCE

Pettigrew, T. J. 1834. *A History of Egyptian mummies.*
    London: Longman, Rees, Orme, Brown, Green,
    and Longman.

Introduction

AIDAN COCKBURN

What is a mummy? For most people, the word immediately brings to mind visions of Egypt and, in particular, pictures of a body wrapped in swaddling bands of cloth. This was the original idea of the term, and indeed from the earliest days of antiquity, the preserved bodies of ancient Egypt have gripped the imagination of all who knew about them, whether rich or poor, educated or not. This was so much the case that when the Romans took over Egypt and found the art of preservation to be badly degenerated, they tried to revive the old ways. But it was too late. The ability to read hieroglyphics and ancient writings had been lost when the Greeks under under the Ptolemies conquered the country and introduced their much superior Greek script. However, some form of body preservation was continued up to the eighth century AD. At that time, the invading Arabs swept all before them in Egypt. To them, the practice of embalming the dead was abhorrent, and they put a stop to it.

Today, the term *mummy* has been extended to cover all well-preserved dead bodies. The majority of these are found in dry places such as the sands of deserts or dry caves, where desiccation has taken place rapidly, doing naturally what Egyptians did by artifice. The basic procedure in either process is the same: water is extracted rapidly from the tissues. There is no mystery in this, for people since antiquity have been preserving fish and meat in the same basic ways, either by drying in the sun or by packing in salt. The Egyptian embalmers used a naturally occurring salt called *natron* instead of common table salt and supplemented this with oils, resins, and bitumen. The word *mummies* derived from the Persian *mumeia* or *mum*, meaning 'pitch' or 'asphalt'. This substance had been used in classical times in medical prescriptions, but medieval physicians introduced a refinement with preparations of pitch from Egyptian mummies. These 'exudations' of mummies became very popular and remained so up to the nineteenth century. The first use of the word referring to medicine dates back to the early fifteenth century

Introduction

(*Encyclopaedia Britannica* 1911). As applied to a preserved body, however, the earliest record is 1615 (*Oxford English dictionary*).

Occasionally, bodies are found preserved in other ways. Most of these are frozen, like an Inca boy who had been sacrificed on a high mountain in Chile. Apparently, he had been drugged and left to freeze. In Siberia, mammoths and extinct horses have been found in the permafrost. In the Altai mountains of Russia, Scythian bodies from about 400 BC have been recovered, encased in ice, from their tombs. The first use of *mummy* applied to a body frozen in ice was in 1727 (*Oxford English dictionary*).

More baffling is the wonderfully preserved corpse of a Chinese princess of 2000 years ago. The coffin in the tomb was hermetically sealed and still contained the preserving fluid, a weak mercurial solution. The tissues were still elastic and the joints could be bent. Whether this survival was attributable to the exclusion of oxygen, as suggested by the Chinese scientists, or to the mercurial solution, or to a combination of both is uncertain.

Serious scientific studies of mummies on an organized basis began in Egypt shortly after the turn of the century (Dawson 1938). This coincided with the period when Egypt was dominated by the British and with the foundation of a school of medicine and the creation of the first Aswan Dam. The two events were interrelated. The first great dam at Aswan was completed in 1902, and the reservoir behind it was filled in the spring of 1903. By this action, the First Cataract on the Nile was obliterated, Philae was inundated, and much of the valley of the Nile was flooded. Many antiquities were ruined and many burials destroyed by the inundation and seepage.

Much public resentment had been expressed at this destruction of historical records, and the pathetic sight of the Temple of Philae, standing half drowned in the muddy water, had appealed to innumerable tourists as a sacrifice of the beautiful and historic on the altar of modern utilitarianism. In 1907, the Egyptian Government proposed to increase the height of the dam by another seven meters. Such a project entailed the flooding of a very large area. The Government wisely decided that before the inundation took place, the area should be thoroughly surveyed and examined. All antiquities were to be recorded; all burials were to be examined, described, photographed, and rescued before the raised Nile could reach them.

(Wood Jones in Dawson 1938)

Coincidental with this event was the founding of the English-language Government School of Medicine in Cairo on the ruins of the former French school, which had become defunct 10 years earlier. The professors at the school were excellent, and three of them shaped the future of the study of mummies for decades. They were Grafton Elliot Smith (anatomy), Armand Ruffer (bacteriology), and Alfred Lucas (chemistry). Elliot Smith left Egypt after 7 years to return to England, but for the rest of his life he continued to develop the ideas he had conceived in Egypt. Ruffer explored means of examining soft tissues, and his techniques are still used today. The world lost a distinguished scientist when he was killed during World War I, while serving in a hospital ship that was sunk. Lucas continued in Egypt; when Tutankhamun's tomb was found, he was called in as a consultant. Elliot Smith made the greatest impact at the time, but today it is Armand Ruffer who reigns supreme in the field of paleopathology.

Elliot Smith began his studies of Egyptian bodies in the Thebaid in 1901, and in 1905 he made the first detailed examinations of the technique of mummification. In early 1903, the tomb of Pharoah Tuthmosis IV was found, and Maspero, the director of the Service des Antiquités, ordered that the mummy of the king be unwrapped and examined. The result was a public spectacle for the elite of Cairo, but the examination had no scientific value. However, Elliot Smith was able to make a later, private examination that included roentgenography. At that time, there was only one X-ray machine in Cairo, so Elliot Smith and Howard Carter took the rigid pharaoh in a cab to the nursing home to have it X-rayed. This was a historic first. Following this, Elliot Smith made a study of all the royal mummies found in the two great caches of Deir el-Bahri (1881) and the tomb of Amenophis (1898). Later he investigated a series of mummies from different periods in order to determine how the embalming process had changed over the centuries. On a visit to his native Australia, he found two mummies of Papuans from the Torres Strait in a museum in Adelaide. These had so many features in common with the mummies of Egypt that he developed his concept of cultural diffusion, claiming that the idea of mummification had spread from Egypt to the Torres Strait. Pretty and Calder discuss this theory in chapter 13.

The investigations that resulted from the raising of the Aswan Dam proved beyond the capacity of the staff of the Government Medical School, so additional assistance, notably that of W. R. Dawson and Frederic Wood Jones, was obtained from England. The task was so great that in one month in one small area, the archeologists uncovered the tombs of 2000 persons. The workers did their best, but by modern standards the whole operation was a very crude and rushed affair. Under similar circumstances, it is doubtful whether we could have done any better today. Regardless of this, the pathologies of ancient Egypt were revealed for the first time. In all, autopsies were performed on about 8000 mummies.

After that initial period of excitement, work on ancient bodies dwindled to almost nothing until recent times, when an even bigger Aswan Dam was built and the whole business of saving ancient relics began anew.

Sir Armand Ruffer's work was not in the blistering heat of the exposed desert, but within the four walls of his laboratory. Whereas Elliot Smith measured bones and studied mummification, Ruffer explored the possibility of restoring ancient tissues to something approximating their condition before death. He was so successful that Ruffer's fluid is still in use today. He was the first to show *Schistosoma* ova in kidneys, bacteria in tissues, and organized structures in organs dead for two or three millennia. We must all salute his memory.

Lucas, a painstaking chemist, analyzed the materials used by ancient Egyptians. By modern standards, his techniques seem old fashioned, but his results have never been surpassed. His work (1962) is a classic that even today is indispensable. He also experimented with mummification. According to Herodotus, the body was immersed in a large vat that contained a solution of natron, although apparently this interpretation depends on the translation of a single word. If the word is taken in its other meaning, the interpretation is different. Lucas doubted that immersion in a solution of natron would produce mummies as we know them today, so he took pigeons, soaked them as described, and found that the flesh became soft and separated from the bones. Typical mummies could be produced by packing dry natron inside the birds and covering them with the salt externally. Treated this way, they dried out quickly. The process was so successful that decades later his mummified pigeons still sit in the Department of Antiquities just as he left them, though kept at room temperature without any special care for so many years.

How many mummies are there in the world? This question is often asked, especially in criticism of the sometimes destructive methods used in an autopsy. The implication is that something irreplaceable is being destroyed, but this is not always correct, for two of the six mummies studied by our group have enhanced in value and are now on exhibition in major museums instead of being hidden in basements.

A head count of mummies is not possible, but some idea of the total number can be gained by a review of their history. In desert areas of North Africa that have been dry for thousands of years, large numbers of bodies must still remain preserved in the sand. In Peru the same applies, with the additional factors of careful burial and wrapping in cotton. So over a period of 2000 or 3000 years, many millions of bodies must have been interred. To start with, artificial mummification in Egypt was probably reserved for the pharaoh, his family, and the nobles; but eventually, as everyone wanted to live for eternity, the practice spread. Even if the population had been no more than 1 million people (and surely it was much more), with an average life expectancy of 40 years, about 1 million mummies would have been laid in the ground every 40 years. In the course of 2000 years this would amount to more than the present population of Egypt.

The question of numbers was discussed in Egypt in 1972 with officials from the Department of Antiquities. They say that tombs containing mummies are discovered almost every time a new road or airfield is constructed. There are so many mummies that those that appear to be of no special interest are reburied in the sand.

On the other hand, Egypt has been exporting or using mummies for centuries, so vast numbers must have been destroyed or dispersed. The process started in the fifteenth century, when it was claimed that ground-up mummy had medicinal properties, and this became an expensive and valued remedy for many diseases. How many hundreds of tons of mummy tissues were swallowed by credulous sufferers, before the practice died out early in the nineteenth century, is anyone's guess.

Another drain on the mummy population in Egypt was caused by lively interest in the Western world, possibly sparked by reports from the savants who accompanied Napoleon to that country. By the end of the nineteenth century, it was *de rigueur* for every museum to have at least one mummy on exhibition. Even today many small towns have a specimen dating from this period, although the larger museums frequently relegate the bodies to the basement. In Canada during the nineteenth century, mummy cloth was used in the manufacture of paper. Because the supply of rags for paper making proved inadequate, Canadian paper manufacturers imported thousands of mummies just for their wrappings. What happened to the bodies is not known.

In *Innocents abroad*, Mark Twain tells of another way in which mummies were destroyed. They were used instead of coal in the engines of the newly constructed railway! Some mummies were destroyed in areas where irrigation was extended and the level of subsoil water rose. This was especially true in the delta region, where silt from the Nile pushed the land increasingly into the Mediterranean and the land sank slightly as a result of the extra weight.

The biggest destruction of mummies came in the period of dam building that began about 1900 and continues to the present. More and more land was covered by water, and any bodies interred there were damaged. Rescue operations touched only the fringe of the problem and in any event, most of the bodies found were simply reinterred after a preliminary examination, then left to the mercy of the rising waters. However, Nubia and the areas above the

Aswan dams were not noted for the practice of artificial mummification, and so far the prime areas have been left undisturbed by this particular form of cultural development.

When all these factors are taken into account, it seems probable that many hundreds of thousands of mummies have been lost; even so, millions still remain in the sands and tombs of Egypt. Add to this figure the millions in Peru and other dry areas of South America, and it becomes clear that a huge store remains for future generations to study.

Of course, mummification was not confined to humans: animals were treated the same way. The Egyptians embalmed specimens of almost every animal in their ecosystem – ranging from bulls through birds, cats, fish, and bats down to shrews – and the numbers were enormous. Their sacred bird, the ibis, may have become extinct simply because every one found was killed and stuffed.

It is in the cold regions, however, that future studies on animals look most promising, especially for the field of biochemistry. The frozen mammoths of Siberia are well known, and a baby mammoth in good condition was recently exposed by a bulldozer in Siberia. Rhinoceroses, horses, and small mammals have also been identified. The permafrost of the Arctic must be a well stocked refrigerator whose contents are virtually unexplored. At the other pole, conditions are different, but the potential is also great. There, the extreme cold and dryness of the air freeze-dry any animals that die on ice or on land. Thousands of dead seals have been found, some thousands of years old, and there are even reports of bacteria remaining alive in the soil after 10000 years. Possibilities like this make the future of mummy research most exciting.

Among the most satisfying discoveries associated with mummies are objects that have been included by chance. Quite apart from the religous ritual and ceremony that appertain to the processing of a body for preservation, objects were occasionally included that were insignificant to the embalmers but shed bright beams of light in corners that would otherwise remain dark for us.

Our own group experienced one such example of serendipity with the finding of a ball of cotton in the wrappings of PUM II. This is the earliest cotton recorded in Western civilization, although the textile was used in both India and America perhaps 2000 years earlier. How it reached Egypt and what it was doing in a mummy's wrappings are matters for conjecture. Meryl Johnson, who was the first to notice it, is inclined to believe that perhaps the ball of cotton was regarded as a valuable object and was included for that reason (see chapter 4).

Another adventitious find was the only example of an Etruscan text that has come down to us (Wellard 1973). It was half a century before any one realized the writing on the shroud was Etruscan, and in that time some 80 percent of the wrappings disappeared. The mummy was bought in 1848 by a Croatian, Michael Barie, who was employed by the Hungarian Chancellery in Alexandria. He took it home with him, and on his death his brother gave it to the museum of Agram (now Zagreb). The museum noted that the wrappings were 'covered with writing in an unknown and hitherto undeciphered language'.

Dr. Heinrich Brugsch, an Egyptologist, viewed the writing and could make nothing of it; he mentioned it to Richard Burton, the famous explorer and linguist, who was at that time British Consul at Trieste. The vice-consul copied part of the text for him, and this was published in the *Transactions of the Royal Society of Literature* in 1882. The previous year Burton had published a book, *Etruscan Bologna*, but in spite of these studies he did not suspect the nature of the writing. In the end, the bandages were sent to the University of Vienna, and there professor Jakob Krall made the proper identification. How this inscribed linen came to be wrapped around a dead Egyptian girl is not known. It has been suggested that the linen had nothing to do with the girl, but that the embalmers simply bought a sheet of second-hand linen and tore it roughly into strips for their purposes. As will be seen in chapter 6, a similar method was used on PUM III. We still do not know what the writing says, though it appears to deal with the religious code of the Etruscan people. Perhaps some day an interpretation will be made that will help us to understand more about these mysterious people.

Why were bodies preserved in this way, to last long periods of time? Naturally preserved bodies have come down to us simply because of accidents or environmental conditions, without deliberate human thought. The general climate or microclimate at the time of death produced a situation in which the tissues were dehydrated or frozen, so that the usual biochemical changes of degradation in dead bodies were inhibited. This occurred in hot dry areas, at high altitudes, or in arctic surroundings.

When, however, deliberate efforts were made to ensure that the body would continue to exist in a form somewhat resembling that of the living person, the question of why this was done and how it was done become matters of considerable interest, going as they do to the very basis of man's attitude to death.

Death is a fearsome thing. Within a brief period – 24 hours in the tropics and a few days elsewhere – a close friend, a relative, or a colleague becomes a bloated, horrifying caricature of the living being; the body melts and eventually turns into a heap of bones. This happened since the origin of life and is a basic fact: everything that lives must die.

The human race has constantly rebelled against this idea, producing various concepts to show that death is not the end and that life in one form or another continues after the physical disintegration of the body. This is the essence of most religions. There are many variations on the theme – the Valhalla of the Vikings, Paradise for Muslims, Resurrection among Christians, the reincarnation beliefs of the Hindus – but the central premise is that death is not final: something better comes afterward.

In most cases where mummies have been preserved deliberately, the objective seems to have been to keep the body intact and recognizable for this afterlife, even to the point of burying with it clothing, food, and utensils for the future. The Egyptians believed that the spirit of a person could not continue to exist if the physical body disappeared; therefore, to attain immortality the body had to be mummified. Eventually, almost all Egyptian bodies were so treated, to universal satisfaction: the people believed they had conquered death.

Not all peoples are afraid of death. One has only to think of Spartans at Thermopylae, Scythian youths going willingly to their deaths at the funeral ceremonies of their kings, sacrificial maidens of the Incas treated with the greatest respect during their lives and dying in full expectation of a magnificent thereafter, Christian martyrs in Roman times welcoming death in a state of ecstasy, or even, in modern times, the kamikaze pilots of Japan. To people like these, death is not a disaster, but the gateway to a better existence in another world.

Looking at the matter on a global scale, we can say that most people believe in some form of life after death and often come to the conclusion that the body of the deceased should be prepared for this continuing existence. This can be achieved either by burying the person along with objects for use in the next life or, better still, by preserving the body itself. It can be noted in passing that almost all dead bodies in the United States are embalmed. This can have no other purpose but to give survivors reassurance that life continues in some way: from the purely public health point of view, it is meaningless.

Throughout the world, nations and tribes have striven to preserve the bodies of their leaders and great men. One unsuccessful effort was that of the Chinese ruler who had a marvellous suit made of small pieces of jade stitched together with gold wires and shaped to enclose his whole body. Jade was believed to preserve bodies, but in this case it was ineffective, and the body inside the suit changed into dust. In Vienna, according to Ekkehard Kleiss (personal communication 1977), there are mummies of the kings and princes of Austria. A peculiar feature here is that in some instances the bodies are kept in one cathedral and the internal organs in another. To this day, the bodies of the Jewish patriarchs and their families are kept in tombs in Israel. It is probable that all of them were mummified as described in the bible.

Among mummies that have been lost are those of the Ptolemies in Egypt. These Greek pharaohs adopted the customs of their conquered country, and that must have included preserving the body after death. The greatest of all the Greek leaders was Alexander, and the site of his tomb in Alexandria has also been forgotten. An active search is even now in progress for the tomb of the world's first known genius, Imhotep, near the pyramid he built for his pharaoh. This step pyramid at Saqqara was the first one, and archeologists feel certain that Imhotep was buried near his master.

Preservation of the body was undertaken not only for the future good of the dead, but often out of fear by the living of the spirits of the dead. If there is life after death, as so many people have believed, then it follows that the ghosts may return to haunt and hurt the living. Therefore, the dead must be placated by adequate care during burial and kept in a friendly state by presents of food and other gifts long after death. The ancestor worship of the Chinese is probably based on such beliefs. The mummies of the Inca rulers were displayed at intervals in the square in Cuzco, as though they were still living, and were offered food and drink.

In many parts of the world, bodies resting in churches, cathedrals, and temples were preserved by accidents of climate or circumstance. I saw one example in the making in 1959 in East Pakistan (now Bangladesh) while fighting a smallpox epidemic. One night in Cox's Bazaar, the district commissioner came to see me and asked if I would visit a monastery 60 km away on a river that formed the boundary with Burma. Some 2000 years ago, there had been 1500 monks there, but now only one was left and he was very ill. On arrival, I was escorted to the temple, but had to enter alone.

The last surviving monk was lying before the statue of Buddha, almost unconscious, scarcely breathing, and with a very feeble heartbeat. His legs were gangrenous, and because this was the hot dry season, they had dried up and were in fact mummified. He could not drink the water I gave him, and it was obvious he was near death: In fact, he died the next day. In time, he would have dried up completely. But in that climate the body could not have stayed mummified for long: with the arrival of the monsoon rains, humidity, insects, rats, and fungi would soon have reduced the soft tissues to dust so that only a skeleton remained.

In many countries, however, bodies like his have survived. A spectacular example is in the Capuchin Catacombs of Palermo, Sicily, where 8000 mummies of men, women, and children, dressed in their best clothes, line the walls, their flesh preserved by the dryness of the air. These mummies represent a cross section of the populace of the nineteenth century, coming from all sections of society. The practice was abandoned in the early twentieth century, but the mummies remain as dressed a hundred or more years ago.

In Venzone, Italy, there are mummies displayed in white sheets in erect positions (one wonders if they survived the recent earthquake that destroyed the town). In Vienna, kings and princes were preserved and their organs distributed among the cathedrals and churches of that city. In Corfu, Greece, the mummy of Saint Spiridion, patron saint of the island, is paraded with full ceremony around the town during his festival. The list is endless.

An advance in embalming technology in which the tissues are infiltrated with paraffin wax first appeared in the Argentine at the beginning of this century. The most superb example of this method is said to be the body of Eva Perón, who appears to be merely asleep in spite of the peregrinations of her remains to Italy and back home again. Many observers have commented on the waxy face of Lenin, and some on that of Stalin, so perhaps they also had paraffin treatment.

This longing for everlasting life has taken a new twist in recent years as a result of advancements in technology. It has long been known that freezing can, to some extent, suspend animation; for example, fish frozen in lake ice sometimes swim away when they thaw out. For decades microbiologists have preserved living viruses, bacteria, and simple organisms by keeping them at very low temperatures. Recently, it was reported from the Antarctic that living bacteria, up to 10 000 years old , have been found deep down frozen in the soil.

It is, therefore, not surprising that a new 'science' of cryogenics has arisen in which the bodies of the dying or recently dead – the time at which the change from life to death takes place is a debatable legal point of considerable importance – are placed into deep freezes for revival in the future.

The reason this procedure is deemed worthwhile is the belief that a disease that kills today is likely to be curable tomorrow. It is hoped that, at some future time, life can be restored and the disease treated. In this way life can be continued, with occasional pauses for renewal, through eternity. Already, numerous bodies have been prepared in this way and stored in lockers at low temperatures. This technique may or may not work, but it will surely supply excellent specimens for research by paleopathologists in the future!

REFERENCES

Dawson, W. R. 1938. *Sir Grafton Elliot Smith*. London: Cape

Lucas, A. 1962. *Ancient Egyptian materials and industries*, 4th. edn. revised and enlarged by J. R. Harris. London: Edward Arnold.

Wellard, J. 1973. *The search for the Etruscans*. New York: Saturday Review Press.

PART I

Mummies of Egypt

I

Mummies of ancient Egypt

WILLIAM H. PECK

In the modern mind no single type of artifact from the ancient world excites more interest than the Egyptian mummy, and no other kind of object is considered more typically Egyptian. The very word *mummy* brings to mind a host of associated ideas – the Egyptian belief in life after death, the seemingly pervasive concern with the notion of death, and the elaborate preparations that were made for it. It is well to state at the outset that religious beliefs made it necessary to preserve the dead, and what seems a preoccupation with death was actually the outgrowth of a love of life and an attempt to prepare for a continuation in the next world of life as it is known in this.

A considerable literature, much of it of a speculative nature, has grown up around the modern interest in the process of mummification. In recent decades the progress of science has done much to dispel earlier misconceptions, but many of these have become firmly fixed and die hard. The process of mummification is still considered to be a 'lost art' by many who would rather remain content with an intriguing mystery than be disappointed with a simple explanation. The process was the result of a continuous development based on trial and error and observable results. The details of technique can now be discussed with some confidence and accuracy.

Modern literature on the subject of mummification is extensive (D'Auria *et al.* 1988; Brier 1994; Taylor 1996); the historic cornerstone of the study in English is Thomas Pettigrew's *History of Egyptian mummies*, published in 1834. For the time at which it appeared, the work was a monumental undertaking. Based on scholarly research and practical experience, Pettigrew's work was a summation of almost all that was known concerning Egyptian funerary practices. He compiled all the ancient sources and commented on them, as well as discussing many examples of mummified remains investigated by or known to him (Figure 1.1). This work is illustrated by engraved plates by George Cruikshank (better known for his satirical drawings) that are the product of careful observation.

Mummies of Egypt

FIGURE I.I. Major sites in ancient Egypt. (Map by Timothy Motz, Detroit Institute of Arts.)

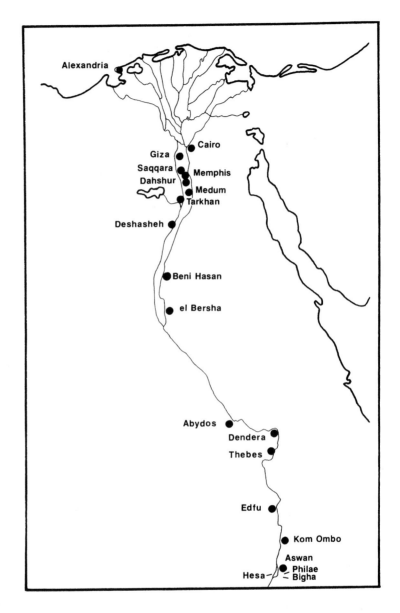

It was not until 1924 that another work of comparable stature appeared. *Egyptian mummies* by G. Elliot Smith and Warren R. Dawson is still a standard text to which the interested reader can turn with confidence. Alfred Lucas was another twentieth-century pioneer in the scientific study of the process of mummification. In addition to many articles on various aspects of the subject, he devoted a chapter to his findings in *Ancient Egyptian materials and industries* (Lucas 1962). His work has been carried on by the Egyptian, Zaki

FIGURE 1.2. Predynastic burial, before 3000 BC, British Museum 32752. The typical flexed position of most predynastic burials is illustrated here, as is the high state of preservation resulting from the dry sand rather than a complicated embalming process. The subject is an adult female.

Iskander (Mokhtar *et al.* 1973).James Harris and Kent Weeks (1973) have published a popular report of the work done on the royal mummies in the Cairo Museum in *X-raying the pharaohs.*

The purpose of mummification in ancient Egypt was twofold. The body of the deceased, it was believed, had to be treated to render it incorruptible. At the same time the physical appearance had to be maintained as nearly as possible to what it had been in life. The Egyptian conception of life after death developed early, as is evidenced by the burials of the predynastic (prehistoric) age. It would seem that the notion of preserving human and animal dead came about naturally in the dry climate of Egypt. Predynastic burials were simple and practical (Figure 1.2). The corpse was placed in a hole in the sand, usually in a contracted position, accompanied by such grave goods as pottery and other useful objects. No embalming process was carried out; in no way was the body prepared (mummified) for the burial, but it was often wrapped in linen, reed matting, or hide. The pit was sometimes lined with matting, boards or bricks, but the cavity that received the body was more grave than tomb. A small tumulus was erected over the grave, never large enough to interfere with the warming effect of the sun. It was the hot, dry sand that served to desiccate the tissue. The result, to be observed in countless examples, is a well preserved corpse. From the simple fact that objects were included with the burial, we can deduce that they were meant to serve the spirit of the dead in some fashion in the next life.

At the beginning of the dynastic age (around 3000 BC), the religious beliefs and accompanying funerary ritual appear to have been already well developed. The tomb structures of early dynastic kings were designed as imitation palaces and fortresses that must have reflected the style of living architecture of the time. The great quantity of funerary offerings in these burials indicates that a king or member of the royal family expected to be able to use such material in a continued existence in the next life. The subsidiary interment of retainers nearby suggests the ability to confer immortality on them, if for no other purpose than to serve their master in the spirit world. As tomb structures became more complex, the position of the body in relation to the surface layers of warm sand was altered; the body was placed lower in the earth, at the bottom of a tomb shaft.

The notion of a 'home' for the spirit continued throughout pharaonic history; the form of the structure underwent many changes, but the fundamental purpose remained the same. In the Old Kingdom the private tomb superstructure became more houselike, providing a protection for the burial, which was placed deep in the earth beneath it. The superstructure also provided the necessary rooms for the conduct of the ritual at the time of the burial and after, as well as a storage area for ritual objects and offerings. Because the development of the tomb resulted in the removal of the body from the surface area of warm sand, it became necessary to invent a technology that would accomplish the preservation of the physical remains, a process that had occurred naturally in more simple times. In all cases where the body of the deceased received 'proper' burial, we can assume that some effort was made to treat the corpse and render it resistant to decay. The key factor in the preservation of the human body, as it was practiced by the Egyptians, is the removal of all body fluids. It is difficult to imagine the impetus for the initial steps in the development of the craft of mummification, but it has been suggested that some accidental knowledge of predynastic burials must have become available to the people of the early dynasties. By simple reasoning, it could have been determined that the removal of body fluid was the most important factor in the preparation of the dead. The inspiration may even have come from observation of the processes of drying meat and fish. In any case, during the first 400 years of pharaonic history, the essential details of Egyptian mummification were evolved.

According to the *Oxford English dictionary*, the word *mummy* is recorded in the English language as early as the fourteenth century. It existed in medieval Latin as *mumia* and was ultimately derived from the Arabic and Persian designations for an embalmed body by way of those for wax or bitumen. In modern usage, the word *mummy* is taken to mean the body of a human or animal that has been embalmed by the ancient Egyptian or some similar method as a preparation for burial. By analogy, many corpses are called 'mummies' even if they have nothing to do with ancient Egypt. As a result, it is common to speak of Peruvian mummies, Aleutian mummies, the mummified Capuchins of Palermo, and the like. In English, the word *mummy* has been used to designate medicinal materials prepared from the mummified bodies of Egypt, a brown pigment from the same source used in oil painting, and, in somewhat more specialized use, as a slang term for Egyptian issues on the English stock exchange. Current in the sixteenth century was the use of the word *mummy* for any dead flesh: 'The water swells a man; and what a thing should I have been, when I had been swel'd? I should have been a mountain of Mummie' (William Shakespeare, *The Merry Wives of Windsor*).

It has been traditional in the past to base any study of mummification on the accounts given by a few classical authors. The few Egyptian texts that can be used to supplement these are tantalizing in the extreme. It is to be hoped that a complete account of the embalming process may be found for some period in Egyptian history, but until now, this has not happened. By accident of preservation, a composition entitled *The ritual of embalming* exists in a fragmentary state in two versions (Goyon 1972). The information it contains is more of a ritual nature than a step-by-step handbook on the technique of mummification. Its material consists of three parts: ceremonial acts to be performed on the mummy, prayers and incantations to be said during the process, and the methods of applying ointments and bandages to some parts of the body (arms, hands, legs, feet, back, and head). If either of the two late Papyri that contain this partial text were more complete, at least a sequence of wrapping the body might be explained. The most important lack is the absence of any information on the earlier stages of the mummification process, including evisceration and desiccation. From a number of minor Egyptian sources on stelae, ostraca, and papyri, the total length of time necessary for the total mummification process is established as 70 days. This includes the long period in which the body was allowed to dry.

The two classical authors who have given the best and most complete account of the process of mummification as they understood it are Herodotus and Diodorus Siculus. The account of Herodotus is by far the better known of the two, probably because the *Persian Wars*, of which it is a part, makes such interesting reading and because his account of Egypt has received such widespread publication. It must always be remembered that he was a Greek from

Halicarnassus writing in the fifth century BC and that he is often accused by modern historians of reporting a considerable amount of what may be termed hearsay evidence. The reliability of Herodotus in regard to his descriptions of Egyptian customs and daily life has been the subject of much contemporary criticism; what he had to say about mummification must be weighed against the physical evidence of the mummies themselves.

Herodotus' account in the Rawlinson translation is as follows:

There are a set of men in Egypt who practice the art of embalming, and make it their proper business. When a body is brought to them these persons show the bearers various models of corpses, made in wood, and painted so as to resemble nature. The most perfect is said to be after the manner of him whom I do not think it religious to name in connection with such a matter; the second sort is inferior to the first, and less costly; the third is the cheapest of all. All this the embalmers explain, and then ask in which way it is wished that the corpse should be prepared. The bearers tell them, and having concluded their bargain, take their departure, while the embalmers, left to themselves, proceed to their task. The mode of embalming, according to the most perfect process, is the following: they take first a crooked piece of iron, and with it draw out the brain through the nostrils, thus getting rid of a portion, while the skull is cleared of the rest by rinsing with drugs; next they make a cut along the flank with a sharp Ethiopian stone, and take out the whole contents of the abdomen, which they then cleanse, washing it thoroughly with palm-wine, and again frequently with an infusion of pounded aromatics. After this, they fill the cavity with the purest bruised myrrh, with cassia, and every other sort of spicery except frankincense, and sew up the opening. Then, the body is placed in natrum for seventy days, and covered entirely over. After the expiration of that space of time, which must not be exceeded, the body is washed, and wrapped round, from head to foot, with bandages of fine linen cloth, smeared over with gum, which is used generally by the Egyptians in the place of glue, and in this state it is given back to the relations, who enclose it in a wooden case which they have made for the purpose, shaped into the figure of a man. Then (Herodotus, *History*, Book II:86) fastening the case, they place it in a sepulchral chamber, upright against the wall. Such is the most costly way of embalming the dead.

If persons wish to avoid expense, and choose the second process, the following is the method pursued: Syringes are filled with oil made from the cedar-tree, which is then, without any incision or disembowelling injected into the bowel. The passage is stopped, and the body laid in natrum the prescribed number of days. At the end of the time the cedar-oil is allowed to make its escape; and such is its power that it brings with it the whole stomach and intestines in liquid state. The natrum meanwhile has dissolved the flesh, and so nothing is left of the dead (Herodotus, *History*, Book II:87) body but the skin and the bones. It is returned in this condition to the relatives without any further trouble being bestowed upon it.

The third method of embalming, which is practiced in the case of the poorer classes, is to (Herodotus, *History*, Book II:88) clear out the intestines with a purge, and let the body lie in the natrum the seventy days, after which it is at once given to those who come to fetch it away.

Herodotus' account may well give a description of the mummification process as it existed in the fifth century and as it may have been related to him, but it must be remembered that over 2000 years of development cannot always be measured by a description of so late a stage. It will be helpful to suggest what can be learned from his account. That the embalmers were a special class of workers we are reasonably certain. The presentation of models of the various classes of mummification to the family cannot be verified, but contained in the description is a reference to 'him whom I do not think it religious to name' (the god Osiris), which may be a reference to small mummiform statues, and an attempted explanation of their purpose. The brain was often removed through the nose, but evidence exists for its removal through the base of the skull and other openings. The incision in the abdomen usually was made on the left side and is seldom found to have been stitched up. Herodotus states emphatically that the body was covered with natron. This part of his description holds the most important key to the process. In earlier translations this was misinterpreted as natron in solution involving a prolonged soaking. It has been proved very satisfactorily that dry natron was used for the important step of desiccating the body and that the 70 days assigned to this stage actually refer to the entire mummification process. If the mummy was given back to the relatives for placement in a coffin, it was probably for an inspection of the embalmer's work. There is little evidence that the mummy was placed standing in the tomb, but mummy cases from the Ptolemaic period do have a baselike section at the foot. Good evidence of the second method exists, for mummies have been found with no abdominal incision, yet with internal organs missing and the anus plugged with linen packing.

Herodotus' account of mummification continues with some details that need not be quoted in full. He says that the bodies of women of high rank or great beauty are not delivered to the embalmers immediately, but after 3 or 4 days to prevent the possibility of intercourse with the dead body. He also adds that the bodies of those that have fallen in the Nile, or have been attacked by crocodiles, must be embalmed by the inhabitants of the nearest city and buried by them. Of the delay in embalming important women there is some evidence, but the second assertion is difficult to prove .

The second important classical source for the process of mummification is the account of Diodorus Siculus. A native of Sicily, as his name implies, he drew heavily on Herodotus, added a few details, and has left us some additional information. Because he was writing in the first century AD and because he agrees so much with Herodotus, it is hard to believe that his account contains an accurate description of mummification in his own time. To Herodotus' statement that embalmers were of a special class, he adds that the occupation was hereditary. This is likely, considering the number of other trades of ancient Egypt that were passed on in families. Diodorus adds designatory titles for the specialists who performed the different stages of the process. He identifies the heart and kidneys as having been left in place in the body when the other organs were removed, which seems to be accurate considering the number of times the heart has been found in mummified remains. He says that the cleansed corpse was treated with cedar oil and other substances, but omits mention of the removal of the brain.

After listing the three grades of mummification, Diodorus describes only the most expensive, but gives prices for all three. Two interesting details are added in his account. According to him, the embalmer who made the incision in the side, even though it was necessary to the embalming process, had to flee to escape the wrath of his fellow workmen. The explanation given is that any injury to the body of the deceased had to be punished, and this suggests that the ritual of protecting the corpse was taken very seriously by the practitioners of the embalming craft. The second addition supplied by Diodorus is a description of the embalmed body, which, according to him, was preserved in every detail. So lifelike was the state of preservation that the body could be kept as sort of a display piece for the edification of the living. This agrees with Petrie's theory that some mummies of the Roman period must have been on view in the home for a considerable time before they were interred. Petrie was referring to mummies that had painted face coverings; the implication in Diodorus is that the face was still visible. The latter would be particularly curious and is not supported by the evidence of existing mummies.

In addition to Herodotus and Diodorus, Elliot Smith and Dawson refer to several papyri that give additional information, such as the prices of the various materials used in the mummification process. They also cite several late references to Egyptian embalming from Plutarch, Porphyry, Augustine, and others. For a somewhat distant source that contains mention of mummification, the Book of Genesis in the Old Testament should be quoted: 'And Joseph commanded his servants, the physicians, to embalm his father; and the physicians embalmed Israel (Jacob)' (Gen. 50:2); 'And forty days were fulfilled for him; and so are fulfilled the days of those which are embalmed; and the Egyptians mourned for him, three score and ten days' (Gen. 50:3); 'So Joseph died, being an hundred and ten years old; and they embalmed him, and he was put into a coffin in Egypt' (Gen. 50:22). These short statements from the Old Testament add little to the Egyptian or classical sources beyond suggesting that the author had some familiarity with, or access to, a tradition concerning Egyptian mummification.

No ancient Egyptian illustrations of the mummification process exist as such. The tomb paintings that have been preserved depict stages in the ritual and the offerings of prayers, but none of the physical treatment of the body itself. There are numerous instances in which the mummy is shown on the funerary bier, while it is being transported to the tomb, and before the tomb entrance at the time of the Opening of the Mouth ceremony, but the physical mummification seems not to have been an appropriate subject for tomb decoration. Any modern study of the process of mummification is dependent, then, on the physical remains of mummified bodies supplemented by the Egyptian, classical, and other references that deal with mummification and that have to be tested against the examples of mummification preserved.

The preservation of buried bodies in the predynastic age has already been commented on. The state of the development of the art of mummification in the early dynastic period is difficult to determine and must be inferred from the evidence of examples of later times. From Petrie's excavation of the Royal Tombs at Abydos came the bones of an arm that was wrapped in linen and still decorated with jewelry, but this indicates only the use of wrapping and gives no indication concerning the other preparations of the body. Quibell found at Saqqara the remains of a female of the Second Dynasty (2780–2635 BC). A contracted burial contained in a wooden coffin, the corpse was wrapped in over 16 layers of linen, but again, the condition of preservation made it impossible to determine exactly how the body had been treated. One important burial from the beginning of the Fourth Dynasty does a great deal more to suggest the state to which the science had progressed. In the early years of this century, the Boston – Harvard expedition, working at Giza under the direction of G. A. Reisner, discovered a tomb of Queen Hetepheres, the wife of Sneferu and the mother of Cheops (c. 2500 BC). Apparently, the remains of the queen had been entombed first at some other location, perhaps Dahshur, for the simple shaft tomb at Giza gave every appearance of a reburial. When the stone sarcophagus was opened, the body was missing, but the compartmented chest that contained the queen's viscera was found undisturbed. The packages of internal organs were still preserved in a solution of natron. The fact that the solution was still liquid after 4500 years was incredible, but the real value of the discovery is the evidence it gives for the developed practice at this early time of the removal of the viscera and their inclusion in the burial in a special container of their own. The course of events to be inferred is obvious. At some point between the end of the predynastic period and the time of Hetepheres' burial, the technique developed of removing from the body those organs that were most likely to decay. It is not surprising that, in the 500 years this historical period covers, methods of embalming should have developed to such an advanced state.

The outward form of such vessels used in the preservation of the viscera varied during the dynastic period. In the case of Hetepheres, the container was a compartmented chest of alabaster. Individual canopic jars of the Fourth Dynasty exist. The idea of sets of four containers (or one divided into four parts) continues throughout much of dynastic history. The form changes – a miniature coffin occasionally replaced the jars – but the central idea was that the parts removed from the body were still a part of it and had to be treated as the body was, as well as being buried with it. The tradition was so strong that in the late period, when organs were returned to the body cavity after being treated, dummy or imitation jars were still included in the burial.

By the Fourth Dynasty, the techniques of mummification had advanced so far that they may be studied in detail. That the process took a considerable time is suggested by the lack of well preserved evidence from the earlier dynasties. A single foot found in the burial chamber of the Step Pyramid at Saqqara, tentatively identified as once a part of the mummy of Zoser, offers no evidence about the techniques of mummification, but it does suggest, from the layers of linen wrapping, that the corpse was padded out in some semblance of a lifelike form.

The number of preserved bodies from the Fourth Dynasty on (and, of course, the number of tombs that have been identified) makes it clear that the preservation process was used for the nobility as well as for royalty. One well-known example found at Medum by W. M. F. Petrie in 1891 was provisionally dated by Elliot Smith and Dawson to the Fifth Dynasty, but they also stated that 'the exact age of this mummy is uncertain. On archaeological evidence, it may be as early as the IIIrd Dynasty, but the extended position and the great advance in technique which it displays would seem to indicate a somewhat later date, probably Vth Dynasty' [2450–2290 BC]. Petrie's description, made at the time of the mummy's discovery, is worth quoting:

The mode of embalming was very singular. The body was shrunk, wrapped in a linen cloth, then modelled all over with resin, into the natural form and plumpness of the living figure, completely restoring all the fullness of the form, and this was wrapped around in a few turns of finest gauze. The eyes and eyebrows were painted on the outer wrapping with green.

(Petrie 1892)

Elliot Smith and Dawson examined this specimen at the Royal College of Surgeons in London, where it had been deposited by Petrie, and they described it as being wrapped in large quantities of linen with the outer layers soaked in resin and modeled to resemble the fine details of the body. Even the genitals were so treated, with such care as to allow the investigators to determine that circumcision had been practiced. They also observed that the body cavity had been packed with resin-impregnated linen, This mummy, found by Petrie at Medum and identified by him as a man named Ranofer, is now dated to the Fourth Dynasty. The descriptions of it give a concrete idea of the attempt that had been made to create a lifelike appearance by modeling and wrapping. The mummy is no longer available for further examination, as it was destroyed in an air raid in World War II (Lucas 1962).

The fully developed intention at the height of the Old Kingdom seems to have been to effect the most lifelike suggestion possible of the original appearance of the body before death. It is a pity that there are not more and better preserved examples of mummification that span the time between the beginning of the dynastic period and the pyramid age. Nevertheless, the conclusion is the same: the practice of preservation was accompanied by a desire to create of the dead body a resemblance to the deceased as he had been in life. One additional example from the Fifth Dynasty adds support to this assertion. The mummy of a man named Nefer, found at Saqqara, is described in *X-raying the pharaohs* as looking like a man asleep. The wrappings of this specimen were soaked in an adhesive and molded to suggest the shape of the body, 'the genitalia were particularly well modeled. Eyes, eyebrows and mustache were carefully drawn in ink on the moulded linen' (Harris and Weeks 1973). From the description, this mummy seems to provide an almost exact parallel to the one from Medum, now destroyed.

The desire to preserve the outward appearance of the deceased took another direction, in addition to the coating of the body with resin and the modeling of the features in that material. Masks of plaster applied over the face are known from as early as the Fourth Dynasty. By the time of the Middle Kingdom, the facial features were often modeled in cartonnage, a combination of either cloth and glue or papyrus and plaster (Figure 1.3). In the Middle Kingdom, the entire body was sometimes covered with cartonnage as a final layer of the wrapping process. The face seems naturally to have been the most important part of the body for realistic treatment. The technique varied from the plaster masks of the Old Kingdom to the flat, painted portraits of the Roman period (Figure 1.7) and includes such notable examples as the solid gold face mask of Tutankhamun. Like the coverings of the face, the style of wrapping in linen bandages varied. At its best-developed stage in the New Kingdom, every individual part, including each finger and toe, was wrapped separately. After this, each larger unit was covered, and finally the total mummy was enwrapped. Single sheets as long as 13 or 17 m have been recorded.

FIGURE I.3. Body of an adult female, twenty-first Dynasty, 1080–946 BC, British Museum 48971. The well-preserved outer wrapping of this mummy is in the typical arrangement for its period. The large outer cloths have been tied in place with a simple but decorative strapping, which is also well preserved.

Changes in the technique of embalming were progressive and continuous, but not until the time of the New Kingdom can the complete sequence of steps in the process be detailed. Working on the basic studies carried out by Lucas, and with continued experimentation, Zaki Iskander (Mokhtar *et al.* 1973) outlined what he considered the complete method employed at its fully developed stage:

1   Putting the corpse on the operating table.
2   Extraction of the brain.
3   Extraction of the viscera.
4   Sterilization of the body cavities and viscera.
5   Embalming the viscera.
6   Temporary stuffing of the thoracic and abdominal cavities.
7   Dehydration of the body.
8   Removal of the temporary stuffing material.
9   Packing of the body cavities with permanent stuffing material.
10 Anointing the body.
11 Packing the face openings.
12 Smearing the skin with molten resin.
13 Adorning and bandaging the mummy.

The following is a commentary on the 13 steps.

1   The body of the deceased was taken to the place of mummification soon after death. The clothing was removed, and the body was placed on a work table for the succeeding processes. Embalmers' tables have been found and recognized as such. Little other comment is needed for what would have been the most obvious first stage of the working procedure.

2   The brain, one of the organs most subject to rapid putrefaction, was probably removed first; this is verified by Herodotus' account and seems practical. A passage was opened, through the nose usually, and the cerebral matter taken out with a hooked metal rod. Implements have been identified as possibly the types used for this operation. The brain was apparently not preserved. There is no mention on any container connected with the mummification process or on the burial material of their use for the brain, but there are certainly many mummies in which it can be demonstrated that the brain is absent.

3   An incision was made in the abdomen, usually on the left side, but it may be found in other locations as well. The abdominal organs were extracted except for the kidneys, but this exception was not consistently observed; the kidneys are also missing sometimes. Next, the diaphragm was cut out and the contents of the thorax, except the heart and usually the aorta, were removed. This is the usual condition of well prepared mummies. In mummification of the less expensive types, there is no incision and the removal of the organs is less consistent. The necessity for this stage in the preservation of the body needs little comment, for the extraction of the soft organs, particularly the intestines, would greatly aid the preservation of the body. The heart was usually left in

place because it was considered the 'seat of the mind'. This may help to explain why the brain seems not to have been preserved. The heart, in any case, is muscle and would not be as apt to decay as the organs that were removed.

4   After the removal of the internal organs, the thorax and the abdomen were cleansed, probably with palm wine, which would have had some sterilizing effect. Diodorus mentions the cleansing of the viscera with palm wine, and it is natural to assume that this would have also been done to the body cavities. The operation would have left no detectable trace, but it is a natural assumption that some sort of internal cleansing was carried out.

5   The viscera were separated, emptied, cleansed, and dried. They were then treated with molten resin, wrapped in separate linen packages, and placed in containers. The so-called canopic jars or chests took different forms at different times, as will be discussed elsewhere. This stage could have been carried out concurrently with the next.

6   After the cleaning mentioned in step 4, the thorax and abdomen were stuffed with packing material to ensure the complete desiccation of the body. There is evidence from refuse material examined by Iskander that such temporary packing existed. Although this step has been doubted by some authorities, it would have been practical and useful, not only for the drying effect, but also for the maintenance of the shape of the corpse. Herodotus mentioned packing the cavities before the complete desiccation, but he did not specifically indicate that it was of a temporary nature.

7   The complete desiccation of the body could now be accomplished. Exactly how this was done has been the subject of considerable debate, but the general conclusion reached in modern scholarship indicates that the process involved the use of dry natron. The body, probably on a slanting bed, was completely covered with natron. This had the effect of removing any remaining body liquid and consequently ensuring against any further putrefaction. The drying-out process lasted 40 days; the total embalming process, 70 days. There is a good deal of evidence to support this time scheme.

8   After the drying-out process, the temporary packing material was removed. It was not discarded, because it had come into contact with the body. Caches of embalmers' material have been found in sufficient quantity to make it clear that the temporary packing was buried near the tomb.

9 Resin or resin-impregnated cloth was put into the cranium. This is often evident in X-rays of the skull, in which the resin can be seen as having reached its own level while liquid and then solidified. The body cavities were stuffed with linen cloth and bags of other materials including natron, sawdust, earth, and occasionally a few onions. The incision was closed with resin, wax, or linen and covered with a plate of metal or wax. The embalming incision is seldom found actually to have been stitched together.

10 The body was presumably anointed at this point with fragrant materials.

11 The orifices of the head were packed with wax or resin soaked linen, and pads of linen were placed over the eyeballs.

12 Liquefied resin was smeared over the whole body. This acted as a preventative against the reentry of moisture and tended to strengthen the skin.

13 Amulets and other jewelry were placed on the mummy. The amount and quality of such materials depended on the wealth and position of the deceased. In a royal mummy, such as that of Tutankhamun, the quantity of objects was very large, including bracelets, rings, necklaces, pectorals, finger and toe coverings, as well as amuletic devices prepared especially for the burial. The mummy was then wrapped in linen bandages, sometimes with resin between the layers. The most complex wrapping began with the individual fingers and toes, proceeded to the limbs, and ultimately encased the total corpse in many layers of linen.

These 13 steps outline the most complete manner of preparing the body for the tomb in the New Kingdom. A mummy such as this would have stood a good chance of being completely preserved (Figures 1.4 through 1.7). There were, undoubtedly, many variations on this model program, but the principal operations of desiccation, washing with palm wine (which contained alcohol), and anointing with resin all resulted in the desired end of rendering the physical remains incorruptible.

One of the most complex arguments about the mummification process was centered around the chemical material used in the desiccation of the body. The principal ingredients that have been considered are salt and natron. To the earlier investigators, salt seemed the most likely desiccating agent employed, probably from actual experience with salted meat and fish. Considerable investigation and study have proved that salt appears only as an adulterant and was not the principal means of preserving the body. For a considerable time, natron was believed to have been used in solution, mainly because of faulty

FIGURE I.4. Body of an old man, Ptolemaic period, 332–30 BC, British Museum 20650. The somewhat rough and wide outer wrapping strips suggest that some further decoration is missing, such as additional bandings, a shroud, or other elements. In the catalog, *Mummies and human remains,* of the British Museum there is mention of beads found in the wrappings; this may indicate that the missing element is a bead netting.

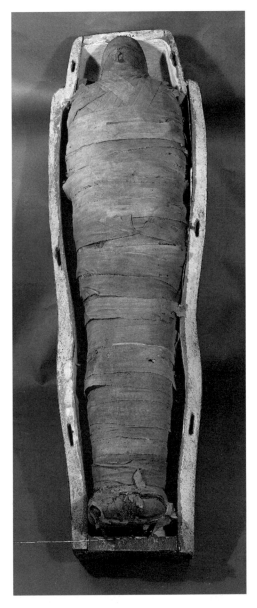

translations of the description of the mummification process in Herodotus. Lucas and others have proved satisfactorily that the body was packed in dry natron, not soaked in a solution. Lucas made a series of experiments in which he treated the bodies of pigeons by four possible methods: salt in solution; dry salt packing; natron in solution; and dry natron packing. The conclusion he reached was that the mummification process depended for its success on the use of dry natron. Zaki Iskander treated a group of ducks using the principle

FIGURE I.5. Body of an old woman, Ptolemaic to Roman period, date uncertain, British Museum 6665. This example illustrates the use, even at a late date, of a modeled face mask on the mummy. The other objects that embellish the front of the body may not belong, and as a consequence, the actual date of the mummy is difficult to determine.

suggested by Lucas. After 30 years, in 1973, he stated that they were 'still in a very good state'. Iskander had kept the mummified ducks in a laboratory under normal conditions of atmosphere and humidity. It can be generally assumed that the packing of the mummy in dry natron, a material abundant in ancient Egypt, was the simplest and most practical method of desiccation. The physical problem of obtaining containers of sufficient size to hold a human body should have long ago ruled out the possibility of a bath, whereas the dry method could have been employed by arranging the remains on a table or matting and simply heaping the natron around it.

Three other arguments for the use of a 'pickling' solution have been propounded. The fact that mummies have been found with separate limbs that did not belong to them suggested that parts had become detached in a soaking process and had been incorrectly reassembled. In fact it is more likely that such cases were the result of a later rewrapping of vandalized bodies. The purpose of finger and toe stalls was, at one time, explained as

31

FIGURE I.6. Body of an adolescent boy, Roman period, probably first to second century AD, British Museum 13595. The typical crossed outer wrapping of narrow strips with gilded metal buttons common on mummies of the Roman period is shown here. The use of a flat, painted portrait is a Greco-Roman contribution to the manner of decorating the mummy.

being to keep the fingernails and toenails in place during soaking. In actuality, these objects were probably more decorative than useful. The third argument for the use of a soaking bath was the apparent lack of epidermis in examples inspected: the theory was that the epidermis had soaked away. The lack of epidermis can usually be explained by its having come away with the wrapping or actually having been present but not recognised as such. The physical state of well preserved mummies, taken together with accurate translations of the ancient texts, makes the use of a liquid bath and prolonged soaking seem unlikely. The use of dry natron for complete packing of the body seems at present to offer the most understandable explanation of how desiccation was carried out.

FIGURE 1.7. Body of an adult male, Roman period, British Museum 6704. An unusual (for its time) treatment of the final wrapping is illustrated here. The limbs are wrapped separately, and the face has had the features painted, a technique going back to the Old Kingdom but no longer common in later Egyptian history.

From the earliest time for which there is evidence, the process of preservation was accompanied by a decided attempt to create a lifelike appearance of the mummy. In the Old Kingdom, this was accomplished mainly by wrapping with sufficient linen to restore the natural contours of the body. Special mention should be made of the practice followed in the Twenty-first Dynasty. Modern taxidermists would find the techniques of the embalmers in this period similar to their own work, for the basic steps outlined above as typical of the New Kingdom were augmented by a process designed to produce an even more natural effect. Stuffings of various materials, principally linen cloth, were inserted under the skin through incisions made for that purpose. The body cavity was filled and the arms and legs rounded out either from inside the trunk or through minor openings made in the limbs. The loss of body mass was made up wherever needed, and the face was stuffed from inside the mouth. Elliot Smith and Dawson suggest that this elaborate treatment of the body occurred at a time of, and may have been responsible for, less emphasis on substitute images of the deceased as alternate dwelling places for the spirit. It is true that during this period there are fewer examples of the ka statues made in the likeness of the dead. In any case, mummies from this time exhibit a definite attempt to restore an appearance of life and can be easily recognized as belonging to this period.

The evolution of the mummification process was accompanied by a development of the necessary funerary 'furniture', such as containers for the body and the viscera. The early pit burial of the predynastic age required no container except for the simple wrapping of the body in cloth, reed matting, or hide. Because the pit or hole was sometimes lined with brick, boards, or matting, it may be considered that this acted as a substitute for a portable container. In the early dynastic period, the notion of a miniature house for the deceased was suggested by the use of small paneled chests or boxes, suitable only for contracted burials. In form, these were imitative of lower Egyptian houses with paneled walls and arched roofs. As religious ritual developed, these small containers gave way to larger rectangular sarcophagi of wood or stone (limestone, granite, or alabaster). As the burial of the remains of Queen Hetepheres has already received some comment above, her sarcophagus can serve as an example of the beginning of Dynasty Four. Made of fine alabaster with a close-fitting lid, Hetepheres' sarcophagus was of a proportion that indicates it was made to accommodate an extended rather than a contracted body. When found by excavators in the twentieth century, it was, unfortunately, empty.

A rectangular container for the body was used throughout the Old Kingdom, but it is in the painted wooden coffins of the Middle Kingdom that the form reached its height as a decorated object. A typical coffin of the Eleventh and Twelfth dynasties was decorated with painted architectural motifs on the outside, which resemble the so-called palace facade design. The left, or east, side was usually decorated with some hieroglyphic texts and with a false door and a pair of eyes to allow the spirit the means by which he could communicate with the outside world. The interior of the coffin was decorated with paintings in registers or horizontal bands. The uppermost of these contained a carefully painted invocation on behalf of the occupant; the middle register, a series of depictions of funerary offerings and necessities for the next life; and the lower areas, a series of finely written prayers, spells, and amuletic sayings drawn from a larger body of religious literature known as the Coffin Texts.

The anthropoid coffin makes its first appearance in the Middle Kingdom. It is probable that the notion of designing the complete container in such a way that it resembles a human figure developed directly from the Old Kingdom tradition of covering the face of the deceased with a lifelike mask. Although the long-hallowed use of a rectangular coffin persisted into the New Kingdom, particularly for royal burials, the body at that time was first enclosed in an anthropoid coffin or a series of nested coffins of such shape. The notion, probably, was that the coffin helped to ensure the preservation of the shape of the body, while the stone sarcophagus served as a house or a shrine within which to contain it. Throughout the history of the anthropoid coffin the face was nearly always modeled in relief (Figure 1.5). The hands, arms, and breasts also were sometimes treated as relief decoration. Wooden examples could be elaborately painted inside and out with a combination of religious texts and vignettes illustrating the funerary ritual, protective divinities, and the progress of the spirit in the next life. Wooden coffins could be items kept in stock, with the name and title of the individual added at the time of use.

The elaborate protection for the mummified body was extended to the internal organs that had been removed from it. They were considered with the same care because they were, in effect, part of the human remains and had to be treated with the same degree of respect. As said above, one of the earliest pieces of solid evidence for the removal of the viscera as part of mummification was the canopic box of Hetepheres. The alabaster box was divided into four compartments, was sealed with a tight-fitting lid, and still contained the embalmed viscera when found.

The division of the viscera, as it was later standardized, was into four parts: the liver, the stomach, the lungs, and the intestines. At most times in the history of mummification, four containers, or symbolic substitutes for them, were provided. These containers are usually called canopic jars because their form, with the lid or stopper in the shape of a head, was thought to resemble the burial of Canopus, the priest of Menelaus, who was revered in the form of a bulging jar with a human head.

During the Old Kingdom, the canopic jar was typically a rough-hewn, slightly bulging limestone jar with a convex lid. There is preserved in the Metropolitan Museum a set of jars of this description found in the burial chamber of the tomb of Pery-neb of the late Fourth Dynasty. Although these four containers are identifiable as to their intended purpose, they were clean inside and were never used. By the beginning of the Middle Kingdom, the identification of the viscera as part of the body was reinforced by the shape of the jar or stopper, which was modeled in the shape of a human head. That the four jars had human heads as late as the end of Dynasty Eighteen is attested to by the four stoppers from the canopic chest of Tutankhamun. As a complete example of the treatment of the viscera in a royal burial, the canopic chest of this king should be described. Inside a gilt wooden chest was found an alabaster chest of a similar shape. This was divided into four interior compartments, each of which was plugged with a stopper fashioned in the likeness of the king's head. In the four compartments were four miniature inlaid gold coffins that actually contained the visceral packets.

In the Eighteenth Dynasty, a second treatment of the four canopic lids developed. One continued to be made in the form of a human head, but the other three were fashioned as the heads of a jackal, a baboon, and a falcon. The four heads identified the viscera as being protected by four genii (called the four sons of Horus). When it became customary to package the organs that had been removed and return them to the body cavities, the tradition of the canopic containers continued, but the jars were false or imitation, often solid, the body and lid carved from the same piece of stone.

The materials from which the canopic containers were made were extremely varied. Clay, limestone, alabaster, wood, faience, and cartonnage were all employed. The canopic jar could be a carefully designed work of art or a crude, roughly fashioned receptacle. As is the case with all aspects of the preparation for burial, the social status and ability to pay of the deceased or his family were the key factors in the choice of the methods and materials employed. This has resulted in a wide variety of tomb goods and, naturally, the method of embalming and wrapping during any one period. What had begun as a necessary precaution during the early dynastic times for the protection and preservation of the king's body had gradually become available to anyone who could pay the price. The number of objects – coffins, papyrus scrolls of the *Book of the dead*, heart amulets – that have been found with the name of the deceased left blank attests to the common practice of producing standard funerary objects to be sold at a price. The place in the text appropriate for the name was intended to be filled in at the time of purchase. In some instances, this was not done, for what reason we shall probably never know.

The religious basis of the mummification process was rooted in the necessity of preserving the physical remains as a resting place for the spirit. What had been accomplished accidentally in the predynastic period was done by a gradually developed process over the centuries. The techniques and procedures, which became more and more complicated through the course of Egyptian history, served this single purpose: the preservation of the human form, and particularly the features of the face, from decay. With the embalming process there grew up attendant aids for the protection of the spirit. The ritual decoration of the mummy, coffin, and sarcophagus, and the amuletic devices placed on and around the body served this end. The mummy has become a symbolic touchstone that conjures up the mysteries of ancient Egypt for modern man. What the physical remains of the ancient Egyptians can tell us through scientific techniques is only now becoming evident.

REFERENCES

Brier, B. 1994. *Egyptian mummies*. New York: William Morrow.

D'Auria, S., Lacorva, P. and Roehrig, C. H. 1988. *Mummies and magic: the funerary arts of Ancient Egypt*. Boston: Museum of Fine Arts.

Diodorus Siculus. 1935. *History*. Transl. C. H. Oldfather. Cambridge, MA: Harvard University Press.

Elliot Smith, G. and Dawson, W. R. 1924. *Egyptian mummies*. New York: Dial Press.

Goyon, J. C. 1972. *Rituels funéraires de l'ancienne Egypte*. Paris: Cerf.

Harris, J. E. and Weeks, K. R. 1973. *X-raying the pharaohs*. New York: Scribner.

Herodotus. 1910. *History*. transl. G. Rawlinson. London: Dent.

Lucas A. 1962. *Ancient Egyptian materials and industries*, 4th edn, revised and transl. J. R. Harris. London: Edward Arnold.

Mokhtar, G., Riad, H. and Iskander, S. 1973. *Mummification in ancient Egypt*. Cairo: Cairo Museum.

Petrie, W. M. F. 1892. *Medum*. London: David Nutt

Pettigrew, T. J. 1834. *A history of Egyptian mummies*. London: Longmans.

Reisner, G. A. 1927–32. Articles on Queen Hetepheres. *Bulletin of the Museum of Fine Arts (Boston)* **25** (1927), **26** (1928), **27** (1929) **30** (1932).

Taylor, J. H. 1996. *Unwrapping a mummy: the life, death and embalming of Horemkenesi*. Austin: University of Texas Press.

2

Disease in ancient Egypt

A. T. SANDISON AND EDMUND TAPP

All men and women share certain experiences. All are born; all suffer illnesses during their lives; and all must sooner or later die, whether from disease, degenerative process, accident, or violence. The historian's overall view of ancient peoples is incomplete if he or she fails to take into account these phenomena of health or disease. The major lines of study of ancient diseases comprise examination of literary sources by scholars in collaboration with physicians, study of artistic representations in sculpture and painting, and study of skeletal remains and mummies by macroscopic examination, supplemented by radiography and by histological examination using light, polarizing, and electron microscopes.

The major literary sources for our knowledge of disease processes in Egypt are the Ebers, Edwin Smith, and Kahun papyri (Dawson 1953). The first deals with medical diseases and includes, among many others, descriptions of parasitic gut infestations and urinary disorders, most certainly including schistosomiasis. The second is surgical and contains accurate prognostic comments on traumatic and certain inflammatory diseases. The third concerns obstetrical and gynaecological disorders. Precise diagnoses are, in many instances, difficult to make from the symptoms listed. Nevertheless, the papyri will continue to engage scholars and medical historians for many years. From these, as well as other literary sources, specialist scholars have adduced evidence of trachoma, seasonal ophthalmia, skin diseases, hernia, haemorrhoids, and so on. Studies of artistic representations have yielded evidence of achondroplastic dwarfism and probable diagnoses of such states as bilateral dislocation of the hips and post poliomyelitic limb atrophy, but the problems associated with interpreting artists' work have been reiterated recently by Nunn (1996).

Macroscopic examination of ancient Egyptian skeletons has revealed a wealth of pathological changes. These have been reviewed by Brothwell and Powers (1968) and Sandison (1968) and additional information from other sources continues to be published (Strouhal 1982; Schultz 1995). In the macroscopic examination of bones, pseudopathological changes are troublesome artifacts; these were fully discussed by Wells (1967) and summarized by Sandison (1968). Such pseudopathological changes may be due to depredation by insects and rodents, effects of plant roots, high winds, pressure of overlying soil or matrix, and impregnation by chemical substances. Other problems associated with the evaluation of such specimens have recently been reviewed (Buikstra *et al.* 1993).

The study of actual mummies by dissection (Ruffer 1921; Elliot Smith and Dawson 1924; Cockburn *et al.* 1975; Hart *et al.* 1977; Tapp 1979a; Tapp and Wildsmith 1992) and histological examination (Ruffer 1911a; Sandison 1955, 1970; Tapp 1979b, 1986) has yielded much interesting information. If dissection is not possible endoscopic examination has proved extremely useful for examining the inside of mummies and in taking biopsies for histological and other examinations (Tapp *et al.* 1984; Tapp and Wildsmith 1986).

Radiological examination of mummies has revealed useful information about disease in ancient Egypt. Gray (1967) has carried out extensive surveys of mummies in several European museums and has discovered evidence of arthritis, arterial calcification, cholelithiasis, and possible bone infarction. It is now clear that artifacts must be carefully excluded; earlier radiographic diagnoses of alkaptonuric arthropathy are now known to have been erroneous (Gray 1967), although Lee and Stenn (1978) have shown a homogentisic acid derivative in material from an Egyptian mummy of 1500 BC. This appears to be a proven case of ochronosis.

If tibial bones are subjected to x-ray examination, transverse (so-called Harris) lines may be seen. They have been thought to indicate episodes of intermittent disease or malnutrition. There is no way of telling what condition was causal, and lines may become absorbed. Nevertheless, the fact that about 30 percent of Egyptian mummies show Harris lines suggests a generally poor state of health in childhood and adolescence in ancient Egypt. More recently, computed tomography has been used to examine Egyptian mummies and some remarkable results have been obtained (Isherwood and Hart 1992, Baldock *et al.* 1994).

After this preamble, we shall look at the evidence of disease in ancient Egypt.

INFECTIOUS DISEASES

Ruffer's (1910b) identification of calcified ova of *Schistosoma* (Bilharzia) *haematobium* in the kidneys of two mummies of the Twentieth Dynasty is

FIGURE 2.1. Larval forms of the worm *Strongyloides* in the intestines of the mummy Asru.

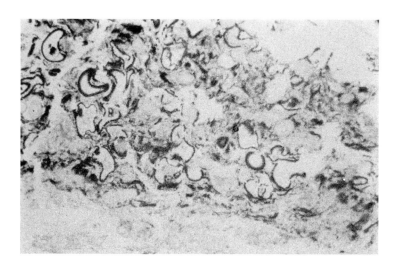

unquestioned. Hematuria was probably common in ancient Egypt. Schistosomiasis has certainly been very common in Egypt in the twentieth century. The Egyptian Ministry of Public Health reported in 1963 that 50 percent of the population harbored parasites, *Schistosoma* commonly included (Ghalioungui 1973); this parasite was undoubtably the cause of hematuria reported in French troops during the campaign of Napoleon Bonaparte in Egypt in 1799–1801. The parasite is small and was not recognized until 1851 by Bilharz, so it is unlikely that the ancient Egyptians ever identified it. More recently, in Toronto, the mummy ROM I has been shown to harbor the ova of *Schistosoma haematobium* and to display changes in the liver that may have resulted from the schistosomal infestation (Hart et al.1977). Evidence of schistosomiasis infection in Egyptian mummies may now be adduced from the presence of specific antigens in their tissues using immunological tests (Deelder *et al.* 1990; Miller *et al.* 1992). Infection with the worm *Strongyloides*, like schistosomiasis, is acquired by immature forms of the worm penetrating unprotected parts of the body, so it is perhaps not surprising that larval forms of this worm (Figure 2.1) were found in the intestines of the mummy Asru (Tapp 1979b).

In addition to showing evidence of schistosomiasis, the mummy ROM I was found to harbor a tape worm of the *Taenia* species. Hydatid cysts (Figure 2.2) have been found in the brain of one Egyptian mummy and in the lungs of another, indicating that the dog tape worm (*Taenia echinococcus*) was also a problem in ancient Egypt (Tapp 1984). Eggs of the roundworm *Ascaris* were present in the mummy PUM II (Cockburn *et al.* 1975). Tapp and Wildsmith (1992) found filarial worms in the soft tissues from the groin of the Leeds

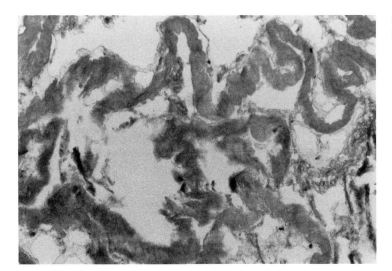

FIGURE 2.2. Part of the wall of a collapsed hydatid cyst.

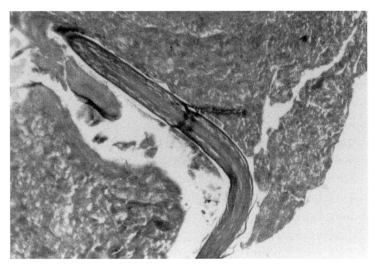

FIGURE 2.3. A filarial worm from the groin of the Leeds mummy.

mummy (Figure 2.3). This worm is known to block the lymphatic channels of the body causing swelling of the legs and genitalia. It is possible that this infestation may be the cause of some cases of elephantiasis in artistic representations from ancient Egypt (Weeks 1970). The remains of a calcified male guinea worm (*Dracunculus medinensis*) were found radiologically in the anterior abdominal wall of mummy 1770 in Manchester (Tapp 1979a). The female of the species, once pregnant, usually migrates to the legs where it may cause extensive necrosis and ulceration. The legs of mummy 1770 had been amputated and it is interesting to speculate that this was necessary due to the infestation.

Ruffer tentatively diagnosed malaria in some Coptic bodies with splenomegaly, but this is not good evidence in a warm country. It would appear, however, that as with schistosomiasis immunological techniques may be of value in determining whether malaria was prevalent in ancient Egypt; very recently Miller and his colleagues (1994) detected an antigen produced by *Plasmodium falciparum* in mummies from all the periods tested.

The case of leprosy in a Coptic Christian (sixth century) body discovered by Elliot Smith and Derry (1910) at El Bigha in Nubia and redescribed by Elliot Smith and Dawson (1924) is unquestioned. This case was reviewed macroscopically by Rowling (1960) and macroscopically and radiologically by Møller-Christensen (1967); both accepted the diagnosis. Sandison examined skin, subcutaneous tissue, and nervous tissue from this specimen but failed to demonstrate acid-fast bacilli. This is not surprising; it is known that even tissues in a paraffin block containing numerous *Mycobacterium leprae* may, after a few years, appear to be free of bacilli. Certainly there is no direct evidence of leprosy in the Pharaonic period and, as Nunn (1996) points out, the evidence for leprosy in the medical papyri is tenuous.

We now turn to the other important mycobacterial disease – tuberculosis. Morse and associates (Morse *et al.* 1964; Morse 1967) have discussed the evidence for its presence in ancient Egypt, and their findings along with additional material have been reviewed by Buikstra and her co-workers (1993). Their conclusions, derived from a critical survey of all available artistic and pathological evidence, are completely acceptable. The famous mummy of the priest Nesperehan of the Twenty-first Dynasty has been unreservedly accepted as a case of typical spinal tuberculosis with characteristic psoas abscess. Morse and associates conclude that there are a total of 31 acceptable cases of skeletal and mummy tuberculosis. Of these, 16 were culled from the literature and 15 were reported for the first time. Not all the dates for these 31 cases are certain, nor is the provenance of the mummies absolutely clear, but the dates probably range from 3700 to 1000 BC. They accept that the fibrous adhesions and collapsed left lung found in a Byzantine Nubian female body from the Island of Hesa are good evidence of pulmonary tuberculosis (Elliot Smith and Wood Jones 1908). This diagnosis is perfectly tenable, but other conditions might lead to similar appearances. These 31 acceptable cases represent only a part of those found in Egyptian sites. Many have doubtless been discarded unrecognized and others may languish in museums unrecognized and undescribed. Some form of granulomatous tuberculosis has probably infected man since Neolithic times and may have resulted from closer contact with livestock, presumably bovine, following the Neolithic

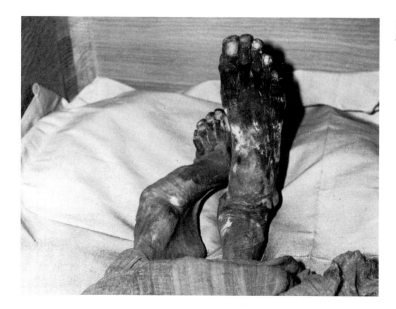

FIGURE 2.4. Probable club foot of Pharaoh Siptah (photograph by James Harris).

Revolution. The contemporary domestic dog may suffer from pulmonary or, less commonly, renal tuberculosis, but this is attributable to a human form of bacillus and is probably derived from contact with the owner. The dog is therefore not likely to have been the source of the origin of Neolithic human tuberculosis.

Another important granulomatous disease is syphilis caused by *Treponema pallidum*. Other treponemal diseases include yaws, pinta, and bejel, and some workers have concluded that all these disease processes may be caused by variants of one organism. This may explain the present obscurity of the origin of syphilis, and there seems little likelihood of a convincing early resolution of the problem. There is no clear evidence of syphilis in the vast amount of material examined in Egypt and Nubia from the ancient period, although venereal syphilis is not uncommon in Egypt at the present time (Buikstra *et al.* 1993).

Poliomyelitis is a virus infection of the anterior horn cells of the spinal cord, and its presence can be deduced only by deformity in persons who have survived the acute stage. In an early Egyptian body from Deshasheh, Mitchell (1900) noted shortening of the left leg which he interpreted as evidence of poliomyelitis. The clubfoot of the Pharaoh Siptah (Figure 2.4) is more probably attributable to a congenital abnormality than to poliomyelitis (Elliot Smith 1912), as is the deformity of Khnum-nakht of the Twelfth Dynasty (Cameron 1910). Some authorities, however, believe that the deformities in the last two individuals may be postmortem artifacts. The portrayal of Roma, a door keeper of the Eighteenth or Nineteenth Dynasty, on his funeral stele is often cited as an example of atrophy in a limb following poliomyelitis in childhood but others believe that the primary lesion was a variety of clubfoot (Nunn 1996). When seeking interpretation of changes found in Egyptian feet, Valenti (1984) studied the feet of 99 mummified Egyptians and believes that the parameters of the ancient Egyptian foot were different from those of today and that they gave the Egyptians a high degree of protection from pedal disorders.

It is possible that smallpox may have existed in ancient Egypt and that unrecorded epidemics occurred. The changes described by Ruffer and Ferguson (1911) in the skin of a male mummy may well have been those of variola, despite criticism of this diagnosis by Unna. Also, the Pharaoh Ramesses V (Figure 2.5) may have been the victim of lethal smallpox (Elliot Smith 1912). Hopkins and his colleagues were recently allowed to take some fragments of scabs from the wrappings of Ramesses V and these were examined immunologically and by electron microscopy. The scab extract had a vague precipitin reaction with smallpox antibody and under the electron microscope two particles were found that looked like smallpox viruses, though the findings were not conclusive (Lewin 1982).

Sandison (1967b) reviewed the evidence for infective ocular disease in ancient Egypt. Seasonal ophthalmia may have occurred. The evidence for ocular disease is purely literary, and no paleopathological evidence is available. Blindness is certainly portrayed in ancient Egyptian art.

BONE DISORDERS

Nonspecific bone inflammation is not rare in human remains from older societies. The evidence for this is overwhelming, and the phenomenon is of interest in view of the opinions formerly held by some morbid anatomists that the inflammatory reaction may have been a late evolutionary acquisition. Similar inflammatory processes are also seen in fossil animals from as far back as the Mesozoic period, but their causes are likely to remain obscure. It has been suggested that many specific infections were probably rare or absent before the gregariousness permitted by the Neolithic Revolution. Nonspecific infections might, however, have been possible without close personal contiguity and might have been caused by a wide range of organisms. Such nonspecific changes are of significant frequency in early cemeteries, but are difficult to interpret.

It is customary to divide bone inflammation into periostitis, osteitis, and

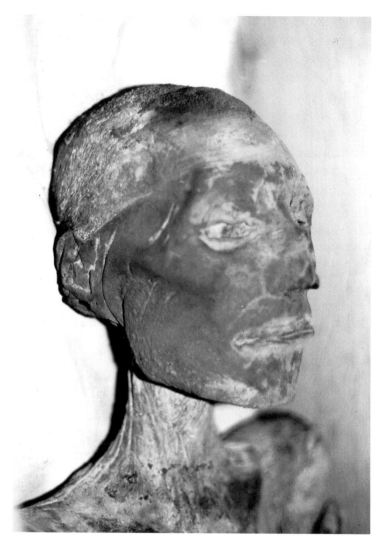

FIGURE 2.5. Head of Pharaoh Ramesses V, showing smallpox vesicles on the face (photograph by James Harris)

osteomyelitis, depending on whether periosteum, bone proper, or bone marrow is most obviously involved. This is to some extent artificial, because bone is a biological unit and not a series of distinct tissue entities. These phenomena may lead one to another; all three may be present together. When confronted with evidence of periosteal reaction in an ancient bone, it is difficult to say with any confidence whether the cause was infection or trauma. It must, however, be conceded that site is important, particularly the tibia, which has a large subcutaneous area. Even here we are on uncertain ground; the subcutaneous tibia is vulnerable to trauma, but also to extension of infection from the skin to the periosteum. Wells (1964) noted that one in six of a group of Saxon agriculturists had tibial periosteal reactions. Compared with Anglo-Saxons, ancient Egyptians showed a lower fracture rate for the leg, and yet a similar rate of periosteal reaction. Wells (personal communication 1970) found that among 92 ancient Egyptian tibiae dating from predynastic to Coptic times, 14 (15.2 percent) had well-marked periostitic changes. He therefore suspected that something other than trauma may be operating, and suggests that in ancient Egypt infection of insect bites or simple abrasions may have been the cause.

There are no recent incidence figures for ancient Egypt other than those of Wells, but there are isolated reports. Derry (1940) noted only dental infection and osteoarthritis in the bones of Pharaoh Psusennes I of the Twenty-first Dynasty; Derry (1942) only arthritis in Pharaoh Amenenopet and no abnormality in Har-Nakht; Derry (1947) no disease in prince Ptah-Shepses of the Fifth and Sixth Dynasties; Batrawi (1947), some evidence of dental and maxillary sinus infection in a middle-aged male and possible post-fracture sepsis of the radius in a middle-aged female from Shawaf, but no disease in Pharaoh Djed-Ka-Re of the Fifth Dynasty; Batrawi (1948), possible dental and air sinus infection of Akhet-Hetep, but only arthritis in his wife; and Batrawi (1951), no evidence of infection in remains from the Northern Pyramid of Sneferu of the Fourth Dynasty. Apart from such isolated reports, we must fall back upon the *Archaeological Survey of Nubia* (Elliot Smith and Wood Jones 1910).

Although occasional bodies gave clear evidence of the cause of death, a very large proportion of this enormous mass of material did not. Elliot Smith and Wood Jones (neither of whom was a pathologist) were therefore left in ignorance of the cause of death in the vast majority of persons buried in ancient Nubia. They reached some important conclusions, in that they believed that examination of 6000 bodies revealed no evidence of tuberculosis, syphilis, or rickets. As we have seen, however, this view had to be revised with regard to tuberculosis. They also believed correctly that malignant disease must have been exceptionally rare. Where the actual cause of death was clear to them, the death had usually resulted from violence. Although some remains showed evidence of disease, it was impossible even to guess at the precise cause of death.

Elliot Smith and Wood Jones concluded that inflammatory diseases of bone were rarely seen in ancient Egyptian skeletons. Even when fractures had been severe and necessarily compound, sepsis rarely seems to have followed. They postulate, in contrast to contemporary experience in surgical practice, that there must have been a remarkable resistance to infection in ancient Nubia.

An alternative explanation might, of course, be that organisms were of lower virulence. In the same report, Elliot Smith and Wood Jones found that neglected dental disease accounted for practically all septic conditions of the facial bones, but in one female skull there were traces of chronic inflammation around the margin of the nares and destruction of the turbinates and part of the nasal septum. There was a direct communication through the hard palate posteriorly between nasal and oral cavities. The remainder of the skeleton was unexceptional, and a diagnosis of long-standing nasal infection was made. The cause of this must remain obscure.

Elliot Smith and Wood Jones (1910) also illustrated two examples of cranial disease, one in the parietal bone and the other in the frontal bone; these showed peripheral reaction and central necrosis, which were attributed to extension of a scalp infection. The appearances are certainly not those of syphilis. An isolated humerus of a child of New Kingdom date showed necrosis of the lower half of the shaft, with a line of heaped-up reactive bone running down the middle of the anterior surface and a more superficial reaction over the lateral area of this line. The internal bone was necrotic and constituted a sequestrum. This appears to have been severe osteomyelitis. Sepsis following fracture appears to have been rare, even in apparently compound fractures. This is especially notable in skull wounds in which the scalp must surely have been severely affected. Nevertheless, in two New Kingdom scapulae there was evidence of reaction in transverse fractures, where there must have been severe soft tissue injury, but death occurred before healing took place.

Of 65 fractures of the upper limb, only one showed evidence of sepsis. This was in a woman of the Christian period, both of whose forearms were fractured; the right ulna had united, but the left showed periostitis. Another skeleton of this period from Hesa showed inflammation and necrosis following fracture of the clavicles, and there were two other ununited clavicular fractures. Of 38 fractures of the lower limb, only two showed septic changes. One early dynastic male with a right-sided fracture of tibia and fibula showed malunion and much inflammatory bone extending as periostitis over the bone shafts below the area of injury. The right femur of a male of the same period had an inflammatory reaction around the fractured lower portion.

Gray (1967) has discovered what appears almost certainly to be an old infarct of bone in a mummy from the Horniman Museum, and Golding (1960) found a further example in a Ptolemaic female mummy from the same museum. Caution is necessary in accepting these findings. Very similar radiographs from clinical cases have been published and in these the lesions have been attributed to arteriosclerosis. Arterial disease certainly occurred in ancient Egypt, and thus a possible aetiological factor is not lacking. Aseptic necrosis, of course, may occur in quite young people who do not have significant atherosclerosis, and such a case is quoted by Strouhal (1982).

Healed fractures are not rare, and splints have been described. The mummy of Pharaoh Seknenre of the Seventeenth Dynasty shows that he was attacked by at least two men armed with axe and spear, possibly while asleep, and suffered severe wounds (Elliot Smith 1912). Wood Jones described judicial hanging and decapitation in Roman Egyptian skeletons and Strouhal (1982) found evidence of punishment amputations. The latter author also found evidence of both blunt force and sharp instrument injuries to bones in his survey of Late Period populations at Abusir. Ulnar injuries (parry fractures) affecting the distal third of the diaphysis were found only in males.

One of the most common diseases found in ancient bones is arthritis. There are numerous accounts from many prehistoric and historical periods by many authors. Arthritis in animal fossils is discussed at length by Moodie (1923). Ankylosed vertebrae have been noted in animal remains over a wide span of time, from fossil reptiles to cave bears and even to domesticated animals from ancient Egypt. Arthritic changes including ankylosing spondylitis have also been noted in human remains during the whole of Egyptian history from predynastic to Coptic times (Elliot Smith and Wood Jones 1908, 1910; Ruffer and Rietti 1912; Bourke 1967; Zorab 1961) but the case for rheumatoid arthritis is less well established. Kilgore (1986) reported a possible case from Sudanese Nubia, but Strouhal (1982) did not find any cases of multi-articular arthritis of the rheumatoid type in his large series.

Rowling (1960) drew attention to specimen number 178A in the Nubian Collection. Hyperplastic new bone on the femora represented the adductor muscles and was more marked on the right side. Some new bone was also formed on the pelvis. There was ossification of the interosseous ligament between radius and ulna. The humeri were normal. There was a small spina bifida with a defect in the first and second sacral vertebrae. The appearances are not those of osteomyelitis or myositis ossificans. Rowling interprets these strange findings as ossification attributable to partial paraplegia consequent on the spina bifida. The forearm changes are difficult to explain, and Rowling suggests that the patient supported himself on his hands. Brothwell believes this is an example of osteogenesis imperfecta and points out the similarity to cases illustrated by Fairbank (1951), but there is no doubt that spina bifida occurred in ancient Egypt (Rabino Massa 1978; Molto 1989).

A metabolic disorder that produces recognizable changes is gout. A classic case reported by Elliot Smith and Dawson (1924) was an old Coptic

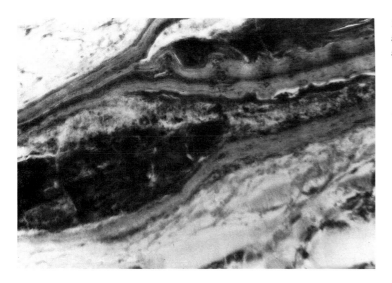

FIGURE 2.6. Frozen section of tibial artery of an elderly female mummy showing lipid in an atheromatous plaques. Sudan Black stain.

male from Philae on the Nile. The radiographs are characteristic and analysis of tophi by W. A. Schmidt showed uric acid and urates. Rowling (1960) reviewed this specimen and agreed with the diagnosis. Because of the intense sunlight, rickets is never seen in Egyptian material.

VASCULAR DISEASE

With regard to vascular disease, we are on firm ground and have direct evidence. Blood vessels are often well preserved in Egyptian mummies and dried bodies. Czermack (1852) described aortic calcification, and Shattock (1909) made sections of the calcified aorta of Pharaoh Merneptah. Elliot Smith (1912) noted this change in his macroscopic description of the royal body, and also described calcification of the temporal arteries in Ramesses II. Ruffer (1910a, 191lb) described histological changes in vessels of Egyptian mummies from the New Kingdom to the Coptic period. Long (1931), examining the mummy of Lady Teye of the Twenty-first Dynasty, described degenerative disease of the aorta and coronary arteries, with arteriosclerosis of the kidney and myocardial fibrosis. Moodie (1923) described radiological evidence of calcification of superficial vessels in a predynastic body. It is often difficult to assess the older descriptions that are unaccompanied by photographs; Sandison (1967a) examined and photographed mummy arteries (Figure 2.6) using modern histological methods. Arteries were tape-like in mummy tissues, but could readily be dissected. Arteriosclerosis, atheroma with lipid depositions, reduplications of the internal elastic lamina, and

FIGURE 2.7. Clefts in the intima of an artery from the Leeds mummy where the atheroma has been largely dissolved by the fat solvents used in processing the tissue.

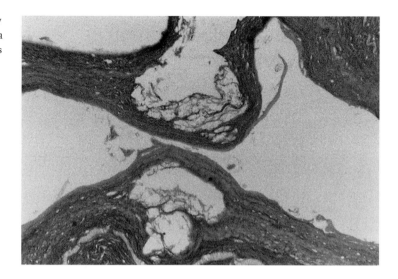

medial calcification could readily be seen. Zimmerman and Mirro (1983) also described the histological appearances of atherosclerosis in three peripheral arteries from different individuals found in the tomb of Nebwenenef but several other vessels including a coronary artery were free from disease. Well-developed plaques of atheroma were also seen histologically in the femoral arteries of the Leeds mummy (Tapp and Wildsmith 1992). Atheromatous lesions in mummy arteries tend to form sectoral clefts, but these should not be interpreted as dissecting aneurysm (Figure 2.7). It is evident that the stresses of highly civilised life are not, at any rate, the sole causes of degenerative vascular disease.

TUMORS

With regard to tumors there is a marked paucity of evidence, possibly because the expectation of life in earlier times was short. With a few exceptions, most examples are to be found in the skeleton. Elliot Smith and Dawson (1924), for example, suggested carcinoma of the ethmoid and of the rectum as causal in the erosion of the skull base and sacrum in two Byzantine bodies; this is slender evidence, but may be correct. Other cases of primary carcinoma are evidenced by destructive changes in bone. These include Derry's case (1909) of probable nasal carcinoma in a pre-Christian Nubian. Elliot Smith and Derry's case (1910) of sacral erosion in a Nubian male may have been attributable to rectal cancer or chordoma. In all these, a prima facie case can certainly be made.

Evidence of primary malignant tumors in ancient bones is rare. This is not entirely surprising, because even at the present time primary malignant tumors of bone are not common; deaths from them constitute less than 1 percent of all deaths caused by malignant disease. On the other hand, many carcinomas metastasize to bone in the terminal phase of the disease, and secondary cancer in bone is common in the necropsy room. Osteocartilaginous exostosis or osteochondroma is not uncommon in clinical practice, and cases are known in ancient material. Perhaps the best known is the celebrated specimen of the Fifth Dynasty ancient Egyptian femur illustrated by Elliot Smith and Dawson (1924) and wrongly diagnosed as osteosarcoma. The contour, absence of periosteal reaction at the base, and lack of spiculation suggest that it is osteochondromatous and quite simple. It is not possible to comment on the two further alleged examples from Fifth Dynasty graves (Elliot Smith and Dawson 1924), as these are neither described nor illustrated. A Roman pelvic tumor from Alexandria, described by Ruffer and Willmore (1914), was of large size and thought by them to be an osteosarcoma. This must remain in doubt. Rowling (1960) thought that osteosarcoma was possible but not certain. Brothwell (1967) considers the tumor may have been chondromatous. Certainly cartilage-forming tumors do occur in the pelvis, but are often malignant. Intracranial meningioma may induce hyperostotic change in the cranium. This has long been known to radiologists. Such a reaction was postulated by Lambert Rogers (1949) in two Egyptian skulls of the First and Twentieth Dynasties. The diagnostic problems arising from osteolitic and osteosclerotic lesions from the skulls of four Egyptian mummies have been discussed by Pahl and his colleagues (1984).

Possibly the most convincing evidence of neoplasm of soft tissues came from Granville (1825), who macroscopically diagnosed a cystadenoma of the ovary, possibly malignant, in a mummy now known to be Ptolemaic. Recently, Tapp (1997) has had the opportunity to examine this tumor histologically (Figure 2.8). The appearances support Granville's naked-eye opinion and show no evidence of malignancy in the tumor. Sandison noted a small squamous papilloma of the skin in a mummy. There are no examples of breast cancer.

KIDNEY DISEASE

Kidney lesions noted by Ruffer (1910a) included unilateral hypoplasia of the kidney; in another Eighteenth to Twentieth Dynasty mummy, the kidney

FIGURE 2.8. Part of the wall of the ovarian cyst from Granville's mummy. The rounded objects attached to the wall are probably the remains of papillary projections that are normally found in these tumors.

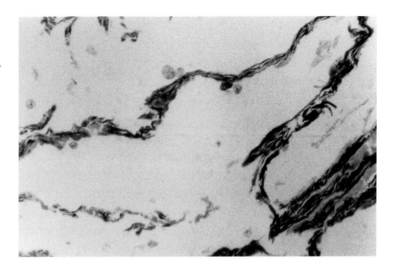

showed multiple abscesses with gram-negative bacilli resembling coliforms. Long (1931) described arteriosclerosis in the kidneys of Lady Teye of the Twenty-first Dynasty. Shattock (1909) described and analysed renal calculi from a Second Dynasty tomb; oxalates and conidia were noted. A vesical calculus found in the nostril of a Twenty-first Dynasty priest of Amun contained uric acid covered by phosphates, and Ruffer (1910a) described three mixed phosphate–uric acid calculi from a predynastic skeleton. More recently, Fulcheri and Grilletto (1988) described a probable renal stone in a mummy from the Old Kingdom.

DISEASE OF THE ALIMENTARY TRACT

Elliot Smith and Dawson (1924) also refer to the finding of multiple stones in the thin-walled gall bladder of a Twenty-first Dynasty priestess. Shaw (1938) noted in the canopic preserved gall bladder of an Eighteenth Dynasty singer that spaces resembling Aschoff–Rokitansky sinuses were present; this suggests chronic cholecystitis. Ruffer (1910a) mentions fibrosis of the liver in a mummy and equates this with cirrhosis, but insufficient evidence is given to evaluate this diagnosis. Little has been written about alimentary disease in mummies. Elliot Smith and Wood Jones (1908) report appendicular adhesions in a Byzantine period Nubian body. These are almost certainly the result of appendicitis. Ruffer (1910a) describes what may well be megacolon in a child of the Roman period and prolapse of the rectum in Coptic bodies. Elliot Smith (1912) mentions two probable cases of scrotal hernia. Ramesses V shows a bulky scrotum now empty after evisceration, and the

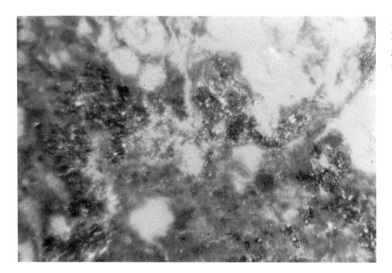

FIGURE 2.9. The normal structure of the lung has largely been destroyed. The photograph has been taken in polarized light to show the doubly refractile sand particles.

scrotum of Merneptah was excised after death by the embalmers, possibly because of the bulk of a hernia. Anorectal problems seem to have been common, as some of the royal physicians were regarded as shepherds of the royal anus.

RESPIRATORY DISORDERS

Some interesting studies of the lung have been published. Anthracosis in Egyptian mummy lungs was described by Ruffer and by Long (1931). Shaw (1938) reported anthracosis in the lungs of Har-mose of the Eighteenth Dynasty, but Har-mose had also suffered from emphysema and lower lobe bronchopneumonia. Rowling (1967) has surveyed the evidence for respiratory disease in Ancient Egypt and accepts Ruffer's (1910a) cases of pneumonia in two mummies, one Twentieth Dynasty and the other Ptolemaic; the latter may have been pneumonic plague, although the evidence is far from complete. Long (1931) reported caseous areas in the lung of a Twenty-first Dynasty lady. As already indicated, these diagnoses must be accepted with reserve in view of the possible confusion between molds and leukocytes. Fibrosis of the lung associated with the presence of the sand particles (sand pneumoconiosis) was noted by Tapp and his colleagues (1975), and since then has been found in biopsies (Figure 2.9) from several other mummies (Tapp 1984). This condition is due to the inhalation of fine sand and is closely allied to silicosis, the disease that occurs in stone masons and coal miners. It is interesting to note that sand pneumonoconiosis is still a problem in some modern desert populations (Bar-Ziv and Goldburg 1974).

ENDOCRINE CONDITIONS

A fairly rare disease that should be readily recognized is acromegaly. This produces characteristic bone changes. Brothwell (1963) illustrates an ancient Egyptian skull that may represent this disease. Aldred and Sandison (1962) gave reasons for their belief that Akhenaten suffered from endocrine disorders. Statues and reliefs show acromegaloid facies and eunuchoid obesity. An alternative diagnosis of Klinefelter's syndrome (XXY) has been suggested but this is untenable if he was the father of his six children. Nunn (1996) suggests that the condition may be one of simple adolescent gynaecomastia. Cameron (1910) describes the bones of two brothers from the Middle Kingdom of ancient Egypt and concludes that the skeleton of Nekht-ankh shows eunuchoid changes but also a curious penile appearance suggesting a subincisional operation. It is not certain, however, if this is a genuine lesion. Male Egyptian mummies show circumcision throughout the dynasties until the practice was abandoned in the Christian period.

GYNECOLOGICAL CONDITIONS

Elliot Smith (1912) described lactating breasts in the recently delivered Queen Makere. Williams (1929) reported an observation by Derry that Princess Hehenhit of the Eleventh Dynasty had a narrow pelvis and died not long after delivery with vesicovaginal fistula. Elliot Smith and Dawson (1924) described violent death in an unembalmed 16 year old pregnant ancient Egyptian girl and postulated illegitimate conception. The *Archaeological Survey of Nubia* listed a deformed Coptic negress, who died in childbirth as a result of absent sacroiliac joints contracting the pelvis. Vaginal prolapse was also noted in a Nubian specimen by Wood Jones (1908). Rabino Massa (1982) has had the opportunity of examining what at first was thought to be a large uterovaginal prolapse in an Egyptian Dynastic mummy, but histological examination of the specimen indicated that this was a total inversion of a post partum uterus rather than a simple prolapse.

REFERENCES

Aldred, C. and Sandison, A. T. 1962. The Pharaoh Akhenaten: a problem in Egyptology and pathology. *Bulletin of the History of Medicine* **36**: 293–316.

Baldock, C., Hughes, S. W., Whittaker, D. K., Taylor, J.,

Spencer, A. J., Tonge, K. and Sofat, A. 1994. Reconstruction of an ancient Egyptian mummy using x-ray computer tomography. *Journal of the Royal Society of Medicine* **87**: 806–8.

Bar-Ziv, J. and Goldberg, G. M. 1974. Simple siliceous pneumoconiosis in Negev Bedouins. *Archives of Environmental Health* **29**: 121–6.

Batrawi, A. 1947. Anatomical reports. *Annales du service des antiquités de l'Egypte* **47**: 97–109.

Batrawi, A. 1948. Report on the anatomical remains recovered from the tombs of Akhet- Hetep and Ptah-Irouka and a comment on the statues of Akhet-Hetep. *Annales du service des antiquités de l'Egypte* **48**: 487–97.

Batrawi, A. 1951. The skeletal remains from the northern pyramid of Sneferu. *Annales du service des antiquités de l'Egypte* **51**: 435–40.

Bourke, J. B. 1967. A review of the palaeopathology of the arthritic diseases. In *Diseases in antiquity*, ed. D. R. Brothwell and A. T. Sandison, 352–70. Springfield, IL: Thomas.

Brothwell, D. 1963. *Digging up bones*. London: British Museum Press.

Brothwell, D. 1967. The evidence of neoplasms. In *Diseases in antiquity*, ed. D. R. Brothwell and A. T. Sandison, 320–45. Springfield, IL: Thomas.

Brothwell, D. and Powers, R. 1968. Congenital malformations of the skeleton in earlier man. In *The skeletal biology of earlier human populations*, ed. D. Brothwell, 173–203. Oxford: Pergamon Press.

Buikstra, J. E., Baker, B. J. and Cook, D. C. 1993. What diseases plagued the Ancient Egyptians? A century of controversy considered. In *Biological anthropology and the study of Ancient Egypt*, ed. W. V. Davies and R. Walker, 24–53. London: British Museum Press.

Cameron, J. 1910. Report on the anatomy of the mummies. In *The tomb of two brothers*, ed. M. A. Murray, 33–7. Manchester: Sherrat and Hughes.

Cockburn, A., Barraco, R. A., Reyman, T. A. and Peck, W. H. 1975. Autopsy of an Egyptian Mummy. *Science* **187**: 1155–60.

Czermack, J. 1852. Beschreibung und mikroskopische Untersuchung zweier ägyptischer Mumien. *Akademie der Wissenschaften Wien* **9**: 427–69.

Dawson, W. R. 1953. Egypt's place in medical history. In *Science, medicine and history*, ed. E. A. Underwood 47–60. London: Oxford University Press.

Deelder, A. M., Miller, R. L., De Jonge, N. and Krijger, F. W. 1990. Detection of schistosome antigen in mummies. *Lancet* **335**: 724.

Derry, D. E. 1909. Anatomical report. *Archaeological Survey of Nubia*, Bulletin 3. Cairo: National Printing Department.

Derry, D. E. 1940. An examination of the bones of king Psusennes I. *Annales du service des antiquités de l'Egypte* **40**: 969–70.

Derry, D. E. 1942. Report on the skeleton of King Amenenopet and Har-Nakht. *Annales du service des antiquités de l'Egypte* **42**: 149–50.

Derry, D. E. 1947. The bones of Prince Ptah-Shepses. *Annales du service des antiquités de l'Egypte* **47**: 139–40.

Elliot Smith, G. 1912. The royal mummies. *General Catalogue of Egyptian Antiquities*. Cairo: Cairo Museum.

Elliot Smith, G. and Dawson, W. R. 1924. *Egyptian mummies*. London: Allen and Unwin.

Elliot Smith, G. and Derry, D. E. 1910. Anatomical report. *Archaeological Survey of Nubia*, Bulletin 6. Cairo: National Printing Department.

Elliot Smith, G. and Wood Jones, F. 1908. Anatomical report. *Archaeological Survey of Nubia*, Bulletin 1. Cairo: National Printing Department.

Elliot Smith, G. and Wood Jones, F. eds. 1910. *Archaeological Survey of Nubia Report for 1907–1908*, vol. 2. *Report on human remains*. Cairo: National Printing Department.

Fairbank, T. 1951. *An atlas of general affections of the skeleton*. Edinburgh: Livingstone.

Fulcheri, E. and Grilletto, R. 1988. 'On a probable renal stone from the Old Kingdom.' Paper presented at the VII European meeting of the Paleopathology Association, Lyon, France. September 1988.

Ghalioungui, P. 1973. *The house of Life per Ankh: magic and medical science in ancient Egypt*. Amsterdam: B. M. Israel.

Golding, F. C. 1960. Rare diseases of the bone. In *Modern trends in diagnostic radiology*, ed. J. W. McLaren, 55–74. London: Butterworth.

Granville, A. B. 1825. An essay on Egyptian mummies. *Philosophical Transactions of the Royal Society* **1**: 269.

Gray, P. H. K. 1967. Calcinosis intervertebralis with special reference to similar changes found in mummies of ancient Egyptians. In *Diseases in antiquity*, ed. D. R. Brothwell and A. T. Sandison, 20–30. Springfield, IL: Thomas.

Hart, G. D., Cockburn, A., Millet, N. B. and Scott, J. W. 1977. Autopsy of an Egyptian Mummy ROM I. *Canadian Medical Association Journal* **117**: 461–73.

Isherwood, I. and Hart, C. W. 1992. The radiological examination. In *The mummy's tale*, ed. A. R. David and E. Tapp, 100–11. London: Michael O'Mara.

Kilgore, L. 1986. 'A possible case of rheumatoid arthritis in a skeleton from Sudanese Nubia.' Paper presented at the 13th annual meeting of the Paleopathology Association, Albuquerque, NM, USA. Abstract in *Paleopathology Newsletter* **54** (supplement): 12–13.

Lee, S. L. and Stenn, F. F. 1978. Characterization of mummy bone ochronotic pigment. *Journal of the American Medical Association* **240**: 136–8.

Lewin, P. 1982. 'Ramses V: smallpox victim?' Paper presented at the 9th annual meeting of Paleopathology Association, Toledo, OH, USA. Abstract in *Paleopathology Newsletter* **36** (supplement): 10.

Long, A. R. 1931: Cardiovascular renal disease: report of a case of 3000 years ago. *Archives of Pathology* **12**: 92–6.

Miller, R. L, Armelagos, G. J., Ikram, S., De Jong, N., Krijgers, F. W. and Deelder, A. M. 1992. Palaeoepidemiology of *Schistosoma* infection in mummies. *British Medical Journal* **304**: 555–6.

Miller, R. L., Ikram, S. and Armelagos, G. J. 1994. Diagnosis of *Plasmodium falciparum* in mummies using the rapid manual Para Site TM-F test. *Transactions of the Royal Society of Tropical Medicine and Hygiene* **88**: 31–52.

Mitchell, J. K. 1900. Study of a mummy affected with anterior poliomyelitis. *Transactions of the Association of American Physicians* **15**: 134–6.

Møller-Christensen, V. 1967. Evidence of leprosy in earlier peoples. In *Diseases in antiquity*, ed. D. Brothwell and A. T Sandison, 295–306. Springfield, IL: Thomas.

Molto, J. E. 1989. 'Spina bifida occulta in skeletal samples from the Dakhleh Oasis.' Paper presented at the 16th annual meeting of the Paleopathology Association, San Diego. Abstract in *Paleopathology Newsletter* **66** (supplement): 8.

Moodie, R. L. 1923. *Palaeopathology: an introduction to the study of ancient evidences of disease.* Urbana: University of Illinois Press.

Morse, D. 1967. Tuberculosis. In *Diseases in antiquity*, ed. D. Brothwell and A. T. Sandison, 249–71. Springfield, IL: Thomas.

Morse, D., Brothwell, D., and Ucko, P. J. 1964. Tuberculosis in ancient Egypt. *American Review of Respiratory Diseases* **90**: 524–30.

Nunn, J. F. 1996. *Ancient Egyptian Medicine.* London: British Museum Press.

Pahl, W. M., Asaad, E., Khattar, N. Y. and El-Maligy, M. 1984. Macroscopic and radiological aspects of tumors of the skull in ancient Egyptians. Abstract in *Proceedings of the V European meeting of the Paleopathology Association*, ed. V. Capecchi and E. Rabino Massa, 259. Siena: Siena University.

Rabino Massa, E. 1978. 'Two cases of spina bifida in Egyptian mummies.' Paper presented at the 2nd European meeting of the Paleopathology Association, Turin. Abstract in *Paleopathology Newsletter* **25** (supplement): 13.

Rabino Massa, E. 1982. Post-partum inversion of the uterus in an Egyptian dynastic mummy. Abstract in *Proceedings of the 4th European meeting of the Paleopathology Association*, ed. G. T. Haneveld and W. R. K. Perizonius, 170. Utrecht: Elinkwijk B. V.

Rogers, L. 1949. Meningiomas in pharaoh's people: hyperostosis in ancient Egyptian skulls. *British Journal of Surgery* **36**: 423–6.

Rowling, J. T. 1960. Disease in ancient Egypt: evidence from pathological lesions found in mummies. Doctoral dissertation. University of Cambridge.

Rowling, J. T. 1967. Respiratory disease in Egypt. In *Diseases in antiquity*, ed. D. Brothwell and A. T. Sandison, 489–93. Springfield, IL: Thomas.

Ruffer, M. A. 1910a. Remarks on the histology and pathological anatomy of Egyptian mummies. *Cairo Scientific Journal* **4**: 1–5.

Ruffer, M. A. 1910b. Note on the presence of *Bilharzia haematobia* in Egyptian mummies of the Twentieth Dynasty (1250–1000 BC) *British Medical Journal* **1**: 16.

Ruffer, M. A. 1911a. Histological studies on Egyptian mummies. *Mémoires sur l'Egypte: Institut d'Egypte* **6**(3): 1–33.

Ruffer, M. A. 1911b. On arterial lesions found in Egyptian mummies (1580 BC–525 AD). *Journal of Pathology and Bacteriology* **15**: 453–62.

Ruffer, M. A. 1921. *Studies in the palaeopathology of Egypt.* Chicago: University of Chicago Press.

Ruffer, M. A. and Ferguson, A. R. 1911. Note on an eruption resembling that of variola in the skin of a mummy of the Twentieth-Dynasty (1200–1100 BC) *Journal of Pathology and Bacteriology* **15**: 1.

Ruffer, M. A and Rietti, A. 1912. On osseous lesions in ancient Egyptians. *Journal of Pathology and Bacteriology* **16**: 439–465.

Ruffer, M. A. and Willmore, J. G. 1914. A tumor of the pelvis dating from Roman times (AD 250) and found in Egypt. *Journal of Pathology and Bacteriology* **18**: 480–4.

Sandison, A. T. 1955. The histological examination of mummified material. *Stain Technology* **30**: 277–83.

Sandison, A. T. 1967a. Degenerative vascular disease. In *Diseases in antiquity*, ed. D. Brothwell and A. T Sandison, 474–88. Springfield, IL: Thomas.

Sandison, A. T. 1967b. Diseases of the eyes. In *Diseases in antiquity*, ed. D. Brothwell and A. T Sandison, 457–63. Springfield, IL: Thomas.

Sandison, A. T. 1968. Pathological changes in the skeletons of earlier populations due to acquired disease and difficulties in their interpretation. In *The skeletal biology of earlier human populations*. ed. D. Brothwell, 205–43. Oxford: Pergamon Press.

Sandison, A. T. 1970. The study of mummified and dried human tissues. In *Science in archaeology*, 2nd edn, ed. D. Brothwell and E. Higgs, 490–502. London: Thames and Hudson.

Schultz, M. 1995. Results of the osteological examination of infant skeletons from Elephantine (Egyptian Nubia). Abstract in *Proceedings of the IX European meeting of the Paleopathology Association*, ed. R. Batista, D. Campillo, and T. Carreras, 359. Barcelona: Museu d'Arqueologia de Catalunya.

Shattock, S. G. 1909. A report upon the pathological condition of the aorta of King Merneptah. *Proceedings of the Royal Society of Medicine* **2**: 122–7.

Shaw, A. F. B. 1938. A histological study of the mummy of Har-Mose, the singer of the Eighteenth Dynasty (c. 1490 BC). *Journal of Pathology and Bacteriology* **47**: 115–23.

Strouhal, E. 1982. Paleopathology of Late Period population of Abusir (Egypt). In *Proceedings of the 4th European meeting of the Paleopathology Association*, ed. G. T. Haneveld and W. R. K. Perizonius, 151–9. Utrecht: Elinkwijk B. V.

Tapp, E. 1979a. The unwrapping of a mummy. In *The Manchester Museum mummy project*, ed. A. R. David, 83–93. Manchester: Manchester Museum Press.

Tapp, E. 1979b. Disease in the Manchester mummies. In *The Manchester Museum mummy project*, ed. A. R. David, 95–102. Manchester: Manchester Museum Press.

Tapp, E. 1984. Disease and the Manchester mummies – the pathologist's role. In *Evidence embalmed*, ed. A. R. David and E. Tapp, 78–95. Manchester: Manchester University Press.

Tapp, E. 1986. Histology and histopathology of the Manchester mummies. In *Science in Egyptology*, ed. A. R. David, 247–350. Manchester: Manchester University Press.

Tapp, E. 1997. The histological examination of an ovarian tumor. In *Irty Senu: Granville's Egyptian female mummy: the autopsies of 1824 and 1994*. ed. W. B. Harer and J. H. Taylor. London: British Museum Press. In press.

Tapp, E. and Wildsmith, K. 1986. Endoscopy of Egyptian mummies. In *Science in Egyptology*, ed. A. R. David, 351–4. Manchester: Manchester University Press.

Tapp, E. and Wildsmith, K. 1992. The autopsy and endoscopy of the Leeds mummy. In *The Mummy's tale*, ed. A. R. David and E. Tapp, 132–53. London: Michael O'Mara.

Tapp, E., Curry, A. and Anfield, C. 1975. Sand pneumoconiosis in an Egyptian mummy. *British Medical Journal* **2**: 276.

Tapp, E., Stanworth, P. and Wildsmith, K. 1984. The endoscope in mummy research. In *Evidence embalmed*, ed. A. R. David and E. Tapp, 55–77. Manchester: Manchester University Press.

Valenti, V. 1984. Palaeomorphology and Palaeopathology of the Ancient Egyptian Foot. In *Proceedings of the V European meeting of the Paleopathology Association*, ed. V. Capecchi and E. Rabino Massa, 355–72. Siena: Siena University.

Weeks, K. R. 1970. 'The anatomical knowledge of the Ancient Egyptian and the representation of the human figure in Egyptian art.' Doctoral dissertation. Yale University.

Wells, C. 1964. *Bones, bodies and disease*. London: Thames & Hudson.

Wells, C. 1967. Pseudopathology. In *Diseases in antiquity*, ed. D. Brothwell and A. T. Sandison, 5–19. Springfield, IL: Thomas.

Williams, H. U. 1929. Human paleopathology. *Archives of Pathology* 7: 839–902.

Wood Jones, F. 1908. The pathological report. *Archaeological Survey of Nubia*, Bulletin 2. Cairo: National Printing Department.

Zimmerman, M. R. and Mirro, J. 1983. The paleopathology of the human remains from Nebwenenef's tomb, Part II. The histologic findings. *Paleopathology Newsletter* **42**: 6–7.

Zorab, P. A. 1961. The historical and prehistorical background of ankylosing spondylitis. *Proceedings of the Royal Society of Medicine* **54**: 415–20.

3

Dental health in ancient Egypt

JAMES E. HARRIS, PAUL V. PONITZ AND BRIAN K. INGALLS

Because any meaningful discussion must include a time span of well over 3000 years, the survey of dental health in ancient Egypt is an ambitious task. A simplified time line would begin with the unification of Upper and Lower Egypt (3100 BC) and end with the conquest of Egypt by the Roman Empire (30 BC). This 3000 year span may be further divided by the dynastic periods of the Old Kingdom (2686–2181 BC), Middle Kingdom (2050–1786 BC) and the New Kingdom Periods (1600–1085 BC); the Late Dynastic Periods (1085–300 BC); and the Ptolemaic Period (300 BC–AD 30).

In reviewing the literature that examines dentistry and dental health in ancient Egypt, it is clear that many authors have based their conclusions on the biological record (mummies) from discrete periods in the 3000 year history. Piccione (1996) has recently completed the Bibliography of Egyptian Medicine, which includes practically every medical and dental publication relating to ancient Egypt. This was a Herculean task given the disparate disciplines and corresponding journals with an interest in some aspect of ancient Egyptian medicine. The problem remains that data are often based on small sample sizes or even single mummies from various museum collections throughout the world. Many of the mummies in museum collections are derived from the later period, particularly the Greek–Roman period, whereas there are fewer examples from the Old or Middle or New Kingdoms. Hence, there is always the danger of over generalization in the discussion of dental health over this vast period of time in Egyptian history.

Unfortunately, although there has always been tremendous curiosity about the Egyptian mummy during most of the history of exploration and excavation of the Egyptian tombs, relatively few mummies have survived intact and identified. In Egypt, substantial collections are housed at the Kasr el Einy Faculty of Medicine (the Derry–Batrawi Collection), The Greek Roman Museum in Alexandria, the Reisner collection at the Giza Plateau, the Nobles and Priests of the XXI Dynasty in the Cache at the Valley of the Kings, and the

Old Kingdom Collection in the Tombs of Aswan. Most of these mummies are no longer identified by title or name, although their general period has been established. There is renewed interest among many current expeditions to include the study of the mummified remains in Egypt, including those of the workers' villages of the Giza Plateau and the Greco-Roman cemeteries in the Fayoum.

In the campaign to save the monuments of Nubia which began in the early 1960s, there was a concerted attempt to preserve the biological record along with the archaeological history of the Nubian people. Many expeditions included the study and even collection of naturally mummified remains before the inundation created by the building of the Aswan High Dam. Extensive cemetery excavations at the old Nubian fortress of Gebel Adda near Abu Simbel Temple resulted in finding several thousand naturally mummified individuals from a period of almost 1300 years (AD 200–1500). This material excavated by Millet and Weeks (in Harris *et al.* 1970) was made available to the University of Michigan expedition in 1966 for investigation by x-ray cephalometry. Ultimately, the Michigan expeditions continued to study the living Nubian descendants of Abu Simbel and Ballana villages for over 20 years (Harris and Ponitz 1996). Extensive investigations into the anthropology and paleo-pathology of the ancient Nubian people (3400–1500 BC) living near the Egyptian–Sudanese border at Wadi Halfa have been reported by Greene (Greene *et al.* 1962; Greene 1982), Calcagno and Gibson (1988), and Carlson and Van Gerven (1979). Large sample sizes provided by the various Nubian expeditions offered the opportunity of utilizing multivariate analyses to examine dental and craniofacial variability over long time periods. These studies have made important contributions to micro-evolution, documenting tooth size reduction and craniofacial skeletal remodeling during those periods.

From the dental point of view, how may the ancient Egyptian be character-ized as far as dental disease is concerned? The greatest single problem was attrition, or wear (Figure 3.1). The teeth were rapidly worn down throughout life by the consumption of a coarse diet. Interestingly enough, the pharaohs of Egypt exhibit this wear just as do the farmers of both modern and ancient Egypt. In time, this wear becomes so extensive that the enamel and dentine are eroded away until the pulp is exposed. The living tissue inside the tooth dies, and the empty root canals become a source of chronic infection and abscess. The teeth of Ramesses II are excellent examples of the effects of old age, attrition, and ultimate abscesses (Figure 3.2). Ghalioungui and El Dawakhly (1965) concluded that the dental surgeon drained these types of abscess through a hollow reed.

FIGURE 3.1. Dental wear or attrition typical of ancient and modern rural Egyptians. This mandible was found in a Nubian cemetery of AD 250.

The second greatest problem from the viewpoint of both ancient and modern Egyptians was periodontitis (disease of the supporting tissue of the teeth). This disease results in loss of the bony support of the teeth and is often associated with plaque resulting in calculus, or tartar, deposits on the teeth. Calculus was often so extensive in the skulls of the ancient Nubians that this deposit frequently held the teeth in place 1500 years after death. Although calculus deposits of any consequence are rarely seen in Americans below 20 years of age, they have been observed in Nubian children in elementary school (Holden *et al.* 1970). The ultimate result is extensive periodontal disease, which results in the loss of bony support, loose teeth, and deep periodontal pockets or even exposed root bifurcations. This in turn leads to infection, abscesses, and loss of teeth.

Dental caries, or cavities, were far less frequently seen in ancient Egyptians or Nubians until the latter population was moved to New Nubia near Kom Ombo and the great sugar cane fields. Neither ancient kings, nor nobles, nor commoners exhibited extensive dental decay, and where observed, the decay was of the pit-and-fissure variety (top of the tooth) rather than interproximal (decay between the teeth), so frequently seen in modern civilization. There are two major environmental causes,one may speculate, that may have resulted in the lack of extensive dental decay. The first is the absence from the diet of refined carbohydrates such as sugar. The second, is the extreme attrition (wear) mentioned earlier, for wear occurs not only on the occlusal surface (top of the teeth), but between the teeth (interproximally) as well. The extensive wear provides a more difficult environment for decay to begin. Leek

FIGURE 3.2. Lateral cephalogram of the mummy of Ramesses II. This pharaoh had a bone age of 70+ years, and the extreme wear of the teeth may be noted, with resulting exposure of the pulp chambers and periapical abcesses. Periodontal disease, or loss of bone support of the dentition, is also apparent.

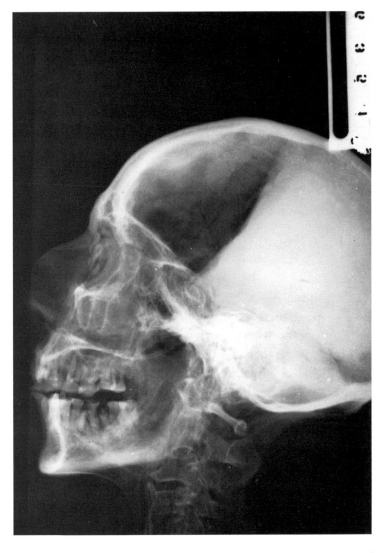

(1967) has related dental wear to the grinding of wheat in the preparation of bread. Ibrahim (1987) in a study of attrition and diet in a period ranging from 5000 BC to AD 500 concluded that there was less attrition over time due to diet but carious lesions and hypoplasia increased over time. He attributed the increase in caries to the availability of honey among the more affluent population.

Although there has been limited discussion of dental morphology in the ancient Egyptian samples, tooth size, eruption sequences, impactions of third molars, supernumerary teeth, congenitally missing teeth, root form, and enamel and dentine dyscrasias have been noted.

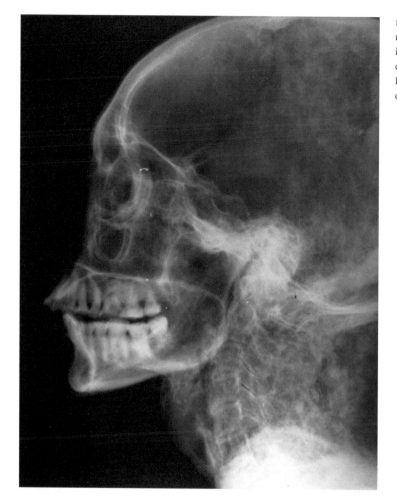

FIGURE 3.3. Cephalometric x-ray of the mummy of the Queen Ahmose Nefertiry illustrating the maxillary prognathism characteristic of the queens of the early Eighteenth Dynasty. Note the attrition of the dentition.

A brief comment on dental occlusion or malocclusion and facial types is appropriate. In general, perhaps owing to extreme wear, the dentition of ancient Egyptians (Old Kingdom) and ancient Nubians rarely exhibited dental crowding. The latter, in fact, tended to have congenitally missing teeth more frequently than supernumerary teeth (Harris and Ponitz 1996). Most modern Egyptians have good molar relationships with moderate to severe crowding. If, however, the queens of the New Kingdom period (early Eighteenth Dynasty) are examined by x-ray cephalometry, many resemble modern Europeans or Americans, with maxillary, or upper jaw, prognathism. This condition may be either hereditary or environmental, i.e., the result of thumb sucking or other oral habits. Queen Ahmose Nefertiry is an excellent example of this type of occlusion (Figure 3.3). In modern Nubia, this same

FIGURE 3.4.
Computerized tracings
of the x-rays of the
mummies of (a)
Thutmose I and (b)
Thutmose IV of the
Eighteenth Dynasty.
These two facial profiles
and anterior dentition
demonstrate the remark-
able heterogeneity among
the pharaohs of the New
Kingdom.

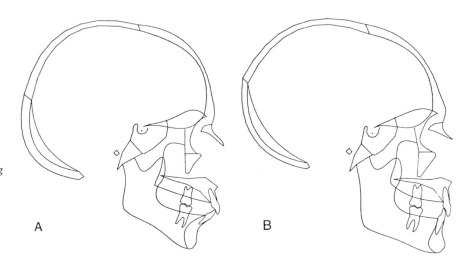

A B

FIGURE 3.4. Computerized tracings of the x-rays of the mummies of (a) Thutmose I and (b) Thutmose IV of the Eighteenth Dynasty. These two facial profiles and anterior dentition demonstrate the remarkable heterogeneity among the pharaohs of the New Kingdom.

condition has been observed, but appears to be the result of functional habits, i.e., tongue thrusting or thumb sucking.

Many of the Kings and Queens of the New Kingdom period in Egypt had little similarity in appearance, contrary to their stylized portraits found in contemporary tombs and temples. Computer tracings of the x-ray cephalograms of the mummies of Thutmose I and Thutmose IV dramatize considerable heterogeneity in the skulls of mummies of the Eighteenth Dynasty (Figure 3.4). The historical record is supported by biological evidence that the pharaohs of the New Kingdom period of Egypt were quite heterogeneous, like the present population of the United States. During the New Kingdom period the Egyptian royal court included many members of royal families from other nations under Egyptian power and influence. These princes and princesses represented potential consorts (Wente 1980; Iskander and Badawy 1965). Except for Tuthmosis I, II, and III, most of the pharaohs of the New Kingdom period had Class I (i.e., neutro-occlusion) molar relationships with straight profiles, but neither their craniofacial skeletons nor their soft tissues suggested homogeneity of appearance.

In contrast, x-ray cephalograms indicated that the nobles of the Old Kingdom studied at Giza (approximately 2400–2000 BC) and those of the New Kingdom (1200–1000 BC) examined at Deir el-Bahri were quite homogeneous. It would therefore appear that admixture was restricted to the royal and noble families and was not readily observable in the skeletal remains of the average Egyptian (Hussien and Shaban 1979; Wente and Harris 1992).

An examination of dental health would not be complete without a discussion of medicine and the medical profession in ancient Egypt. Many authors such as Leek (1967), Hoffmann-Axthelm (1979), and Reymond (1984) feel there is not a sufficient body of evidence to indicate dental specialization . On the other hand, Ghalioungui and El Dawakhly (1965), Harris, Iskander, and Farid (1975), Weeks (1980) and Chohayeb (1991) conclude that there were dental specialists. Greater weight must be perhaps given to scholars such as Ghalioungui and El Dawakhly (1965), Weeks (1980) and Reymond (1984) who have translated directly from the ancient Egyptian texts. Ghalioungui and El Dawakhly (1965) and Weeks (1980) recall that Hesy-Re (Third Dynasty), the oldest person in history who ever carried the title of physician, even in the time of Imhotep, two thousand years before the war of Troy, called himself 'Chief of Dentists' (Figure 3.5). The time would date back to the Old Kingdom, and there are many medical papyri, such as the famous Ebers papyrus (Ebell 1937), that prescribe medicines to relieve dental pain and even describe how to fix loose teeth.

In 1975, Harris, Iskander, and Farid reported the discovery of a dental bridge from the Fourth Dynasty of the Old Kingdom, about 2500 BC (Figure 3.6). This bridge replaced a maxillary right lateral and central incisor and was attached to the left central incisor and cuspid. The bridge consisted of pre-pared natural teeth, which had very fine holes drilled through them, and gold wire, which was used in a skillful manner to attach the substitute teeth to the abutment teeth. This find, together with the written evidence of the medical papyri, suggests that Ghalioungui and El Dawakhly (1965) were correct when, speaking of the remarkable specialization of medicine, they cited 'Men-kaou-Re-ank who was called a maker of teeth (iry-ibh), to distinguish him from Ni-ankh-Sekhmet who figures on the same stele as a tooth physician.'

Weeks (1980) lists the only six Egyptian dentists known to us, but strangely only one, Psammetik-seneb of the Twenty-sixth Dynasty, is not from the Old Kingdom. Weeks speculates that the specialty of dentistry may have peaked in the Old Kingdom (2400–2000 BC).

In short, Egypt has the most complete biological record documented by history of any country in the world. Comparisons of the ancient Egyptians with modern Egyptians suggest that attrition and periodontal disease are common to both populations. Only in recent times, with the development of refined sugars, has dental decay become a major problem in urban areas of Egypt. The ancient pharaohs and queens of Egypt show in their dental occlusion and craniofacial skeleton, as revealed by x-rays, the diversity and heterogeneity one might assign to modern Western communities with a history of racial admixture. The Egyptian nobles and the Nubian people present a much

FIGURE 3.5. Portrait and Titles of Office of Hesy-Re, Chief Physician and Chief of Dentists, inscribed on wooden panels from the Old Kingdom (2650 BC), Egyptian Museum.

more homogeneous facial skeleton with good occlusion, and moderate bimaxillary protrusion sometimes associated with dental crowding (Harris 1989, Harris and Ponitz 1996).

The study of dental health and disease in ancient Egypt is at best sporadic and incomplete. Until sufficient samples are examined from throughout the

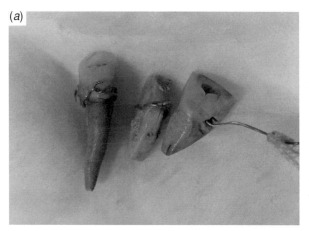

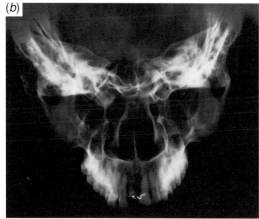

long inhabitation of the Nile Valley, the findings of the present literature must be considered tentative and incomplete, although a valuable beginning. The question of whether or not there was a dental specialty founded upon a body of knowledge that included formalized treatment procedures, surgery, medications, and even dental restorations remains to be answered.

FIGURE 3.6. (a). Dental bridge from the Old Kingdom (2500 BC) consisting of artificially prepared natural teeth and gold wire. (b). X-ray of anterior bridge attached by silver wire from late period (approximately 300 BC).

REFERENCES

Calcagno, J. M. and Gibson, K. R. 1988. Human dental reduction: natural selection or the probable mutation effect. *American Journal of Physical Anthropology* **77**: 505–17.

Carlson, D. S. and Van Gerven, D. P. 1979. Diffusion, biological determinism, and biocultural adaptation in the Nubian corridor. *American Anthropology* **81**: 561–80.

Chohayeb, A. A. 1991. The dental heritage of ancient Egypt. *Bulletin of the History of Dentistry* **39**: 65–9.

Ebell, E. 1937. *The Papyrus Ebers, the greatest Egyptian medical document* (translation), 103. Copenhagen: Levin & Munksgaard.

Ghalioungui, P. and El Dawakhly, Z. 1965. *Health and healing in ancient Egypt*, 12. Cairo: Egyptian Organization for Authorship and Translation.

Greene, D. L. 1982. Discrete dental variations and biological distances of Nubian populations. *American Journal of Physical Anthropology* **58**: 75–9.

Greene, D. L., Ewing, G. H. and Armelagos, G. J. 1962 Dentition of a Mesolithic population from Wadi

Halfa, Sudan. *American Journal of Physical Anthropology* **27**:41–55.

Harris, J. E. 1989 The Nubian people of the Nile Valley: past and present. *Paleopathology Newsletter* **67**: 9–13.

Harris, J. E. and Ponitz, P. V. 1996. The Egyptian Nubian people of Kom Ombo. In *Genetic disorders among Arab populations*, ed. E. S. Teebi and T. I. Farag, 411–31. Oxford: Oxford University Press.

Harris, J. E., Iskander, Z. and Farid, S. 1975. Restorative dentistry in ancient Egypt: an archaeologic fact. *Journal of the Michigan Dental Association* **57**: 401–4.

Harris, J. E., Ponitz, P. V. and Loutfy, M. S. 1970. Orthodontic's contribution to save the monuments of Nubia: a 1970 field report. *American Journal of Orthodontics* **58**(6): 578–96.

Hoffmann-Axthelm, W. 1979. Is the practice of dentistry in Ancient Egypt an archaeological fact? *Bulletin of the History of Dentistry* **29**: 71–7.

Holden, S., Harris, J. E. and Ash, M. 1970 Periodontal disease in Nubian children. In *International Association* of *Dental Research Program and Abstract of Papers*, 65. Chicago: American Dental Association.

Hussien, F. H. and Shaban, M. M. 1979. On the homogeneity of the pyramid builders as evidence of their endogenous origin. *Egyptian Journal of Anatomy* **2**: 133–42.

Ibrahim, M. A. 1987. A study of dental attrition and diet in some ancient Egyptian populations. Doctoral dissertation, University of Durham, UK.

Iskander, Z. and Badawy, A. 1965. *Brief history of ancient Egypt*, 5th edn, 207. Cairo: Madkour Press.

Leek, F. F. 1967 The practice of dentistry in ancient Egypt. *Egyptian Archaeological Journal* **53**: 51–8.

Piccione, P. A. 1994. Bibliography of Egyptian Medicine, University of Chicago. Manuscript.

Reymond. E. A. 1984. From an ancient Egyptian dentist's handbook. In *Mélanges Adolphe Gutbub, l'Institut d'Egyptologie, Université Paul Valery*, 183–9. Montpellier: Université de Montpellier.

Ruffer, M. A. 1908. Abnormalities and pathology of ancient Egyptian teeth. *American Journal of Physical Anthropology* **3**: 335–82.

Weeks, K. R. 1980. Ancient Egyptian Dentistry. In *An x-ray atlas of the Royal mummies*, ed. J. E. Harris and E. F. Wente, 99–121. Chicago: University of Chicago Press.

Wente, E. F. 1980. Genealogy of the Royal Familes. In *An x-ray atlas of the royal mummies*, ed. J. E. Harris and E. F. Wente, 124–62. Chicago: University of Chicago Press.

Wente, E. F. and Harris, J. E. 1992. Royal mummies of the Eighteenth Dynasty. In *After Tut'ankhamun: research and excavation in the royal necropolis at Thebes*, ed. C. N. Reeves, 2–20 London: Kegan Paul International.

4

A classic mummy: PUM II

AIDAN COCKBURN, ROBIN A. BARRACO, WILLIAM H. PECK
AND THEODORE A. REYMAN

The traditional Egyptian mummy is one on which all the arts of the embalmers have been employed; the organs have been preserved, the body is wrapped in linen, and everything is contained in a highly decorated sarcophagus. Such was mummy PUM II. It belongs to the Philadelphia Art Museum and was lent to the Paleopathology Association for dissection and study through the courtesy of David O'Connor of the Pennsylvania University Museum, thus its name PUM II, being the second mummy from that museum. PUM II is now on display at the Pennsylvania University Museum, complete with the sarcophagus and photographs of the unwrapping and the autopsy findings.

Little is known of the provenance of this mummy (Figure 4.1). It was brought to America about the turn of the century by John T. Morris, a wealthy Philadelphian, who donated it to the Philadelphia Art Museum (Cockburn and Ballard 1992), but its origins in Egypt are unknown. The sarcophagus was highly decorated but lacked the name and any details of the person inside (Figure 4.2). The unwrapping and autopsy of PUM II took place on February

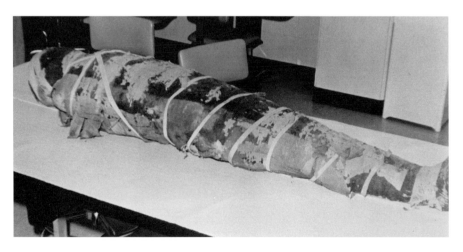

FIGURE 4.1. PUM II, the mummy before unwrapping (Photograph by Nemo Warr, Detroit Institute of Arts).

1, 1973, as part of a symposium (Death and Disease in Ancient Egypt) that was held at Wayne State University Medical School, Detroit, Michigan (Cockburn 1973). Radiographic and xerographic examinations at Mt Carmel Mercy and Hutzel Hospitals, Detroit, were performed prior to and following the autopsy (Kristen and Reyman 1980). The mummy seemed to be well preserved. The brain had been removed and replaced with resin, which formed a pool in the skull before it solidified, appearing in the radiographs as a 'water level'. An

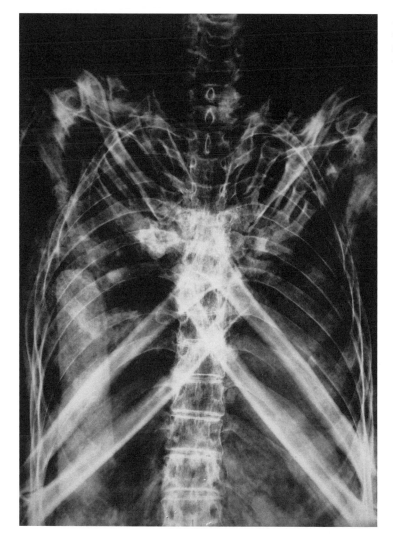

FIGURE 4.3. An elongated visceral package containing internal organs is seen in this radiograph in the right side of the chest and upper abdomen.

erroneous diagnosis of fractured skull was the result of several deep scratches in the resin that covered the scalp, being interpreted as linear defects in the bone prior to unwrapping. Four visceral packages were seen in the body cavities (Figure 4.3). No amulets or relics were visible in the wrappings. There was a transitional or sixth lumbar vertebral body that might have made stooping painful and difficult during life. The right fibula and adjacent tibia had pathological thickenings resembling periostitis (Figure 4.4). Polytomographs of the skull showed the hole punched through the cribriform plate for removal of the brain (Figure 4.5). The temporal bones appeared normal.

FIGURE 4.4. Right fibula of PUM II, showing an irregular cortical margin (1). A small similar area is seen on the lateral tibia (2). Note growth arrest (Harris) lines (3).

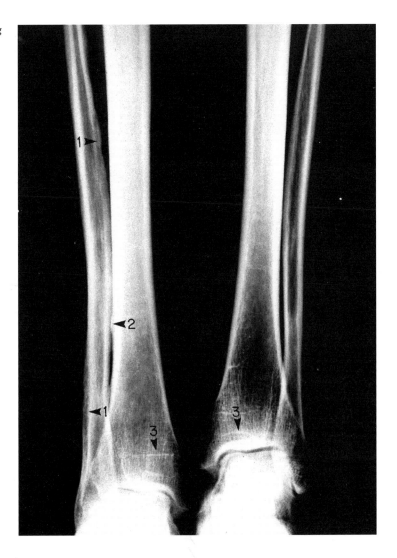

REMOVAL OF WRAPPINGS AND GENERAL EXAMINATION

There proved to be about 12 layers of linen wrapping of varying qualities of cloth. The outer layers were generally larger sheets or strips of fine weave. Hot liquid resin had been poured liberally over the body at many stages so that most of the wrappings had been converted into a hard, solid mass, which could be removed only with a hammer and chisel or cut through, several layers at a time, with a Stryker saw. After the general broad wrapping had been removed, it was found that limbs and even individual fingers and toes were wrapped separately. As many as nine people worked simultaneously,

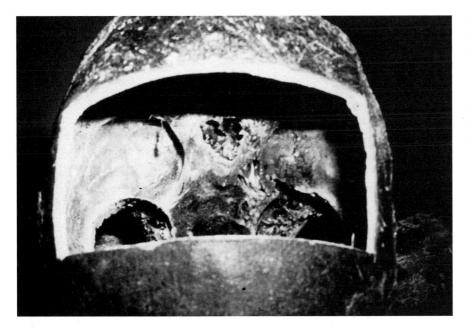

FIGURE 4.5. Skull. The openings in the base are two circular ones made by the Stryker saw used in dissection; the foramen magnum is in between; and the irregular opening above these was made by the embalmers.

but it still required almost seven hours to strip away all the bandages completely.

The wrappings were examined by Meryl Johnson (1974). As expected, the cloth was linen with a simple weave, but a complete surprise was the discovery of a ball of cotton enclosed between two pieces of linen. It was adherent to the linen and was partially coated with some nondescript material that could have been unguent or tissue juice. As cotton has not been recorded in the Mediterranean world before Christ, the earliest find being from a Roman grave about AD 200, there was much speculation about the find. Cotton has been found in cultures of the Indus Valley and South America dating back to about 2000 BC, but how did it arrive in Egypt by 200 BC? By the time of the Romans, there was considerable trade with India, and indeed the Romans had several trading posts in southern India (Miller 1969). Could the Egyptians have used one of those trade routes to import cotton as early as 200 BC? As Meryl Johnson speculated, cotton was so rare and valuable that the ball found in PUM II may have been included as a form of amulet.

THE GENERAL AUTOPSY

The skin and tissues were as hard as plastic and were cut with a Stryker saw. When the blade cut through the resin, the resin burned with a most fragrant

FIGURE 4.6. The embalmers' incision. The abdomen has been opened, and the layers of wrappings, congealed into one mass, can be seen. (Photograph by Nemo Warr, Detroit Institute of Arts.)

FIGURE 4.7. Visceral package containing lung covered by fly pupae, which are covered with resin. (Photograph by Nemo Warr, Detroit Institute of Arts.)

odor. The anterior abdominal wall and the incision made by the embalmers in the left side were cut out and removed (Figure 4.6). Inside the abdominal and thoracic cavities there were four visceral packages. Hot resin had been poured in, covering both the packages and the floors of the thorax, abdomen and pelvis. The packages were removed with a chisel and were found to be covered with pupae (Figure 4.7) preserved by the resin; further study showed that one package contained spleen and some intestine and the other three contained only lung. Some of the aorta and a piece of heart tissue were found *in situ*. The liver, kidneys and urinary bladder were not identified. The penis was intact, held in an upright position with support from a small piece of wood (Figure 4.8). There had been no circumcision. The testes were not identified. The right leg appeared to be swollen with impressions of the

FIGURE 4.8. The penis was supported by a small wooden slat. (Photograph by Nemo Warr, Detroit Institute of Arts.)

bandages on the skin (Figure 4.9). The hands and the feet were in excellent condition. The nails were painted red with henna and the soles of the feet were white with lime. Radiographs taken before the autopsy had shown a fluid level pattern in the skull, so a window was cut in the cranium above that point. It was found that resin had been poured into the cranial vault through a hole punched through the base of the skull by a tool forced up the left nostril. Presumably, the brain had been removed through this hole before the resin was introduced. Originally, we had supposed that the brain would simply

FIGURE 4.9. Lower part of the legs. The right leg is swollen and shows the marks of the bandages. (Photograph by Nemo Warr, Detroit Institute of Arts.)

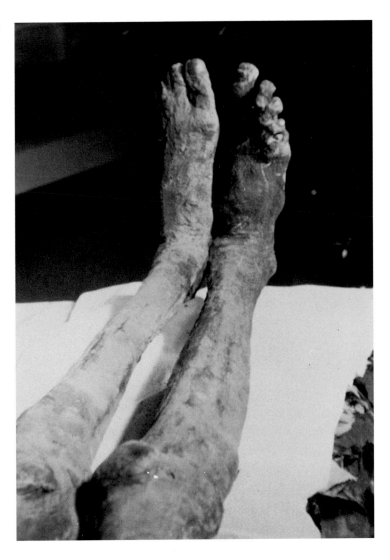

liquefy after death and could be drained away. However, this does not happen. Brain tissue, if undisturbed, retains its general shape and shrinks to about one-third its original volume, as was the case in mummies ROM I, PUM I and PUM IV (see chapters 5 and 6).

The eyes were intact and upon removal appeared normal although shrunken. The temporal bones containing the auditory structures were removed with a circular saw and taken out through the window in the skull (Figure 4.5). The spinal canal was opened but no spinal cord was present. P. K. Lewin noted that the color of the mummy's skin had changed from a light brown to dark brown after 24 hours. Within a few days, the skin was almost black. J. L. Angel estimated the age of the individual as between 35 and 40 years and his height as approximately 162 cm (5 ft 4 in.).

SPECIAL STUDIES

There has been speculation that organisms such as seeds and bacterial spores might survive long dormant periods, as we have seen with anthrax and other hardy organisms. Despite the possibility of present day contamination, cultures were taken from the abdominal cavity in areas remote from the opening. All were sterile. In two previous mummies, Reyman had found the tissues to be riddled with fungi. In this case, none was found. The explanation is probably the abundant use of resin, which was obviously very hot and fluid when it was applied and which may have innate antimicrobial properties. The hot fluid penetrated not only into the large visceral cavities but also into the mastoid air cell via the foramen of the eighth nerve, into the middle ear through a perforation in the tympanic membrane, and even trickled from the skull down the entire length of the spinal canal.

THE RESIN

Specimens of the resin were distributed to a number of laboratories. One scientist was intrigued by the fragrant odor produced when the resin was cut by the Stryker saw and wanted to test this fragrance in his studies of smell. However, when a sample was set on fire, the resin melted and burned, giving off thick, black smoke that was most unpleasant.

An analysis of trace elements was undertaken by Nunnelley and his colleagues (1976). Their report, given later in this chapter, indicated that the resin had penetrated all the tissues of the body.

Another analysis was made by Coughlin (1977). Using mass spectroscopy, she found that the PUM II resin had completely polymerized into one vast and continuous molecular form. This polymerization was attributable to a combination of aging and electromagnetic properties of natural botanical products. The result was a kind of organic glass, an intermediate with respect to amber. This condition of being a 'glass' has been confirmed by x-ray diffraction.

The major constituent of PUM II mummy resin identified by those x-ray diffraction studies is the oil of a coniferous evergreen tree, *Juniperus*. This genus consists of approximately 35 species of evergreen trees or shrubs whose distribution ranges from the Arctic Circle to Mexico, the West Indies, the Azores, the Canary Islands, North Africa, Abyssinia, the mountains of East Africa, China, Formosa and the Himalayas. *Juniperus* is one of the few northern forms found in the southern hemisphere. These juniper trees have a fragrant wood, and a red to reddish-brown oil can be expressed from the wood, leaves and shoots.

Two additional, although minor, constituents were separated by means of an organic extraction and filtration technique. One of the additional components identified by thin-layer chromatography was an oil from the aromatic tree, Lauraceae, *Cinnamomum camphora*. This is the camphor tree, whose enlarged base, twigs and bruised leaves have a marked camphor odor. The tree is found in Ceylon and Asia. The third component detected was myrrh, the fragrant gum resin exuded from special resin ducts in the bark of the myrrh tree, Burseraceae, *Commiphora myrra*. This tree is native to only two parts of the world – southern Arabia and northern Somalia.

Although minute quantities of other botanical products, such as spices or flowers, may be present, the principal components of the resin are the oils of juniper and camphor trees and the gum resin myrrh.

THE PACKAGES

Peck described earlier (chapter 1) how the Egyptians preserved certain organs either in canopic jars or by wrapping them in linen and replacing them in the mummy's abdominal cavity. The process of extracting water with natron shrank the organs considerably, some being one tenth their natural weight. Traditionally, the organs treated in this way were the lungs, liver, stomach and intestines. PUM II had the four customary packages but Reyman discovered that three of them contained only lung and the fourth only spleen plus a small piece of intestine. This lent support to the opinion that although the form of mummification had followed the traditional lines, it had suffered some debasement. The embalming obviously was expensive, yet the embalmers had handled organs in a slipshod way.

Some of the pupae found embalmed on the packages have been studied by the US Department of Agriculture at its Systematic Entomology Laboratory, Washington, DC. The entomologists at this laboratory pointed out that certain insects have specialized in breeding on decaying flesh and other organic material. Indeed, in PUM IV, a child eight years of age autopsied in Detroit in 1976 (Chapter 6), the insect larvae within the wrappings had been so numerous that they had penetrated to all parts of the body, including the brain, and had left large holes in bones and tissues.

In the case of PUM II, the process had not progressed to that point. The insects certainly had laid their eggs on both body and packages, larvae had hatched out and eaten their fill and some had turned into pupae; but at that point, the embalmers had poured in hot, liquid resin, which killed and embalmed them all in an instant, including one found on the left eardrum. The insects from PUM II so far identified (Cockburn *et al.* 1975) are: *Dermestes*, probably *frischii*; *Piophila casei*; *Atheta* sp.; and *Chrysomya* sp.

HISTOLOGY

In general, it can be said that the tissues from PUM II, such as bone, cartilage and muscle, were found to be in good condition with normal microstructure. The skin was preserved and showed intact glandular structures (but without nuclei), hair follicles, and an intact basal layer with melanin pigment and ghost forms of nuclei.

The lung tissue from the visceral packages contained intact bronchi and bronchioles with normal cartilage and connective tissue. Although there were areas of normal alveoli and septa, areas of diffuse and nodular fibrosis were also present. Within these fibrotic zones, there were anthracotic (carbon) and silicotic (silica) deposits (Figure 4.10a). The silica content of the lung was 0.22 percent; the normal value has an upper limit of 0.20 percent and is usually less than 0.05 percent. These findings indicate that the man had pneumoconiosis, probably from inhaling sand during desert dust storms. Whether PUM II had symptoms of this pulmonary disease is difficult to assess.

One of the packages housed spleen and a small portion of intestine. The spleen, with recognizable capsule and trabeculae, was normal. The intestinal tissue contained a single fragment of partially digested meat (muscle) fiber with residual striations. Also present in this tissue was a single parasite egg. This ovum has been studied by a number of helminthologists, who are agreed that it probably is *Ascaris*; some state definitely that it is *A. lumbricoides* (Figure 4.10b). This finding was not a complete surprise, for the ubiquitous *Ascaris* has already been reported from many locations in antiquity. Sometimes, there were millions of ova in the feces, as noted in ancient cesspits in Winchester, England (Biddle 1967).

Both eyes were collected, and the whole section of one revealed the lens to be present, although the cornea had disappeared. The choroid and the ciliary body were intact and contained melanin pigment, but there was no trace of the retina. Large nerves, probably those to the extrinsic eye muscles, were well preserved in the retrobulbar fat.

FIGURE 4.10.
Photomicrographs, all
Trichrome stain. (a) Lung
tissue showing dark
carbon pigment and
bright silica particles with
polarized light; (b) *Ascaris*
(probably) *lumbricoides*
ovum from the intestine
of PUM II; (c) atherosclerotic plaque (arrow) in the
aorta; (d) cross section of
fibula showing periosteal
new bone growth (arrow).
(Courtesy of the New York
Academy of Medicine.)

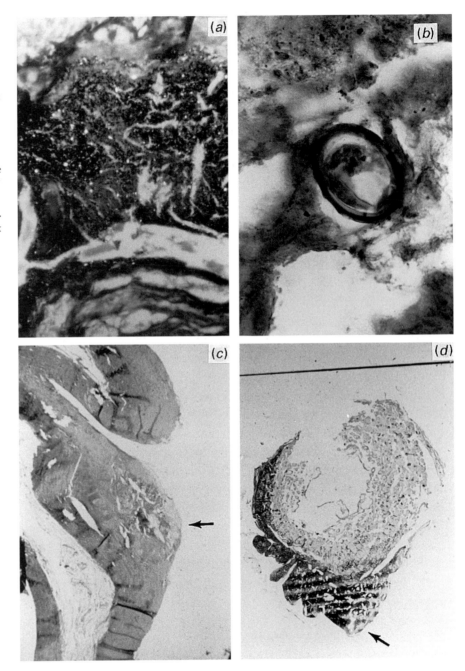

Portions of the aorta and other vessels were found in the visceral packages; large and small arteries and arterioles showed areas of intimal fibrosis with fatty plaques, typical of atherosclerosis (Figure 4.10c). In some of the vessels, partially and completely intact red blood cells could be seen.

It had been noted by the radiologists that the right leg was abnormal in that there appeared to be periostitis of the fibula and the adjacent part of the tibia. This abnormality was confirmed when the body was unwrapped, for the right leg was swollen compared with the left. The bandages wrapped around the right leg had left distinct marks, suggesting that it had been edematous at the time of mummification. The right toes were curled back and led to some dispute but it was finally agreed that this was a postmortem effect caused by the tightness of the wrappings. Microscopic sections of the right fibula (Reyman *et al.* 1976) revealed excessive periosteal new bone growth in the thickened areas (Figure 4.10d).

Benitez and Frost (1993), studying undecalcified sections of the right fibula and sections of rib, indicated that PUM II had osteopenia as a result of some chronic debilitating illness. This was supported by the finding of several Harris lines in the long bones, seen radiographically (Figure 4.4). The areas of periosteal new bone growth in the fibula had features of increased bone turnover, indicating a chronic reactive disorder localized to the right leg. The pattern is one of chronic venous and lymphatic obstruction and reinforces Aidan Cockburn's suggestion that this might be the result of a guinea worm (*Dracunculus* sp.) infestation.

Benitez was able to examine the auditory apparatus from both temporal bones (Figure 4.5). His histological findings indicated that the mastoid air cells were normal and that there was no evidence of otosclerosis. He did identify a smooth, oval perforation in the posterior inferior quadrant of the right tympanic membrane that had gross and microscopic features of an antemortem defect (Figure 4.11). Sections of the edge of the perforation showed healing, consistent with otitis media (Benitez 1988).

BIOCHEMICAL STUDIES

It is well known that amino acids are stable for immense periods of time. It is, therefore, not surprising that various workers have reported amino acids and even peptides from Egyptian mummies. However, it had usually been assumed that macromolecular proteins would break down into component parts over any significant length of time. Cockburn (1963) suggested that this might not necessarily be the case and that gamma globulin and even

FIGURE 4.11. Oval perforation in the tympanic membrane probably due to acute otitis media.

antibodies might persist under favorable conditions. It was to test this speculation that Barraco set out to isolate proteins from the tissues of PUM II.

Using standard biochemical techniques (Barraco 1980), he was able to extract what appeared to be pure protein of a molecular weight of 150 000 daltons (which is the same as gamma globulin), but subsequent testing indicated it to be biologically inactive. Trace amounts of intact, immunoreactive albumen were previously identified from PUM II by Reyman (Cockburn *et al.* 1980).

In the meantime, startling advances in the isolation and identification of macromolecules have been made and include the ABO blood group antigens (Allison *et al.* 1976; Hart *et al.* 1977; Henry 1980), HLA tissue antigens (Stasny 1974) and most recently both native and infectious DNA via the polymerase chain reaction (see chapter 16).

Another problem to be tackled was the question of whether any given mummy had been treated with natron. Mummies DIA I and PUM II quite obviously had been so treated, but the others remained in doubt. Some were simply wrapped in linen without preliminary dehydration. Barraco (1975) found that the salt content of the tissues of PUM II was very high, perhaps 10 times that of normal tissues, but the salt content of an untreated mummy (ROM I) was the same as in normal living tissues. This provides a future test for the use of natron. It also incidentally demonstrated that the natron, like the resin, had penetrated into all the tissues.

DATING

Several techniques are available for dating a mummy. First, radiocarbon dating was done by Stuckenrath (1975), using linen from the wrappings. The date he obtained was 170 BC±70 years. The coffin should give valuable information for dating, but Strouhal (personal communication 1973) reported that about 10 percent of the 180 mummies he examined in Czechoslovakia appeared to be in coffins not originally intended for them. Angel measured PUM II and concluded that his size was consistent with the assumption that the coffin was made for him. Photographs of the coffin taken by Angel were studied by Fischer (1975), who described it as Greco-Roman. The Apis bull carrying a dead man seen on the lower half of the coffin is a late motif. Fischer also noted that the slight garbling of the hieroglyphs and the absence of any name for the dead man suggest a stock coffin rather than one that was custom-made.

An estimate based on cultural features was given by E. Strouhal (personal communication 1973). At first sight, it appeared that the methods of mummification (packaging the organs, removing the brain, painting the nails with henna and the soles of the feet with lime, crossing the arms) indicated a mummy of the Third Intermediate period, perhaps about 700 BC. Later evidence showed that the organs were packaged carelessly, with three packages containing lung and one spleen and intestine, instead of lungs, liver, stomach and intestines being placed in separate packages. Circumcision had not been performed. These facts suggested that the methods were a debased form of those used in an earlier period.

The linen wrappings were examined by Johnson (1975), who believed them to be Ptolemaic. In short, all the evidence points to the Ptolemaic period, about 170 BC.

TRACE ELEMENTS

Early tests were made to see whether the concentration of metals from vertebral bone could be estimated by using neutron activation and atomic absorption techniques. Unfortunately, the overwhelming amount of calcium in

Table 4.1. *Trace element concentrations of PUM II tissue and resin (parts per million dry weight)*

Element	PUM II muscle	PUM II skin	PUM II tendon	PUM II resin	Modern muscle	Mammalian muscle
K	1,500±300	3,500±1,000	1,400±300	580±160	11,600±1,800	10,500
Ca	500±90	83,000±16,000	520±90	760±170	570±80	105
Mn	2.1±0.6	<8	2.9±0.4	7.4±1.3	<1.7	0.21
Fe	145±8	27±4	111±6	600±50	110±30	140
Ni	3.0±0.3	<3	2.6±0.2	7.3±0.7	—	0.008
Cu	4.1±0.3	<2	3.4±0.3	5.8±0.4	1.8±0.8	3.1
Zn	86±3	37±2	56±2	4.9±0.3	170±30	180
As	0.12±0.006	<0.5	0.06±0.03	0.31±0.08	<0.3	0.16
Se	0.29±0.04	—	0.25±0.03	0.04±0.03	—	2.5
Br	13.9±0.3	6.0±0.3	12.1±0.3	8.9±0.3	—	4
Rb	2.0±0.1	0.6±0.2	1.34±0.08	0.82±0.06	9±5	24
Sr	4.3±0.1	78±2	4.3±0.1	10.1±0.3	0.13±0.006	0.05
Y	0.04±0.03	—	0.08±0.02	0.27±0.4	—	—
Zr	0.36±0.03	<0.9	0.32±0.03	1.82±0.08	—	<0.3
Nb	0.03±0.02	—	0.019±0.016	0.82±0.04	—	—
Mo	1.64±0.05	<0.3	1.32±0.03	4.0±0.1	0.06±0.01	<0.2
Sn	0.57±0.06	<0.6	0.68±0.04	1.37±0.08	—	<0.2
Pb	0.33±0.06	<1.2	0.41±0.04	3.4±0.2	0.8±0.5	<0.2

Note:
Dash indicates concentration not measurable.
Source: From Nunnelley et al. (1976).

relation to the other heavy metals interfered with the test. Of the 20 metals sought, only calcium could be measured. Smith (1975) tested for lead and mercury in bone using atomic absorption and found a lead level of 0.6 parts per million (ppm) and a mercury concentration of 0.43 ppm (dry weight). According to Kehoe (1961), the lead content of modern flat bone averages 6.55 ppm and that of long bone 18.0 ppm, so PUM II had only a fraction of the lead load of modern people. The mercury level in bone from PUM II, however, is about the same as that in modern bone, which ranges from 0.03 to 1.04 ppm with a mean value of 0.45 ppm (Goldwater 1972).

Using atomic absorption, Reyman obtained similar results from mummy PUM I. His heavy metal values for soft tissue were (in ppm): lead, 1.3; copper, 1.9; arsenic 6.2; and mercury 0.3. The values for long bone were: lead, 2.5; copper, 2.3; mercury, 0.1; and arsenic, none detected.

Nunnelley and colleagues (1976) also reported on the trace elements in PUM II. Specimens from skin, tendon, muscle, and resin were selected, ashed at 410 degrees centigrade and analyzed using x-ray fluorescence. Modern tissue samples of similar type were examined in the same manner. The results are shown in Table 4.1. Many elements are more concentrated in the resin than in the tissues. This complicates the interpretation of the tissue concentrations. The more exotic elements in muscle and tendon such as yttrium, zirconium, and niobium are possibly attributable entirely to contamination from the resin. Because the resin is so rich in trace elements, it may be possible to develop trace element profiles of other resins to help distinguish the origin of, or treatment with, different resin samples. The skin of PUM II is rich in calcium and strontium (a chemical homolog of calcium), possibly the result of postmortem calcium soap formation in the subcutaneous fat. In those cases where resin has been applied, skin will have a different trace element profile from either the muscle or tendon, because the skin is in direct contact with the resin and the deeper tissues are not. Also shown in Table 4.1 are the average results from three modern human muscle samples as well as the typical values for mammalian muscle reported by Bowen (1966). Compared with modern values, PUM II tissues appear to be low in potassium. Because potassium is an essential component of tissue cells, the depressed values in PUM II tissues suggest some removal process, possibly something that occurred during the preparation of the mummy. Also, the modern value for zinc concentration in muscle is about 170 ppm. The zinc level in PUM II is about half the modern value. This suggests that PUM II could have had a deficiency in this essential element, but much caution should be used in describing endemic zinc deficiencies in ancient populations until a larger number of mummies has been studied and the effect of long-term storage on trace elements has been investigated.

Many disease states are correlated with trace element abnormalities. Examples include anemia caused by iron deficiency or the lack of vitamin B12 being absorbed in the form of cobalt porphyrin from the intestinal tract. In modern Egypt, retarded growth and the failure of adolescent males to reach sexual maturation have been associated with endemic zinc deficiency.

Such analyses of mummy tissues may enable us to study long-term trace element body burdens. These studies may also help delineate diet and possible disease states of a given individual before death.

DISCUSSION OF THE FINDINGS

Discoveries made during the autopsy of PUM II cover a broad variety of disciplines. Some merely confirm what had been reported earlier, but some are new. The presence of silica in the lungs was surprising only because it had not been reported before. At certain times of the year, in many areas of Egypt, it is almost impossible to avoid breathing in sand; the air is full of it and so, inevitably, are the mouths and nostrils of the people living there. Shortly after the first report on PUM II appeared, Israeli workers (Bar-Ziv and Goldberg 1974) recorded finding sand in the lungs of Negev Bedouins, a condition now know as Negev Desert Lung (1974). A similar condition was reported from a mummy in Manchester, England (Tapp *et al.* 1975). Munizaga and associates (1975) found similar changes in ancient Chilean miners.

Pulmonary anthracosis, or carbon particles in the lung, has been reported from most mummies whose lungs have been examined. Air pollution is not a modern development. It was just as severe in antiquity and must have followed quickly after the discovery of fire making, for people would take fire with them into their homes, whether cave, tent, hut, or igloo. As none of them had proper chimneys, they would fill with smoke almost to the point of asphyxiation.

Atheromatous disease of the arteries is also a common finding in mummies. Nowadays, a great deal of emphasis is placed on the stress of modern life or on modern diet as factors in the high incidence of this disorder in our present-day industrialized civilization, but the etiological influences were certainly there in the ancient world, and this fact should be taken into account in any theorizing regarding causation.

At the time the autopsy was performed, the perforated eardrum and middle ear disease in PUM II were the earliest known records of these conditions. Since then, additional finds have been reported by Benitez and Lynn (1975) and by Horne and associates (1976) in Egyptian mummies, and the same condition was discovered in the Chinese Princess, the Marquise of Tai (Group for research of the Han Cadaver 1976). In many areas of the ancient world, otologic and temporal bone disease were apparently not uncommon.

Barraco's recovery of protein with a molecular weight of 150 000 daltons was a major step forward in the biochemistry of ancient tissue and was the forerunner of astounding studies of tissue antigens and macromolecules such as ribosomal DNA (see chapter 16).

The periostitis of the right fibula and tibia was thought to be reactive, and the work of Benitez and Frost (1993) reinforces the suggestion of Aidan Cockburn that it might be the result of guinea worm infestation. Also, their findings of osteopenia and the presence of Harris lines in the long bones indicate that PUM II was, perhaps, chronically ill prior to his demise. A second parasitic infestation was ascariasis, and we begin to see a picture of a young man with a variety of potentially disabling diseases, a picture that was not uncommon in ancient populations.

In two separate studies, Nunnelley and Smith (both in Cockburn *et al.* 1980) found considerably less lead in PUM II tissues than in similar modern tissues, suggesting that there is more environmental pollution today with this element than in ancient Egypt. The low zinc levels noted by Nunnelley may be an indication of zinc deficiency in PUM II, a condition not uncommon in Egypt today. Obviously, one should not use data from a single mummy as a basis for conclusions regarding a whole population, Still, the data are interesting. More recent chemical studies have shed light on the dietary regimes of individuals or groups (Ubelaker *et al.* 1995) and help even further in reconstructing life styles in these ancient populations (see chapter 16).

The mystery of the small cotton ball has still not been solved. The possibility that it had been carelessly dropped among the wrappings during the autopsy was negated by the way it was firmly affixed to the linen (Figure 4.12), and any doubt we might have felt was removed in 1979, when visual inspection of the cartonnage (the decorated layer that protects the wrapped, mummified body) found a matching wad of cotton attached with the same adhesive (a mixture of some protein substance with a natural ester resin that could have been used in any period) to the linen directly above the right toes. There was even a small smear of reddish pigment, which matched the red of the cartonnage (Cockburn 1984). Contamination as a source of the cotton could therefore be dated back conclusively to some time prior to the autopsy.

Although a few written references to cotton survive from the period, cotton

FIGURE 4.12. A ball of
cotton found within the
wrapping is adherent to
the linen.

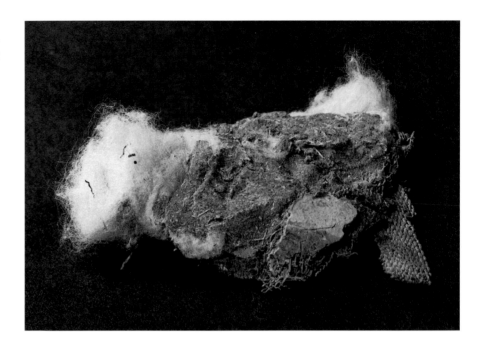

itself has never been found in an archaeological context in Ptolemaic Egypt.
The ball itself had been ginned from its seeds (in other words, it was not a
cotton boll), so no genetic material remains, and it has been reported that
ginned cotton wads were used in the packing and shipping of artifacts during
the late nineteenth and early twentieth centuries. Under the microscope, the
fibers appear modern and unaged, and it is quite probable that the cotton was
Egyptian, but contemporary with the acquisition of the mummy by John
Morris, rather than contemporary to the embalming of the body. Modern
Egyptian cotton production had developed during the reign of Pasha
Muhammad Ali (born 1767, died 1849), and this ball may have been used in
preparing the mummy for trans-Atlantic shipment to Philadelphia at the turn
of the century (Cockburn and Ballard 1992). None of the options so far
studied has been completely satisfying.

The analysis of the resin by Coughlin is a fine piece of work, for she not
only named the components of the resin by tree, but located their sources. All
were imported and expensive, reinforcing our ideas regarding the quality of
the mummification process. The physical properties of the resin as a form of
organic 'glass' resulted in the superb preservation of PUM II's tissues. This is
a tribute to the knowledge and skills of the Egyptian embalmers. There is
little sign of decay in PUM II. Embedded in glass, as it were, there is no reason
why this body, as long as it is kept in either a dry warm or a cold place, should

not survive to the end of time. For a parallel, we can look at insects embalmed in amber from the Baltic Sea, preserved for 30 million years. PUM II, if left undisturbed, could do the same. And that, after all, was the promise of the God Osiris.

REFERENCES

Allison, M. J., Houssaini, A. A., Castro, N., Munizaga, J. and Pezzia, A. 1976. ABO blood groups in Peruvian mummies: an evaluation of techniques. *American Journal of Physical Anthropology* **44**: 55–62.

Barraco, R. A. 1980. Preservation of proteins in mummified tissue. *Paleopathology Newsletter* **11**:8.

Bar-Ziv, J. and Goldberg, G. M. 1974. Simple siliceous pneumoconiosis in Negev Bedouins. *Archives of Environmental Health* **29**: 121–6.

Benitez, J. T. 1988. Otopathology of Egyptian mummy PUM II: final report. *Journal of Laryngology and Otology* **102**: 485–90.

Benitez, J. T. and Frost, H. M. 1993. 'Undecalcified sections study from the right fibula of Egyptian mummy PUM II.' Paper Presented at the Twentieth Annual Meeting of the Paleopathology Association (Toronto), April 1993. Abstract in *Paleopathology Newsletter* **82** (supplement): 6–7.

Benitez, J. T. and Lynn, G. E. 1975. Temporal bone studies: findings with undecalcified sections in a 2000 year old Egyptian mummy. *Journal of Laryngology and Otology* **89**: 593–9.

Biddle, M. 1967. Health in medieval Winchester: the evidence from excavations. In *Infectious diseases: their evolution and eradication*, ed. T. A. Cockburn, 58–60. Springfield: Charles C. Thomas.

Bowen, H. J. M. 1966. *Trace elements in biochemistry.* New York: Academic Press.

Cockburn, E. 1984. Cotton in Ancient Egypt: an unfinished story. In *Science in Egyptology*, ed. A. R. David, 469–73. Manchester: Manchester University Press.

Cockburn, E. and Ballard, M. 1992. Cotton in Ancient Egypt: a unique find. In *Proceedings of the I World Congress on Mummy Studies*, 625–31. Santa Cruz de Tenerife: Museo Arqueológico y Etnográfico de Tenerife.

Cockburn, T. A., ed. 1963. *The evolution and eradication of infectious diseases.* Baltimore: Johns Hopkins University Press.

Cockburn, T. A. 1973. Death and disease in ancient Egypt. *Science* **181**: 470–71.

Cockburn, T. A., Barraco, R. A., Reyman, T. A. and Peck, W. H. 1975. Autopsy of an Egyptian mummy. *Science* **187**: 1155–60.

Coughlin, E. A. 1977. Analysis of PUM II mummy fluid. *Paleopathology Newsletter* **17**: 7–8.

Fischer, H. 1975. Quoted in Cockburn, A., Barraco, R. A., Reyman, T. A. and Peck, W. H. Autopsy of an Egyptian mummy. *Science* **187**: 1155–60.

Goldwater, L. J. 1972. *Mercury: a history of quicksilver.* Baltimore: Fork.

Group for research of the Han Cadaver of Mawangti, Shanghai Institute of Biochemistry, Academica Sinica, and Hunan Medical College. 1976. The state of preservation of the cadaver of the Marquise of Tai found in the tomb no.1 in Mawangti near Changsha as revealed by the fine structure of the muscle and other tissues. *Scientia Sinica* **19**: 557–72.

Hart, G. D., Kvas, I. and Soots, M. L. 1977. Blood group testing: autopsy of an Egyptian mummy. *Canadian Medical Association Journal* **117**: 461–73.

Henry, R. L. 1980. Paleoserology. In *Mummies, disease, and ancient cultures*, ed. A. and E. Cockburn, 327–34. New York: Cambridge University Press.

Horne, P. D., Mackay, A., John, A. F. and Hawke, M. 1976. Histologic processing and examination of a 4000 year old human temporal bone. *Archives of Otolaryngology* **102**: 713–15.

Johnson, M. 1975. Quoted in Cockburn, A., Barraco, R. A., Reyman, T. A., and Peck, W. H Autopsy of an Egyptian mummy. *Science* **187**: 1155–60.

Kehoe, R. A. 1961. The metabolism of lead in man in health and disease. *Journal of the Royal Institute of Public Health and Hygiene* **24**:1–40

Kristen, K. T. and Reyman, T. A. 1980. Radiographic examination of mummies with autopsy correlation. In *Mummies, disease, and ancient cultures*, ed. A. and E.

Cockburn, 287–300. New York: Cambridge University Press.

Miller, J. I. 1969. *The spice trade of the Roman Empire*. London: Oxford University Press.

Munizaga, J., Allison, M. J., Gerszten, E. and Klurfeld, D. M. 1975. Pneumoconiosis in Chilean miners of the 16th century. *Bulletin of the New York Academy of Medicine* **51**: 1281–93.

Negev Desert Lung. 1974. *British Medical Journal* **4**(5945): 614

Nunnelley, L. L., Smythe, W. R., Trish, J. H. V. and Alfrey, A. C. 1976. Trace element analysis of tissue and resin from Egyptian mummy PUM II. *Paleopathology Newsletter* **12**: 12–14.

Reyman, T. A., Barraco, R. A. and Cockburn, T. A. 1976. Histopathological examination of an Egyptian mummy. *Bulletin of the New York Academy of Medicine* **52**: 506–16.

Smith, R. G. 1975. Quoted in Cockburn, A., Barraco, R. A., Reyman, T. A. and Peck, W. H. Autopsy of an Egyptian mummy. *Science* **187**: 1155–60.

Stasny, P. 1974. HLA antigens in mummified pre-Columbian tissues. *Science* **183**: 864–6.

Stuckenrath, R. 1975. Quoted in Cockburn, A., Barraco, R. A., Reyman, T. A. and Peck, W. H. Autopsy of an Egyptian mummy. *Science* **187**: 1155–60.

Tapp, E., Curry, A. and Anfield, C. 1975. Sand Pneumoconiosis in an Egyptian mummy. *British Medical Journal* **2**: 276.

Ubelaker, D. H., Katzenberg, M. A. and Doyon, L. G. 1995. Status and diet in precontact Ecuador. *American Journal of Physical Anthropology* **97**(4): 403–11.

5

ROM I: mummification for the common people

NICHOLAS B. MILLET, GERALD D. HART,
THEODORE A. REYMAN, MICHAEL R. ZIMMERMAN
AND PETER K. LEWIN

Herodotus noted that the least expensive form of mummification was where no treatment was given and the body was simply wrapped in linen. ROM I, autopsied in Toronto in August 1974, was just such a mummy. The name is shorthand for the Royal Ontario Museum, to which the mummy belongs. The autopsy was an international operation, demonstrating cooperation among members of several disciplines from the Royal Ontario Museum, the Toronto Academy of Medicine, the University of Toronto and the Detroit group of the Paleopathology Association (Lewin et al. 1974; Hart et al. 1977a). The study arose as the result of a lecture on PUM II given by Aidan Cockburn and Theodore Reyman in February 1974 at the Academy of Medicine in Toronto. The following day, Eve Cockburn suggested a joint Canadian–United States project, and a day later Nicholas B. Millet offered to provide a mummy from the collection of the Royal Ontario Museum.

Following the unwrapping by Millet and his staff, the examination of ROM I was carried out in the anatomy department of the Medical Sciences Building, University of Toronto. Radiographic examination had been completed by D. F. Rideout prior to the unwrapping. The autopsy was directed by Reyman, Zimmerman and Lewin. Specimens obtained from the dissection were distributed to qualified participants and observers as this had the advantage of ensuring greater coverage in the search for abnormalities.

THE MUMMY

In the winter of 1904–1905, C. T. Currelly, founder of the Royal Ontario Museum, was attached to the Egypt Exploration Fund's expedition at Deir-el-Bahri, across the river from modern Luxor, where he assisted at the excavation of the funerary temple of Menthuhotep II, a king of the Eleventh Dynasty (c. 2010 BC). All the tomb chambers in the temple area had been robbed in antiquity, and many had been used in later times by humbler people. It was in

FIGURE 5.1. Hieroglyphics on the coffin, describing Nakht. (From Hart *et al.* 1977.)

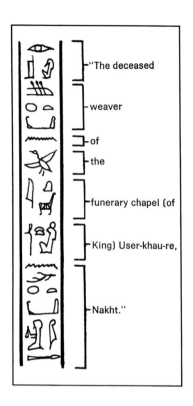

"The deceased

weaver

of

the

funerary chapel (of

King) User-khau-re,

Nakht."

one of these that the coffin of Nakht was found. Although the date the mummy was acquired by the museum is not known, we must assume that its acquisition was directly attributable to Currelly's presence at the time of the excavation.

The coffin was built in the traditional manner, with planks and small pieces of wood, probably sycamore (Lucas and Harris 1962). The lid, which was carved in anthropoid shape, showed the deceased wearing a long wig striped in blue; his forearms and clenched fists were executed in relief. The whole exterior of the coffin, except the bottom, was covered with a thin coating of gypsum plaster and gaily painted with the usual scenes and inscriptions. The text inscribed on it (Figure 5.1) tells us the owner was a male named Nakht, invariably described as 'weaver of the *kny*-temple of User-khau-re'. User-khau-re was the throne name of king Setnakht, the first ruler of the Twentieth Dynasty, who died about 1198 BC after a brief reign, leaving the throne to his son, the great Ramesses III. The latter established a funerary cult and chapel in memory of his father on the west bank at Thebes. The word 'kny' means 'armchair' and 'carrying or sedan chair', referring to either a statue of the god-king in a palanquin or an empty throne chair over which the spirit of the dead ruler was thought to hover. The chapel was maintained for many years and the inclusion of a weaver suggests that some of the land was used to grow flax, linen being the common cloth of the time. The style of Nakht's coffin suggests that it was made in the first half of the twelfth century BC. From the historian's viewpoint, Nakht's mummy was a natural choice for autopsy; there is a good account of its provenance and date. The simple title 'weaver' shows that Nakht was a person of the laboring class and was far more representative of the great mass of the ancient population than most mummies, which tend to be from the aristocracy. Finally, we are probably better informed about Nakht's times – the last century of the New Kingdom – than we are about any other period in Egyptian history.

Nakht's lower-class family had apparently been able to afford a relatively fine coffin because he had not undergone the expensive process of mummification. He had simply been washed and wrapped in linen. By omitting extensive mummification practices, they were able to spend their meager resources on the coffin itself, which would have cost approximately 31 g of silver, about 10 percent of a family's yearly income. The grieving parents must have been willing to sacrifice a great deal to see their son suitably interred.

Although the body had been carefully wrapped in linen in the traditional manner, the amount of linen used was noticeably less than in many mummies of the period. The bandages were in good condition and came away easily, chiefly because none of the sacral oils had been poured over the body. The manner in which the bandages and filling pads had been arranged suggests familiarity with ritual custom and hints at a professional hand, but the poor people of Thebes may have attained a certain expertise in wrapping their dead simply from economic necessity. The wrappings were well preserved in all parts of the mummy except the head where they had broken through entirely, probably as a result of the collapse of the cranial vault (Figure 5.2). Several of the pads contained in the wrappings proved to be more or less complete garments; two large, sleeveless tunic-like robes of a type familiar to us from wall paintings and sculpture of the period as representing the characteristic male costume of the day. Their size is about right for Nakht himself, and his family probably contributed some of his clothing to provide wrapping material.

Surviving records of the community, labor rolls, and fragments of official day books tell us something of the physical conditions under which Nakht lived during his short life. Nakht's house was probably not at Deir el-Medina but nearer his place of burial in the Asasif valley below the Deir el-Bahri temple and nearer the cultivation on the east. Because he was in his middle teens when

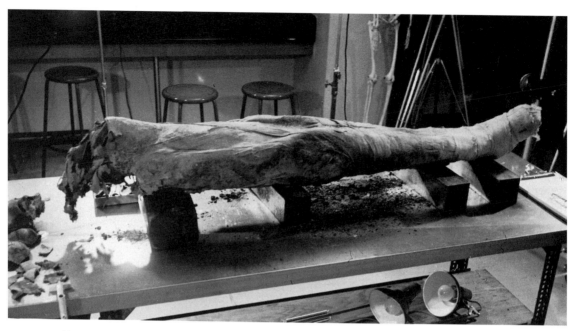

FIGURE 5.2. Mummy before unwrapping. Note the broken skull.

he died, he was probably what the official records describe as a 'mnh' or 'stripling', a youth of employable age but still unmarried and living in his parents' home and drawing a smaller ration allowance (wages being paid in kind) than the head of a family. The house in which he lived was probably similar to excavated samples, consisting of two or three rooms of mud brick with a flat roof of earth on rafters of palm logs, plus a small courtyard. His diet and general standard of living would have been better than most of the peasant cultivators who composed the bulk of the population. By any reckoning, he must have been in the upper ranks of the working class. In addition, he enjoyed the security derived from being attached to a permanent and prestigious institution, which may have exempted him from military service, forced labor or the economic uncertainties that afflicted the kingdom of his time.

RADIOLOGIC FINDINGS

Radiographic studies by Rideout (1977) indicated that the subject was a male teenager, but more exact determination of age was difficult because desiccation had widened some epiphyseal lines and narrowed others, so that the hip joints suggested age 18 and the knees age 14. The left knee showed unfused epiphyses and Harris lines suggesting episodes of infection or malnutrition during life. The hands were not well shown because they overlapped the pelvis but, as far as could be seen, they corresponded with an age of 14. Therefore, it was reasonably certain that Nakht was between 14 and 18 years of age at the time of his death. The wisdom teeth were well developed but unerupted. All the other teeth were accounted for and in good condition.

The pelvis was of male configuration and appeared to show protrusio acetabuli. Xeroradiographs, however, showed this to be an artifact due to postmortem change; this was substantiated at autopsy. Radiographs of the chest showed a mass in the center and to the right that was too large for a desiccated heart and was assumed to represent the heart and the liver adhering to each other. Patchy opacities in both hemithoraxes suggested the remains of lung tissue adhering to the posterior chest wall. Tomography confirmed the position of these masses within the body cavity and also showed an intact diaphragm between abdomen and thorax.

Between the shrunken tissues and the wrappings, there was an air-containing gap up to 4 cm across. This indicated that desiccation occurred after the wrappings were applied. Harris lines in the lower 1.5 cm of the distal femoral metaphyses suggested recurrent severe illness in the last two years of his life. Radiographic examination gave no indication that Nakht had been eviscerated or even embalmed. He had desiccated naturally in the dry, hot air of Thebes. Apart from the rather nonspecific evidence of the Harris or growth arrest lines, there was no radiographic clue to the cause of death.

GROSS ANATOMY

A general study showed that the wrappings of the head had been removed earlier and that the skull had been damaged (Figure 5.2). In addition, the cranial sutures had not united and all the skull bones had collapsed inward; the facial features had disintegrated.

The body showed no evidence of artificial preservation by means of natron, oils or bitumen. The body was firm and boardlike, weighing only 5.13 kg and measuring 143.1 cm in length. Circumferential measurements of the extremities confirmed the extensive soft tissue shrinkage noted on the radiographs. The skin was a light café-au-lait color and had a tough, leathery consistency. At areas of soft tissue fissuring, the muscles were visible and had a friable consistency. The whorls and ridges on the fingers and toes were preserved as were the fingernails and toenails.

The autopsy began with a study of the head. The loose skull bones were carefully reconstructed. On some areas of the frontal and parietal bones, the scalp with 2 mm long hairs was still adherent. The imprints of the ears were

95

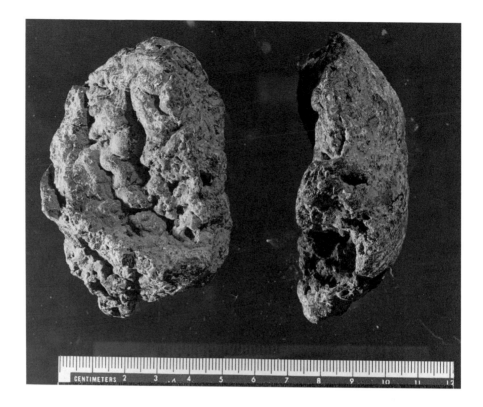

present in the head wrappings, where many loose hairs were also found. The left eye socket was covered with a thin, transparent film on which eyelashes were also identified. The teeth showed some wear but were well preserved and without caries. Three upper incisor teeth had become dislodged post-mortem and were recovered from the wrappings.

The cerebral hemispheres were found lying in the base of the cranial cavity (Figure 5.3). The left hemisphere weighed 61.6 g and measured $9 \times 7 \times 2.5$ cm and the right weighed 66.15 g and measured $8 \times 6 \times 2.5$ cm. The hemispheres were dark brown, firm and had a soapy feel. The convolutions were preserved and best seen on the inferior surfaces. The sigmoid sinus contained rusty, brown material suggesting dried blood adhering to the inner lining. There was a postmortem transverse fracture of the neck of the mandible just below the condyle.

The thorax was opened with a Stryker saw, cutting through the leathery tissue at the anterior lateral margins of the ribs so that the anterior chest plate could be removed in *toto*. The ligaments were preserved but the fat had disappeared. The pericardium appeared as a tent tethered between the sternum and the thoracic spine. The lungs had collapsed and it was not possible to dis-

FIGURE 5.4. The shrunken but otherwise normal heart of Nakht.

tinguish the lobes. They were grey-black and friable. The aortic arch was transected and the heart and mediastinum were removed. The heart (Figure 5.4) and great vessels weighed 17.7 g. The trachea was identified and removed along with the thyroid cartilage. The intact diaphragm was dark brown, firm and leathery. The diaphragm and anterior abdominal wall were removed in *toto* (Figure 5.5). The liver was shrunken but retained its shape and had a sharp leading edge. It measured 12.5 × 7.5 × 3 cm and weighed 106.3 g. Portions of the gall bladder were removed. The spleen was present and, taking into account the amount of shrinkage of the other organs, appeared to be enlarged. It was very friable and was not weighed. The posterior walls of the splenic bed were discolored, possibly representing blood from a ruptured or very congested spleen.

The intestines were paper-thin and collapsed. The urinary bladder was a sac-like hollow structure measuring 6 cm at its widest point. The prostate

FIGURE 5.5. Trunk and hands after removal of the organs.

was not identified. The rectum passed through the pelvic cavity, being desiccated and friable. The sacral nerve plexus was preserved. The penis was uncircumcised. The scrotum was intact but testes were not identified.

HISTOLOGIC FINDINGS

The heart and brain were not processed in detail, being retained for permanent display. All other tissues were rehydrated in modified Ruffer's solution and processed in the same manner as fresh tissue (Reyman and Dowd 1980). Sections were stained with Masson's trichrome, periodic acid-Schiff, acid fast, Grocott's methenamine silver, elastic tissue and alizarin red staining techniques and examined with polarized light microscopy. Histological detail was preserved to varying degrees, although distinct cel-

FIGURE 5.6. Ovum of *Schistosoma haemato-bium* with terminal spine.

lular outlines were generally lost. Many tissues were infiltrated with bacteria and fungi.

In the lungs, the alveolar structure was partially preserved and there was marked deposition of anthracotic pigment within connective tissue. Throughout the lungs, bright birefringent particles were present and electron microscope microprobe diffraction analysis by E. Pooley, University of Cardiff, Wales, suggested that these particles are granite.

The muscle coats of the intestinal tract at various levels were preserved and within the lumens of both small and large intestine were numerous ova of *Schistosoma* and *Taenia* sp. Some of the *Schistosoma* ova had large terminal spines (Figure 5.6). No adult worms of either type were seen but the *Taenia* ova (Figure 5.7) were clumped together suggesting the site of degenerated proglottids.

The liver revealed preservation of cords of indistinct hepatic parenchyma intersected by interlacing thick and thin bands of fibrous tissue, occasionally surrounding small nodules of parenchyma (Reyman 1976). Some portal areas contained calcified *Schistosoma* ova with terminal spines similar to those noted in the intestine and typical of *Schistosoma haematobium*. The spleen was poorly preserved and showed heavy postmortem microbial contamination. No malarial pigment was seen. Sections of gall bladder and brain tissue revealed

FIGURE 5.7. Clustered ova of *Taenia* species; note internal hooklets.

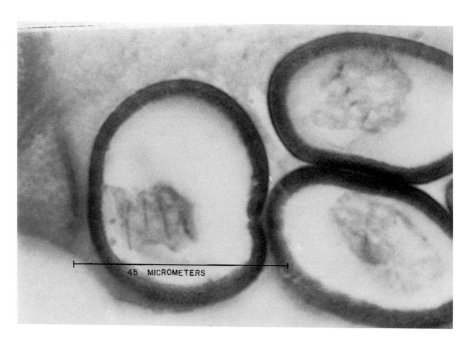

45 MICROMETERS

extensive degenerative changes. Sections of myocardium, coronary artery and aortic valve were normal. The parenchyma of the kidneys was not well preserved but several *Schistosoma* ova were seen. The urinary bladder revealed remnants of epithelium but no ova or changes suggestive of inflammation. A few well preserved red blood cells present on the mucosal surface suggested haematuria during life. Electron micrographic studies of the dustlike intestinal contents and a small section of skin from the sole of the right foot were performed (Horne and Lewin 1977; Millet *et al.* 1980). The epidermis of the skin was well preserved and cellular elements were easily recognized. The intestinal contents contained several ova of *Taenia* sp. which at the ultrastructural level demonstrated in great detail the striated embryophore of an egg with its hooklets (Figure 5.8). Intact blood cells were also noted.

The temporal bones were removed and examined by Lynn and Benitez (1977) using tomography and the operating microscope. The foramen of Huschke was an obvious defect in the temporal bone but its pathological significance, if any, is unknown. The ossicles in both ears were displaced but were normal anatomically, suggesting postmortem dislodgment. There was no evidence of temporal bone disease, chronic otitis media, cholesteatoma or other destructive lesions of the middle ear.

Thus, the postmortem examination of this 3200 year old mummy of a teenage Egyptian boy revealed a variety of disease processes. He had at least

ROM I: mummification for the common people

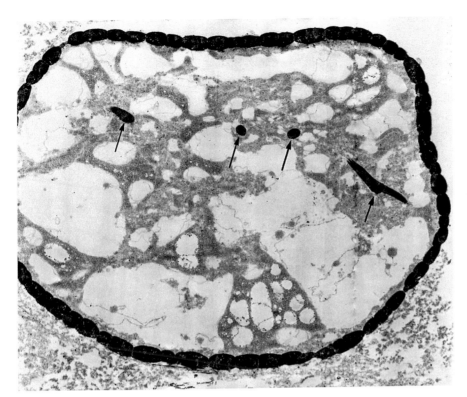

FIGURE 5.8. Electron micrograph of *Taenia* ovum showing hooklets (arrows), three in cross section and one in full view, ×5800.

two parasitic infestations, both of which could have produced severe complications. Numerous ova of *Taenia* sp. were found in the intestinal tract. As the ova of T. *solium* and T. *saginata* cannot be differentiated and no scolex was found, no final decision can be made concerning the type of infestation that existed. Many schistosomal ova were also found, several with large terminal spines diagnostic of *Schistosoma haematobium* and others without obvious spines. These ova may be degenerated forms or may be *Schistosoma mansoni*. Both forms of schistosomiasis are endemic in modern Egypt, and S. *haematobium* has been reported in other Egyptian remains (Ruffer 1910). There was evidence of early cirrhosis of the liver and congestive splenomegaly, possibly with terminal rupture. Schistosomal ova were found in the liver, suggesting that the cirrhosis was secondary to hepatic schistosomiasis. Although S. *mansoni* is the commonest offending parasite, S. *haematobium* may give the same picture in the liver. The calcified ova in the kidney and the presence of blood in the urinary bladder also indicate involvement of this system with S. *haematobium*. Finding tapeworm ova is also of interest, implying as it does that Nakht ate meat, and probably meat that was not well cooked. Meat fibers were found in the intestine of another mummy

(PUM II), so ancient Egyptians were not strict vegetarians. In any case, the associated malnutrition probably contributed to the youth's demise. The presence of Harris lines in the leg bone supports this thesis.

An incidental finding, present in almost all ancient remains, is pulmonary anthracosis, which is attributable to air pollution from cooking and heating fires and from oil lamps in small, poorly ventilated rooms. It is also possible that this boy had pulmonary silicosis from inhaling sand during sandstorms.

Another parasitic infestation was discovered in one of the intercostal muscles in the form of a small cyst just visible to the naked eye with characteristics of a parasite. At first, *Cysticercus cellulosae* (the larva of *T. solium*) was considered, but these cysts are about 5 mm in diameter and much larger than the muscle fibers. The cyst is somewhat small to be that of *Trichinella spiralis* but it is appropriate when compared with the size of the muscle fibers and the small size may be the result of shrinkage during drying. *Trichinella* infestation, like cystercercosis, is caused by eating inadequately cooked pork and this, with other findings, suggests that Nakht ate pork. Today, cystercercosis and other parasitic diseases transmitted by pigs are virtually nonexistent in Egypt because of strict religious dietary laws.

BLOOD GROUP TESTING

Splenic material and the brown substance from the sigmoid sinus were tested by Hart and associates (Hart *et al.* 1977b) using the serological micromethod (SMM) and the inhibition agglutination test (IAT). The SMM test on splenic material was complicated by hemolysis of the absorbed group O cells, possibly due to the heavy fungal infiltration in the splenic tissue. The IAT on splenic material and both SMM and IAT tests on sigmoid sinus blood gave reactions indicative of blood group type B. The histological findings of preserved red blood cells in this and other mummy autopsies (Zimmerman 1971; Riddle 1980) give us confidence that our results are bona fide and that Nakht's blood type is B.

CHEMICAL STUDIES

Various chemical studies were performed on the tissues of Nakht (Barraco 1977; 1980). Because there appears to be a relationship between the use of natron during mummification and the preservation of tissue elements (Barraco 1975), sodium levels in Nakht's muscle were determined and found to be similar to modern fresh, human muscle, indicating that Nakht had not been treated with natron. Protein extracts contained amino acid components of about 17 000 daltons, similar to PUM II, but there were no large proteins in the range of 150 000 daltons as noted in PUM II, indicating a more severe degradation of these macromolecules in Nakht's tissues. No specific proteins were identified although the molecular weight of the proteins in the range of 17 000 daltons might be attributable to myoglobin in the muscle samples.

OTHER STUDIES

Various tissues from Nakht were cultured aerobically and anaerobically but were negative for microbial growth. The soil and other contaminants adherent to the wrapping were high in manganese. Electron microscopy of liver tissue did not reveal any viral particles and radioimmunoassay of liver extracts was negative for Hepatitis B antigen. Craniofacial characteristics and dentition were investigated at the Faculty of Dentistry, University of Toronto, but no significant abnormalities were noted.

Computerized transaxial tomography (CTT) scans done on the intact brain at the Hospital for Sick Children showed that the gray and white matter had been preserved and that the lateral ventricles were intact. Calcified cysts suggesting cerebral cysticercosis or other abnormalities were not identified and further destructive needle or tissue biopsies were felt unnecessary. This is the first time CTT had been used in paleopathology (Lewin and Harwood-Nash 1977).

Many of the findings detailed in this report are now part of a teaching exhibit on disease in ancient times, sponsored by the Royal Ontario Museum and the Academy of Medicine. The mummy itself is on display at the Royal Ontario Museum.

An additional finding has surfaced in the study of tissues from Nahkt. Miller and associates (personal communication 1996) have identified yet another infectious disease in this young lad. A test for the histidine-rich protein antigen 2 (Miller *et al.* 1994) of *Plasmodium falciparum* (quartan malaria) was positive and indicated that Nakht had malaria at one point, possibly in the latter stages of his short life.

DISCUSSION

The importance of ROM I is that the mummy can be accurately located in time and place in ancient Egypt. To have actual facts like these is a rare luxury when dealing with antiquity, so the data are priceless. We can now state that in the twelfth century BC, on the bank of the Nile opposite modern day Luxor, there existed a focus of infection of the parasite *Schistosoma haematobium*. This has been proven. Speculations about the epidemiology of the infection in Egypt can begin with this firm base.

The same may be said about the presence of *Plasmodium falciparum* antigens in Nakht's tissues. The identity of the tapeworm is less certain, for it could be either the pork or the beef parasite. However, the cyst of what is probably *Trichinella spiralis* is definitely pork related and the tapeworm may be the same. This raises the interesting subject of eating pork. In the Middle East today, eating the flesh of the pig is taboo, but many people think that in some cases, as with the cows in India, the animal in question was once regarded as sacred. According to Fraser in his *Golden Bough*, the pig in Egypt was the totem animal of Osiris. Osiris was killed, rose from the dead, reigned over life after death, and was represented as a mummy. The flesh of the pig was forbidden except on the holy day of Osiris. On that day, everyone ate pork, and even the poor who could not afford meat made cakes resembling pigs and ate them instead. Certainly, the findings from ROM I indicate that 3000 years ago at least one Egyptian ate pork on at least one occasion.

The most likely explanation for the pork taboo is a religious prohibition, probably going back long before Moses to the dawn of Egyptian history. A modern explanation linking it with hygienic reasons and trichinosis can be dismissed. The parasite *Trichinella spiralis* was not discovered until 1834, and its association with pigs came two decades later. The human disease was not recognized before that time, nor was its association with eating uncooked pork. The hygienic theory is probably a modern rationalization for an otherwise inexplicable taboo.

What we see in this young boy is an all too common picture of multiple parasitism, any one of which would be debilitating and possibly fatal, particularly the malaria. They are surely the cause of death in this youth.

ACKNOWLEDGMENTS

Special sections were contributed by the following: trichinosis, U. de Boni, M. M. Lenczner, and J. W. Scott; electron microscopy, L. Spence, P. K. Lewin and P. D. Horne; nuclear medical techniques, B. N Ege and K. G. McNeil; dentition, A. Storey and D. W. Stoneman; computed transaxial tomography, D. Harwood-Nash.

REFERENCES

Barraco, R. A. 1975. Preservation of proteins in mummified tissue. *Paleopathology Newsletter* **11**: 8.

Barraco, R. A. 1977. Analysis of protein extract: autopsy of an Egyptian mummy. *Canadian Medical Association Journal* **117**: 474.

Barraco, R. A. 1980. Paleobiochemistry. In *Mummies, disease, and ancient cultures*, ed. A. and E. Cockburn, 312–26. New York: Cambridge University Press.

Hart, G. D., Cockburn, A., Millet, N. B. and Scott, J. W. 1977a. Editorial: autopsy of an Egyptian mummy. *Canadian Medical Association Journal* **117**: 461.

Hart, G. D., Kvas, I. and Soots, M. L. 1977b. Blood group testing: autopsy of an Egyptian mummy. *Canadian Medical Association Journal* **117**: 476.

Horne, P. D. and Lewin, P. K. 1977. Electron microscopy of mummified tissue: autopsy of an Egyptian mummy. *Canadian Medical Association Journal* **117**: 472–73.

Lewin, P. K. and Harwood-Nash, D. C. 1977. X-ray computed axial tomography of an ancient Egyptian brain. *International Research Communication System* **5**: 78

Lewin, P. K., Mills, A. J., Savage, H. and Vollmer, J. 1974. Nakht, a weaver of Thebes. *Rotunda* **7**: 15–19.

Lucas, A. and Harris, J. 1962. *Ancient Egyptian materials and industries*. London: Edward Arnold.

Lynn, G. E. and Benitez, J. T. 1977. Examination of ears: autopsy of an Egyptian mummy. *Canadian Medical Association Journal* **117**: 469.

Miller, R. L., Ikram, S. and Armelagos, G. J. 1994 Diagnosis of *Plasmodium falciparum* in mummies using the rapid manual Para Site TM-F test. *Transactions of the Royal Society of Tropical Medicine and Hygiene.* **88**: 31–52.

Millet, N. B., Hart, G. D., Reyman, T. A., Zimmerman, M. R. and Lewin, P. K. 1980. ROM I: mummification for the common people. In *Mummies, diseases, and ancient cultures*, ed. A. and E. Cockburn, 71–84. New York: Cambridge University Press.

Reyman, T. A. 1976. Schistosomal cirrhosis in an Egyptian mummy. *Yearbook of Physical Anthropology* **20**: 356–8.

Reyman, T. A. and Dowd, A. M. 1980. Processing of mummified tissue for histological examination. In *Mummies, disease, and ancient cultures*, ed. A. and E. Cockburn, 258–73. New York: Cambridge University Press.

Riddle, J. M. 1980. A survey of ancient specimens by electron microscopy. In *Mummies, disease, and ancient cultures*, ed. A. and E. Cockburn, 274–86. New York: Cambridge University Press.

Rideout, D. M. 1977. Radiologic examination: autopsy of an Egyptian mummy. *Canadian Medical Association Journal* **117**: 463.

Ruffer, M. A. 1910. Note on the presence of *Bilharzia haematobia* in Egyptian mummies of the Twentieth Dynasty (1250–1000 BC). *British Medical Journal* **1**: 16.

Zimmerman, M. R. 1971. Blood cells preserved in a mummy 2,000 years old. *Science* **180**: 303.

6

Egyptian mummification with evisceration per ano

THEODORE A. REYMAN AND WILLIAM H. PECK

The Egyptian embalmers were masters of their art. The trial and error method they employed for 2000 years resulted in a scientific discipline for preserving bodies (Mokhtar *et al.* 1973). These embalming techniques required long hours of toil, expensive medicants, and fine linen wrappings. The costs were necessarily high. Because the majority of people who were mummified in the early dynasties were royalty or the rich and influential of the time, cost had little importance. As the poorer segments of the populace were allowed the privilege of mummification, these costs became prohibitive. For this and possibly other reasons, modifications were made in the classical mummification process, most being aimed at reducing the cost. The external form and appearance of the mummy remained the same but the fact is that mummification for the poor became less a preservative and more a symbolic exercise. Two examples of a common alternative method are presented: mummification with evisceration per ano. Both mummies were provided by David O'Connor, Department of Egyptology, Pennsylvania University Museum. Neither had known provenance or coffin. The first, designated PUM III, was an adult female; the second, a male child called PUM IV. They will be described separately.

PUM III

Radiography

Before the unwrapping, the mummy was examined radiographically (Kristen and Reyman 1980). The body arrived with the head unwrapped and separated from the body at the level of the fifth cervical vertebra, probably occurring postmortem. There was a healed fracture of the left second rib. Harris lines were present in the distal femora. The chest cavity revealed central densities suggesting the heart and lungs. The diaphragm clearly separated the thorax and abdominal cavities. A right upper abdominal mass appeared to be the

Egyptian mummification with evisceration per ano

FIGURE 6.1. The wrapped body of PUM III. The head was detached and the wrappings were missing.

liver. The remainder of the abdominal cavity contained irregular, speckled opacities. In the pelvis, a double shadow centrally suggested the urinary bladder with an air contrast lumen and the uterine body behind it. There were numerous air contrast lines in the thigh muscle, suggesting fissuring.

The wrappings

Because the head was separated and the head bandaging was missing, there was no way of knowing how the head was wrapped (Figure 6.1). The outer layers of the body wrapping were without decoration and consisted of medium quality linen. Most of these outer bandages were complete strips with a woven end and a fringed end that had been torn from a larger sheet six or seven meters long. Intermixed with the first few layers were small, folded pads of a darker, slightly finer linen which were used to fill out the body outline. By the fifth layer, deterioration was obvious, possibly from liquids used in wrapping. Deeper layers were large sheetlike strips that had been laid on lengthwise to cover the entire body. The spaces between the arms and body were filled with linen wads and wood chips, and reeds and fibers were present. The legs were bound together with a figure-of-eight continuous bandage. Circular strips bound the right arm to the body but not the left. The fingers and toes were not individually wrapped. The wrapping immediately next to the body was crossed over the shoulders and through the pelvic area, having been wound from top to bottom. Radiocarbon dating of the cloth by Robert Stuckenrath, Smithsonian Institution, Washington, DC gave a date of 810 BC (2785 BP±70 years).

FIGURE 6.2. The larger of
two hieroglyphic inscrip-
tions on the wrappings.
See text. (Photograph by
Nemo Warr, Detroit
Institute of Arts.)

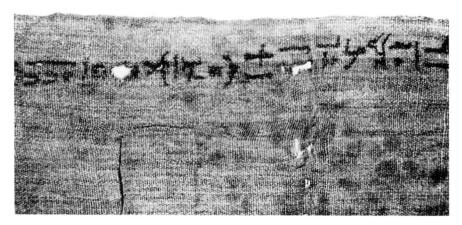

The most remarkable part of the wrapping consisted of two pieces of linen that had ink inscriptions. The translation of the writing on the larger piece (Figure 6.2) indicated that the owner of the linen was the priest Imyhap, son of Wah-ib-Re, and appeared not to pertain to the subject mummy, apparently being reused fabrics. A disturbing feature was that the ink inscribed fabric disintegrated within a few days of exposure to air, leaving only holes where the inscriptions had been.

Autopsy findings

There was extensive degeneration of most tissues. The hair, scalp and external ears were missing. There was what appeared to be an antemortem, post-infectious perforation of the left tympanic membrane described by Benitez and Lynn (1980). The eyes had either been removed or were so degenerated that they were not recognizable; the orbits were stuffed with granular packing. The teeth were intact and there were no apparent cranial fractures. The calvarium was removed and there was an irregular 2 cm hole in the cribriform bone communicating with the left nostril. A small mass of brown, granular material near the occiput was thought to be residual brain but when processed by Riddle (1980) was found to be blood with intact red and white blood cells.

The skin over the rest of the body was degenerated as were the larger muscles. Flattened, discoid breasts were present but nipples were not identified. The external genitalia were female. There was a large, irregular defect involving the labiae, perineum, anus and rectum. The overall configuration of the body was otherwise normal and no flank or abdominal incision was noted.

The chest plate was removed and the heart, mediastinal tissue and lungs were removed *en bloc*. The collapsed lungs were black and brittle, and fragmented easily during removal. Each lung measured $10 \times 6 \times 1$ cm with small discrete holes that suggested bronchi. The heart was an ill-defined mass without detail. The diaphragm was covered in part by a thin layer of black, resinous material.

When the abdominal skin was removed, the entire abdominal cavity was found to be full of large wads of black, resin soaked linen. The liver was pressed against the right hemidiaphragm and there was a defect in the left hemidiaphragm with linen protruding into the thoracic cavity. No intestines or other abdominal organs could be found. In the pelvis, the urinary bladder was ovoid with a central lumen and measured 6 by 4 cm. The uterus with intact broad ligaments could be identified. There was a large pelvic defect in the area of the rectum and anus, apparently the passage for insertion of the linen wadding and resinous material. Any visceral removal would have occurred through this defect.

After the autopsy, the head was examined by Richard Wesley and Edwin Secord, School of Dentistry, University of Detroit (Figure 6.3). Their report indicated that there was extensive occlusal attrition, probably due to a coarse and gritty diet. A moderate amount of alveolar bone loss was present around all teeth but no calculus or caries were noted. There was congenital absence of all third molars. The skeletal maturation and the occlusal wear suggested that PUM III was in the third or fourth decade of life at the time of death.

Examination of bones

Michael Finnegan, Kansas State University, noted that PUM III had a wide greater sciatic notch of the innominate bone, suggesting the mummy was female. Well developed but eroded preauricular sulci in radiographs of the sacrum also suggested femaleness. The subpubic angle, the fine morphology of the pelvis (Phenice 1969), and the left femoral head diameter of 40.5 mm all indicated a female individual. Because suture closure is not a reliable method of age estimation (Brooks 1955), he removed the pubic symphyses for examination in his laboratory, and he arrived at a Todd's (1921) phase 7, suggesting an age of 35 to 39 years. A portion of the right femur was studied by D. J. Ortner, Smithsonian Institution, using thin-section techniques, and resulting in an age estimate of 42 years, although he felt that this might be a little high.

The stature of the mummy was calculated using the data shown in Table 6.1. Based on the Trotter and Gleser (1958) formula for white females, a stature of 155.86 cm (61.36 in.) was obtained. Using this value, an estimation of the living body weight was made. Because the dry weight (Sunderman and Boerner 1949) and the mummified weight would be very similar (25–30

FIGURE 6.3. Skull. (a) Estimated soft tissue profile based on bony structure (Richard Wesley, University of Detroit Dental School); (b) profile of the head (photograph by John Levis).

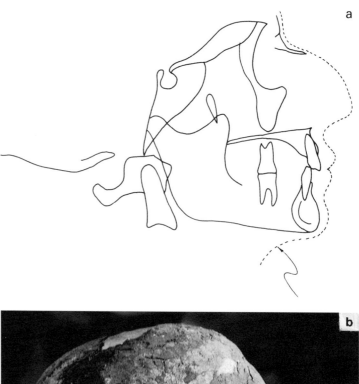

percent of living weight), a mummy weighing 11.35 kg would have weighed 37.8 to 45.4 kg during life, a close approximate of the expected 43.2 to 52.3 kg for a female 155.86 cm tall.

Histological examination

Electron micrographs by Jeanne Riddle (1980) of an insect larva found on the body were interpreted by G. C. Steyskal and J. M. Kingsolver, Systemic

Table 6.1. *Measurements and indices of
PUM III (in millimeters)*[a]

Head length	182
Head breadth	142
Minimum frontal breadth	93
Bizygomatic breadth	130
Total face height	110
Nose height	55
Cephalic index	78.02
Frontoparietal index	65.49
Total facial index	84.62
Left femur physiological length	412
Left femur maximum head diameter	40.4
Right femur midshaft diameters	
Mediolateral	23.6
Anteroposterior	23.3

Note:

[a] These are standard measurements used in
physical anthropology.

Entomology Laboratory, US National Museum, Washington, DC, as *Thelodrias
contractus* Motschulsky, family Dermestidae, a cosmopolitan species.

The tissues obtained during the autopsy were processed for microscopic
examination (Reyman and Dowd 1980). Unfortunately, the poor preservation
noted grossly was even more pronounced microscopically. Even those organs
that were identifiable at the time of the autopsy were virtually without
histological detail. A single exception was a small sample taken from the
lateral margin of the left breast. Within the friable tissue was a 1 cm nodule
that remained intact (Figure 6.4). The nodule was composed of connective
tissue, not fat, and within the tissue were slitlike spaces containing moderately preserved cuboidal cells with recognizable nuclei. The overall pattern
suggested that this was a fibroadenoma of the breast. The woman's age, the
size of the tumor and its lateral position in the breast support this thesis.

Summary: PUM III

PUM III was female with an estimated age of 35 years at the time of her death in
810 BC. She was 156 cm tall and weighed approximately 41 kg. The linen wrappings were modest and parts were reused linen. Two small hieroglyphic
inscriptions were present within the wrappings. She had a healed fracture of the

FIGURE 6.4. (a) Round one cm piece of breast tissue from PUM III consisting of connective tissue without fat; (b) Vacuolated cells that appear to be epithelial cells. Elastic tissue stain.

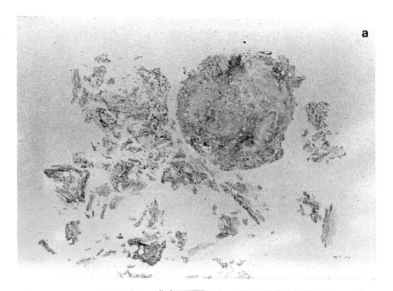

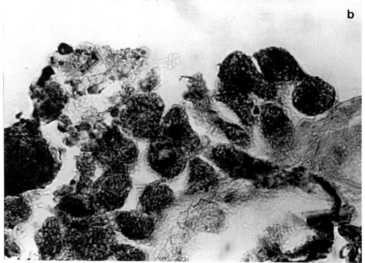

second left rib and all third molars were congenitally absent. Partial evisceration had been performed per ano and the brain had been extracted through the left nostril. The body tissues were poorly preserved with the exception of a fibroadenoma of the left breast and a small blood clot in the cranial cavity.

PUM IV

Radiography

From its size, the second mummy was obviously a child. As with PUM III, the radiographic studies were performed by Karl Kristen (Kristen and Reyman

1980) at Mt Carmel Mercy Hospital, Detroit. His studies indicated that the child was normally developed (Figure 6.5). Within the wrapping, posteriorly, there was a body-length opacity with the density of wood. There were bilateral basal and inferior occipital skull fractures without healing that are possibly postmortem damage. There were no visible healed fractures or developmental anomalies. No Harris lines were seen. The epiphyses were open and there were several unerupted teeth, including some of the central incisors. The child's age was estimated to be eight years at the time of death.

The wrappings

Overlying the wrappings was a ropelike cord that proved to be a fishnet in a square-knot pattern. The first layer of wrapping consisted of a painted covering that normally would be termed a shroud (Figure 6.6), except that it extended only from the head to the ankles and did not meet in the back. It was made of coarse linen, assembled from several pieces in a neat patchwork. The area of the textile that had covered the face was severely damaged and no painted portrait remained. The rest of the covering was in a badly damaged and fragmentary condition, but traces of paint remained. These were interpreted as geometric patterning and, in the lower left-hand corner, there was the figure of a seated Anubis jackal. This covering was stitched to the lower sides of the torso and across the top of the head with a thin strip of cloth.

Under the net and painted covering, the first layer of wrapping consisted of narrow linen strips that crossed the body at right angles to the trunk and did not conceal the next layer, which was composed of similar strips running vertically from the feet to the neck. Then the pieces of linen became larger, almost random in their application, of no standard size, and of varied quality. Some had been torn roughly from large shapes, and some showed obvious signs of wear, as if they had been used for cleaning or other rough work. Little attempt had been made to round out the mummy to a lifelike shape except for some folded material applied to the sides of the head. Interspersed with the partial layers of this wrapping were loose cord ropes applied in a diagonal spiral, perhaps to hold the wrappings in place.

After the 'random' wrapping had been removed, the body was found to have been tied to a full-length board that was broken in its midportion at the level of the pelvis. The mummy was now seen to be dressed in a short tunic, a simple, flat garment with a neckhole cut in the middle, placed over the head and extending down the front and back to the waist. The neckline of the tunic had been rolled and stitched and the tunic had been decorated with two vertical bands of near black color that extended completely down the front and

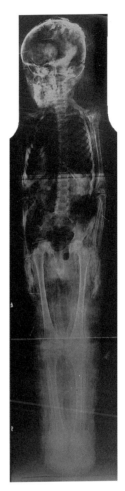

FIGURE 6.5. Large format radiograph of the child attached to a wooden board.

FIGURE 6.6. The wrapped body of the child PUM IV. (Photograph by John Levis.)

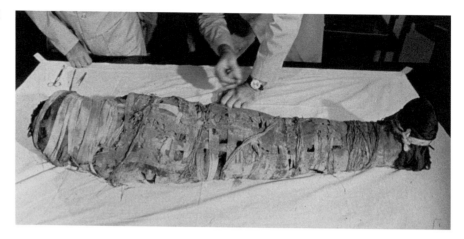

back, passing over the shoulders on either side. These bands had been added to the linen tunic in a tapestry weave. Near the two edges of the tunic were borders of the same color as the solid bands but the borders were composed of four threads with spaces between them.

Beneath the tunic, the body was enveloped in three shroud-like garments with neckholes. These may have been made expressly for the burial, as the edges were not hemmed, the neckhole was crudely stitched and the fabric was rather narrow. In contrast, the decorated tunic could well have been used in life. Around the neck and wrist, next to the skin, were knotted cords of one strand. A small fragment of painted cartonnage was found in the wrapping with what appeared to be a sliver from the eye decoration of a face mask. The impression was that the mummy had been prepared from the contents of the embalmer's scrap bag and the cartonnage fragment had been simply included.

Autopsy findings

At the time of autopsy, the unwrapped body weighed 3.5 kg. The head circumference was 50.7 cm (Figure 6.7). The body length of 106 cm, even considering shrinkage, is small by modern standards for an 8 year old. The skin was very dark, severely degenerated and full of holes varying from 1 mm to 1 cm. There were numerous scarab beetles and insect larvae on almost all areas of the skin, similar in type to those seen in other autopsies. Many areas of the skin were partially covered with brown granular material. The eyes had been depressed into the orbits by wads of cloth packing and a black tarry substance; they had assumed a cuplike configuration but appeared otherwise normal. The external ears were poorly preserved. The scalp was partially

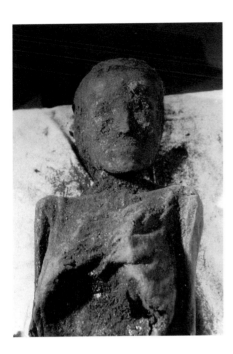

FIGURE 6.7. The head and upper torso showing severe degeneration and granular packing material. (Photograph by John Levis.)

covered by dark hair, matted by the brown to black material. The teeth were well preserved with the central incisors appearing to be baby or milk teeth. No caries were noted.

The external genitalia were those of an immature male with a 5 × 1 cm uncircumcised penis. The scrotum was intact but testes were not identified. There was a large defect in the anorectal area that contained a moderate amount of granular packing material and a 5 cm wad of cloth that partially sealed the defect. The anterior chest and abdominal walls were removed. No abdominal or flank incision was present. There were no recognizable organs in the body cavities, which were filled with large masses of granular packing material, possibly sawdust. Large numbers of dried insect larvae were present. Sections through the neck tissue revealed residual structures resembling the trachea and/or esophagus. When the calvarium was removed, two large, brown granular cerebral hemispheres were present and measured 10 × 4 cm each (Figure 6.8). During the dissection, virtually every bone of the skeleton became loose and separated. There was no evidence of trauma or other pathological process.

The tissue removed during the autopsy was so degenerated that processing for histological examination was not possible. All tissue crumbled into amorphous material when rehydrated. A determination of the cause of death was not possible.

Summary: PUM IV

The data on the mummified male child indicated that he was 8 to 10 years old at the time of death, probably in the first century AD. His height was 106 cm, short by modern standards for a child of this age. The wrappings and filler were crude. The body had been eviscerated per ano but the brain had not been removed. The body was so severely degenerated that no microscopic examination was possible.

SUMMARY: PUM III AND PUM IV

The mummification of these two bodies was less than classical and was haphazardly done. Both bodies had been eviscerated per ano but to varying degrees. PUM III, the adult female, had partial abdominal evisceration as well as removal of the brain but no removal of organs from the chest cavity. PUM IV had total abdominal and thoracic evisceration but the brain was not removed. The wrapping had been done in similar fashion for both; the outer wrappings were circular bandages around the body and the deeper layers consisted of larger sheets or pieces of clothing. Various artifacts and assorted fragments of unrelated wrapping and decorated material had been included in the deeper wrapping. PUM III had been treated sparingly with resin and the body cavities packed with resin-soaked linen wads. PUM IV had been packed with what appeared to be sawdust mixed with a colorless oily substance. Both bodies had severe tissue degeneration.

PUM III had been mummified in approximately 810 BC and it appeared that some care had been taken with the preparation of the mummy, although still less than classical. PUM IV perhaps demonstrated the ultimate debasement of the mummification process. Both bodies were small for their estimated age and may reflect poor nutrition or the effects of disease. This may have been the result of low socioeconomic status, which is suggested by the methods of mummification employed.

REFERENCES

Benitez, J. T. and Lynn, G. E. 1980. Temporal bone studies. In *Mummies, disease and ancient cultures*, ed. A. and E. Cockburn, 301–11. New York: Cambridge University Press.

Brooks, S. T. 1955. Skeletal age at death: the reliability of cranial and pubic age indicators. *American Journal of Physical Anthropology* 13: 567–90.

Kristen, K. T. and Reyman, T. A. 1980. Radiographic examination of mummies with autopsy correlation. In *Mummies, disease and ancient cultures*, ed. A. and E. Cockburn, 287–300. New York: Cambridge University Press.

Mokhtar, G., Riad, H. and Iskander, Z. 1973. *Mummification in ancient Egypt*. Cairo: Cairo Museum.

Phenice, T. W. 1969. A newly developed visual method of sexing the os pubis. *American Journal of Physical Anthropology* 30: 297–301.

Reyman, T. A. and Dowd, A. M. 1980. Processing of mummified tissue for histological examination. In *Mummies, disease and ancient cultures*, ed. A. and E. Cockburn, 258–73. New York: Cambridge University Press.

Riddle, J. M. 1980. A survey of ancient specimens by electron microscopy. In *Mummies, disease, and ancient cultures*, ed. A. and E. Cockburn, 274–86. New York: Cambridge University Press.

Sunderman, E. W. and Boerner, F. 1949. *Normal values in clinical medicine*. Philadelphia: Saunders.

Todd, T. W. 1921. Age changes in the pubic bone: II The pubis of male Negro–white hybrid; III The pubis of the white female; IV The pubis of the female Negro–white hybrid. *American Journal of Physical Anthropology* 4: 1–70.

Trotter, M. and Gleser, G. 1958. A reevaluation of estimation of stature based on measurements taken during life and of long bones after death. *American Journal of Physical Anthropology* 16: 79–123.

PART II

Mummies of the Americas

7

Mummies and mummification practices in the southern and southwestern United States

MAHMOUD Y. EL-NAJJAR, THOMAS M.J. MULINSKI
AND KARL J. REINHARD

Mummification was not intentional for most North American prehistoric cultures. Natural mummification occurred in the dry areas of North America, where mummies have been recovered from rock shelters, caves, and overhangs. In these places, corpses desiccated and spontaneously mummified. In North America, mummies are recovered from four main regions: the southern and southwestern United States, the Aleutian Islands, and the Ozark Mountains of Arkansas. This chapter is limited to a discussion of burial practices and a tabulation of the location of mummies in the southwestern United States with some comments on mummies of the southern United States, including the Ozarks (Figure 7.1).

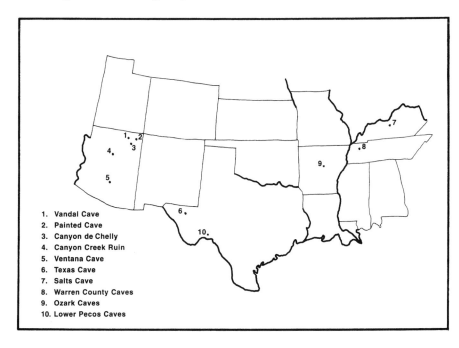

1. Vandal Cave
2. Painted Cave
3. Canyon de Chelly
4. Canyon Creek Ruin
5. Ventana Cave
6. Texas Cave
7. Salts Cave
8. Warren County Caves
9. Ozark Caves
10. Lower Pecos Caves

FIGURE 7.1. Sites where mummies have been found in the southern and southwestern United States. (Map by Timothy Motz, Detroit Institute of Arts, modified by K. Reinhard.)

SOUTHWESTERN UNITED STATES

Mummies are associated with several cultures in the southwestern United States. The oldest mummies are from the Archaic cultures in western Texas, primarily from the Rustler Hills and the lower Pecos region at the confluences of the Rio Grande and Pecos Rivers, and the Rio Grande and Devils River (Turpin *et al.* 1986). Mummies are also associated with later agricultural populations of Arizona, Colorado, New Mexico, and Utah. These mummies come from three main localities: northeastern (Anasazi), east-central (Sinagua) and southern (Hohokam) Arizona. Mummies vary in how they are positioned. In the Four Corners area, they are usually tightly flexed, with the arms and knees drawn to the chest and the head bent forward. In southern Arizona and west Texas, however, the position varied. Some were tightly flexed, but some were buried in extended position.

From northeastern Arizona, mummies have been recovered from Canyon de Chelly, Canyon del Muerto, Vandal Cave, and Painted Cave. Canyon de Chelly and its major tributary, Canyon del Muerto, have yielded some of the best preserved desiccated bodies in the New World. Only a few of these have been conserved to the present day. The majority of these (n=10) is housed at the American Museum of Natural History, New York City. Four of these mummies were studied at Case Western Reserve University, Cleveland, Ohio (El-Najjar *et al.* 1980). A partial mummy and an Anasazi child were studied at the Human Variation Laboratory, Arizona State University, Tempe.

The earliest of the Anasazi are known as the Basket Makers, a semi-nomadic group of hunters and gatherers who lived in the caves and rock shelters between AD 100 and 700. The diet of the Basket Makers was a mix of agricultural products and gathered foods (Reinhard 1992). Mummies of Basket Makers show that they were short and had coarse black hair with a tendency to be wavy, little body hair, and brown skin (Wormington 1973).

Basket Maker corpses mummified when placed in pits or stone-lined cysts that had originally been constructed for storage in caves. Occasionally, however, a body was left in a corner on the floor of a cave or was placed in a crevice. This was probably done immediately after death occurred, before the body had stiffened. It is possible that the small size of the cyst led to the custom of flexing, in which the knees are drawn up to the chest and the arms are extended at the side. The bodies were usually wrapped in fur blankets, but occasionally tanned deerskins were used. Bodies of infants and small children were wrapped in a pad-like mass of soft fiber made from the leaves of yucca plants and shrouded either in fur, skin, or feather cloth blankets.

Mortuary offerings included baskets, sandals, beads and ornaments, weapons, digging sticks, cone shaped pipes, and a variety of personal possessions. Among the unique finds associated with Basket-Maker mummies is a pair of unworn sandals which are double soled, somewhat cupped at the heel, with a square toe, and usually ornamented with a fringe of buckskin or shredded juniper bark (Wormington 1973).

One of the most unusual mummies recovered from the American Southwest is a young Pueblo child approximately three years of age. The Pueblos were the Anasazi descendants of the Basket Makers and lived in large communal houses in the same area between AD 700 and 1300. The child died during the eleventh century (El-Najjar et al. 1975). The desiccated body had been laid flat on an elaborate cradleboard with a cottonwood bark sunshade in place around the head. There was also a worn textile fragment round the neck and a bracelet round the right wrist. This burial contrasts markedly with other burials recovered from the same site. None of the others had a grave cover or had as many or as elaborate grave goods. The child's death has been attributed to severe anemia (El-Najjar and Robertson 1976). The diagnosis was based on macroscopic, radiographic, and histochemical analysis. No other evidence of pathology was found. In an earlier paper, El-Najjar et al. (1975) conclude that the child was probably unable to walk and was unable to participate in normal activities and/or was mentally retarded.

Autopsies have been performed on two Canyon del Muerto mummies, an adult male and an infant (El-Najjar et al. 1980). The researchers found dried red powder, thought to be blood, in the thoracic cavity of the adult mummy. After immunologic analysis there was the suggestion of degraded IgG in the powder. This material was very unstable and may be the result of proteolytic enzyme activity after rehydration. They also conducted hair and fecal analysis. No abnormalities could be found in the hair samples. The feces contained eggs of the pinworm *Enterobius vermicularis*, which has been shown to be the most common parasite of the Anasazi (Reinhard 1990).

Reporting on mummies from Ventana Cave, southern Arizona, Haury (1950) found two types of burial practice: flexed and extended bodies. Haury further states that the degree of flexure varies, from doubling up the legs without drawing them up to the chest to tight flexing, the latter being more common. In the former cases, there is a binding about the legs. Here, as elsewhere in the Southwest, the mummies were entirely the result of natural desiccation.

One of the largest mummy collections is stored at the Arizona State Museum (Table 7.1). This includes mummies from Vandal Cave and Painted

Table 7.1. Sites with mummies in the collections of the Arizona State Museum (ASM)

Site name	Site number[a]	Total number of burials	Number of mummies in ASM collections	Time period[b]	Cultural affiliation[b]	Archeological reference
Vandal Cave	Ariz. E:7:1	11	8	AD 500–700 AD 1150–1250	Anasazi	Haury (1936)
Painted Cave	Ariz. E:7:2	3	2	AD 1150–1250	Anasazi	Haury (1945)
Canyon Creek Ruin	Ariz. V:2:1	40	5	AD 1300–1350	Anasazi	Haury (1934)
McCuen Cave	Ariz. W:13:6	21(?)	10	Undoubtedly prehistoric	?	None
Ventana Cave	Ariz. Z:12:5	39	11	AD 1000–1400[c]	Hohokam	Haury (1950)
Texas Cave	Texas 0:7:3[d]	2(?)	2	?	?	None
Miscellaneous	Various places in Arizona and Colorado	?	5	Probably prehistoric	?	None

Notes:

[a] Except when noted, sites are designated according to the system employed by the Architectural Survey of the ASM (Wasley 1964).

[b] Information on the time period and cultural affiliation of Vandal Cave, Painted Cave, Canyon Creek Ruin, and Ventana Cave comes from Haury (personal communication).

[c] Ventana Cave was occupied off and on for thousands of years, beginning more than 10 000 years ago. However, all the burials except three (nos. 20, 35, and 36), and all the mummies, date from the period AD 1000–1400.

[d] This designation is according to the system employed by the no-longer-existing Gila Pueblo Archeological Foundation.

Cave, northeastern Arizona, as well as those from east-central and southern Arizona. The mummies from Ventana Cave were reburied in 1992. Pertinent information on each mummy is provided in Tables 7.2 through 7.8. It is necessary to point out two things. First, when the burial number of a mummy is not known, the Arizona State Museum (ASM) catalog number of the specimen is used in its place in order to distinguish individuals. The catalog number always appears in parentheses. Second, the age and sex of each mummy were estimated by Mulinski and Birkby (unpublished data).

As noted above, dry conditions resulted in spontaneous mummification, i.e., the soft tissues dried before putrefaction destroyed them. In connection with this, it is interesting to note that the integument of the head is usually the first to disintegrate. For example, mummies had generally intact skin on the torso and extremities, but the covering of the head, especially of the face, has not been preserved or has a significantly lesser percentage of skin still intact. This phenomenon is undoubtedly related to differences in the thickness of the soft tissues surrounding the skull and post-cranium.

Very few biological studies on the mummies in the ASM collections have been carried out. Gabel (1950) examined the human remains from Ventana Cave but made no specific studies of the mummies. On the other hand, two unpublished studies on the Ventana Cave mummies are mentioned by Haury (1950). One of these concerned the paleopathology of valley fever (coccidioidomycosis). Radiographic attempts to define pathology related to valley fever were inconclusive. A second study involved a search for ABO antigens. Nine mummies were positive for type O and one for AB.

Other research projects focussing on diet and parasitism have been done. Reinhard and Hevly (1991) analyzed feces from Mummy 5 from Ventana Cave, a child who died between 4 and 5 years of age. No parasites were found, but two meals were identified. One was composed primarily of mesquite and the other of Saguaro cactus seeds and pollen. A coprolite from an adult female mummy from Ventana Cave, Mummy 11, was studied. No intestinal parasites were found, but the sample contained evidence that buds of saguaro or organ pipe cactus were eaten. The use of buds from these cacti has never before been noted. Birkby has undertaken an examination of the head hair from several mummies for ectoparasites His results are presented in Table 7.9. Of 18 individuals with a sufficient amount of hair to be analyzed, 8 (44.4 percent) had head lice (*Pediculus humanus capitis*). In all instances, only the nits were found.

Analysis of coprolites from partially mummified bodies from Utah and Arizona provides insights into the prehistoric use of medicinal plants, especially willow, Mormon tea, and creosote (Reinhard *et al.* 1991).

Table 7.2. *Mummies from Vandal Cave*

Burial number	Burial position	Condition of mummy	Sex	Age (yr)	Comments
2	Flexed	Complete, but no nails or hair present	Female (?)	Old adult, (>40)	Part of shroud still covering legs
7	Flexed	Complete, but no nails present; small amount of hair present	?	Infant (1–2)	Bracelet still in place on right wrist
9	Flexed	Complete, but no nails present; very small amount of hair present	Male (?)	Adult	Part of burial blanket still covering lower torso
10	Semiflexed	Apparently complete; nails and fair amount of hair present	?	Adult	Body still almost entirely covered with burial blanket and encrusted with soil
?(0–485)	Flexed/semiflexed	Complete; nails, but only very small amount of hair present	?	Infant (0.5–1.0)	Buried on flexible cradleboard
?(0–487A)	Flexed	Complete, although head detached from rest of body; some nails and very small amount of hair present	?	Infant (1.5–2.5)	Cranium with occipital deformation
?(0–487B)	?	Partial; only right forearm and hand and right leg and foot present	?	Infant (0.5–1.5)	
?(0–487C)	?	Partial; only lower part of left leg and foot present	?	Infant (birth–0.5)	

Table 7.3. *Mummies from Painted Cave*

Burial number	Burial position	Condition of Mummy	Sex	Age (yr)
?(o–514)	Semiflexed (?)	Partial: left leg and foot missing, part of right foot missing; anterior walls of thoracic and abdominal cavities almost completely disappeared; nails absent; some hair present	?	Infant (0.5–1.5)
?(o–515)	Flexed	Complete, but skin rather worm-eaten in appearance; nails and some hair present	Male	Child (3.5–4.5)

ARCHAIC MUMMIES FROM TEXAS

In the last decade, mummies from the lower Pecos region of Texas have been most intensively studied. Mummies from this area come from caves and natural shafts where corpses were placed in prehistory. A great number of mummies is known from the regions, and the burial practices have been summarized by Turpin and associates (1986). These mummies are from hunter–gatherer cultures and provide an idea of the hazards of hunter–gatherer life in the area. One such hazard was seasonal starvation, as documented by Banks and Rutenburg (1982). Their radiographic analysis of a child mummy reveals a series of growth arrest lines that are probably the result of seasonal fluctuation in food abundance. The other main health hazard for the region was dental pathology. Dental attrition and dental caries with resulting tooth avulsion was the most consistent health problem faced by ancient Texas hunter–gatherers (Hartnady 1986; Marks *et al.* 1988; Turpin *et al.* 1986). The cause of this severe dental pathology was a reliance on desert succulent plants (Huebner 1991). These plants have been found to have a remarkably high concentration of abrasive crystals called phytoliths which are harder than enamel and which wore the teeth to point of exposing the pulp chamber (Danielson 1993).

SOUTHERN UNITED STATES

Another collection of naturally mummified prehistoric American natives comes from Kentucky. The best known of these is Little Alice (Watson 1969). Little Alice's desiccated body was recovered by two local men in 1875 near what is now known as Mummy Valley. Little Alice was displayed in commercial

Table 7.4. Mummies from Canyon Creek Ruin

Burial number	Burial position	Condition of mummy	Sex	Age (yr)	Comments
13	Extended (?)	Indeterminate, but no skin left on exposed part of head	?	Infant (1–2)	Body still wrapped in shroud(s); buried on cradleboard
20	?	Partial: only bones of right leg and both feet present, with some tissue also present	?	Adult	Osteitis observable on tibia and fibula; both feet in sandals
22	Extended (?)	Indeterminate, but does not appear to be much tissue left	?	Probably infant	Body still wrapped in shrouds(s)
32	?	Partial: skeleton disarticulated; very little tissue remaining	?	Infant (birth–0.5)	Body still wrapped in shroud(s); buried on cradleboard
33	?	Partial: skeleton disarticulated and incomplete; with no skull and very little postcranium remaining; very little tissue left	?	Fetal–newborn	

Table 7.5. *Mummies from McCuen Cave*

Burial number	Burial position	Condition of mummy	Sex	Age (yr)	Comments
Mc:1—4	?	Partial: body jumbled mass, but some tissue present	?	Fetal–newborn	
?(0–483)	Extended	Complete, although head detached from rest of body; a few strands of hair present	?	Infant (1–2)	Body still somewhat covered by shroud(s)
?(0–493)	?	Partial: only some lumbar vertebrae, pelvis, and lower extremities present; only small amount of tissue present	Male	Adult	
?(0–494)	?	Partial: head, upper extremities (except for left humerus), and feet missing; fair amount of tissue still remaining	Female	Adult	
?(0–500)	Extended	Complete; abundant amount of hair present	?	Infant (birth–0.5)	Body still wrapped in shroud(s); buried on cradleboard
?(0–502)	Flexed	Complete, although head detached from rest of body and skin not well preserved; no hair present	?	Infant (1–2)	
?(0–503)	Extended	Complete; some hair present	?	Fetal–newborn	Body still wrapped in shroud(s); buried on cradleboard
?(0–512)	?	Partial: only head, some vertebrae, and rib fragments present; some tissue preserved, but no hair present	Female	Adult	Cranium exhibits lambdoid deformation
?(0–750A)	?	Partial: only both legs and feet present; some tissue preserved	?	Adult	Feet in sandals
?(0–750B)	?	Partial: only left leg and foot present; some tissue preserved	?	Adult	Foot in sandal

Table 7.6. *Mummies from Ventana Cave*

Burial number	Burial position	Condition of mummy	Sex	Age (yr)	Comments
3	Flexed	Complete, although right upper extremity disarticulated at elbow; some hair present	Female	Old adult (>50)	Most of head hair present is gray; calculus present on anterior mandibular teeth; periodontal disease evident
5	?	Partial; skeleton fairly complete, but disarticulated; some tissue remaining, including very small amount of hair	?	Young child (5–6)	
6	Extended	Complete, although left upper extremity disarticulated at elbow; some hair present	Female	Young child (4–5)	Wooden block wrapped with textiles placed under head of this individual when buried
9	Extended	Complete; small amount of hair present, but no nails	Male	Adult	Nose plug and earrings still present; most of torso and upper extremities covered with shroud; grave goods included skin quiver containing cord with attached shell, nose plug, projectile points, four bone awls, human-hair wig, cactus-spine needle, and several fragments of preserved sandals, and miscellaneous cotton cloth fragments
11	Extended	Complete; nails and hair absent	Female	Adult	Body covered with cotton robe when buried
15A	?	Partial: skeleton fairly complete, but disarticulated; very little tissue	?	Infant (1.5–2.5)	

Burial	Position	Condition	Sex	Age	Comments
		remaining; extremely small amount of hair present			
15B	?	Partial: only left forearm and hand present; some tissue remaining	?	Young child (5–6)	
16	?	Partial: only skull, some cervical vertebrae, and right talus present; some tissue remaining, including very small amount of hair	Male (?)	Old adult (>40)	
24	?	Partial: skeleton fairly complete, but somewhat disarticulated; some tissue remaining	?	Infant (0.5–1.5)	Body placed in twined bag and buried in grass nest
25	Semiflexed	Complete; fair amount of hair present	?	Probably infant/young child	Body still almost entirely covered with shroud
29	Semiflexed	Complete, although head detached from rest of body; fair amount of tissue remaining; very small amount of hair remaining	?	Infant (1.0–1.5)	Body buried in fur robe shroud

Table 7.7. *Mummies from Texas Cave*

Burial number	Burial position	Condition of mummy	Sex	Age (yr)	Comments
?(0–740)	?	Partial: skeleton fairly complete, although somewhat disarticulated; some tissue remaining	?	Infant (birth–0.5)	
?(0–759)	Extended	Complete; large amount of hair present	?	Infant (birth–0.5)	Body still covered with burial blanket; buried on mat

caves for many years after the original discovery. In 1958 she was brought to the University of Kentucky, where detailed studies were made. The presence of external genitalia showed the desiccated body to be that of a young male about 9 to 10 years of age and Little Alice is now known as Little Al. According to Robbins (1971), the body is in an excellent state of preservation, except for slight fungus growth as a result of its exposure to the outside atmosphere. Radiocarbon dating using abdominal and lower thoracic tissue produced an age of 1960 ± 160 years BP. On the basis of cultural and physical anthropological data, Robbins concluded that Little Al may have belonged to a group of Woodland Indians who were the recent human occupants of the cave.

Several other desiccated bodies have been found in the Mammoth Cave area. Most of these were discovered by saltpeter miners early in the nineteenth century in Short Cave. Between 1811 and 1815, at least four mummies were found (Meloy and Watson 1969). The Mammoth Cave mummy known as Fawn Hoof was found in Short Cave in 1813. She was sitting in a stone box grave, of the kind commonly found in Tennessee and neighboring counties in Kentucky to the south of Short Cave. Physically, the body was well preserved; the flesh was dry, hard and dark. Fawn Hoof was dressed in several finely fashioned animal skin burial garments (Robbins 1974) and was accompanied by a variety of grave goods. Fawn Hoof is the only one of the mummies that definitely seems to have been accompanied by grave goods (Watson 1969). According to Watson, Fawn Hoof and several items found with her were given to the American Antiquarian Society in Worcester, Massachusetts, about 1817. She was then exhibited at the US National Museum in 1876. Her body has been dissected, and the clean bones are stored at the Division of Physical Anthropology, Smithsonian Institution.

Table 7.8. *Mummies from several localities in the Southwest*

Location	Burial position	Condition of mummy	Sex	Age (yr)	Comments
Slab House Ruin, Duggagei Canyon, Arizona (0–200)	?	Partial: legs and feet missing; no skin left anteriorly and only small amount remaining posteriorly	?	Infant (1–2)	Cranium exhibits rather extreme lambdoid deformation
Yellow Jacket Canyon Colorado (0–245)	?	Partial: skeleton fairly complete, but almost completely disarticulated; some tissue remaining	?	Infant (1.5–2.5)	
Cliff House, Tonto Basin, Arizona (0–498)	?	Partial: skeleton fairly complete, but for most part disarticulated; some tissue remaining	?	Infant (birth–0.5)	
Cottonwood area, Arizona (0–501)	?	Partial: most of face and lower extremities missing	?	Infant (birth–1)	
Duggagei Canyon, Arizona (0–511)	?	Partial: only skull, some cervical vertebrae, and innominates present; small amount of tissue present	Female	Adult (15–20)	

Table 7.9. *Findings of examination of head hair from certain North American Indian mummies in ASM collections for head louse, Pediculus humanus capitis*

Site	Number of mummies with lice	Number of mummies without lice
Vandal Cave	0	3 (burials 7, 9, 10)
Painted Cave	2 (0–514, 0–515)	0
McCuen Cave	0	3 (Mc:2, 0–500, 0–503)
Ventana Cave	6 (burials 3, 5, 9, 15A, 16, 25)	2 (burials 6, 29)
Texas Cave	0	2 (0–740, 0–759)
Total	8	10

Source: W. H. Birkby (unpublished data).

Another mummy, known as the Scudder mummy, was also recovered from Short Cave. Deerskin wrappings on the body and deerskin items found with it indicated that it was from the same population as Fawn Hoof (Robbins 1974). The Scudder mummy, thought to be an adolescent boy, showed evidence of a fracture of the occipital bone that may have contributed to his death.

The remains of a mummy known as Lost John were recovered from Mammoth Cave in 1935. The desiccated body was found lying partially crushed under a boulder. Apparently, Lost John was the victim of a prehistoric mining accident. Neumann (1938) believes that the miner was kneeling when the boulder fell, its impact forcing him to fall on his right side. The cultural items found near the body indicate that this individual was involved in mining activities at the time of death (Robbins 1974). The body is well preserved, with flesh and internal organs present except for areas where rodent activities are evident. Lost John was a male in his forties. Textile material, evidently some sort of a blanket or robe of open twined weave, was tied with a braided cord around the body, and a mussel shell pendant was suspended from the neck by a piece of two strand twisted cord. A crude limestone hammer, bundles of reeds tied with grass, sticks, parts of gourds, a fragment of bagging, a stout pole that was probably used as a ladder, some hickory nuts, and human coprolites are the only other materials in the cave (Neumann 1938). On the basis of cultural and geological evidence, Neumann suggests a date for John's death of about 500 years ago .

Mummies have also been found in caves in Tennessee. Holmes (1891–2) reported on two mummies found in 'a copperas cave' in Warren County, West Tennessee. The bodies, a male and a female, were discovered in 1810. Both had been placed in large cane baskets and buried in the cave floor. The female, like the bodies in Short Cave, was wrapped in a succession of materials, including hides, a feather cloak, and a piece of plain textile. According to Holmes (1891–2), a scoop net, a moccasin, a mat (all made of bark thread), and a turkey feather fan were also found.

Robbins (1974) suggests that the interment of the Short Cave mummies exhibits a pattern similar in some ways to mummies found in Tennessee, though it is different in others. In both areas mummies were wrapped in deerskin and accompanied with grave goods. Robbins further suggests that the Tennessee mummies differ in that some were disarticulated at the hips before being wrapped or dressed.

The most significant mummy discovery was made in Florida, where a peat bog had preserved brain tissue from a hunter–gatherer occupant dated to between 7000 and 8000 years ago. The site is known as Windover Pond and its discovery and excavation was a major sensation in the mid-1980s. No soft tissue other than the brain was preserved, but it provided the oldest sample of human DNA recovered at that point (Doran *et al.* 1986).

The mummies in the Ozark Mountains along the Arkansas–Missouri border belong to the bluff-dwellers who inhabited the shelters for centuries. Of the large number of burials found, a few mummified bodies have been identified and these have been studied sparingly (Riddick 1992). The mummies were not intentional, but were simply preserved by the dry climate in the limestone caves. Radiocarbon dating of agricultural material from these caves gave values ranging from 2960±40 BP to the most recent at 280±100 BP, although dating of charcoal from one site gave a value of approximately 10 000 BP. Analysis of coprolites from one mummy revealed traces of sumac, ground acorns, charcoal, and other vegetable material. Radiographic studies including three dimensional and standard CT scans were performed on several wrapped mummies, identifying those bodies that might be suitable for further study.

SUMMARY

Although mummies have been recovered from the southwest and southeast United States for many years, very few scientific studies on prehistoric health have been completed. During the past decade, Texas has been the scene of the most active mummy research, with a variety of analyses shedding light on the paleopathology in that region. In the 1990s, the potential for analysis decreased due to repatriation efforts on the part of Native American tribes. One of the most significant collections of mummies, that from Ventana Cave, has been reburied and is lost for future study. This is a strong indication that the door has been shut on mummy studies in the Southwest and can be opened only by concerted efforts to educate and cooperate with Native American tribes in the region.

REFERENCES

Banks, K. and Rutenburg, G. 1982. *A childhood bundle burial from Val Verde County, Texas.* Dallas, TX: Texas Archaeological Foundation.

Danielson, D. R. 1993. Phytolith Analysis of Coprolites from the Prehistoric Southwest. Master's Thesis, Department of Anthropology, University of Nebraska, Lincoln.

Doran, G. H., Dickel, D. N., Ballinger, W. E., Agee, O. F., Laipis, P. J. and Hauswirth, W. W. 1986. Anatomical, cellular and molecular analysis of 8,000-yr-old human brain tissue from the Windover archaeological site. *Nature* **323**: 803–6.

El-Najjar, M. Y. and Robertson, A. 1976. Spongy bones in prehistoric America. *Science* **193**: 141–3.

El-Najjar, M., Benitez, J., Fry, G., Lynn, G., Ortner, D., Reyman, T. A. and Small, P. A, 1980. Autopsies on two Native American mummies. *American Journal of Physical Anthropology* **53**: 197–202.

El-Najjar, M. Y., Morris, D. P., Turner, C. G. and Ryan, D. 1975. An unusual pathology with high incidence among the ancient cliff-dwellers of Canyon de Chelly. *Plateau* **48**: 13–21.

Gabel, N. E. 1950. The skeletal remains of Ventana Cave. In *The stratigraphy and archaeology of Ventana Cave*, ed. E. W. Haury, 473–520. Tucson: University of Arizona Press.

Hartnady, P. 1986. Premature Tooth Loss in the Archaic Trans-Pecos of Southwest Texas. Master's Thesis, Department of Anthropology, University of Arkansas, Fayetteville.

Haury, E. W. 1934. *The Canyon Creek ruin and the cliff dwellings of Sierra Ancha.* Medallion Papers, No. 14. Globe, AZ: Gila Pueblo

Haury, E. W. 1936. Vandal Cave. *Kiva* **1**(6): 1–4.

Haury, E. W. 1945. *Painted Cave, northeastern Arizona.* Dragoon, AZ: Amerind Foundation.

Haury, E. W. 1950. *The stratigraphy and archaeology of Ventana Cave.* Tucson: University of Arizona Press.

Holmes, W. H. 1891–2. Prehistoric textile art of the eastern United States. In *Thirteenth annual report of the Bureau of American Ethnology*, 3–55. Washington, DC: Smithsonian Institution Press.

Huebner, J. A. 1991. Cactus for dinner, again! An isotopic analysis of late Archaic diet in the lower Pecos region of Texas. In *Papers on Lower Pecos prehistory.* ed. S. A. Turpin, 175–90. Austin: Texas Archaeological Research Laboratory, University of Texas.

Marks, M. K., Rose, J. C. and Buie, E. L. 1988. Bioarchaeology of Seminole Sink. *Plains Anthropologist* **33**: 75–116.

Meloy, H. and Watson, P. J. 1969. Human remains: 'Little Alice' of Salts Cave and other mummies. In *The prehistory of Salts Cave, Kentucky*, ed. P. J. Watson, 65–9. New York: Academic Press.

Neumann, G. K. 1938. The human remains from Mammoth Cave, Kentucky. *American Antiquity* **36**(2): 36 201–6.

Reinhard, K. J. 1990. Archaeoparasitology in North America. *American Journal of Physical Anthropology* **82**: 145–62.

Reinhard, K. J. 1992. The impact of diet, and parasitism on anemia in the prehistoric West. In *Diet, demography and disease: changing perspectives of anemia*, ed. P. Stuart-Macadam and S. Kent, 219–58. New York: Aldine deGruyter.

Reinhard, K. J. and Hevly, R. H. 1991. Dietary and parasitological analysis of mummy 5, Ventana Cave, Arizona. *Kiva* **56**: 314–25.

Reinhard, K. J., Hamilton, D. H. and Hevly, R. H. 1991. Use of pollen concentration in paleopharmacology: coprolite evidence of medicinal plants. *Journal of Ethnobiology* **11**: 117–34.

Riddick, R. B., Jr. 1992. The Ozark Bluff-dweller mummies. In *Proceedings of the I World Congress on Mummy Studies*, vol. 2, 837–9. Santa Cruz de Tenerife: Museo Arqueológico y Etnográfico de Tenerife

Robbins L. M. 1971. A Woodland 'mummy' from Salts Cave, Kentucky. *American Antiquity* **36**(2): 201–6.

Robbins L. M. 1974. Prehistoric people of the Mammoth Cave area. In *Archeology of the Mammoth Cave area*, ed. P. J. Watson, 137–62. New York: Academic Press

Turpin, S. A., Henneberg, M. and Riskind, D. H. 1986. Late Archaic mortuary practices of the Lower Pecos River region, Southwest Texas. *Plains Anthropologist* **31**: 294–316.

Wasley, W. W. 1964. *The archaeological survey of the Arizona State Museum*. Tucson: University of Arizona Press.

Watson, P. J. 1969. *The prehistory of Salts Cave, Kentucky*. Reports of investigation no. 16. Springfield: Illinois State Museum.

Wormington, M. 1973. *Prehistoric indians of the Southwest*. Colorado Museum of Natural History, Series 7. Denver: The Museum.

8

Alaskan and Aleutian mummies

MICHAEL R. ZIMMERMAN

In contrast to the many mummies that have been studied from other parts of the world, only a few mummified bodies from the Arctic have been subjected to paleopathologic examination. The frigid climate of Alaska proper has resulted in the production of frozen mummies with remarkable preservation of histologic detail. In contrast, the cool damp climate of the Aleutian Islands would seem to be poorly suited to mummification but cultural practices have supervened in this area to produce artificial mummies.

The oldest preserved bodies from Alaska are mammals of the late Pleistocene (15 000–25 000 years BP) from the area of Fairbanks, recovered during gold mining in the late nineteenth century. Studies of a mammoth and other animals revealed gross preservation of the organs, with some preservation of histologic structure, including cross-striations in the skeletal muscle of the mammoth and the fibrous tissue framework of a rabbit liver (Zimmerman and Tedford 1976). The preservative effect of freezing and subsequent mummification by desiccation was thus demonstrated to last much longer than had previously been suspected. The degree of tissue destruction did indicate that a significant period of time had elapsed between the death of the animals and their entombment in the permafrost, countering a popular notion that Arctic mammals were killed and preserved instantaneously by a catastrophic climate change (Sanderson 1960).

A 1600 YEAR OLD FROZEN ESKIMO MUMMY

In October 1972, the frozen body of a woman washed out of a low beach cliff at Kialegak Point on the Southeast Cape of Saint Lawrence Island in the Bering Sea. The body was found by three Eskimo hunters, the Gologergan brothers of the village of Savoonga. A visiting National Park Service (NPS) anthropologist, Zorro Bradley, was notified of the find and, with the permission of the Eskimos of the island, the body was transported to Fairbanks.

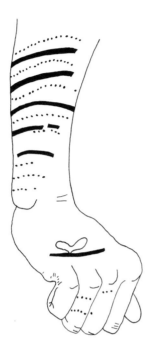

FIGURE 8.1. Pattern of tattooing on the right forearm of a 1600 year old frozen body from Saint Lawrence Island, Alaska. (Drawing courtesy of George S. Smith, National Park Service.)

Using facilities arranged by Robert Rausch at the federal Arctic Health Research Center (no longer in operation), the author and George S. Smith of the NPS and the Anthropology Department of the University of Alaska, performed a complete autopsy (Zimmerman and Smith 1975). Tattooing noted on the arms indicated some degree of antiquity, as this practice had been discontinued on St Lawrence Island by the 1930s (Geist 1928). Radiocarbon dating, at AD 405±70 years, placed the body in the Old Bering Sea Phase on St Lawrence Island, AD 200–500 (Birkit-Smith 1959). Examination of the tattoos (Smith and Zimmerman 1975), which were confined to the arms, was undertaken in an effort to provide an archaeologic date. As is usual with bodies long dead, the skin was dark brown, obscuring the tattoos, but they were defined by infrared photography. The right forearm tattoos consisted of rows of dark blue to black dots with alternating lines and a flanged heart shape attached to a horizontal line (Figure 8.1). There were also rows of dots on the fingers. The tattooing on the left arm was even more elaborate, with multiple flanged hearts attached by vertical and horizontal lines. The left hand showed ovals within ovals and dots on the fingers.

The process of tattooing on St. Lawrence island was described by Otto Geist in a letter (1928). The pigment was made from soot mixed with urine and was applied with steel needles. One technique involved threading a

FIGURE 8.2. Coronary artery showing atherosclerotic plaque. Hematoxylin and eosin. ×95.

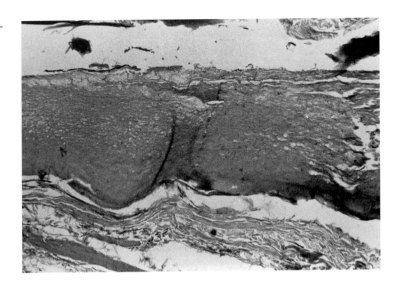

pigment soaked string through the skin in small segments; the other was to prick the skin with the needle, which was dipped in the pigment each time. Collins (1937), in illustrating decorative motifs of Old Bering Sea Style 2, has drawings of artifacts with motifs very similar to these tattooing designs. The artistic motifs of the tattooing thus correlate with the radiocarbon dates in placing this individual within the Old Bering Sea Phase of Alaskan prehistory.

The body of this elderly woman was well preserved, weighed about 25 kg, and showed mild scoliosis. The right side of the face was partially crushed. Several teeth were missing, as was the left lower leg, apparently postmortem. The internal organs were noted to be somewhat desiccated but generally well preserved. There was a moderate degree of coronary atherosclerosis but no evidence of myocardial infarction, acute or healed. The lower lobes of both lungs showed adhesions to the chest wall and diaphragm and the lungs were markedly anthracotic. The smaller bronchi of both lungs were packed with moss, forming casts of the bronchi. A calcified carinal lymph node was found. Moderate aortic atherosclerosis was noted. Atrophic internal genitalia confirmed that this was an elderly woman.

Tissue samples were rehydrated with Ruffer's solution (Ruffer 1921) for light microscopic examination. The coronary arteries showed the atheromatous lesions that had been seen grossly (Figure 8.2). The myocardium was less well preserved. The lungs showed the patchy deposition of anthracotic pigment observed in modern patients with centrilobular emphysema (Figure 8.3). The alveolar architecture was generally preserved, with many of the

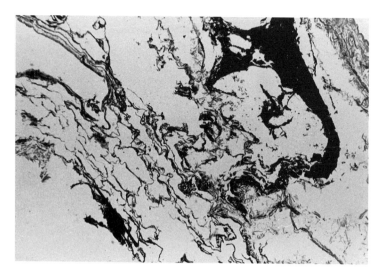

FIGURE 8.3. Centrilobular deposition of anthracotic pigment in the lungs. Hematoxylin and eosin. ×37.5.

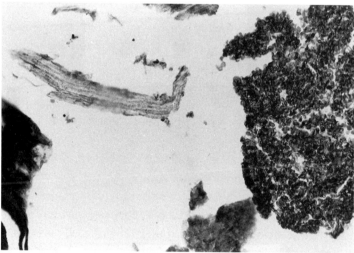

FIGURE 8.4. Aspirated moss fiber with hemorrhage in the bronchial lumen. Masson's trichrome. ×95.

alveoli coalescent. Moss fibers seen in the bronchi were associated with hemorrhage (Figure 8.4). The liver showed a distinction between portal triads and parenchymal cells, which contained a brown pigment that failed to stain for iron or bile and almost certainly represented lipofuscin, an aging change. The thyroid contained well-preserved follicles and colloid. The calcified carinal lymph node and identical splenic lesions were interpreted as healed granulomas (Figure 8.5). Examination with polarized light was negative for silica and results of staining for acid-fast bacilli were negative. Stains for fungi revealed a *Candida* species, which was found in other tissues and appears to be a postmortem invader. Although fluorescein-labeled

FIGURE 8.5. Fibrocalcific granuloma in a carinal lymph node. Hematoxylin and eosin. ×95.

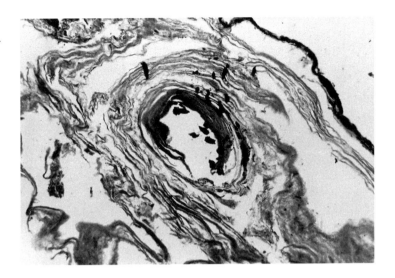

Histoplasma capsulatum antiglobulins that had been absorbed with cells of *Candida albicans* did not demonstrate H. *capsulatum*, this lesion probably is histoplasmosis, based on the anatomical distribution of the lesions and geographical incidence of the disease. Examination of the feces revealed the ova of a fish trematode, *Cryptocotyle lingua*. The ova of this parasite have been reported in modern Eskimos (Rausch *et al.* 1967) but the adult helminth has not been identified in humans.

Microscopic fracture of the right temporal bone was also seen, with associated hemorrhage indicating that this was an antemortem fracture and confirming the role of trauma in this woman's death (J. Benitez, personal communication). Based on this evidence of trauma and the moss found in the bronchi, it appears that this elderly woman had been trapped in her semisubterranean house by a landslide or earthquake, buried alive and asphyxiated. The body was unclothed and in life Eskimos are unclothed only in their houses; after death, if burial is deliberate, the bodies are clothed. In view of the preservation of the body, one would have expected any clothing to have been preserved as well. Aspiration of foreign material into the bronchi is known to occur in accidental inhumation and has been demonstrated in persons buried in heaps of coal (Gonzalez *et al.* 1954). The microscopic finding of hemorrhage associated with the moss fibers in the bronchi is consistent with asphyxiation. It is not unusual for blood cells to be preserved for extended periods. Preserved erythrocytes have been reported in the tissues of Peruvian (Allison *et al.* 1975) and North American Indian (Zimmerman 1973) mummies.

THE FROZEN FAMILY OF UTQIAGVIK

In July 1982 the remains of five people were found in a crushed winter house in the ancient village of Utqiagvik on a bluff overlooking the Arctic Ocean (Zimmerman and Aufderheide 1984; Zimmerman 1985) in the modern town of Barrow, the northernmost point of Alaska. Their deaths were attributed to the well documented phenomenon of *ivu*, an enormously powerful inland incursion of large amounts of broken sea ice driven by winds and tides (Kovacs and Sodhi 1981). Radiocarbon dating of AD 1510±70 years was consistent with the artifacts found within the house.

Three of the bodies, a 20 year old female, a 13 year old male and an eight year old female had been skeletonized. The others, two females, one in her forties and the other in her mid-twenties, were very well preserved. Both showed fatal crushing chest injuries. The older woman was found near the exit from the house, with the roof collapsed on her and fractures of all her ribs. Her lungs were collapsed, with a significant volume of fluid in the chest cavities. The younger woman, found under the sleeping platform, showed similar changes, with a skull fracture, rib fractures and chest fluid containing a small amount of hemoglobin, preserved for almost 500 years.

The lungs of both bodies showed massive anthracosis and there was severe demineralization of the bones, which could easily be cut with a scalpel. Histologic examination confirmed the finding of osteoporosis. Atherosclerosis was not seen in the younger woman but was present in the older woman, affecting coronary arteries and aorta. The older woman was also reproductively active. Her breasts, prominent on gross examination, showed the histologic appearance of lactation and other evidence indicated that she had delivered some two to six months before death. No infant's body was found. Calcification was found in one of the older woman's heart valves, the mitral valve. On the basis of the appearance and location of the lesion, the most likely diagnosis was a healed bacterial endocarditis, or inflammation of the lining of the valve. This infection was usually fatal before the use of antibiotics. Adhesions of the lungs to the chest wall suggested pneumonia as a source of the blood-borne bacterial infection, and the kidneys showed healing from acute tubular necrosis, a form of renal failure that complicates a variety of serious illnesses, including endocarditis. The full pathological sequence may have consisted of pneumonia and pleuritis, complicated by bacteremia, acute mitral endocarditis and kidney failure, followed, rather surprisingly, by recovery. The older woman showed cystic structures in the diaphragm indicating trichinosis, currently thought to infect Arctic populations through the meat of the polar bear. Humans are more likely to become infected when the meat is undercooked, as sometimes occurs because of a scarcity of firewood in the Arctic (Rausch 1970). Healed granulomas in her lungs and lymph nodes were probably caused by histoplasmosis.

STARVATION AND CHRONIC ILLNESS IN AN 800 YEAR OLD THULE MUMMY

In the summer of 1994 the frozen body of a young Eskimo girl was found at Ukkuqsi in the old whaling village of Utqiagvik, adjacent to the site of the frozen family described above. At the request of the Barrow Elders, and with initial funding through the Commission on Iñupiat History, Language and Culture and ultimate funding through a supplemental grant from NSF's Office of Polar Programs, an archaeologic team under the direction of Glenn Sheehan and Anne Jensen of Bryn Mawr College, Pennsylvania and Gregory Reinhardt of the University of Indianapolis, Co-principal Investigators of an ongoing National Science Foundation funded project, 'Archaeology of the North Alaska Coast: A Settlement Pattern Study', excavated and conducted research on the body and the site. The archaeological context and radio-carbon dates suggest that the little girl was a member of the semi-nomadic Thule culture (c. AD 800–1200). She had been buried in a meat cellar dug partly through an abandoned house floor.

The author was invited to perform an examination of the child's body at Providence Hospital in Anchorage. The body, intact inside a birdskin parka, was that of a female Eskimo child weighing 6.025 kg, in a knee-chest position with the arms drawn up to the chest. The intact parka, consisting of birdskins with the feathers on the inside, had a hood with several small points, indicative of the female sex, and a fur ruff. Full juvenile dentition showed a moderate amount of wear. X-rays showed a number of growth arrest lines in the distal tibia and indicate an approximate age of 5–6 years. There was no evidence of trauma. Several small (0.5 cm and less) ovoid opaque bodies were noted in the lower abdominal cavity.

The body was opened through a standard autopsy incision, revealing watery fluid, with some blood, in the thoracic and abdominal cavities. The bones were markedly osteoporotic and, on microscopy, the bone spicules were very thin with minimal calcification, a pattern similar to that seen in the other Eskimo mummies. The organs were intact and sampled for histologic examination. The stomach contained a small amount of granular, sand-like material with fragments of hair. The large intestine was noted to be full of

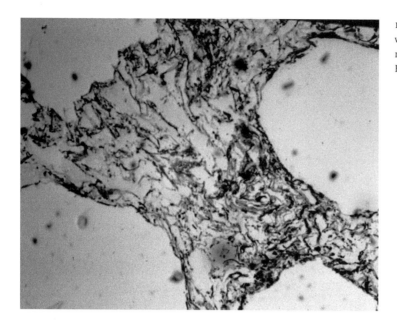

FIGURE 8.6. Interstitial fibrosis consistent with emphysema in the 1000 year old mummy of a 6 year old Eskimo child. Hematoxylin and eosin. ×100.

pebbles, corresponding to the radio opacities noted previously, fragments of gravel and fecal material, with masses of large deeply pigmented hairs that appeared to be of animal origin. No parasites were seen, grossly or microscopically.

The heart showed no pathologic change. The lungs showed extensive anthracosis and a one centimeter air filled bleb in the upper portion of the right lower lobe. The left lung was less well aerated than the right. Anthracotic hilar lymph nodes were identified. The usual alveolar architecture was distorted by marked coalescence and interstitial fibrosis (Figure 8.6). Edema fluid was noted within many of the alveoli. There was no evidence of pneumonia. The chest fluid tested positive for hemoglobin. The liver showed extensive scarring (Figure 8.7) and accumulation of an abnormal pigment in the liver cells. The rest of the organs were well preserved and showed no abnormalities. This six year old girl appears to have died of starvation about 800 to 1000 years ago. Her lower intestine was filled with gravel, sand, pebbles and animal hair, indicating that normal food sources were unavailable. Isotopic analysis performed on the young girl's hair by Roy Crouse, Department of Physics, University of Calgary, Alberta, Canada, indicated that her diet was derived from marine food resources, similar to those of other ancient marine populations.

The terminal event was pulmonary edema, probably secondary to hypoproteinemia, with the accumulation of bloody fluid in the chest cavities and

FIGURE 8.7. Cirrhosis due to alpha-1
antitrypsin deficiency in the Eskimo child.
Hematoxylin and eosin. ×100.

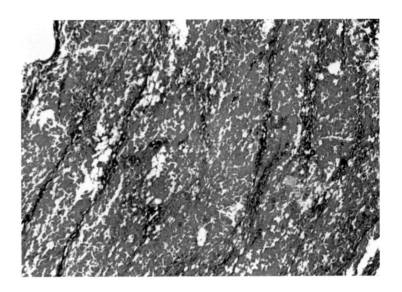

collapse of the left lung. A severe degree of emphysema was a contributing cause to her death. Emphysema, common in elderly cigarette smokers, is rare in children. This child's emphysema was a complication of a rare genetic disorder, alpha-1 antitrypsin (A1AT) deficiency, as evidenced by the accumulation in her liver of an abnormal form of the A1AT. The gene for A1AT has been identified in a specific site on chromosome 14. Roughly two in 10 000 of the United States population suffer from this disorder. It is seven times more frequent in Scandinavians, which raises the possibility that this may represent a circumpolar disorder. The pathogenetic sequence in this condition is initiated by lung infection. Inflammatory cells enter the lungs from the blood and release destructive enzymes such as trypsin aimed at the invading bacteria. To prevent destruction of the lung itself by trypsin, A1AT is released by the liver into the blood stream. Individuals with an inherited deficiency of A1AT are unable to inactivate trypsin and other destructive enzymes in their lungs. Unchecked activity of elastase leads to destruction of elastic tissue in the walls of the pulmonary alveoli, resulting in continued stretching of the airspaces and the development of emphysema (Cotran *et al.* 1989).

A1AT is a glycoprotein synthesized in the liver. In the deficiency state, a mutant protein accumulates in the liver cells, creating cytoplasmic globular inclusions that stain strongly positive with a special stain called PAS, which also stains the glycogen normally present in hepatocytes. However, glycogen does not stain after the tissue is exposed to an enzyme called diastase, which splits sugars. The inclusions of A1AT deficiency are PAS positive and diastase resistant. The pattern seen in the Eskimo child's liver is very similar to that seen in modern patients, including the development of scarring in reaction to the accumulation of the abnormal material.

Clinical liver disease is also associated with this disorder (Cotran *et al.* 1989). The disease may present with respiratory disease due to emphysema or liver disease at any time from birth to adulthood. At birth or a few months later, it may be discovered because of laboratory evidence of abnormal liver function or overt hepatitis with jaundice. Later in adolescence it may take the form of hepatitis or cirrhosis but in other instances it remains silent until cirrhosis appears in middle to later life. Attacks of hepatitis may subside with complete recovery or they may become chronic and lead progressively to cirrhosis or liver cancer. The role of the accumulation of the abnormal A1AT in the induction of liver disease remains to be completely elucidated.

This disease accounts for the multiple bouts of illness she undoubtedly suffered during her brief life, as evidenced by numerous growth arrest lines (Harris lines) observed by x-ray in her long bones. A sled buried with the child was probably used when she was too weak or ill to walk. Her deliberate burial is a rare finding in ancient Eskimo populations and it is clear that this chronically ill child was kept alive and treated with care in life and in death.

MUMMIES FROM AN ALEUTIAN ISLAND

The cold, damp climate of the Aleutian Islands would appear ill suited to the practice of mummification, which is generally based on desiccation. Hrdlička (1945) attributed the development of mummification by the Aleuts to a reluctance to part with the deceased. Laughlin (n.d.) points to the anatomic interests of the Aleuts in conjunction with their desire to preserve and use the spiritual power residing in the human body. The Aleuts who studied comparative anatomy, using the sea otter as the animal most like humans, conducted autopsies on their dead and had an extensive anatomic vocabulary. Mummification as an Aleut funerary practice was an extension of their pragmatically oriented culture.

The technique of mummification varied with the social status of the deceased (Jochelson 1925; Dall 1945; Veniaminov 1945). The bodies of hunters and tribal leaders were eviscerated through an incision in the pelvis or over the stomach. Fatty tissues were removed from the abdominal cavity, which was stuffed with dry grass. The body was then put in running water, which completed the removal of fat, leaving only skin and muscle, and then bound in a flexed position, the habitual leisure posture of the Aleuts. The flexed body was then air-dried by carefully and repeatedly wiping off exuded moisture, the cords were removed, and the mummy was wrapped in its best clothes, usually a coat of aquatic bird skins, followed by a waterproof coat of sea lion intestines and then various layers of seal, sea lion or otter skins and perhaps some matting. The entire bundle was then tied and removed to a burial cave, where the mummies were placed on platforms or suspended from the ceiling to avoid contact with the damp ground. The cave in which the mummies were found was heated by volcanic vents, creating a preservative warm dry atmosphere. The burial caves were probably used for only a few hundred years before the Russian contact of the early eighteenth century.

An Aleut tale (Jochelson 1925) explaining the use of the warm cave, tells of a rich headman, Little Wren, who lived near the cave on Kagamil Island. His young son was accidentally killed by Little Wren's son-in-law. In the subsequent funeral procession, Little Wren's daughter slipped on a rock and suffered a fatal miscarriage. As the season was snowy and cold, the chief decided to place the bodies of his children in the nearby cave, which had previously been used for storage. The chief declared that the cave would become a mausoleum for his entire family and, when he died of grief shortly afterward, he was interred there with all his possessions.

A number of bodies (believed to include Little Wren) were removed from the warm cave in 1874 by Captain E. Hennig of the Alaska Commercial Company and the remainder by Hrdlička in 1938. Many of the bodies were skeletonized by Hrdlička and blood group determinations performed, showing a distribution similar to that of Eastern Siberian tribes (Candela 1939). In 1969, a group directed by the author examined one of the remaining mummies, fortunately that of a common man who had not been eviscerated (Zimmerman et al. 1971). Radiologic examination of the fur-wrapped bundle revealed the outlines of the heart and lungs. The brain presented as an occipital opacity. Pathologic changes were limited to minimal arthritic changes in the vertebral column and evidence of dental attrition and periodontal disease. A number of radiopaque masses, subsequently found to be fecal material, were seen in the left side of the abdomen.

The outer five wrappings were sea otter skins and the innermost layer was an eider down parka, numerous birdskins sewn together with the feathers on the inside, with a spotted fur collar. No incision was seen in the body, which was that of a 165 cm adult male weighing approximately 10 kg. The skin was dark brown, dry and leather like. The face was partially covered by a birdskin, probably a cap that had slipped down. There was some balding and the hair appeared singed, suggesting that the body had been suspended over a fire for desiccation. A mustache and full beard were present. There was a full complement of teeth, in normal occlusion. Lodged between the left forearm and the left side of the abdomen was an empty birdskin pouch.

A Stryker electric autopsy saw was used to remove the rigid tissues of the anterior chest and abdominal wall. A few pleural adhesions were noted and the lower lobe of the right lung was consolidated. The abdominal viscera were poorly preserved, only the distal large intestine and rectum, which were filled with coprolites, being identified. The abdominal aorta and iliac vessels were seen, the right iliac artery showing atherosclerosis. The brain, found to be shrunken into the posterior fossa of the cranial cavity, was roughly rectangular, measuring 14 by 10 by 5 cm and was covered by a fine crystalline material. The upper left maxillary dentoalveolar process was removed *en bloc*. Extreme dental attrition was present to a point slightly beyond the interdental contacting tooth surfaces. Heavy dental calculus and periodontal bone loss were evident.

Histologic examination revealed the pulmonary architecture to be well preserved, although cellular detail was lost. The right lower lobe was completely destroyed, consisting of free gram-negative bacilli and clumps of gram-negative material. Multiple small aggregates of crystalline material, containing gram-negative bacilli, were found in these areas, and in similar foci in the other lobes of the lungs, the heart, trachea, and kidneys. A moderate amount of interstitial anthracotic pigment was seen throughout. The iliac artery plaque was composed of cholesterol crystals with minute calcific foci. A similar plaque was noted in the inferior labial artery.

The hard tooth structures were well preserved. Ground tooth sections showed complete histologic properties of enamel and dentin. Secondary dentin measured about 350 nm in thickness and was separated from the reparative (tertiary) dentin by a prominent basophilic line. The reparative dentin was 1 to 2 mm in thickness under the worn cuspal areas where attrition had abraded through the enamel into the dentin of the teeth. In spite of the severe attrition, structurally sound enamel remained in the intercuspal areas. Because of the excellent reparative response to attrition and the absence of periapical dental disease, it was assumed the teeth were vital.

The blood group was type O. Cultures of the lung failed to reveal viable organisms. The tissues showed almost total preservation of protein content but loss of enzymatic activity. Neutron activation analysis showed no evidence of heavy metal poisons. The crystalline areas in the tissues were subjected to x-ray crystallographic analysis, which revealed them to be composed of acid–ammonium–sodium–phosphate hydrate and apatite, a calcium–phosphate compound. The coprolites were negative for ova and parasites. No adipocere was found in the body. Chondrocytes were found to be well preserved by electron microscopy (Yeatman 1971).

It was concluded that this 200 to 300 year old mummy was that of a middle aged man who had died of lobar pneumonia involving the right lower lobe, caused by a gram-negative bacillus, probably *Klebsiella pneumoniae*, and complicated by septicemia and diffuse metastatic abscesses. Pulmonary anthracosis was related to open fires for cooking and heating. Severe masticatory dental stress resulted in marked dental attrition and reparative processes.

A second Aleutian mummy, from the collection of the Peabody Museum of Archaeology and Ethnology of Harvard University was examined by a group of scientists (Zimmerman *et al.* 1981) sponsored by the Museum and the Paleopathology Association (Cockburn 1978). This mummy, one of the group removed from Kagamil Island in 1874, was a middle aged female, wrapped in sea otter and sea lion skins and tied into a flexed position. Archaeologic dating was to the early eighteenth century. X-ray examination revealed loss of maxillary and most of the mandibular teeth, a postmortem fracture of the left forearm, an old injury to the right clavicle, and degenerative joint disease of the upper extremities. Autopsy revealed the organs to be poorly preserved; only the lungs, liver, intestinal tract, kidneys, and brain were identified and removed for histologic examination. Gross pathologic changes noted were pleural adhesions in the upper lobe of the left lung and the diaphragm, congestion of the renal medulla, and osteophytosis of the vertebrae and joints of the arms.

Microscopic examination revealed extensive infiltration of the tissues by fungi, plants, and insects. The poorly preserved lungs showed anthracosis, focal bronchial dilation, and pulmonary and pleural fibrosis. The aorta showed calcific atherosclerosis. The kidneys were remarkably well preserved, with the glomeruli reduced to masses of basement membrane material, the cells having degenerated. The lining cells of the tubules were preserved in areas and many of the tubules contained small deposits of iron and calcium, a change seen in the recovery phase of acute tubular necrosis and very similar to that seen in the mummy of the older woman from the Utqiagvik site. The larger arterioles showed minimal sclerotic changes.

The temporal bones, studied with an operating microscope, showed a large, kidney-shaped perforation in the right tympanic membrane. The margin of the perforation was smooth and well circumscribed. The ossicles were in place and there was bilateral mastoid sclerosis, more severe in the antrum. The left tympanic membrane was not present.

Age at death was determined by photon-osteon analysis to be 51 ± 6 years.

This age was consistent with age-specific changes of erosion and erratic ossification on the faces of the pubic symphysis, which also showed evidence of parturition. No lead was detected in tibia and rib bone samples. Unlike the osteoporotic Eskimo bodies, the bones of this Aleut woman were robust. The scalp contained numerous adult lice and ova of *Pediculus humanus capitis*, attached to the hair and visible to the unassisted eye. Examination by scanning electron microscopy showed extraordinary preservation of surface detail. These 200 year old lice showed no essential difference from modern lice. The scalp itself showed excoriations consistent with such an infestation.

Final diagnoses were as follows: pleural adhesions, possible pneumonia or bronchiectasis, recovery phase of acute tubular necrosis, aortic atherosclerosis, arteriolar nephrosclerosis, bilateral chronic mastoiditis, right otitis media with perforation of the tympanic membrane, pediculosis capitis and degenerative joint disease.

CONCLUSION

Study of these Eskimo and Aleut mummies has demonstrated our ability to determine cause of death and to illustrate the hazards of life in these extreme environments. Such studies also provide information on the history of several disease processes.

The mummies of Eskimos and Aleuts, far removed from the stresses of modern technological society, show evidence of coronary artery disease. These cases not only confirm the antiquity of coronary atherosclerosis but also exhibit its occurrence in preliterate society. Although mammal meat constituted a relatively small proportion of the Aleut diet, both Aleut mummies showed atherosclerosis, as do the mummies of ancient Egyptians, who also ate little meat (Breutsch 1959; Sandison 1967, 1970; Zimmerman 1977). These paleopathologic observations raise some questions as to the associations that have been suggested among stress, diet, and atherosclerosis.

The finding of severe anthracosis can be attributed to lifetimes spent around open cooking and heating fires. For example, winter houses in the prehistoric area of Barrow were semisubterranean, with a tunnel entrance below the floor level of the house and heating by small seal oil lamps. The hot air in the house would not sink into the tunnel when the door, in the floor of the house, was opened. This effect also trapped smoke in the house. In addition, it was the duty of the women to trim the lamp at night; sleeping next to the lamp increased the exposure to smoke, resulting in severe anthracosis at an early age and lung damage, including bronchiectasis and emphysema.

Similar findings reported in many other mummies make it clear that air pollution, at least on a local level, is not a recent phenomenon.

Osteoporosis poses a major health problem for modern Eskimos. With the antiquity of osteoporosis in this region established by the bodies from Barrow, it now appears that the westernized diet of modern Eskimos is not a direct factor and further investigation is needed. The disorder has been attributed to the Eskimos' meat based diet. In contrast, the Aleuts' wide selection of sea mammals, fish, invertebrates and land and marine plants appears to have resulted in osteological robusticity.

Two of the Eskimo mummies showed granulomatous lesions suggestive of histoplasmosis, but whether it may have been a common disease in ancient Alaska cannot be determined on the basis of such a small sample. Tuberculosis is considered to have been nonexistent in Alaska prior to the introduction of the disease by the Russians in the early eighteenth century. Of the human fungal diseases characterized by granulomatous reaction, only histoplasmosis is thought to occur in Alaska. Less than one percent of modern Eskimos have a positive skin test for the infection (Sexton *et al.* 1949; Comstock 1959). *Histoplasma capsulatum* was not demonstrated in these mummies but the distribution of the granulomas is most consistent with the diagnosis of healed histoplasmosis.

Although the freezerlike conditions of the Arctic would seem to provide for excellent preservation of soft tissues, bodies are in fact preserved only under extraordinary circumstances. The frozen ground makes winter burials impossible and the permafrost layer, only a few centimeters below the surface, discourages deep burials even in summer. Cycles of freezing and thawing tend to bring summer burials to the surface, exposing any bodies to the ravages of animals and weather. Rare finds such as those described above give a glimpse into prehistoric Alaska, showing health hazards shared by past and present inhabitants of a once remote area.

REFERENCES

Allison, M. A., Klurfield, D. and Gerszten, E. 1975. Demonstration of erythrocytes and hemoglobin products in mummified tissue. *Paleopathology Newsletter* **11**: 7–10.

Birkit-Smith, K. 1959. *The eskimos*, 2nd edn. London: Methuen.

Breutsch, W. L. 1959. The earliest record of sudden death possible due to atherosclerotic coronary occlusion. *Circulation* **20**: 438–41.

Candela, P. B. 1939. Blood group determinations upon the bones of thirty Aleutian mummies. *American Journal of Physical Anthropology* **30**: 361–83.

Cockburn, T. A. 1978. Paleopathology and its association. *Journal of the American Medical Association* **40**: 151–3.

Collins, B. 1937. *Archaeology of St. Lawrence Island, Alaska.* Smithsonian Institution Miscellaneous Collections **96** (1): 82.

Comstock, G. W. 1959. Histoplasmin sensitivity in Alaskan natives. *American Review of Tuberculosis and Pulmonary Disease* **79**: 542.

Cotran, R. S., Kumar, V. and Robbins, S. L. 1989. *Robbins pathologic basis of disease,* 4th edn, 769–70, 955–6. Philadelphia: Saunders.

Dall, W. H. 1945. Quoted in A. Hrdlička, *The Aleutian and Commander Islands and their inhabitants,* 184–91. Philadelphia: Wistar Institute.

Geist, W. W. 1928. *Diary.* Fairbanks: University of Alaska Archives.

Gonzalez, T., Vance, M., Helpern, M. and Umberger, C. J. 1954. *Legal medicine: pathology and toxicology.* New York: Appleton.

Hrdlička, A. 1945. *The Aleutian and Commander Islands and their inhabitants.* Philadelphia: Wistar Institute.

Jochelson, W. 1925. *Archaeological investigations in the Aleutian Islands.* Washington, DC: Carnegie Institute.

Kovacs, A. and Sodhi, D. S. 1981. Ice pile-up and ride-up on arctic and subarctic beaches. *Coastal Engineering,* **5**: 247–73.

Laughlin, W. S. The use and abuse of mummies. Manuscript. Storrs: University of Connecticut. n.d.

Rausch, R. L. 1970. Trichinosis in the Arctic. In *Trichinosis in man and animals,* ed. S. E. Gould, 348–73. Springfield, IL: Charles C. Thomas.

Rausch, R. L., Scott, E. M. and Rausch, V. R. 1967. Helminths in the Eskimos in western Alaska, with particular reference to Diphyllobothrium infection and anemia. *Transactions of the Royal Society of Tropical Medicine and Hygiene,* **61**: 351–7.

Ruffer, M. A. 1921. *Studies in the paleopathology of Egypt.* Chicago: University of Chicago Press.

Sanderson, I. T. 1960. *Saturday Evening Post,* June 16, 39.

Sandison, A. T. 1967. Degenerative vascular disease. In *Diseases in antiquity,* ed. D. Brothwell and A. T. Sandison, 474–88. Springfield, IL: Charles C. Thomas.

Sandison, A. T. 1970. The study of mummified and dried human tissues. In *Science in archaeology,* 2nd. edn, ed. D. Brothwell and E. Higgs, 490–502. New York: Praeger.

Sexton, R. L., Ewan, J. R. and Payne, R. C. 1949. Determination of the specificity of histoplasmin and coccidioidin as tested on 365 Aleuts of the Pribilof Islands. *Journal of Allergy* **20**: 133–5.

Smith, G. S. and Zimmerman, M. R. 1975. Tattooing found on a 1600 year old frozen, mummified body from St Lawrence Island, Alaska. *American Antiquity,* 40:434–7.

Veniaminov, I. 1945. Quoted in A. Hrdlička. *The Aleutian and Commander Islands and their inhabitants,* 182–4. Philadelphia: Wistar Institute.

Yeatman, G. 1971. Preservation of chondrocyte ultra-structure in an Aleutian mummy. *Bulletin of the New York Academy of Medicine* **47**: 104–8.

Zimmerman, M. R. 1973. Blood cells preserved in a mummy 2000 years old. *Science* **180**: 303–4.

Zimmerman, M. R. 1977. The mummies of the tomb of Nebwenenef: paleopathology and archaeology. *Journal of the American Research Center in Egypt* **14**: 33–6.

Zimmerman, M. R. 1985. Paleopathology in Alaskan mummies. *American Scientist* **73**: 20–5.

Zimmerman, M. R. and Aufderheide, A. C. 1984. The frozen family of Utqiagvik: the autopsy findings. *Arctic Anthropology* **21**: 53–64.

Zimmerman, M. R. and Smith, G. S. 1975. A probable case of accidental inhumation of 1,600 years ago. *Bulletin of the New York Academy of Medicine* **51**: 828–37.

Zimmerman, M. R. and Tedford, R. H. 1976. Histologic structures preserved for 21,300 years. *Science* **194**: 183–4.

Zimmerman, M. R., Trinkaus, E., LeMay, M., Aufderheide, A. C., Reyman, T. A., Marrocco, G. R., Ortel, R. W., Benitez, J. T., Laughlin, W. S., Horne, P. D., Schultes, R. E. and Coughlin, E. A. 1981. The paleopathology of an Aleutian mummy. *Archives of Pathology and Laboratory Medicine* **105**: 638–41.

Zimmerman, M. R., Yeatman, G., Sprinz, H. and Titterington, W. P. 1971. Examination of an Aleutian mummy. *Bulletin of the New York Academy of Medicine* **47**: 80–103.

9

Mummies of Peru

JAMES M. VREELAND, JR

Mummified impeccably on an icy Andean mountain top, the remains of an adolescent Inca girl captured the attention of people all over the world in 1995, when news of her recovery became known. Yet Peruvian mummies have been the object of anthropological and historical interest for more than four centuries. In 1560, long before Egyptian pharaohs were put on public display in Cairo's Museum of Archaeology, curious Europeans had already been queuing up in Lima's San Andrés Hospital to view several of the marvelously preserved mummies of Peru's legendary Inca kings (Acosta [1590, bk. V, chap. VI] 1954:146; Riva-Agüero 1966:397). Struck by what seemed to them an idolatrous but fascinating custom, the early Spanish chroniclers of Andean culture noted that the practice of mummifying principal lineage heads and local chiefs was widespread in western South America.

Today, studies of pre-Hispanic mortuary practices draw heavily on these richly detailed ethnohistorical accounts, as well as on the wealth of cultural and biologic materials preserved in the arid coastal zone of Peru. Here, despite the absence of written history until the arrival of Pizarro in 1531, the archaeological record of mummification, stated as 6000 years old in the first edition of this volume, has now been extended back another 3000 years.

The origins of this practice remain unclear; naturally mummified bodies [1] occur in Peruvian graves from before Andean societies became sedentary and stratified. They may well have provided models for subsequent experimentation with methods of artificially preserving human flesh. The importance of specialized techniques to retard decay of the remains of local secular and theocratic elite individuals probably increased with the emergence of complex societies and clearly represents an intensification of the ancient Andean practice of ancestor worship (Trimborn 1969). Venerated as living corpses, the mummified bodies of clan ancestors of chiefs often served as community or tribal fetishes, and in the case of the Inca rulers, as historical gods. By the end of the pre-Hispanic epoch, grave goods accompanying the mummy of a high-status figure often included the mummified bodies of his wives, retainers, and slaves (Steward 1948).

Although the term mummy is repeatedly used to describe the often extraordinarily well preserved human remains recovered from Peruvian cemeteries, there is in fact little agreement on what constitutes a Peruvian mummy and how it was actually produced. The term mummification will be used here to refer to all natural and artificial processes that bring about the preservation of the body or its parts. Such methods include drying by air, sun, or fire (with or without evisceration); covering with plastic materials (such as clay); filling body cavities with plant or other materials; and embalming with chemical or other substances (Dérobert and Reichlen, n.d).

In 1980 for the first edition of this volume, I proposed that three principal types of mummification could be identified in pre-Columbian America (Dawson 1928b; Comas 1974). This typology has proven valid, and has been employed by other researchers and applied cross culturally to the twelfth to nineteenth century Japanese Buddhist mummies of northeastern Japan (Zasshi 1993). This simple classification is as follows: Type I, natural mummification, caused by a number of factors (either singly or in combination) such as dryness, heat, cold, or absence of air in the burial unit or grave; Type II, intentional natural mummification, brought about through the intentional exploitation or deliberate enhancement of natural processes, such as those listed above; Type III, artificial mummification, produced by a variety of techniques including evisceration, fire and smoke curing, and the application of such embalming substances as resins, oils, herbs, and other organic materials.

In Peru, the combined archaeological and ethnohistorical evidence indicates that the large majority of mummies known are of Types I and II.[2] The skin, when preserved, has generally been modified to a tough, almost leathery consistency. Although connective tissue frequently remains, most or all of the internal organs have disintegrated to a fine powder, often filling much of the abdominal cavity. Mummified bodies with nearly intact intestinal tracts have been found in several coastal regions where natural preservation was particularly favorable (Stewart 1973; Allison et al. 1974).

Geographically, the central Andean cultural area consists of the coast and highlands of Peru and the adjacent highlands of Bolivia, southern Ecuador, and parts of the north coast and highland regions of Chile (Figure 9.1). The Peruvian littoral, a narrow desert zone crosscut at nearly regular intervals by fertile river valley oases, supported a number of densely populated regions, some of which grew to the status of large chiefdoms and states. Despite the

FIGURE 9.1. Central
Andean cultural area.
(Revised map.)

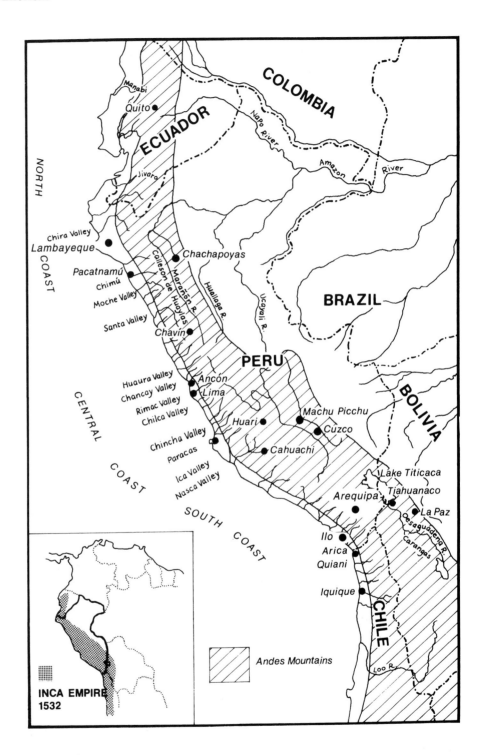

Table 9.1. *Major cultural periods and phases for the central Andes. The dates opposite each period indicate its beginning*

Period	Time	Culture
Colonial	AD 1534	Spanish Conquest
Late Horizon	AD 1476	Inca Empire
Late Intermediate	AD 1000	Ica, Chimú, Chancay
Middle Horizon	AD 600	Huari, Tiahuanaco
Early Intermediate	200 BC	Nasca, Moche, Paracas-Necropolis
Early Horizon	900 BC	Paracas-Cavernas, Chavín
Initial	1800 BC	Africa, Santo Domingo
Preceramic	10000 BC	Tres Ventanas
	20000 BC	Ayacucho

periodic saturation of the surface air layer and occasional winter drizzles (*garúa*), precipitation is negligible and rarely penetrates more than a few centimeters into the ground. Not all areas are equally conducive to the preservation of organic materials; some sites may have been specifically chosen as burial precincts because of their optimal conditions for preservation. The preservative effect of the uppermost soil horizon, when enriched with certain salts, has long been cited as an important additional factor in the mummification process (Rivero and von Tschudi 1854; Mead 1907).[3]

In contrast to the coast, the highland zone is far less homogeneous, characterized by a series of complex gradients of climate and vegetation. In the treeless high altitude valley and plateaus, or altiplano, a marked rainy season delivers as much as 800 mm of precipitation annually. Near or below freezing temperatures are recorded through much of the year, especially on the upper slopes (over 4300 m), where frost is an almost nightly occurrence. Both the rarefied atmosphere and cool temperatures of the altiplano were doubtless key factors in mummification processes.

Any description of Andean mummification practices must move in two dimensions: time and space. Prehistoric Andean cultural chronology is customarily broken down into seven major periods, beginning with a long preceramic sequence dating back over 20 millennia and closing with the Spanish conquest of the Inca empire in 1534 (Table 9.1). The first ceramic period, beginning about 1800 BC, also marks the emergence of the 'Peruvian cultural tradition' (Bennett 1948), characterized by the appearance of widespread maize agriculture, irrigation, terracing, complex religious iconography, and marked ancestor worship (Willey 1971).

Following this so-called Initial Period, a series of three Horizon styles developed, each typified by a complex of more or less homogeneous traits or features, separated by two Intermediate Periods when regional culture eclipsed and superseded the unifying Horizon styles (Rowe 1967). Most authorities generally agree that the three pan-Peruvian cultures evolved from three highland sites, Chavin de Huantar, Huari or Tiahuanaco, and finally Cuzco. From these centers, certain diagnostic styles are seen to have spread outward through most of the central Andean area. Increasingly persuasive arguments supporting a tropical forest inception for the first of these highland cultural matrixes have induced some investigators to look east of the Andes for archaeological evidence of the origins of Peruvian civilization in this moist lowland region (Lathrap 1974).

PRECERAMIC AND INITIAL PERIODS (20 000–900 BC)

Although numerous burials containing skeletons wrapped in skins, hides, and vegetable fiber fabrics have been described for the coastal regions, and to a much lesser extent for dry highland cave sites, little evidence of mortuary practices involving mummification occurs before the fifth millennium BC. Engel (1970, 1977) recovered four naturally mummified bodies, two adults and two juveniles, from Tres Ventanas Cave in the upper Chilca Valley (4000 m), dating from about 4000 to 2000 BC. In contrast to the tightly flexed adult bodies placed on their sides, the position of the subadults was semiflexed, lying on their backs. The bodies had been wrapped in camelid mantles or cloaks bearing traces of a red pigment and were found with fragments of netting and twined and looped fabrics. The skin and hair appear sufficiently well preserved by the high altitude tomb matrix and we might justly term these individuals among the oldest mummies so far reported from Peru.

Recent research by Arriaza (1995) and his colleagues in northern Chile indicates that the earliest remains of a naturally mummified individual can be radiocarbon dated by association to some 9000 years ago. Much better documented and quite complex mummified remains are associated with the Chinchorro culture, which extended from Ilo in southern Peru to Antofagasta in northern Chile (see Arriaza, chapter 10), from about 5000 to 1500 BC. Of the 282 mummies so far recovered in this preceramic culture, over half, 149, were artificial Types II and III (Figure 9.2), the others 'the work of nature' (Arriaza 1995) or Type I (Uhle 1918; Skottsberg 1924; Nuñez 1969; Munizaga

FIGURE 9.2. Chinchorro child with artificial mummification (Red style). Body housed at the Museo de Historia Natural de Valparaiso, Chile. (Photograph courtesy of Bernardo Arriaza.)

1974). Curiously, the earliest remains are those of children. Special attention had been given to the preparation of mummies of infants, described by Bird at the site of Quiani: 'In all cases the viscera and brains appear to have been removed; the legs, arms and body reinforced by sticks inserted under the skin or in the flesh; the faces coated with thin clay and painted; a wig of human hair fastened over the head; and [frequently a] sewn leather casing wrapping the body' (Bird 1943).

The presence of several coats of paint on a similar mummy from Punto Pichalo suggests that the body had not been buried immediately following death, but may have been stored or displayed for a considerable time before final interment.[4] In 1917 Skottsberg, working at the preceramic cemetery of Los Gentiles in Arica, found a bundle containing the remains of two infants similarly mummified (Skottsberg 1924).

A second variety of mummification existed during this same period and appears to represent a form of secondary burial. The extended cadaver was flayed, and the skin was replaced with a thin coating of clay or 'cement' and then wrapped in a reed matting. Bodman (in Skottsberg 1924) analyzed such a brownish cement and found it to contain sand and a certain agglutinate, mixed with an unidentified material. Although Skottsberg reported that the mummy had been eviscerated, no clear evidence of evisceration or embalming was found by Alvarez Miranda (1969) in similar interments at Arica.

EARLY HORIZON TO EARLY INTERMEDIATE PERIODS (900 BC–AD 600)

The abundant archaeological information from the Paracas-Ica area of the south coast of Peru indicates that by the end of the Early Horizon period a major transformation in burial practices had taken place in that region. At least as early as 400 BC, sedentary farming communities had developed a keen interest in enhancing the preservation of the dead, which were wrapped in an upright position inside mummy bundles up to 1.5 m in height. The most spectacular finds of this period include 429 mummy fardels recovered from the Necropolis at Paracas, of which approximately one half have been opened (Tello 1929). Nearly all the bodies examined were elderly males showing a distinctive type of cranial deformation (Tello 1959, 1980; Vreeland 1978a).[5]

Seated in a coiled basket or gourd, the flexed cadaver was generally covered with a simple cotton shroud and wrapped with plain weave cloth, often alternated with polychrome patterned fabrics widely acclaimed for their intricately embroidered designs. Naturally mummified remains of parrots, cavies, foxes, dogs, cats, and deer have also been found in Paracas period mummy bundles. In the larger bundles, four discrete layers of ceremonial garments and wrapping cloths normally occur (Yacovleff and Muelle 1934; Bennett 1938; Tello 1959).

Convincing evidence of artificial mummification (Type III), the subject of a heated debate for decades, is generally indirect and exceedingly difficult to recognize in archaeological contexts. Strong (1957) has argued that the presence of large areas of calcined earth and ashes at the temple complex of Cahuachi suggests that the site had been used as a massive mummy processing area about 2000 years ago. No mummies were recovered from Cahuachi, but bundles belonging to the same cultural period were found at the Necropolis by Mejía Xesspe in 1927–1928. Following his examination of the largest and best preserved units, Tello concluded:

> After extracting the viscera and a great part of the muscles, the body has been subjected to a special mummifying treatment. At times the head has been removed from the body, the brain tissue being extracted through the foramen magnum. The thorax is opened nearly always across the sternum and the lungs and heart pulled out . . . In certain cases they have made incisions in the extremities to pull out the muscles. . . The body is [then] subjected to a process of mummification through the use of fire and perhaps various chemical substances, as indicated by the carbonized appearance of certain parts of the body, and by the salty efflorescences of the chemical substances employed.
>
> (Tello 1929)

Unfortunately, no large intact bundles are now available against which to check Tello's findings. Unable to determine ABO blood groups from muscle tissues extracted from Paracas mummies opened by Tello, Candela (1943) attributed the negative results to the presence of some gummy, resinous substances which he suggested had served as preservatives. In an independent study, Yacovleff and Muelle argued that mummification of the Paracas cadavers had been caused by natural desiccation (Type II) without any artificial treatment:

> To explain the preservation of these mummies, it is not necessary to revert to an hypothesis involving the use of fire and certain chemical substances, because the physical conditions of the place suffice to impede the decomposition of organic material . . . The nearly complete absence of vegetation for twenty kilometers round about is due to the perpetual aridity; the rich salinity of the dry soil and the constant on shore wind; the relative height of the cemeteries above possible ground water; the constant action of the sun – all this makes special treatment for the preservation of the bodies unnecessary.
>
> (Yacovleff and Muelle 1932)

This view is also shared by Mahler and Bird (n.d.), who examined a single large Necropolis bundle in 1949. They found no evidence of foreign material inside the body cavity; the brain had not been removed, and no appreciable dehydration of the tissues appeared to have occurred before burial.

Recent examinations of smaller Necropolis cadavers have also failed to produce any convincing evidence of artificial preservation (Allison and Pezzia 1973; Rivero de la Calle 1975; Vreeland 1976). The leathery consistency and dark brown color of the skin, which is drawn tight over the upper portions of the skeleton, indicate that the bodies probably had been desiccated intentionally, at least in some cases. Nonetheless, sufficient body fluids or putrefaction products resulting from autolytic decomposition seem to have induced extensive rotting in the lower sections of the bundles. The internal soft tissues had in most cases been reduced nearly to powder, and only bits of fibrous connective tissues remained attached to the walls of the body cavities and extremities. Furthermore, the presence of large numbers of pupa cases of necrophagous insects attests to the lack of any immediate and complete mummification treatment, especially one requiring the use of fire and embalming substances such as those described by Tello. However, tissues taken from one recently opened small bundle, which are presently under microscopic examination, show what appear to be artificially preserved, fire-dried, and in places, burned tissues, found in association with several small pieces of charcoal (Vreeland 1978a). Nevertheless, in the absence of further studies of large units, the theory that the presumably elite individuals wrapped in such bundles had in fact been accorded a complex, Type III mummification must remain moot.

Little is known regarding mummification practices from other regions during the Early Intermediate period, but available archaeological information suggests that a pattern distinct from that described for the south coast occurred in other areas. On the north coast, the Mochica buried their high status dead in cane coffins placed in chamber tombs filled with diverse grave offerings (Larco Hoyle 1946). One exceptional (and very late) tomb excavated at the site of Pacatnamú yielded three mummies, all fully extended and placed on their backs (Ubbelohde-Doering 1966).[6] One of these, an 18–year-old woman, was found with skin 'like fine old parchment and black hair' and tattooing on the right forearm. In contrast to the Type III treatment described during the previous period on the Chilean north coast, no evidence of artificial mummification has been reported from postceramic periods in that area.

MIDDLE HORIZON PERIOD (AD 600–1000)

During this period two highland kingdoms emanating from the sites of Huari and Tiahuanaco spread differentially through much of the central Andes, bringing with them significant changes in mortuary practices that in some areas persisted until 1534. Although no mummies clearly dating from this period have been reported in the damp altiplano region, several excellently preserved bundles have been found on the coast (Reiss and Stübel 1880–87; Allison *et al.* 1974). Unfortunately, no comprehensive study of these remarkable fardels has yet been made, but examinations of several large coastal Huari bundles from the Ica-Nasca area by the author decades ago provide a general conception of the mortuary treatment involved.

Tightly flexed and covered in a cloth shroud or poncho, the cadaver was generally seated on a firmly rolled and coiled cotton disc about 50 cm wide. A more or less cylindrical bundle was then built up around the body by alternating layers of cotton lint with plain weave textiles and with tightly interworked cord superstructures. Other packing materials such as grass, reeds, and leaves were also used. Protruding from the top of the 'body' was a slightly conical false head constructed of alternating fiber and fabric layers, frequently decorated with metal or shell 'eyes', and 'nose', a human hair wig, and a woven cap or sling headband. A tapestry tunic was then placed over the completed, bottle shaped bundle (Vreeland 1977; Figure 9.3). Examination of the undigested plant materials recovered in the abdomen of one mummy showed the presence, for the first time in pre-Hispanic times, of three genera of fungi, identified in order of abundance as *Nigrospora* (?), *Lasiodiplodia* and *Brachysporium*, common plant pathogens that may have posed a threat to agricultural societies (Vreeland and Korf 1978).

Examinations of the human remains from the central and southern Peruvian coast areas (Allison and Pezzia 1973; Vreeland 1976) and northern Chile (Le Paige 1964) showed no evidence of Type III mummification. Desiccation by means of natural agents had probably been utilized in some cases. Preservation was also enhanced by the tightly wrapped and highly absorbent cotton layers, which would have helped draw off bodily decomposition fluids. This process is demonstrated in radiographs taken of the bundles before they were opened; the radiopaque oval areas below the skeleton correspond to the cotton discs, apparently hardened by the absorption of internal moisture (Vreeland 1976; Figure 9.4).

LATE INTERMEDIATE PERIOD (AD 1000–1476)

Despite the decline of the Huari and Tiahuanaco cultural influences in the central Andes, throughout much of Peru numerous characteristics of Middle Horizon mortuary practices continued, with regional variations, until the

FIGURE 9.3. High status Middle Horizon mummy bundle. Anthropomorphic features include false head and hair, face mask, cap, headband, necklace, and poncho shirt. Probably from the Nasca area. Collection Museo Nacional de Antropología y Arqueología, Lima.

Spanish Conquest. The most common form of interment continued to be the bundle burial, except in the eastern sierra, where the body was cut in sections or cremated (Tello 1942). In the western sierra the cadaver was wrapped in several ways: in a cactus fiber net, in twisted grass cords, or in a deer or camelid hide bag. The body was always tightly flexed in adult burials, with knees drawn up against the chest, hands opened flat over the face, and arms and legs bound in place with additional cords (Figure 9.5). The wrapping cords often covered the entire mummy, with the exception of a rectangular opening over the face and a smaller aperture for the toes (Figure 9.6).

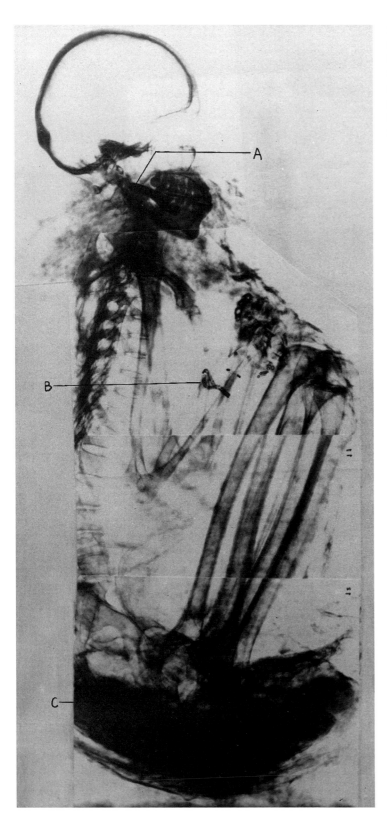

FIGURE 9.4. Composite print of radiograph taken of a Middle Horizon bundle similar to the one in Figure 9.3, showing slightly flexed mummy with metal offering in mouth (A), stone or metal bracelets on wrist (B), and seated on a cotton disc (C) heavily impregnated with radiopaque body decomposition fluids.

FIGURE 9.5. Elderly adult mummy, not eviscerated. Note cotton fiber in orbits and remains of string laced between fingers. No provenance; probably coastal Late Intermediate to Late Horizon period. Collection Museo Nacional de Antropología y Arqueología, Lima.

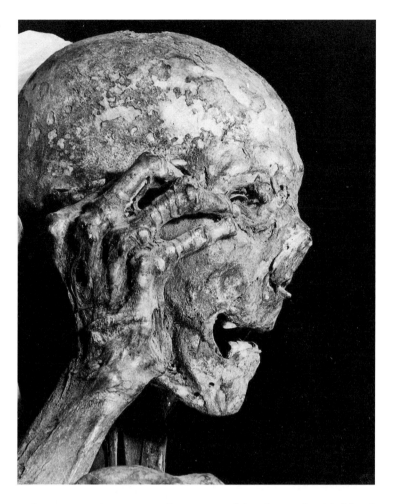

Although complete mummies are rarely preserved in the moist highland zones, hair, usually faded from its natural black to a reddish color, is often encountered. The hair of male mummies appears to have been kept relatively short, and louse eggs are quite common (Villar Córdoba 1935).

The mummy burial also predominated in the coastal areas, where the bundles were normally topped with false heads and masks in Middle Horizon style (Figure 9.7). Some of the larger units weigh over 100 kg (Waisbard and Waisbard 1965). In the northern sierra, the mummy bundle was covered with a layer of mud to form a conical structure and was crowned with a modeled and painted clay mask simulating the human head. Some of the larger mummy casings are from 1 to 1.5 m high, weighing over 125 kg (Savoy 1970).

Mummies on the north Peruvian coast were generally extended and fully clothed (as in the Early Intermediate period Mochica burials), in contrast to

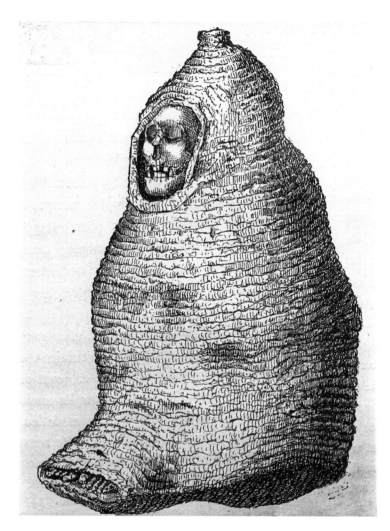

FIGURE 9.6. Sketch of highland mummy wrapped in cords with apertures for hands and feet. Cuzco area, probably Late Intermediate or Late Horizon period. (After Weiner 1880.)

the flexed and shroud covered mummies (Figures 9.8 and 9.9) from other coastal regions (Donnan and Mackey 1978; Rowe 1995).[7] Preparation of these large, plain-weave cotton shrouds required considerable amounts of energy and raw material. One large central coast bundle contained an estimated 265 km of single-ply yarn, requiring some 4000 hours of spinning and plying time, used to weave the 60 square meters of cotton wrapping shrouds alone. Another very large and well preserved unit from the Lima area, containing the remains of an 18 to 20 year old woman, had been wrapped with over 150 kg of cotton cloth; one of these textiles, having a complete warp length of 40.40 m, is the longest single web fabric known from prehistoric America (Vreeland 1978b).

FIGURE 9.7. Large mummy bundle from Lima areas. Late Intermediate period. False head and face mask follow typical Middle Horizon pattern. Collection Museo Nacional de Antropología y Arqueología, Lima.

LATE HORIZON PERIOD (AD 1476–1534)

The final period of the Andean prehistoric sequence begins with the effective consolidation of the Inca empire and concludes with the destruction of its highland capital, Cuzco, by the Spanish in 1534 (Rowe 1946). Although the burial ritual accompanying the Inca elite appears to depart from preexisting patterns, mortuary practices evidenced throughout most of Peru show general regional variations characteristic of the preceding periods (Vreeland 1980). Supplementing the very limited available archaeological data from the highlands is a rich corpus of ethnohistorical information written during the

FIGURE 9.8. Classic Lambayeque period (c. AD 800–1200) mummy from Collus, Lambayeque Valley, north coast of Peru. Dressed with fabrics decorated in Middle Horizon style, the mummy was interred in extended position typical of mortuary pracitices on the coast prior to Middle Horizon influence there. Brüning Museum, Lambayeque.

early part of the Colonial period. These sources indicate that the practice of mummification was largely conditioned by two factors: local traditions and social rank or status of the deceased. One of the fullest accounts of this regional variation is provided by the Indian chronicler Guamán Poma, who not only described but also illustrated at the beginning of the seventeenth century the prevailing customs of the four Inca *suyos* (quarters) constituting the Inca empire (Guamán Poma de Ayala [1613] 1956).[8]

In Condesuyo (i.e., the central highlands) the body of the deceased was

FIGURE 9.9. Pottery vessel depicting funeral procession and extended mummy inside coffin. North Peruvian coast. Late Intermediate period. Collection Museo Nacional de Antropología y Arqueología, Lima.

placed either in a burial tower or in a sepulcher located on a high mountain ridge or peak. Guamán Poma noted that the cadaver was eviscerated and that certain balsamic substances were used to preserve it. In the Yungas (lowlands or coastal) regions, on the other hand, the body was covered with a simple cotton funeral shroud, then wrapped in cloth or cord ropes, forming a netlike superstructure. The upper portion of the mummy bundle was painted or decorated to suggest the human head and face. Apparently, the viscera and sometimes even the flesh were removed from the bones and placed in freshly made ceramic vessels buried next to the mummy bundle.

An early account of Type III mummification is also given in a document written about 1580, describing the mortuary ritual of the Pacajes, an ethnic group inhabiting the Bolivian altiplano region to the southwest of Lake Titicaca:

(Jiménez de la Espada 1965)

The manner in which these Pacajes bury their dead is to remove the viscera, and to throw them in a pot which they bury next to the cadaver, bound with ropes of straw . . . The deceased was buried with the best clothing and plenty of food.

This practice is in part corroborated by Ponce Sanginés and Linares Iturralde (1966), who examined 10 mummies from the Bolivian province of Carangas. Three had been eviscerated through an incision made in the abdominal wall.

170

The cadavers were subsequently mummified by the naturally dry, cool atmos-phere of the Bolivian altiplano, where it appears that this type of mummifica-tion may have been extensively practiced in the Late Horizon period and possibly earlier.

Social status also conditioned mortuary practices to a significant degree. According to the Jesuit chronicler Blas Valera, the common Indian was gener-ally buried with the few possessions he owned in a simple grave in outlying community fields. In contrast, a member of the *kurakas*, or regional nobility, was often interred in a multiroom sepulcher with certain of his wives, ser-vants, and others selected to serve him in the afterlife. These victims were sacrificed (some not unwillingly) and embalmed in the same fashion as the *kuraka* (Valera [1609] 1945). Guamán Poma ([1613] 1956) added that whereas gold or silver offerings were placed in the mouths of the *kurakas*, clay offerings were customarily used in the interments of common Indians.[9] In Chachapoyas, burial in conical clay casings apparently was reserved for the principal members of local descent groups; individuals of lower status were simply buried in the ground.[10]

Evidence reflecting the stratification of social rank in Chachapoyas burial customs was recently confirmed in a spectacular find as yet to be fully docu-mented in Laguna de los Condores, about 2754 meters above sea level near Leimebamba, Department of Amazonas, in northern Peru. Here, some 80 mummies were packed into two storied quadrangular stone mausoleums (Figure 9.10). Measuring some 0.9 to 1.00 meters tall and about 0.4 meters in diameter, the bundles enclose masses of well preserved textiles, clothing, musical and craft instruments, wooden instruments, and other objects. On special balconies constructed above the funerary chamber, half a dozen cane coffins and twice as many larger mummies were found, accompanied by finer textiles, feather crowns, cord accounting devices called *quipus*, and other adornments indicating the higher status of the individuals interred. Although the bundles have not yet been opened, archaeologists interviewed indicated that the bodies were interred in the fetal position, and that the human tissues seem extremely well preserved. Some 70 percent of the finds appear to be totally intact.

Funeral ceremonies following the death of an Inca sovereign were proba-bly the most elaborate rituals of their kind performed in prehistoric Peru (Figure 9.11). The combined ethnohistorical descriptions, though not uniform in detail, indicate that the cadaver of the king was placed on a special seat or throne in a flexed position, arms crossed over the chest, and head positioned over the tightly drawn up knees. Bits of silver or gold were placed

FIGURE 9.10. The recent discovery of over 80 intact Chachapoyas mummies in flexed position, wrapped with knotted cords and cotton cloth, will vastly improve our knowledge of this previously poorly documented highland culture from northern Peru. Photograph courtesy of National Institute of Culture, Amazonas, Peru, 1997.

in the mouth, fists, and on the chest. The body was then dressed in the finest vicuña cloth and wrapped in great quantities of cotton, and the face covered.[11]

One month after death, the body of the Inca was placed in the royal funeral sepulcher, or *pucullo*, along with great quantities of fine cloth, woven by special crafts personnel expressly for the royal funeral. Tributed or bestowed from the four suyos of the vast empire, this exquisite cloth was either folded and placed next to the body or under the funeral shrouds, or burned. Food and drink were also included with the dead ruler's armaments, symbols of power and office, and bags containing all his used clothing, nail parings, hair, and even the bones and corn cobs upon which he had once feasted. Llamas were sacrificed, as were some of the Inca's principal wives, concubines, and retainers.[12]

Upon conclusion of the ceremonies in Cuzco, the royal mummies were reclaimed by the lineage groups of the dead king and were cared for by male and female attendants. These specially appointed custodians knew not only when to give food and drink to the king's mummy, but also acted as spokesmen for the dead ruler's personal desire. They carried out routine chores such as whisking the flies from the mummy's brow, changing and washing its clothing, calling in visitors with whom the Inca wished to 'speak', and lifting

FIGURE 9.11. Mummified
bodies of Inca king
Huayna Capac, his queen,
and a retainer carried on a
litter from Quito to Cuzco
for burial. (From Guamán
Poma [1613] 1956.)

the bundle when its occupant needed to 'urinate' (Polo de Ondegardo [1554] 1916a; Pizarro [1571] 1939; Imbelloni 1946). Ordinarily, none but these professional cult personnel was permitted to look on the royal mummies, except when these relics were removed from their sepulchers and exhibited in Cuzco during certain religious and state ceremonies, such as the two solstice festivals and the coronation of Inca rulers (Molina [1575] 1916; Estete [1535] 1938).

The earliest known account of an Inca royal mummy is that recorded by Pizarro's secretary, Pedro Sancho de la Hoz, who less than 10 years after the Conquest described the mummy of Huayna Capac who died in 1525 as being nearly intact, wrapped in sumptuous cloth, and missing only the tip of the nose (Sancho de la Hoz [1543] 1938). Garcilaso de la Vega, who saw several royal mummies collected by the Spanish licentiate Polo de Ondegardo in Cuzco in 1559, provides a more detailed description:

> The bodies were so intact that they lacked neither hair, eyebrows nor eyelashes. They were in clothes just as they had worn when alive, with llautus (bands) wrapping their heads, but no other sign of royalty. They were seated in the way Indian men and women usually sit, and their eyes were cast down . . . I remember touching the finger of Huayna Capac. It was hard and rigid, like that of a wooden statue. The bodies weighed so little that any Indian could carry them from house to house in his arms or on his shoulders. They carried them wrapped in white shrouds through the streets and plazas, the Indians dropping to their knees, making reverences with groans and tears, and many Spaniards removing their caps.

(Garcilaso de la Vega [1609] 1987)

The bodies of at least three Inca kings and the ashes of another, as well as the bodies of two *coyas* (queens),[13] were sent to Lima in 1560 by Polo de Ondegardo. Some 20 years later, the Spanish priest Acosta noted that they were still wonderfully preserved, causing great admiration among the people of that city (Acosta [1590] 1954).

Despite these provocative accounts, little information on the actual mummification process employed by the Incas can be gleaned from the available ethnohistorical reports. Both early chroniclers of Indian descent, Garcilaso de la Vega and Guamán Poma stated that the bodies of Inca rulers and their principal wives were embalmed and, except for the special properties of the natural highland environment, no preservation processes are mentioned. Blas Valera, on the other hand, specifically described a Type III treatment, including both evisceration and embalming. This was effected with a variety of balsam brought from the province of Tolú.[14] When applied with some unspecified substance, Valera remarked, 'the body thus embalmed lasted four to five hundred years' (Valera [1609] 1945). He further noted that when Tolú balsam was unavailable, the embalmers resorted to a kind of bitumen prepared with an unidentified material that preserved the flesh, apparently with some success. Acosta also reported that the bodies of the royal mummies had been dressed with a certain bitumen (Imbelloni 1946). Father Cobo imaginatively described a mummy that was so well cured and prepared that it seemed to be alive, its face was so well formed and complexion full of color, and then went on to tell us how this was done: 'The preservation of the face ... was effected by means of a piece of calabash placed under each cheek, over which the skin had become very taught and lustrous, with false open eyes' (Cobo [1653] 1964).

Unfortunately, the accounts of these three Jesuit fathers, Cobo, Acosta, and Valera, are all somewhat late to be completely reliable and may not in fact represent entirely independent sources. It is unlikely that Cobo ever saw a royal mummy. Garcilaso de la Vega's narrative was written in Spain some 40 years after he witnessed the mummies in Cuzco as a young man. Valera, like Acosta, may well have seen the Inca mummies brought back to Lima, where he began his novitiate in 1568. But his papers, lost in 1596, are known to us only through the writings of Garcilaso de la Vega, which are remarkable for their impressionistic detail rather than their veracity. Furthermore, the descriptions of Acosta and Valera presumably refer to mummification procedures applied only to Inca nobility and are hardly confirmed by examinations of highland mummies of presumably non-noble status recovered from the Cuzco area.

The use of certain herbs and plant materials in the embalming process mentioned by the Augustinian friar Ramos Gavilán ([1621] 1976) in references to highland Colla burial practices, has also been suggested by Cornejo Bouroncle (1939), who claims to have identified the remains of the fragrant plant muña[15] stuffed inside a number of lower status Inca period cadavers in the Cuzco museum. Lastres (1953), after examining mummies in both the Cuzco and Lima archaeology museums, found no evidence of evisceration and was of the opinion that mummification had been caused predominantly by natural agencies, with the occasional use of herbs and balsam applied to the skin. On the other hand, McCreery (1935) examined about 20 mummies in Cuzco and stated that they were all rather well preserved, of all ages and sexes, and that no evidence of artificial mummification could be found. From these conflicting reports it is clear that additional research is urgently needed to document adequately the nature and range of mummification practices in Late Horizon burials.

HUMAN SACRIFICE, TROPHY HEADS, AND HUMAN TAXIDERMY

Because ritual sacrifice and mummification appear to be closely related, especially in the later pre-Hispanic periods, a brief review of human sacrifice and the practice of preserving the body or its parts seems appropriate. Types I and II mummification have been cited in reference to burials (usually of juveniles) in the 6000 meters and higher zones of the central Andes in what

Table 9.2. *Recorded finds of high altitude Inca sacrificed mummies*

Mountain	Province, Country	Height (m)	Bodies	Sex	Age	Date found
Aconcagua	Mendoza, Argentina	5300	1	m	7	1985
Ampato	Arequipa, Peru	5300	3	ffm	9–14	1995
Cajon	Salta, Argentina	5468?	1	f	25	1924
Coropuna	Arequipa, Peru	5150	1	m?	adult	1965
Chañi	Salta, Argentina	6060	1	m?	6	1905
Chachani	Arequipa, Peru	6057	1	f	15	1896
Esmeralda	Iquique, Peru	905	2	f	9, 18	1976?
Pichu Pichu	Arequipa, Peru	5630	3	ffm?	15	1963, 1996
Plomo	Santiago, Chile	5400	1	m	8	1954
Qehuar	Salta, Argentina	6100	1	m?	14	1974
Toro	San Juan, Argentina	6200	1	m	20	1978
Sara Sara	Ayacucho, Peru	5500	1	m	15	1996

Sources: From Conklin 1995, with contributions by Jose Antonio Chavez, Catholic University of Arequipa; also Linares 1978; Mostny 1956; Reinhard 1996, 1997; Schobinger, 1995.

clearly appear to be cases of human sacrifice. The most celebrated of such interments are those of the frozen Inca girl, 'Juanita', found on Mount Ampato near Arequipa in 1995, and the earlier discovery on Cerro El Plomo near Santiago, Chile, in 1954, when the frozen body of an 8 to 10 year old boy, dressed in a camelid poncho, was recovered with several metal ornaments and figurines from an Inca period sepulcher (Medina Rojas 1958).[16] Mummies of several other subadults have been reported in similarly inaccessible high altitude funeral cairns (Schobinger 1966), where the youths had probably been intoxicated with alcoholic corn beer, chica, or with the narcotic coca leaf (*Erythroxylon coca*) and either sacrificed by strangulation or simply left there to die (Ramos Gavilán [1621] 1976).[17]

Various chroniclers affirm the fact that adolescents of each of the provincial nobility were sacrificed on the death of an Inca ruler following an elaborate ceremony. The youth chosen for sacrifice was brought to Cuzco, there dedicated to the dead Inca's mummy, honored with presents and then returned in an elaborate procession to the home province where the individual was sacrificed and buried in a simple stone cairn on an isolated mountain peak. This ritual offering has been described in numerous archaeological and ethnohistoric accounts, the most important of which are summarized in Table 9.2. Certainly the most spectacular are those of Cerro el Plomo in Chile and recent frozen mummies recovered by Johan Reinhard and Jose Antonio Chavez on Ampato Mountain in Arequipa, Peru. The actual means of death remains conjectural. Schaedel (personal communication 1997) suggests that the elaborate ceremonial offerings of both these finds indicates that their probable source of manufacture was Cuzco itself.

On the Peruvian coast, mummy bundles containing the remains of dismembered bodies also suggest human sacrifice, possibly to obtain entrails for purposes of divination (Allison *et al.* 1974; Walter 1976). A different motive is indicated by the partial immolation found in a recently opened unit from the Lima area, dated to the Late Intermediate period. The bundle contained a pair of well calloused, naturally mummified feet and lower legs, torn off at the knees (Vreeland 1978b). In a bundle from the same area Jiménez Borga found a mummified left foot (Waisbard and Waisbard 1965). Both bundles were relatively large and constructed in a manner identical to those containing entire mummified bodies.

Type III mummification of sacrificed individuals is amply documented for the late pre-Hispanic periods by several early ethnohistorical references. On the eve of the Spanish entry into northern Peru in 1531, Estete reported that in the coastal Ecuadorian village of Pasao (Manabí province), the Indians flayed the bodies of the dead and burned off the remaining muscle tissue. The skin was then 'dressed like a sheep's hide' and stuffed with straw. Thus 'crucified', the body with arms crossed was hung from the temple room (Estete [1535] 1938). The Chanca Indians of the central Peruvian highlands, as well as the Incas, practiced a similar kind of human taxidermy, displaying the stuffed skins of their war captives in temples, making their stomachs into drums (Métraux 1949). According to Estete ([1535] 1938), the heads of the dead in Pasao were also mummified with certain balsamic substances and shrunken in a process similar to that described for the Jíbaro of the eastern Ecuadorian mountain slopes (Tello 1918; Figures 9.12 through 9.15).

SUMMARY AND CONCLUSIONS

Why Peruvian dead were artificially mummified is a question that cannot be comprehensively answered until more archaeological and ethnohistorical information is made available. Based on the present evidence, one can tentatively state that religious, cult, and magical motives, some clearly derived from political and economic contexts, were all contributing factors in Andean mummification practices. As noted earlier, artificial enhancement of soft tissue preservation, which occurs naturally under proper conditions, and the desire to maintain the body in a more or less lifelike state, presumably represent an intensification of the mortuary cult and an extension of the widespread

FIGURE 9.12. Mummified hand showing tattoing. Probably central coast, Late Intermediate period. Collection Museo Peruano de Ciencias de Salud, Lima.

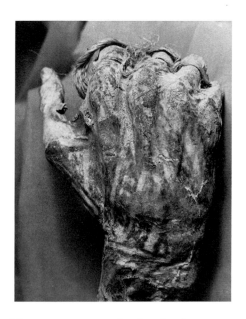

Andean custom of ancestor worship. The aperture over the face in the wrappings of many highland mummies, tubes leading from the tomb to the ground surface, washing and changing the ritual mummy clothing, and the false heads and face masks of the coastal bundles from the Middle Horizon period on, signify further elaboration of the concept of the living dead, enabling, in effect, the deceased to participate in its own mortuary cult.[18] The mummified corpse thus represented a physical entity with human characteristics, and also served as an intermediary for symbolic communication between the worlds of the living and the dead. In some areas such active and periodic participation in ritual activity also presented a threat to the conservation of the mummy bundle and its contents. Mummification therefore may also have provided a solution to the problem of body disarticulation during transport and display. [19]

Insect remains associated with human remains of the Paracas (AD 86), Epigonal Middle Horizon (AD 1231) and Huancho (AD 1240) cultures yield further insights into pre-Hispanic mummification practices (Riddle and Vreeland 1982). Adult beetles (Anobiidae, or 'drug store beetle', also identified in association with the Egyptian mummy PUM IV, c. first century AD; Riddle 1980) of three distinct genera were found with foods wrapped in the bundle, and flies (Diptera) were also found and assigned to two different families (Muscidae and Calliphoridae). The presence of dipterous larvae, puparia and adults in these bundles suggests that the developmental cycle of these flies was completed in the host during or after the preparation of the mummy bale. The infestation must have occurred before the bundle was interred in its

Figure 9.13. Adult male mummy with cranial deformation. Note tattooing on wrist, cords used to bind the cadaver in flexed position and textile impression from mortuary shroud on right knee. Probably from coast, Late Intermediate to late Horizon period. Collection Museo Nacional de Antropología y Arqueología, Lima.

anaerobic burial matrix (sandy soil and refuse). Numerous fly puparia of *Cochliomyia macellaria* found directly associated with dried body fluids indicate that the infestation of maggots or other muscids may have accompanied the burial ceremony of the body, most of whose soft tissues had decayed.

During the Late Horizon, mummies of the Inca kings served an important state function. Preserved by royal privilege in sanctuaries on family estates,

FIGURE 9.14. Posterior view of adult male mummy showing no signs of evisceration. Probably coastal Late Intermediate period. Collection Museo Nacional de Antropología y Arqueología, Lima.

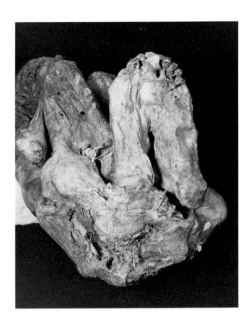

the mummies not only provided unequivocal testimony to the previous existence of those rulers, but also ensured their continued worship as semideified clan ancestors, whose cult was maintained by their descendants and specially appointed retainers. In a similar manner, possession of the mummified body of an important clan ancestor or of a political or religious figure constituted a powerful religious talisman that could often be exploited by the lineage or community owning it.

Even though the origins of Andean artificial mummification still remain unclear, it is nonetheless likely that natural mummification (Figure 9.16) may have directly inspired the prehistoric Peruvians to experiment with intentional mummification for a variety of cultural reasons, with motives growing more varied as complex societies emerged. The possibility that some forms of artificial preparation may have been introduced from the tropical lowlands to the east of the Andes should not be eliminated. A variant of Type II treatment, appearing relatively early in the pre-Hispanic sequence on the north coast of Chile, is frequently mentioned in later periods, especially on the periphery of the central Andean area (northern Chile, the Bolivian highlands, parts of Ecuador and southern Colombia, and the Peruvian montaña), where contacts with tropical forest cultures apparently were more continuous and extensive. Whatever their origins, if complex embalming techniques had been utilized by the Cuzco elite for religious and political reasons, these practices soon fell into disuse and were forgotten as a result of the Spanish cam-

FIGURE 9.15. Mummified trophy head showing perforation in forehead and cactus spine through the lips. Nasca area. Early Intermediate period. Collection Museo Peruano de Ciencias de Salud, Lima.

paign to baptize Inca nobility quickly and forcibly.

In summary, the range of possible agencies or processes noted for each of the three types of mummification considered here are:

TYPE I *Natural mummification*

1   Perpetually dry or frozen tomb matrix.
2   Hot (coastal) or cold (highland) temperatures throughout much of the year.

FIGURE 9.16. Four century old copper miner mummified naturally by copper salts. Chuquicamata, Chile. (Negative # 311244, Courtesy Department of Library Services, American Museum of Natural History.)

3   Anaerobic tomb environment (e.g., direct burial in sand).

4   Local soil characteristics (salinity, alkalinity, etc.).

5   Highly absorbent substance (e.g., sand) in direct contact with the cadaver.

TYPE II *Intentional natural mummification*

1   Body intentionally dried by rarefied and/or cold sierra atmosphere.

2   Body intentionally desiccated by warm coastal climate.

3   Body intentionally wrapped with materials of highly absorbent nature (e.g., cloth, cotton fiber, leaves, grass).

4   Intentional location of cemeteries in areas having favorable natural conditions for preservation of organic materials.

TYPE III *Artificial mummification*

1   Evisceration of internal organs and/or other soft tissues.

2   Replacement of soft tissues with plastic materials (e.g., clay).

3   Removal of all or parts of skeletal material and replacement with sticks, grasses, or other reinforcing materials.

4   Fire desiccation.

5   Smoke curing.

6   Use of bitumen, balsam, or other resinous substances.

7   Filling of body cavity with herbs or other materials having antiseptic chemical properties.

NOTES

1   Naturally mummified individuals in non-burial contexts have also been reported from several areas in the central Andes. Sénechal de la Grange found the naturally mummified body of a woman in a pre-Columbian copper mine in Chuquicamata, Chile, where the body was accidentally preserved in part by the action of the copper salts (Boman 1908: 757). Imbelloni (1956: 282) mentioned that a number of mummies of individuals who died in cave accidents are presently found in various Argentine museums. In 1903 a child was found buried in, and subsequently mummified by, a natural salt formation in the Argentine altiplano (Casanova 1936: 264).

2   Outside the central Andean area, evidence of artificial mummification is extensive (see in particular Steward 1949: 721 and Linné, 1929). Among the northern Andean and circum-Caribbean peoples, the body of the chief was desiccated, placed in a hammock and later cremated (Caquetío); disemboweled, desiccated, and kept as an idol or buried with several wives (Antillean Arawak); desiccated, temporarily buried, then roasted and reburied (Pititú). In southern Panama it was customary to bury the common people in the ground, but to desiccate and preserve the remains of the chief, which were slung in a hammock and mummified over a slow burning fire (Lothrop 1948: 147). The Ecuadorian Quijo eviscerated, smeared with tar, and smoked the bodies of their dead chiefs, and then filled the abdominal cavity with jewels (Steward and Métraux 1948: 655). Dawson (1928a: 73–74) examined two mummies from Colombia, both of which appeared to him to have been eviscerated – one via a perineal incision, the other through a cut in the abdominal wall – and then smoke-cured.

3   In such arid zones almost anything buried in the sand will dry out to a naturally mummified state. For example, during the restoration of a series of Republican period forts constructed around Lima during the war with Chile, a number of Chilean soldiers were recovered from mass graves scooped in the sand. With buttons still shiny, documents intact, and soft external tissues remarkably preserved after nearly 100 years, the cadavers were sent back to Santiago, where they purportedly were returned to their families. Naturally mummified animal carcasses have even served as landmarks to travelers on old Peruvian roads (Rivero and von Tschudi 1854: 209).

4   Bird (1943: 246). This form of mummification (Type III) appears to extend as far south as Iquique and may have continued briefly into the succeeding cultural phases (Schaedel 1957: 21–25 and Appendix IV; cf. Nuñez 1969: 130 ff.).

5   Tello (1929: 120–125) posited that the slightly earlier Cavernas phase mummies at Paracas contained predominantly the remains of adult females, that all the mummies recovered had deformed crania (40 percent of them trephined), and that they had probably belonged to a single, stratified ethnic group.

6   Hollow cane tubes have been found leading from the tomb to the ground surface to permit, it is speculated,

the passage of food and drink to the 'living corpse' buried in the shaft tomb below (see Larco Hoyle 1946; Trimborn 1969: 119–120). Similar tubes (ushnu) have been reported in ethnohistorical literature bearing on Late Horizon Inca burial practices (Zuidema n.d.).

7 Extended burials are also reported from the far northern Chira Valley, as well as from the Huaura, Chancay, and Rimac Valleys on the central coast, and Chincha on the south coast of Peru (Mead 1907: 8; Williams 1927: 1; Tello 1942: 121; Reichlen 1950; Cieza de Leon [1553, bk. I, chap. LXIII] 1959: 312; and Buse 1962: 261).

8 Original dates for the ethnohistorical sources are given in brackets.

9 Gold palatal offerings in Peruvian mummies are found at least as early as the Salinar phase of the Early Intermediate period on the north Peruvian coast (see Larco Hoyle 1946).

10 This status distinction is perhaps no more graphically illustrated than in the case of the burial of a Chachapoyas chief named Chuquimis, who was convicted of regicide after allegedly having poisoned the Inca king Huayna Capac in 1525. Chuquimis died before the death sentence could be carried out, but desiring to desecrate the noble Chachapoyas lineage completely (and thereby set an example for other would-be assassins), the Incas ordered that the mummified cadaver of Chuquimis be exhumed from its clay casing and buried in the ground 'like any other common Indian' (Espinoza Soriano 1967: 246).

11 Acosta ([1590, bk. V, chap. VII] 1954: 147); Garcilaso de la Vega [1609, pt. I, bk. V, chap. XXIX] 1963: 190); Cobo ([1653, bk. XIV, chap. XIX] 1964: 274–275).

12 Garcilaso de la Vega [1609, pt. I, bk. VI, chap. V] 1963: 199). The burial of the Inca king Huayna Capac was supposed to have been accompanied by the sacrifice of no less than 1000 individuals throughout the 80 Inca provinces (Polo de Ondegardo [1567] 1916b: 9). Polo de Ondegardo also informs us that part of Atahualpa's ransom delivered to his Spanish captors at Cajamarca was obtained through the looting of jewels and precious metals from Huayna Capac's mummy in Cuzco (Polo de Ondegardo [1561] 1940: 154).

13 There is considerable confusion among the ethnohistorical sources regarding how many and precisely which of the royal mummies were actually discovered by Polo de Ondegardo. Imbelloni (1946), after examining the various testimonies, tends to favor the version given by Garcilaso de la Vega, holding that the mummified remains of three kings (Huiracocha, Tupac Yupanqui, and Huayna Capac) and two queens (Mama Runtu and Mama Ocllo) were recovered from the villages around Cuzco, where they were still the object of great veneration in 1559. The identification and ultimate fate of the mummies will probably never be known, but informative and fascinating studies have been published by some of Peru's eminent historians, including Juan Toribio Polo (1877) and José de la Riva-Agüero (1966). It is certain, however, that the royal mummies brought to Lima were not provided Christian reburials (Von Hagen 1959: 189, note 2). Rather, after some two decades of exhibition, they were probably unceremoniously buried in a patio or courtyard of the Hospital San Andrés, Lima, sometime after 1580 (see Riva-Agüero 1966: 397).

14 'Tolú' probably refers to Santiago de Tolú, located in the archbishopric of Cartagena, Colombia (Bernal 1970), 'donde se coge muy oloroso balsamo, sangre de drago, y otras resinas, y licores medicinales' (Vázquez de Espinoza [1628] 1948: 249). Peruvian balsam probably originated in Colombia, where it is typed as *Myroxylon balsamum* or *M. toluifera*, and is known to have magnificent antiseptic properties. It grows in the montaña and moist lowland regions of tropical South America and is also found in Peru at Tarapoto, Pozuzo, Huánuco, Loreto, Huallaga, Iquitos, and other regions (MacBride 1943: 241–242). As early as 1887, Peruvian balsam was found interred with a mummy at the Necropolis at Ancón (Safford 1917: 22), a sample of which is now in the National Museum of Natural History, Washington, DC (catalog no. 132613), where spectrographic analysis has recently been conducted on it. However, it should be pointed out that the hardened, blackish resin had been stored inside a crescentia gourd container and was not recovered directly from the mummified bodies.

15 *Mithostachis mollis?* In the sierra of Huancayo, Lima, and Ancash, among other regions not high enough to permit the customary freeze-drying of potatoes, muña leaves are used as a preservative for these tubers. The plants are found between 2400 and 3700 m along

permanent waterways where they grow in an uncultivated state (E. Cerrate, personal communication, Museo de Historia Natural, Lima 1977).

16 The nematode *Trichuris trichiura* was found in the boy's intestine (Stewart 1973: 46).

17 In the case of the Cerro el Plomo mummified boy, Schaedel (personal communication 1997) reported that numerous examinations of the body tissue were carried out, but unfortunately none that would reveal the presence of alcohol or narcotics; nor was there evidence of strangulation. In the opinion of the alpinists who assisted in the recovery of the body, the boy was asleep on the afternoon he was carried across the glacier and placed in his cairn, in which, after a few hours of sub-freezing temperatures, a painless death would have been produced.

18 This concept is partially illustrated by an incident recorded by Bennett (1946: 618) several decades ago. In the center of an underground family mausoleum used since pre-Hispanic times in northern Chile, a table had been set up, and around it the mummies of the family ancestors were arranged. A member of the family who was seriously ill was carried into the chamber, seated at the table, and surrounded by offerings of food and gifts. A ceremonial dance was then given by his relatives in order to help him 'die well'.

19 Perhaps such a situation is suggested in a pre-Hispanic north Peruvian coast myth of an important local *kuraka* who died *en route* to his homeland after an extended stay in Cuzco as an Inca prisoner. His corpse was mummified over a funeral pyre at Pacatnamú and borne home on a litter by his retainers (Kosok 1965: 175–176).

REFERENCES

Acosta, J. de 1954 [1590]. *Historia natural y moral de las Indias.* Madrid: Biblioteca de Autores Españoles.

Allison, M. J. and Pezzia, A. 1973, 1974. Preparation of the dead in pre-Columbian coastal Peru. *Paleopathology Newsletter* **4**: 10–12; **5**: 7–9.

Allison, M. J., Pezzia, A., Gerszten, E. and Mendoza, D. 1974. A case of Carrión's disease associated with human sacrifice from the Huari culture of southern Peru. *America Journal of Physical Anthropology* **41** (2): 295–300.

Alvarez Miranda, L. 1969. Un cementerio preceramico con momias de preparación complicada. *Rehue* **2**: 181–90.

Arriaza, B. 1995. Chile's Chinchorro mummies. *National Geographic* **187**(3): 68–89

Bennett, W. C. 1938. If you died in old Peru. *Natural History* **41** (2): 119–25.

Bennett, W. C. 1946. The Atacameño. In *Handbook of South American indians*, vol.2, ed. J. H. Steward, 599–618. Bureau of American Ethnology, Bulletin 143. Washington, DC: Smithsonian Institution Press.

Bennett, W. C. 1948. The Peruvian co-tradition. In *A re-appraisal of Peruvian archaeology*, ed. W. C. Bennett, 1–7. Menasha,WI: Society for American Archaeology.

Bernal, S. 1970. *Guía bibliográfica de Colombia.* Bogotá: Universidad de los Andes

Bird, J. B. 1943. Excavations in northern Chile. *Anthropological Papers* **38** (4): 173–318.

Boman, E. 1908. *Antiquités de la région andine de la République Argentine et du desert d'Atacama.* Paris: Imprimerie Nationale.

Buse, H. 1962. *Perú 10,000 años.* Lima: Colección 'Nueva Crónica'.

Candela, P. B. 1943. Blood group tests on tissues of Paracas mummies. *American Journal of Physical Anthropology* **1**: 65–8.

Casanova, E. 1936. El altiplano andino. *Historia de la nación Argentina* **1**: 251–75.

Cieza del Leon, P. de. 1959. *The Incas of Pedro de Cieza de Leon* [1553], ed V. Von Hagen, trans. H.de Onis. Norman: University of Oklahoma Press.

Cobo, B. 1964. Historia de la Nuevo Mundo [1653]. In *Obras P. Bernabe Cobo*, vol.2. Biblioteca de Autores Españoles, ed. F. Mateos. Madrid: Ediciones Atlas.

Comas, J. 1974. Origenes de la momificacion pre-hispánica en America. *Anales de Antropologia* **11**: 357–82.

Conklin, William J. 1995. 'Ampato Textile Conservation Notes.' Manuscript. n.d.

Cornejo Bouroncle, J. 1939. Las momias Incas: trepanaciones cráneas en el antiguo Perú. *Boletín del Museo de Historia Natural Javier Prado* **3** (2): 106–15.

Dawson, W. R. 1928a. Two mummies from Colombia. *Man* **53**:73–4.

Dawson, W. R. 1928b. Mummification in Australia and in America. *Journal of the Royal Antropological Institute* **58**: 115–38.

Dérobert, L. and Reichlen, H. n.d. *Les momies*. Paris: Editions Prisma.

Donnan, C. R. and Mackey, C. J. 1978. *Ancient burial patterns of the Moche Valley, Peru*. Austin: University of Texas Press.

Engel, F. 1970. La Grotte du mégatherium à Chilca et les écologies de Haut-Holocene Péruvien. In *Echanges et communications*, ed. J. Pouillon and P. Miranda. The Hague: Mouton.

Engel, F. 1977. Early Holocene funeral bundles from the central Andes. *Paleopathology Newsletter* **19**: 7–8.

Espinoza Soriano, W. 1967. Los señores étnicos de Chachapoyas. *Revista Historica* **3**: 224–332.

Estete, M. de. 1938. Noticia del Perú [c. 1535]. In *Los cronistas de la Conquista*, ed. H. Urteaga, 195–251. Paris: Biblioteca de Cultura Peruana.

Garcilaso de la Vega, I. 1987 [1609]. *Royal commentaries of the Incas*, part 1, transl. H. V. Livermore. Austin: University of Texas Press.

Guamán Poma de Ayala, F. 1956. *Nueva corónica y buen gobierno* [c. 1613], ed. L. F. Bustios Galvez. Lima.

Imbelloni, J. 1946. Las momias de los reyes cuzqueños. *Pachakuti IX, Humanior (sección D)* **2**: 183–96.

Imbelloni, J. 1956. *La segunda esfinge indiana*. Buenos Aires: Libreria Hachette.

Jiménez de la Espada, M. ed. 1965. *Relaciones geográficas de Indias*, vol. I, 183–5. Madrid: Biblioteca de Autores Españoles.

Kosok, P. 1965. *Life, land and water in ancient Peru*. New York: Long Island University Press.

Larco Hoyle, R. 1946. A cultural sequence for the north coast of Peru. In *Handbook of South American indians*, vol. 2, ed. J. H. Steward, 149–75. Bureau of American Ethnology, Bulletin 143. Washington, DC: Smithsonian Institution Press.

Lastres, J. B. 1953. El culto de los muertos entre los aborígenes Peruanos. *Perú Indígena* **4** (10–11): 63–74.

Lathrap, D. W. 1974. The moist tropics, the arid lands and the appearance of great art styles in the New World.

Special Publications **7**: 115–58. Lubbock: Museum of Texas Tech University.

Le Paige, G. 1964. El precerámico en la cordillera atacameña y los cementarios del período agro-alfarero de San Pedro de Atacama. *Anales de la Universidad del Norte*, no. 3.

Linares Malaga, Eloy. 1978. Noticias acerca de un fardo funerario del nevado Coropuna. *Revista del C. I. ADA. M. No. 3*, San Juan, Argentina

Linné, S. 1929. Darién in the past. The archaeology of Eastern Panama and Northwestern Colombia. Handlingar Fjärde Földjen, Series A, Band 1(3). Göteborg: Göteborgs Kungl. Vetenskaps och Vitterherts Samhälles.

Lothrop, S. K. 1948. The archaeology of Panama. In *Handbook of South American Indians*, vol. 4, ed. J. H. Steward, 143–67. Bureau of American Ethnology, Bulletin 143. Washington, DC: Smithsonian Institution Press.

MacBride, J. F. 1943. The flora of Peru. In *Botany*, vol. 12, part 3, no. 1. Chicago: Field Museum of Natural History.

Mahler, J. and Bird, J. B. n.d. Mummy 49: A Paracas Necropolis mummy. Manuscript. American Museum of Natural History, New York.

McCreery, J. H. 1935. The mummy collection of the University of Cuzco. *El Palacio* **39** (22): 118–20.

Mead, C. W. 1907. *Peruvian mummies and what they teach*. Guide leaflet 24. New York: American Museum of Natural History

Medina Rojas, A. 1958. Hallazgos arqueológicos en el Cerro El Plomo. In *Arqueología Chilena*. Santiago: Centro de Estudios Antropológicos, Universidad de Chile.

Métraux, A. 1949. Warfare, cannibalism, and human trophies. In *Handbook of South American indians*, vol. 5, ed. J. H. Steward, 383–409. Bureau of American Ethnology, Bulletin 143. Washington, DC: Smithsonian Institution Press.

Molina, C. de (of Cuzco). 1916. Relación de las fábulas y ritos de los Incas [1575]. In *Colección de libros y documentos referentes a la historia Peruana*, series 1, no. 1, ed. H. Urteaga and C. A. Romero, 1–103. Lima.

Mostny, G. 1957. La momia del Cerro el Plomo. *Boletín del Museo Nacional de Historia Natural*, Tomo XXVII, Santiago

Munizaga, J. R. 1974. Deformación craneal y momificación en Chile. *Anales de Antropología* **11**: 329–36.

Nuñez, A. 1969. Sobre los complejos culturales Chinchorro y Faldes del Morro del Norte de Chile. *Rehue* **2**: 111–42.

Pizarro, P. 1939. Relación del descubrimiento y conquista de los reinos del Perú [1571]. In *Los cronistas de la Conquista*, series 1, no. 2, ed. H. Urteaga, 265–305. Paris: Biblioteca de Cultura Peruana.

Polo, J. T. 1877. Momias de los Incas. *Documentos Literarios del Perú* **10**: 371–8.

Polo de Ondegardo, J. 1916a. Errores y supersticiones de los indios [1554]. *Colección de libros y documentos referentes a la historia del Perú*, series 1, no. 3, ed. H. Urteaga and C. A. Romero. Lima.

Polo de Ondegardo, J. 1916b. Instruccion contra las ceremonias y ritos que usan los indios conforme al tiempo de su gentilidad [1567]. *Colección de libros y documentos referentes a la historia del Perú*, series 1, no. 3, ed. H Urteaga and C. A. Romero. Lima

Polo de Ondegardo, J. 1940. Informe . . . al licenciado Briviesca de Muñatones . . . [1561]. *Revista Historica* **13**: 125–96.

Ponce Sanginés, C. and Linares Iturralde, E. 1966. *Comentario antropológico acerca de la determinación paleoserológica de grupos sanguíneos en momias pre-hispánicos del altiplano boliviano*. Publication no.15. La Paz: Academia Nacional de Ciencias de Bolivia.

Ramos Gavilán, A. 1976. *Historia de nuestra señora de Copacabaña* [1621]. La Paz: Academia Boliviana de la Historia.

Reichlen, H. 1950. Etude de deux fardeux funéraires de la côte centrale de Pérou. *Travaux de l'Institut Français d'Etudes Andines* **1**: 39–50.

Reinhard, J. 1996. Peru's icemaidens: unwrapping the secrets. *National Geographic Magazine* **189**: 62–81.

Reinhard, J. 1997. Mummies of Peru. *National Geographic* **191**: 36–43.

Reiss, J. W. and Stübel, M. A. 1880–87. *The necropolis of Ancón in Peru: a contribution to our knowledge of the cultures and industries of the empire of the Incas, being the results of excavations made on the spot*, transl. A. H. Keene. Berlin: Ascher.

Riddle, J. M. 1980. A survey of ancient specimens by electron microscopy. In *Mummies, disease and ancient cultures*, ed. A.and E. Cockburn, 274–86. New York: Cambridge University Press.

Riddle, J. M. and Vreeland, J. M., Jr 1982. Identification of insects associated with Peruvian mummy bundles by using scanning electron microscopy. *Paleopathology Newsletter* **39**: 5–9.

Riva-Agüero, J. de la. 1966. *Obras completas de José de la Riva-Agüero, vol.5, Sobre las momias de los Incas*. Lima: Pontífica Universidad Católica del Perú.

Rivero, E. M. and von Tschudi, J. J. 1854. *Peruvian antiquities*, transl. F. Hawks. New York: Barnes.

Rivero de la Calle, M. 1975. Estudio antropológico de dos momias de la cultura paracas. In *Ciencias*, series 9, Antropología y prehistoria no. 3. Havana.

Rowe, J. H. 1946. Inca culture at the time of the Spanish Conquest. In *Handbook of the South American indians*, vol. 2, ed. J. H. Steward,183–330. Bureau of American Ethnology, Bulletin 143. Washington, DC: Smithsonian Institution Press.

Rowe, J. H. 1967. Introduction. In *Peruvian archaeology: selected readings*. ed. J. H. Rowe and D. Menzel, 31–7. Palo Alto: Peek.

Rowe, J. H. 1995. Behavior and belief in ancient Peruvian mortuary practices. In *Tombs for the living: Andean mortuary practices. Proceeding of symposium at Dumbarton Oaks*, ed. T. D. Dillehay, 27–42. Washington, DC: Dumbarton Oaks Research Library and Collection.

Safford, W. E. 1917. Food-plants and textiles of ancient America. In *Proceedings of the 19th International Congress of Americanists* (1915), 12–30. Washington, DC: The Congress.

Sancho de la Hoz, P. 1938. Relación para SM de lo sucedido en la conquista y pacificación de estas provincias de la Nueva Castilla y de la calidad de la tierra [1543]. In *Los cronistas de la Conquista*, series 1, no. 2, ed. H. Urteaga, 117–93. Paris: Biblioteca de Cultura Peruana.

Savoy, G. 1970. *Antisuyo*. New York: Simon and Schuster.

Schaedel, R. P. 1957. Informe general sobre la expedición a la zona comprehendida entre Arica y La Serena. In *Arqueología Chilena*, ed. R. P. Schaedel. Santiago: Universidad de Chile.

Schobinger, J. ed. 1966. La 'momia' del Cerro El Toro. *Anales de Arqueología y Etnología* (supplement), 21.

Schobinger, J. 1995. *Aconcagua: un enterratorio Incaico a 5,300 metros de altura.* Mendoza, Argentina: Inca Editorial.

Skottsberg, C. 1924. Notes on the old Indian necropolis of Arica. *Meddelanden fran Geografiska Forenningen i Göteborg* **3**: 27–78.

Steward, J. H. 1948. The circum-Caribbean tribes. In *Handbook of South American Indians*, vol. 4, ed. J. H. Steward, 1–41. Bureau of American Ethnology, Bulletin 143. Washington, DC: Smithsonian Institution Press.

Steward, J. H. 1949. South American cultures, an interpretive summary. In *Handbook of South American Indians*, vol. 5, ed. J. H. Steward, 669–772. Bureau of American Ethnology, Bulletin 143. Washington, DC: Smithsonian Institution Press.

Steward, J. H. and Métraux, A. 1948. Tribes of the Peruvian and Ecuadorian montaña. In *Handbook of the South American Indians*, vol. 3. ed J. H. Steward, 535–656 . Bureau of American Ethnology, Bulletin 143. Washington, DC: Smithsonian Institution Press.

Stewart, T. D. 1973. *The peoples of America.* New York: Scribner.

Strong, W. D. 1957. Paracas, Nazca and Tiahuanaco cultural elements. *Memoirs of the Society for American Archaeology* 13

Tello, J. C. 1918. Es uso de las cabesas humanas artificialmente momificadas y su representación en el antiguo arte peruano. *Revista Universitaria* **1**: 477–533.

Tello, J. C. 1929. *Antiguo Perú.* part 1. Lima: Excelsior.

Tello, J. C. 1942. *Orígen y desarrollo de las civilizaciones prehistoricas andinas.* Lima: Librería Gil.

Tello, J. C. 1959. *Paracas*, part 1, Lima: Empresa Gráfica Scheuch

– 1980. *Paracas*, part 2, *Cavernas y necrópolis.* Lima:Universidad Nacional Major de San Marcos.

Trimborn, H. 1969. South Central America and the Andean civilizations. In *Pre-Columbian American religions*, ed. E. O. James. History of Religion Series. New York: Holt.

Ubbelohde-Doering, H. 1966. *On the royal highways of the Inca.* New York: Praeger.

Uhle, M. 1918. Los aborígenes de Arica. *Revista Historica* **6**: 5–26.

Valera, B. 1945. Las costumbres antiguas del Perú y la historia de los Incas [1590]. In *Los pequeños grandes libros de historia americana*, series 1, vol. 8, ed. F. Loayza. Lima: Miranda.

Vásquez de Espinosa, A. 1948. Compendio y descripción de las Indias Occidentales [1628]. *Smithsonian Miscellaneous Collections* 108. Washington, DC: Smithsonian Institution Press

Villar Córdoba, P. E. 1935. *Arqueología del departamento de Lima.* Lima.

Von Hagen, V. ed. 1959. *The Incas of Pedro de Cieza de Leon.* Norman: University of Oklahoma Press.

Vreeland, J. M., Jr 1976. Second Annual Report: Projecto de investigación textil 'Julio C. Tello'. Research report presented to the Secretariat for Technical Cooperation, OAS. Washington, DC.

Vreeland, J. M., Jr 1977. Ancient Andean textiles: clothes for the dead. *Archaeology* **30** (3): 166–78.

Vreeland, J. M., Jr 1978a. Paracas. *Américas* **30** (19): 36–44.

Vreeland, J. M., Jr 1978b. Prehistoric Andean mortuary practices: a preliminary report from central Peru. *Current Anthropology* **19** (1): 212–4.

Vreeland, J. M., Jr 1980. *Prácticas mortuorias andinas: perspectivos teóricas para interpreta el material textil pre-hispánico*, vol. 3. Lima: Actes del Tecer Congreso del Hombre y de la Cultura Andina.

Vreeland, J. M., Jr and Korf, R. P. 1978. Fungal spores from a Peruvian mummy ca. 800 AD *Paleopathology Newsletter* **21**: 11–12.

Waisbard, S. and Waisbard, R. 1965. *Masks, mummies and magicians.* Edinburgh: Oliver and Boyd.

Walter, N. P. 1976. 'A child sacrifice from pre-Inca Peru.' Paper presented at the annual meeting of the Southwestern Anthropological Association, San Francisco, April 1976.

Weiner, C. 1880. *Pérou et Bolivie: récit de voyage.* Paris: Librairie Hachette.

Willey, G. R. 1971. *An introduction to American archaeology*, vol. 2, South America. Englewood Cliffs, NJ: Prentice-Hall.

Williams, H. U. 1927. Gross and microscopic anatomy of two Peruvian mummies. *Archives of Pathology and Laboratory Medicine* **4**: 1–33.

Yacovleff, E. and Muelle, J. C. 1932. Una exploración de
    Cerro Colorado. *Revista del Museo Nacional* **1**(2):
    31–102.
Yacovleff, E. and Muelle, J. C. 1934. Un fardo funerario de
    Paracas. *Revista del Museo Nacional* **3** (1–2): 63–153.
Zasshi, Kaibogaku. 1993. Buddhist mummies in Japan.
    Journal of Anatomy **68** (4): 381–98.
Zuidema, R. T. n.d. Shaft tombs and the Inca empire.
    Manuscript, University of Illinois, Urbana.

10

South American mummies: culture and disease

BERNARDO T. ARRIAZA, FELIPE CÁRDENAS-ARROYO,
EKKEHARD KLEISS AND JOHN W. VERANO

BLACK AND RED CHINCHORRO MUMMIES OF PERU AND CHILE

Bernardo T. Arriaza

Many scholars have emphasized that the preceramic Chinchorro fishers of southern Peru and northern Chile had the oldest system of artificial mummification in the world (Bittmann and Munizaga 1976; Allison *et al.* 1984; Arriaza 1995a). Although this is interesting, the anthropological significance of the Chinchorro society and its mummies has greater relevance.

The Chinchorros lived year round along the Atacama coast. They were not nomadic or semi-nomadic bands as was previously suggested by various scholars (Nuñez 1969; Bittmann 1982; Rivera 1991). The debate over early Chinchorro sedentism is significant because an evolutionary model is often evoked for preceramic societies. They have been seen as highly mobile groups in constant search of food, following the groups of animals they hunted. In contrast, sedentism allowed a population to increase its birth rates, life expectancy, and population density. Higher population density normally increased socioeconomic and political competition, and craft specialization became a necessity. On the negative side, sedentism and high population density might contribute to environmental contamination and epidemics.

The Chinchorro archaeological evidence also was interpreted using this preceramic model. Mostny (1944) even suggested that the Chinchorros transported the mummies when they moved along the coast, but the presence of cemeteries, the high energy input of artificial mummification, external auditory exostoses (lesions associated with chronic auditory canal irritations due to continuous underwater shellfishing and fishing) and specialized maritime tool kits all point to sedentism. The Chinchorros were living on the coast year round and were quite successful at exploiting maritime resources.

Direct evidence of continuous coastal subsistence was demonstrated by chemical analyses of the mummies' bones. Aufderheide and Allison (1992) found that 89 percent of the Chinchorro diet came from maritime products, five percent from terrestrial meat, and six percent from terrestrial plants. Moreover, 21 percent of late Chinchorro people suffered from external auditory exostoses (Standen *et al.* 1984, 1985). These lesions were found mostly in males, which suggested that males were doing most of the underwater food gathering. The findings of Reinhard and Aufderheide (1990) provided further evidence of a maritime diet. They noted 19 percent of the late Chinchorros were infected with tapeworm parasites, *Diphyllobothrium pacificum*, a consequence of eating raw or poorly cooked fish. Finally, consistent with a coastal diet low in carbohydrates and high in abrasive materials, dental cavities among the Chinchorros were practically nonexistent.

Thus, long before agriculture and centralized power developed in the Andes, the rich resources along the Pacific coast of the Atacama desert gave the Chinchorros the option of becoming sedentary on the basis of maritime specialization. As a consequence of a stable and abundant food supply, sedentism allowed the Chinchorros the time for creating mummies and elaborately venerating their ancestors.

The complexity of the Chinchorro mummies implied the existence of specialists during the preceramic period. The suggestion was first made by Bittmann (1982), and is especially interesting because archaeologists have traditionally postulated that craft specialization appeared with the emergence of agriculture and social stratification. The Chinchorro case shows us otherwise; specialization can be the result of factors like ritualistic mortuary needs (body preparation, reed mat making, etc.) which probably developed from a profound sense of grief, and abundant resources to support specialization, rather than social inequalities.

Black and red mummies: how they differ

Chinchorro morticians were remarkable artisans and prepared the bodies in the black and red styles described by Arriaza (1994; 1995a,b). The black mummies were the older and more complex, beginning about 5050 BC and lasting about two and a half millennia. These were anthropogenically reconstructed bodies, statuelike. The black style can be summarized as follows. After defleshing and evisceration, the mortician used sticks and grass ropes for internal reinforcement of the major joints of the skeleton. The volume and body contour were regained, although not to exact anatomical proportions, using a gray soil paste. Often the skin was replaced and painted black with a manganese pigment, hence the name black mummies (Figure 10.1). On the head, the morticians added a short human hair wig and a facial mask of gray soil paste. The facial skin, which was skillfully put back in place, was coated with a paste of manganese and the facial features were insinuated. The sexual organs were modeled also.

In contrast, during the red style, which began about 2500 BC and lasted about 500 years, the morticians prepared the body without much disarticulation. Instead, incisions were made in the abdomen and shoulders to remove organs and to dry the cavities. The head was decapitated to remove the brain. Sticks slipped under the skin added rigidity and the body cavities were stuffed with soils and camelid fibers to regain some of the lost volume. The head was reattached and a long wig was added, made of black human hair tassels, up to 60 cm long. The wig was secured with a black clay helmet that subsequently was painted red. After suturing the incisions, the whole body was painted with red ocher, except for the face which was often left black (Figure 10.2). In a few cases the skin was replaced bandage style.

Recently, Hapke (1996) suggested that females were the morticians during the early black period, and males took over during the red period. These speculations were based on the universality of female cooperation versus male competitiveness. The black style represented a more communal effort; the mummies were less individualistic, more generic. The communal cooperation may account for the long duration of the period. In contrast, the striking red style, of short duration, was more individualistic and probably prepared by male morticians attempting to gain prestige. Regardless of which sex prepared the black and red mummies, their sophistication shows that during the Andean preceramic period there was an ingenious specialization in the art of making human effigies. Mortuary needs, rather than sociopolitical needs, could have been the primordial cultural force leading to the development of work specialization.

The black Chinchorro mummies, though they are the oldest in the world as far as we know, were made by an egalitarian society. Yet one of the working paradigms in archaeology is that complex treatment of the dead, including providing coffins and graves and thus having high energy expenditure, reflects the existence of social inequalities in life and in death (Binford 1971; Chapman *et al.* 1981). To paraphrase this, present archaeological models indicate that we should not find complex mortuary treatment in nonstratified societies. In Arica, at the Morro 1 site, 62 percent of the bodies were artificially mummified and 38 percent were not; thus Rivera (1991) has argued for the presence of social distinctions. Arriaza (1995b) debated that this dichotomy

FIGURE 10.1. Adult
female, Black style
Chinchorro mummy.
(Photograph by Raúl
Rocha.)

FIGURE 10.2. Red style Chinchorro mummy (infant) housed at the Museo Arqueológico San Miguel de Azapa, Arica. (Drawing by Raúl Rocha.)

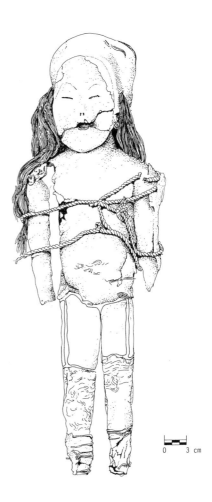

of artificial versus natural mummification was not related to rank, but rather to temporal changes of mummification styles. During the black and red periods, everybody was artificially mummified. In death everyone was treated alike and few worldly possessions were used as grave goods. It was democracy in death.

Social rank can be inherited or earned through individual achievements. Thus, children with lavish burial treatments may represent inherited or ascribed rank (Brown 1981). At the Morro 1 cemetery, 57 percent of those artificially mummified were subadults, including newborns. Arriaza (1995b) demonstrated that the high incidence of mummification of embryos and newborns is another reason to argue against the existence of inherited rank during Chinchorro times. Individuals of high social status should be few. That is, children with inherited rank would not be in the majority as is the case of Morro 1. Chinchorro mummification was apparently independent of the social persona (age, sex and status) of the deceased.

Chinchorro mortuary treatments had more to do with religious beliefs and grief than social inequalities. Using ethnographic data from forty cultures, Fox (1996) found no significant differences in the treatment of children between egalitarian and stratified societies. The key factor was not age or the political complexity of the society, but whether or not a child was incorporated into the society through a rite of passage. If the child was given a name, then he/she was considered an equal member deserving social recognition and the same mortuary treatment as an adult. For adults, however, social status was definitely a factor that affected their burial disposal. Because the Chinchorros mummified even fetuses, this would imply Chinchorro children were always considered part of their society.

The Chinchorro mortuary evidence shows that nonstratified societies can have elaborate mortuary rituals and craft specialists. Complex or lavish mortuary treatments of children were probably the result of parental grief rather than social position of the deceased or their families.

The mummies as a reflection of religion and art
The sophistication of the Chinchorro bodies with artificial mummification demonstrates that Chinchorro religious life was spiritually complex. This proposition challenges the common view that early egalitarian societies had simple social and spiritual existences. Elsewhere, due to poor preservation of preceramic human remains, most archaeological studies have been biased toward the reconstruction of economic and sociopolitical interactions. The understanding of religious ideology has been dwarfed by the economic focus of most scholars.

According to Uhle (1922), Bittmann (1982) and Rivera (1991) the genesis of Chinchorro artificial mummification was elsewhere, not in the Atacama region. Recently, various scholars have challenged this diffusionistic view (Schiappacasse and Niemeyer 1984; Standen 1991; Guillén 1992; Arriaza 1995b), suggesting instead that the anthropogenically made Chinchorro mummies were a local invention that developed in the Arica–Camarones area about 5050 BC and disappeared about 1700 BC. The long duration of three millennia for the black and red mummies reveals an intense religious worship where the cult of the dead and supernatural forces were central to the Chinchorro social and spiritual existence. In contrast, Wise (1991) proposed that the cult of the mummies was tied to territoriality and competition for coastal resources. For a better understanding of the religious and political role of the dead in ancient societies, one must look at modern analogies. For example, in the Andes, indigenous people believe ancestors never die, but they are only transformed from the soft mortal body to a hard imperishable mummy (Salomon 1991).

To the Incas the mummies were considered sacred living entities (*huacas*) that needed to be fed and cared for by their successors. It was a metaphysical system of reciprocity, the living fed the dead and in return the dead, or mummy-huacas, furnished the living with fertility and good crops. The Andean cult of the dead was so strong that the Spanish conquistadors and priests alike systematically destroyed, burned, or buried hundreds of mummies to implant their Catholic religion (Arriaga 1968; Cobo 1964). Urioste (1981) said that the native Andean people were devastated when the Spanish buried their mummies. Being unable to feed or talk to the mummies directly, they imagined the departed relatives as facing terrible suffering and starvation. Interestingly enough the red Chinchorro mummies have an open mouth. This feature may be an indication of the mortician's attempt to give a more life-like appearance and to provide an opening so the mummies could be symbolically fed and given the ability to communicate. The living could talk to the dead and vice versa to assuage spiritual and social grief. As such, the mummies were functional and powerful religious icons.

It is proposed here that the bodies with artificial mummification, in particular the black and red styles, were also artistic outlets for the Chinchorro people. The mummies were reconstructed with great internal and external sophistication. For the black style, the removal of internal organs and muscle tissue, the skeleton encased in clay, the long poles and cord wrappings, fillings of clay, camelid fibers, and wild reeds needed extensive processing and careful selection of materials. The style requiring internal and external treatment and use of colors also implied choices and creativity. It was a remarkable and enduring artistic tradition of mortuary art. This artistry can best be seen in the red mummies, which are most striking. In particular, the head with its long black wig, its polished red clay helmet, and the black facial mask with an opened mouth conveying a lifelike expression are visually powerful.

Surprisingly enough, mummies have also inspired modern artists. Paul Gauguin's famous paintings *Life and Death* and *Eve* (1889) were based on the crouched position of a Peruvian mummy (c. AD 1100–1400) displayed at the Musée de l'Homme in Paris (Thomson 1987). Edvard Munch visited Paris in 1889 and the 'expression of agony' of this mummy, a consequence of the natural dislocation of the jaw, possibly inspired the series of paintings titled

The Scream which he started to paint in 1893. The skull-like face of *The Scream* certainly resembles the face of a naturally desiccated mummy. It is an interesting parallel that thousands of years ago, Andean morticians also were using mummies to create and convey powerful visual messages about life and death.

The Chinchorro black and red mummies are fascinating. They need to be preserved and studied in detail, not only because they are now the oldest examples of intentionally mummified human remains on earth, but also because they represent the earliest manifestations of Andean art and the spiritual beliefs and grief of preceramic people.

MUMMIES FROM COLOMBIA AND OTHER SOUTH AMERICAN AREAS: AN ARCHAEOLOGICAL CONTEXT

Felipe Cárdenas-Arroyo

The study of ancient funerary practices provides us with relevant data regarding the socioeconomic, political and religious structure of past societies. When studied within the greater archaeological context of cultural regional interaction, funerary patterns are important because they add data to the basic archaeological record regarding social hierarchies and social complexity. Recent developments in archaeology stress this approach (Beck 1995), and its application to Colombian archaeology shows the benefits of introducing a regional perspective on mortuary analysis combined with data on subsistence, settlement patterns, and demography (Drennan 1995).

Unfortunately, the study of mummified human remains in Colombian archaeology eludes this perspective, mostly because preserved human bodies have been found out of context – many have been recovered by treasure hunters – and because they are so few that they are not useful for population studies. Within these limitations, however, the available data are susceptible to serious interpretation both from the biological and cultural points of view, and I shall attempt here to give the most relevant synthesized information regarding mummies and mummification in ancient Colombia and selected other areas of South America (Figure 10.3).

Preserving complete human bodies and parts of bodies was a common practice among Colombian aborigines in pre-Hispanic times. Whether for ritual, political, or religious reasons, human remains were symbolically important. For example, human heads were taken after battles, smoke dried, transformed into trophies, and placed at the entrance of dwellings. Bodies were defleshed and the skin preserved by using hot ashes, then supported

FIGURE 10.3. Map of South America indicating known places where artificial mummification was practiced and location of some natural mummies.

with canes and wooden sticks, and placed in huts and communal houses. There are even reports of how human entrails were kept hanging from wooden beams after being smoke dried (Cieza de León 1962 [1553]). In 1542, a Spanish soldier by the name of Pero López was eyewitness to the battles of conquest taking place in southern Colombia, an area known today as Alto Magdalena. Thirty years later, in Europe, López decided to write about his impressions (López 1970 [1572]), and among many stories, recalls the following:

> We arrived to the province of Pirama (the chief) . . . We battled with the Indians and took more than fifty heads they kept in their houses as trophies . . . They preserved them with a bitumen which they do well . . . The [heads] were at the tip of spears . . . next to the doors.

Still more impressive is a narration by the famous chronicler of Peru, Pedro Cieza de León, when describing the territory of the Lile Valley and the Indian town of Petecuy in southwestern Colombia, near the modern city of Cali:

In the middle of this town there is a great wooden house, very tall and circular . . . and, high above, there was a wooden plank from side to side, and on it there were orderly placed many bodies of dead men . . . and they would open them with flint knives, and deflesh them, and once they had eaten the meat they filled the skin with ashes and then made masks out of wax on their heads, and placed them on the plank so they would look like living.

(Cieza de León 1962 [1553])

Descriptions such as these are to be found in many accounts of the conquest, and when viewed within the contextual framework of socio-political and religious perspectives they allow a complex interpretation of ideological aboriginal systems. With the aid of anthropological theory, Arriaza (1995) has presented a very interesting discussion as to the social dimensions of mortuary ritual in ancient societies that is pivotal for understanding the purpose of preserving a mummified body; whether this was done for ritual cannibalism, religious symbolism, or political demonstrations of power, mummification played an important role in social interaction and in maintaining and reproducing the established social order.

Ancient mummies from Colombia are of two kinds: naturally desiccated bodies and artificially prepared mummies. The first are rather common in areas of low relative humidity and enclosed funeral settings, such as natural caves. The two together provided an environment that allowed relatively good preservation of bodies. Low relative humidity areas alone are not sufficient for preserving mummified bodies in good condition. Most of those found in dry but unprotected environments will usually exhibit only traces of soft tissue and evidence of being damaged by animals. Artificial mummification was practiced in four areas: (1) The central Andean highlands, corresponding to the present political provinces of Cundinamarca and Boyacá; (2) the area of Darién, a dense tropical rain forest lowland area in the present day border of Colombia and Panama; (3) the Cauca River valley, in the province of Valle del Cauca (these are strongly associated with a cannibalistic context); and (4) the southwestern corner of Colombia, mainly in the territory of Popayán. I shall not include those areas in which there was a clear intention of preserving the bodies through means that were not successful in the end.

Naturally desiccated mummies
Naturally desiccated mummies in Colombia come from semi-arid environments. Most have been found in the province of Santander, in an area known

as Mesa de Los Santos and inhabited in the past by the Guane Indians. Two main cave sites have been found with mummies: the Cueva de Los Indios and the Cueva de La Loma, both explored by archaeologists in 1939 (Schottelius 1946) after extensive looting by treasure hunters had damaged the original archaeological contexts. Nevertheless, the Cueva de Los Indios proved to be one of the most important burial sites in northeastern Colombia. Four mummies, three partially mummified skulls and several fragments of mummified bodies and skeletal remains were collected (Schottelius 1946). Some of these specimens were kept in private collections and others sent to the Archaeological Museum in Bogotá (now The National Museum) and the Museo Casa Bolivar in the city of Bucaramanga. Schottelius remarks that the cave had originally contained hundreds of bodies, many of which seem to have been well preserved. According to one description by an alleged discoverer of the cave before it was ransacked, there were many mummies bundled with blankets and piled up in the extended position. These were not buried in the soil but placed on the floor or over rock cornices inside the cave. A different burial pattern was also observed: buried in the soil were the cremated remains of various individuals, as well as skeletonized burials.

The importance of the Cueva de Los Indios is also confirmed by the remarkable textiles accompanying the mummies and skeletons; these have also been found in other locations. They have been fully described (Cardale Schrimpff 1986) and it has been observed by the same author that some design patterns probably correspond to ethnic groups different from the Guanes. This corroborates the fact that cotton blankets were an important trade item in pre-Hispanic Colombia, and the use of textiles produced by other ethnic groups implies shared cultural traits among aboriginal Colombians.

It is difficult to estimate whether or not artificial mummification was practiced by the Guanes. Many indigenous tribes in ancient Colombia did attempt to preserve dead bodies by artificial means, but not all were successful. The few mummies still available from the Cueva de Los Indios are not fully preserved, and considerable portions of their bodies are skeletonized, held in anatomical position by patches of soft tissue. However, according to Schottelius, it is clear that a different disposal of the dead took place in this cave, as those buried directly in the ground were not preserved as mummies. Furthermore, the early sixteenth century Spanish chroniclers never mention artificial mummification in Guane territory. Let us outline an ethnographic analogy in a nearby area inhabited by the Yuko ethnic group. These Indians live on the eastern flanks of the Sierra de Perij, on the border between

Table 10.1. *Radiocarbon dates, sites and cultural affiliation of Colombian mummies in museum collections*

Museum catalogue no.	Site/cultural affiliation	Lab sample no.	C-14 date (years BP)	Date (AD)[b]
ICAN 42-IX-3956	Chiscas/Lache	OxA-2829	1480±100	470
G-194	Los Santos/Guane	GrN-19191	1325±160	625
BM 1838-11-11-1	V.Leyva/Muisca	OxA?	1100±60	850
BM 1842-11-12-1	Gachantivá/Muis	OxA?	790±60	1160
ICAN 38-1-776	Unknown/Muisca	OxA-2815	750±60	1200
ICAN 38-1-777	Unknown/Muisca	OxA-2816	710±60	1240
ICAN 423-A-423	Ubaté/Muisca	OxA-2830	480±110	1470
MO-1	Pisba/U'wa?-Muisca?	OxA-2833	430±100	1520
ICAN 41-III-2536	Los Santos/Guane	OxA-2832	390±100	1560
ICAN 42-IX-3957	Chiscas/Lache	Pitt-0453	—[a]	1750

Note: OxA: Oxford Radiocarbon Acceleration Unit. Pitt: Pittsburgh Radiocarbon Laboratory. GrN: Gröningen C-14 Laboratorium. [a]This date was given in years AD and not in years BP by the Lab. [b]Dates given in years AD in the fifth column are calculated with reference to 1950 AD. ICAN=Instituto Colombiano de Antropología (Santafé de Bogotá); BM=British Museum (London); MO=Gold Museum (Santafé de Bogotá); G=Museo Casa Bolívar (Bucaramanga).

Sources: Cárdenas-Arroyo (1994), Holden (1989), Correal & Flórez (1992).

Colombia and Venezuela. The Yuko practice a very complex funeral ritual that includes artificial mummification by heat desiccation, wrapping the body in textiles and vegetal fibers, and finally burial two years after death (Reichel-Dolmatoff 1945). The bodies are relatively well preserved. After the preparation was finished, the mummy bundle was placed in a remote cave in a cliff with other dead members of the social group. This setting is quite similar to the Cueva de Los Indios, which is also located in a remote cliff.

Artificial mummies

Artificial mummification in ancient Colombia was not technically refined, although the final results were very good. The earliest radiocarbon date available places this practice in AD 470 (Table 10.1), among the Lache Indians, a relatively small group located on the eastern slopes of the Andes. These people practiced mummification for hundreds of years, and continued to do so during the late colonial period in the eighteenth century. The Spanish banned artificial mummification as well as all beliefs contrary to the Catholic church, but still the Indians would find their way to preserve the bodies of

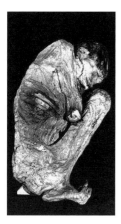

FIGURE 10.4. Artificial mummy of a young person, approximately 14 years of age at death. Probable Muisca affiliation (AD 1200). Extensive burning on the right costal area and right elbow, due to its closeness to the fire during desiccation. (Ican 38–I-776. Collection Instituto Colombiano de Antropología.)

their kin. Early descriptions suggest evisceration was carried out by opening the thorax and abdomen with a knife, and then removing the internal organs. The empty cavity was filled with gold objects, emeralds, precious stones and cotton ritual objects. Only one eviscerated mummy from Colombia is known to exist today, and this is curated at the British Museum (Cárdenas-Arroyo 1990; Dawson 1928; Holden 1989). This body has an extensive incision on the left ventral side extending from the thorax to the lower abdomen. Some of the gut remains can still be seen, attesting to a not very careful evisceration process, and descriptions from Friar Pedro Simón, a sixteenth century eyewitness, confirm the fact that eviscerated bodies were filled with precious metals.

The central Andean highlands of Colombia were inhabited by the Muisca, a general term given to complex socially ranked agricultural chiefdoms, for whom the preferred method of mummification was desiccation by heat. The Muisca mummified their principal leaders in two ways: (1) heat drying by fire with evisceration through abdominal incisions; and (2) heat desiccation by fire without any other type of artificial methods for the preservation of the body or its internal contents. According to data furnished by research conducted at various museums, evisceration was not a common practice; rather, heat dehydration was the preferred method. Some of the mummies in the Colombian collections show signs of having been placed very close to the fire and suffering burns (Figure 10.4). Their state of conservation is remarkable, as many still have intact internal viscera. Some early accounts as well as recent archaeological reports have speculated that the Muisca Indians employed a special tar-like substance for embalming the body and preserving the outer soft tissue. This became an almost unquestionable issue based exclusively on the reports of the sixteenth century chroniclers, but it seems not to have been the case. Confusion originated in descriptions given to the use of a plant known in Muisca language as *moque*. This *moque* produced an inflammable resin that was usually burnt during ritual occasions and was added to the fire when a body was being dried. The Spanish observers interpreted this as a special substance for embalming, but it was never used in that way.

On careful analysis, the accounts indicate that *moque* was always burnt in ritual circumstances, whether a mummy was being prepared or not. In present day Amazonian societies, the related term *moquear* is used to refer to smoke drying fish, suggesting a continuation of the word within the context of drying. Once dried, the mummies of chiefs were placed in temples, ceremonial houses, and even in small isolated huts serving as sanctuaries. These buildings were destroyed by the European colonizers, and the Indians were forced through torture to declare their locations. In one particular document from the year 1595 (Guzmán and Gómez-Garzón 1988 [1595]), an Indian declared, under threat of torture, that he had concealed a sanctuary containing the remains of his uncle, who had been a chief in life, and that he would go there from time to time to pay his respects. It is also known by the most renowned chroniclers of the early years of the conquest that the Muisca had a major temple in the city of Sogamoso, where the mummies of important leaders were displayed. This temple was burned to the ground during a Spanish night raid, turning the mummies into ashes.

Muisca mummies are carefully preserved. After being dehydrated, the bodies were bundled in many blankets, sometimes up to seven, splendidly decorated either by painting or weaving patterns. The bodies were adorned with necklaces made from stone or shell beads, some transported thousands of miles from the Caribbean and Pacific coasts to the Andean highlands, as can be confirmed from two specimens: one, the mummy of a child (Figure 10.5) at the Colombian Institute of Anthropology in Bogotá, and the other an adult female at the British Museum in London (Cárdenas-Arroyo 1989). Other mummies were tightly bound, holding objects in their hands or arms, and still others were placed in caves with weapons by their side or in their hands. Their bodies are usually flexed, imitating the sitting position; indeed that was intentional, as can be discerned from the Spanish descriptions. Symbolically, the Muisca mummies played an important political role in society. According to one Conquest eye witness, the mummies were carried into the battlefields as symbols of the power and military control of the chief.

Further to the north, the Cueva Indians of the Darién Gap area practiced artificial mummification with the bodies of their chiefs. Not one Cueva mummy has ever been found, as that area is one of the most humid tropical rain forests in the world, and organic material such as a mummy would have no chance of surviving for more than a few years. Yet, the Cueva seem to have practiced a most intricate funeral ritual. According to Gonzalo Fernández de Oviedo, an early sixteenth century chronicler:

The Cueva desiccated by heat the bodies of their noble dead, without opening nor mutilating them, and conserved the mummies well bundled with blankets in their houses.

(1851 [1532])

One possible reason for practicing artificial mummification, to use Malinowski (1974) as a theoretical framework, is to deny death. As we have seen, the concept of the living dead is constantly reiterated in different aboriginal societies in which mummification was performed. The mummies took an active part in daily life, as is seen in several examples. They were

FIGURE 10.5. Child mummy from the central highlands of Colombia, partially covered with a cotton blanket (Ican 00–OS-0006. Collection Instituto Colombiano de Antropología).

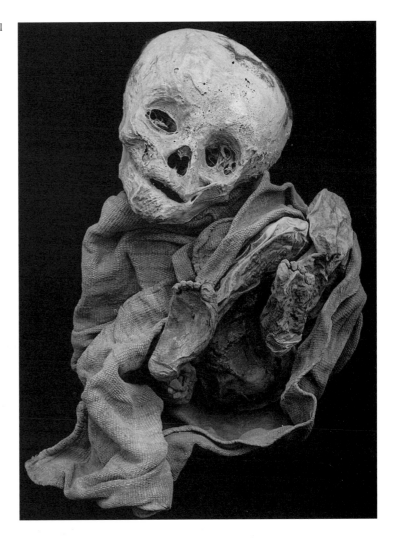

carried to the battle fronts and placed sitting in ceremonial houses and living quarters. They were also symbolically fed and kept warm close to the fire in living quarters; they were dressed and adorned with golden artifacts and precious stones, and consulted about religious matters. Mummies in ancient Colombia, then, were not simply passive cultural artifacts but rather played a crucial role in maintaining social structures and social alliances through their use as symbols of political power (Langebaek 1992; Cárdenas-Arroyo 1992).

In his discussion about complex chief-ruled societies in the Alto Magdalena region of southern Colombia, Drennan (1995) suggests that, despite the presence of monumental funerary architecture of stone statues and monolithic stone slabs, the Regional Classic Period in the San Agustín area (AD 1–800) was characterized by an individualized type of society under chiefs prior to a more elaborate institutionalized society. The source of chief's power in that area is seen by Drennan as originating more in his ability to control the religious sphere than a true control over economic resources. Mummies in Muisca territory, on the other hand, seem to have been an element of political cohesion in a society that had already institutionalized death as a means of social control, although an important religious element also permeates the political symbolism of mummies.

Modern methods of analysis

Colombian mummies have been the object of serious scientific research. Nondestructive techniques have been favored, although internal sampling has been carried out. Computed tomography (CT) has been of great help in these studies, allowing the precise location of internal organs and other material that has been carefully collected and extracted either through the anal aperture or through previously naturally occurring openings in the bodies. Correal-Urrego and Flórez (1992) conducted radiographic studies of two Guane mummies from the Cueva de Los Indios. One belongs to an adult female (G-194), the other to an infant (G-12.980). The female mummy showed marginal osteophytic alterations in C4 through C6, as well as facet arthrosis in the same vertebrae. Two apparently calcified nodules were observed in CT scan images of this same mummy. They are both localized in the left thoracic cavity, one subpleural and the other parenchymatous. These have been interpreted by the authors as possible evidence of tuberculosis (TBC) granulomas (Correal-Urrego and Flórez 1992), although they also call attention to a lack of skeletal involvement that could, if present, have given further support for diagnosing the disease. Up to today, TBC has not been convincingly proven in archaeological material from Colombia, and diagnosis based on limited evidence should be taken with caution. The similar characteristics of different *Mycobacterium* species and related genera must be taken into consideration in all TBC differential diagnosis with archaeological materials, as has been clearly presented by Salo and co-workers (1994); Vreeland and Cockburn (1980) stress the fact that granulomatous abnormalities do not necessarily imply the presence of TBC.

The question about the origins and genetic affinity among Amerindian populations has long been a subject of inquiry by Americanists. During the first half of the twentieth century, Paul Rivet carried out one of the most extensive and scholarly studies on this subject from the point of view of aboriginal linguistics. Today studies of ancient DNA bring us closer to understanding

FIGURE 10.6. Artificial mummy, probably from Muisca territory (AD 1240). Reddish brown body paint can be seen on the face. Originally wrapped in blankets as can be inferred from the impressions left on the soft tissue. CT scan showed a large gall stone. (Ican 38–I-777. Collection Instituto Colombiano de Antropología.)

this phenomenon. In a search for the possible presence of Asian markers, mitochondrial DNA (mtDNA) was extracted from soft tissue samples of Colombian mummies from the Guane region (Monsalve *et al.* 1994) and the Muisca region (Monsalve *et al.* 1996). Some theories regarding the early colonization of South America supported the view of a bottleneck at the Isthmus of Panama (Schurr *et al.* 1990), based on the fact that an Asian specific marker (9–bp COII/tRNA^{Lys} intergenic deletion) is present in some Arizona and mesoAmerican aboriginal tribes, but absent in Indians from northwestern Amazonia. The results obtained from Colombian mummies and present Amazonian and Quechua speaking Indians indicate that such a marker is present in these populations. Contrary to the proposed theory, this suggests that South America was populated by multiple migrations and that such markers necessarily entered South America from Central America, via the Isthmus (Monsalve *et al.* 1994, 1996). Furthermore, three mummies from the eastern Cordillera in Colombia (one of them belonging to the Lache and one possibly to the Uw'a ethnic group) show DNA lineages that have not been identified before in native Americans, suggesting a greater number of ancient descent lineages than previously thought (Monsalve *et al.* 1996).

CT scans were of great value in the detection of pathological conditions in an adult mummy (Figure 10.6) of possible Muisca affiliation (ICAN 38-I-

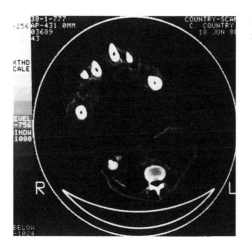

FIGURE 10.7. CT scan image of gallstone in mummy Ican 38–I–777.

777). These were carried out in Bogotá by G. Echeverry and A. Vélez. The abdominal area showed a circular calcified image suggesting the presence of a gallstone (Figure 10.7). After a careful incision performed by T. Holden, a stone measuring 5.0 cm × 3.5 cm was removed. Few stones have been reported in the paleopathological literature, mostly because they are difficult to find in archaeological excavations in which only skeletal remains are present. Artificial cranial deformation was also seen in four of our mummies (Ican 38-I-777, BM 1838-11-11-1; G-194 and an uncatalogued fourth from the Museo de La Merced, Cali), as well as the many partially mummified skulls from the Cueva de Los Indios. The mummies present the tabular–oblique type of deformation, whereas most deformed skulls show the circular (or annular) type. Body paint as decoration was seen in two of the mummies; one (Ican 38-I-777) has extensive paint on the face, eyelids and eyebrows and part of the head. The second specimen (no number), originating from the area of Santander, has red designs in parallel lines (medio-laterally oriented) in the lower half of the left tibia.

Colombian mummies are a rich resource for biocultural data. They represent a very characteristic funeral context and method of mummification in northern South America, which could be seen even up until 40 or 50 years ago. Their study is of great value for understanding biological phenomena, pathology and social features of ancient Amerindians.

The South American picture

Evidence for artificial mummification in areas of South America other than Peru and northern Chile is quite scarce. Ecuador has hardly any mummified specimens, in spite of lying between Colombia and Peru, two important areas in which mummification was a common occurrence. No artificially preserved human body is found in Ecuadorian archaeological collections, despite the fact that it was a major center of socioeconomic, religious and political activity, and an area of paramount importance with regard to trade and exchange between the Andean region, the tropical Amazon lowlands, and the Pacific coastal plains. Inca domination over this territory extended north of the capital city, Quito, and yet no Inca mummies have been found here.

In the early twentieth century, Anthony and Rivet (1908) made a striking discovery in southern Ecuador: the archaeological site of Paltacalo. It consisted of various rock shelters containing several human burials, both skeletal and mummified. Unfortunately, excavations were not carefully conducted, and the material recovered was neither systematically recorded nor fully excavated. Anthony and Rivet described the mummies quite superficially, and took only a few skulls to deposit at the Museum of Natural History in Paris (Salazar 1995), after which the entrance to the rock shelter was closed by an artificial pile of rocks. Inside were the bones of many individuals, and one mummy was said to be in a fully flexed position with its knees under the chin. Another similar body was described for Paltacalo, and still another from the rock shelter of Mano, which the authors did not actually see but knew about from verbal communication (Anthony and Rivet 1908, Spanish translation by Salazar 1995). They noted that the dryness of the environment allowed perfect conservation of the bodies, including hair, articular ligaments and parchment-like skin. Although Rivet later concluded that the Paltacalo individuals belonged to an early human group, it has been argued that his observations were inaccurate because he biased his sample by selecting only those skulls that seemed to fit into his model of an early paleoAmerican biotype (Salazar 1995). The associated ceramics and the burial pattern from the Paltacalo area actually fit better into a later time period.

Although mummies are rare in Ecuadorian archaeological contexts, early burial patterns are interesting (Ubelaker 1981; Villalba 1988; Stothert 1988). Las Vegas culture, one of the most important early archaeological contexts from coastal Ecuador, is represented by several sites in the Santa Elena peninsula, 140 km west of the city of Guayaquil. Radiocarbon dates place Las Vegas between 10 840±410 BP and 6600±150 BP at site OGSE-80 (Stothert 1988). Human remains were analyzed by Ubelaker (1980). Careful excavation showed three types of burials: (1) Regular primary burials; (2) Primary burials of one or two individuals accompanied by a rectangular package of disarticulated human bones belonging to other individuals; (3) Secondary burials of commingled human remains – some with signs of being cremated

– but with the skulls placed in order (Stothert 1988). From this site come the famed 'Sumpa Lovers', an adult male and female inhumed together, the male with his right arm on the female's waist, and his right leg on her pelvis. Other skeletons showed evidence of being decorated with ochre pigment and accompanied with objects such as sea shells, indicating the importance of dead body treatment from very early times on the Ecuadorian coast and the Andean highlands.

Scattered documentary information can be found in hundreds of accounts from early conquest times. Heat drying was the favored method for desiccation, which seems to have been common in a wide area of the tropical rain forests and the Venezuelan coast. Near the Gulf of Paria in Venezuela, there is an interesting account from Spanish writer Pedro Mártir de Anglería, during the second half of the sixteenth century, regarding the Haraia Indians:

> The bodies of the chiefs are laid at full length on a staging, underneath which slow fires are kept up so that the flesh is gradually consumed whilst the bones and the skin remain. The bodies thus desiccated are carefully preserved and kept as a sort of penates.
>
> (Mártir de Anglería 1944 [1574])

Christopher Columbus mentioned preserved human bodies in the westernmost area of Panama, as described by his men during an expedition:

> The most remarkable things they saw were in a great wooden palace covered with canes several tombs, in one of which there was a dead body dried up and embalmed; in another, two bodies wrapped up in cotton sheets . . .
>
> (C. Columbus in S. Linné 1929)

There is also documentary evidence for heat dehydration in eastern Brazil among the ancient Maue, near the junction between the Taipajós and Jamanxim Rivers, people probably of Tupí-Guaraní linguistic affiliation, and two others north of the Amazon River, the Uajurú and the Oyana (Linné 1929), for which there is only a passing reference to bodies being artificially desiccated. In the southern cone, reports indicate smoke drying by the Huilliche and Calchaki of Argentina. Naturally desiccated human bodies found in caves in the Argentinean area of the Gran Chaco are at present curated in the Museo de La Plata, but their state of conservation is critical. These infants and adults were placed in a sitting position, but are so dismembered that it is difficult to tell how they were originally.

Mummification by heat drying and smoking seems to have been a widely used method in South America, in both Andean highlands and tropical rain forest lowlands. This practice may have been associated with ritual consumption of human flesh and entrails, as was the case in the Colombian Cauca River Valley, and possibly among tribes of the eastern Brazilian forests. Taking all this evidence together, the context of human mummification should be extended to include all mortuary practices aimed at preserving the body, even when this was not achieved. The intention to preserve the body, including decorating parts of it, should be taken into consideration as a major element in the interpretation of archaeological burial contexts.

SHRUNKEN HEADS

Ekkehard Kleiss

The head is undoubtedly one of the most important parts of the anatomy of vertebrate animals, especially humans. Headhunting was, therefore, as prevalent in primitive warfare as decapitations were crucial in the administration of justice throughout the history of humanity.

The origin of headhunting goes back to the oldest times in the development of the human race, and is intimately related to the 'cult of the head', ubiquitous among primitive people, and deeply interwoven with magic beliefs and superstitions, but also with fertility rites and the veneration of deceased ancestors. Such talismans (i.e., the preserved head of a forefather) brought to the family of the owner and even to his whole tribe the spiritual properties and powerful attributes of the deceased. This assumption was extended later to the skulls of slain enemies or foreigners (which meant the same for many primitive people). In the life of early man, the killing of animals was an imperative need in order to survive, and as animals killed other animals, why should man refrain from doing the same and killing other men, if he was able to do it according to his strength, weapons, or skill. For the same reason, the slaughter was frequently combined with cannibalism, although anthropophagy was only sometimes due to the lack of food. In most cases, it had a religious and/or magic background: to acquire the physical and spiritual qualities and faculties of the slain person. We can be sure of the existence of prehistoric headhunting and cannibalism, because so many archaeological discoveries confirm this concept.

A tentative but incomplete list of examples of headhunting throughout the history of mankind might start with the neolithic headhunters who caught, slew and beheaded a remnant group of at least 38 mesolithic persons, including 14 children, who inhabited the area of Tiefenellern, Franconia, Germany. The remains of the victims were found in the Jungfernhöhle (Cave of the Virgin). Split and broken bones indicate the probability of cannibalism.

Analogous discoveries exist in prehistoric China and India, among several Bronze Age Cultures of the Asiatic Steppes, and in Ancient Persia, Scythia and Crimea. Herodotus tells about headhunters in Asia who did their grisly work during or after the battles. According to Aztec Codices, we find the custom of cutting off the head of the slain enemy in Ancient Mexico and also in the realm of the Incas (Kleiss 1984).

Even in modern times, there are cases of headhunting not only among primitive tribes in remote parts of the earth, but also in 'civilized' societies. Thus, we can mention the skulls in the wall of a tower near the town of Nish in southeast Serbia, skulls of Serbians who were killed by the Turks during the battle of Kamenica (Hansmann and Kriss-Rettenbeck 1966, Figure 593). The victors put them in the wall to demonstrate their power or perhaps for apotropaic reasons. Before World War I, the Montenegrins, fierce inhabitants of the southern part of former Yugoslavia, used to cut off the heads of their victims, carrying home those trophies of their victory by a lock of hair. Later on during the Balkan war of 1912–1913, they seem to have changed their method of headhunting and cut off only the nose and the upper lip with the moustache, the latter being an important sign of virility and bravery (Kleiss 1984).

The method of taking only part of the head as a trophy instead of the whole one is quite ancient and was already practiced in pre-Columbian America. A typical example is the Huastecs, violent Indians who protected the Mesoamerican High Cultures against the invasion of wild nomads from the North; they stripped off the scalp together with the skin of the face of their victims, as can be seen on a vessel of clay from their epoch. The Conquistador Hernán Cortés subjugated them after several assaults, and found in their temples such trophies taken from the heads of the Spanish soldiers killed by the Huastecs.

We should also mention here the North American Indians who took the scalp rather than the whole head of their victims when fighting against the white settlers, keeping such trophies in their wigwams. According to their beliefs, the 'soul' (i.e., the spiritual force) was located in the hair. The enormous magical importance of hair can be observed all over the world and during any period of our history. A scalp found in a grave near Lima and now in the private collection of the eminent Ecuadorian archaeologist Jacinto Jijón y Caamaño is much older than the North American Indians. This fact might indicate that 'scalping', in very ancient times, was already part of the widely disseminated custom of taking skin trophies instead of the whole head (Gusinde 1937; Paredes Borja 1963).

Of the modern headhunters who practiced their grisly custom in the first half of the 20th century, and continue even today, we can mention here only a few examples, as their number is greater than one might suppose (Cranstone

1961; Gusinde 1937; Heine-Geldern 1924; Kleiss 1966, 1975, 1981/82). Many hill tribes in northeastern India, especially in Assam, as well as several tribal groups in Burma, in the Malay Archipelago (e.g., the Ibans and formerly also the Kadazans of Borneo) and in Indonesia in general, still devoted themselves to all kinds of human sacrifices, combined nearly always with decapitation and frequently with cannibalism. The Igorots and Tagalogs of Luzon, Philippines, abandoned such practices in the middle of the twentieth century. The Asmat (Sowada 1968) and other southwestern Papuans reverted during World War II to tribal fighting and headhunting, which they had formerly given up, and the practice still persists locally in New Guinea as well as in other parts of Oceania, sporadically associated with cannibalism. Several tribes in Nigeria and other African tribal groups frequently carry out human sacrifices similar to the headhunting customs of Indonesia, along with cannibalistic rites. With regard to South American headhunters, one can suppose that those ferocious tribes came from the Caribbean area and extended their domains to pre-Andean and trans-Andean regions. Several groups of these Indians use the boiled and cleaned skulls of their victims as trophies, hanging them in their huts. Our special interest is in the Jíbaros (or Jívaros, sometimes also called Shuara) of the basin of the High Amazon River (Karsten 1923; Kleiss and Simonsberger 1964). These brave warriors and headhunters had a great influence on other tribes long before the arrival of the Conquistadores. Their skill in preparing shrunken heads or Tsantsas (Figure 10.8) is shared by other Indians, from early Mexico and other Central American countries (e.g., Costa Rica) to the Nazca area of Southern Peru, as can be observed on many human figurines that carry a shrunken head as a trophy (Baudez 1970, Figures 144 and 146). Even in modern times, the Jíbaros successfully resisted all attempts to suppress headhunting. Although officially the preparation of tsantsas is strictly forbidden, no one can really enforce the law in the jungle, and so ancient customs probably persist even nowadays.

The Indonesians and other headhunters dried, smoked or mummified the whole head of their foe, sometimes preserving tattoo marks and even the actual features of the victim. They also skinned the head and painted the skull with ash, chalk and ocher, in this way preparing trophies of a macabre beauty. But all these trophies are more or less the original size of the human head. The Jíbaros, however, shrink the tsantsa to the size of a fist or the head of a small monkey, maintaining during all this reduction the original features like a portrait or a caricature.

The basic principle of the technique is to flay the skin of the whole head

FIGURE 10.8. Tsantsas. (Courtesy of Dr. Etta Becker-Donner, Völkerkundemuseum, Vienna)

and neck entirely. The preparation of a tsantsa is a laborious process. First, the head has to be cut as near to the trunk as possible, preserving all the skin of the neck. If the victim was slain near the village of the head hunters, the preparation starts immediately, and this, according to the opinion of some experts, gives the best results. On the other hand, transportation of the head through the jungle for several days undoubtably produces a certain degree of putrefaction, which facilitates the next step, the separation of the skin from the skull. After receiving authorization from the chief of the tribe to make the tsantsa (this is given in a solemn ceremony), the head hunter, sometimes assisted by more experienced fellow tribesmen, makes an incision in the midline of the scalp, from the crown to the occipital bone or even down the whole dorsal portion of the neck. Then he separates the scalp from the roof of the skull. This is quite simple, as the tissues can be separated easily with the bare hands. The halves of the scalp hang outward like two inverted sacks. The more complicated part of the dissection is to separate the skin from the bones of the face, a process for which Indians use sharp bamboo knives, shells, or flint stones. Sometimes they break the bones to facilitate their extraction. Great care must be taken to preserve the eyelids, lips, nose and ears. Preparation of the neck is similar.

The process of shrinking the head is another toilsome task. If the head was fresh, the natural retraction of the skin at once reduces the mask to half its original size or less. In any case, to avoid further delay, the head is put in a bowl for several days with a decoction of plants, probably rich in tannins and other coagulating agents that will preserve and shrink the tissues at the same time. Sometimes the prepared skin is boiled in these extracts of plants and barks. Then the openings of the mouth and eyes are sewn with plant fibers, often fixed to small, painted wooden sticks; with religious rites this closure avoids the evil spirits, execrations, or other calamities that might come out of the orifices. The cut in the scalp and neck is also sewn, practically disappearing under the abundant hair. The head has now been transformed into a sort of sack, open only where the neck was severed from the trunk.

Into this sack, the Jíbaro carefully pours hot sand that has been heated in the shard of a used pottery vessel (both details are important for the success of the preparation); some tribal groups also use three hot pebbles taken from the next river and rolled around in the inside of the sack. This ritual is to avoid any evil reaction from the spirit of the victim. At the same time, it burns away any excess of connective and other tissues, thus helping to shrink the skin in a proportioned way. On the outside, the skin of the face is frequently anointed with vegetable oils or fat, and the features are constantly modeled as their size is gradually reduced. Because of the smoke from special plants or woods, the plant extracts, and the powdered charcoal, this whole procedure produces the dark color typical of tsantsas, even if the victim had been a white man. This can be proved, at least in some cases, by the hair distribution – e.g., mustache – and by other details of the features (Kleiss and Simonsberger 1964, Figure 13).

During the whole time the head is being prepared, the head hunter must observe strict rules of fasting and other rituals, otherwise the spiritual success of the preparation would be in danger. When the work is finished, there is a big fiesta for the tribe, with special purification rites for the successful head hunter and introduction ceremonies for the tsantsa, which nearly always belongs to the whole clan as a sort of talisman.

This ideological framework demonstrates clearly that head hunting in general and the making of tsantsas in particular are not at all the result of bloodthirst or cruelty, but of spiritual concepts, as is typical of primitive religions. Although we cannot discuss here all the details of the ideas or beliefs that induced primitive men to practice head hunting, basically there is a concept of the existence of a material soul. This 'soul matter' has its seat in the head and can be stored and added to the existing stock of an individual or of the whole tribe. Its possession transfers to the owner of the head trophy certain qualities of the victim; strength, courage, sagacity, and so on. Similar ideas are associated with cannibalism, because the eaten parts of the foe's body transfer analogous qualities to the eater, an idea still believed by many primitive populations. Human sacrifices of any kind, including headhunting, are intimately related to fertility rites (the cycle of life), to the initiation of boys to manhood, to better status in the other world, where the head of the victim will assure his services to the owner, and to immanent or real power in the widest sense of the word – for example, related to the building of a new house or the launching of a war canoe. The special importance of hair has been mentioned already and may be compared to the biblical story of Samson and the use of amulets, arm rings, and necklets made from the hair of slain foes and therefore of magic virtue. In the British Museum in London, there is a tsantsa of a sloth, considered by the Jíbaros and other South American tribes as the forefather of mankind, probably because of its hairy aspect. Because of the reduced size of tsantsas, the hair of the head, which was practically never cut during the life span of the victim, seems extremely long and is frequently braided and/or adorned with feathers or beads (Kleiss 1984, 1989).

Because of the commercial interest in tsantsas all over the world, fake ones made from heads of monkeys or with the hairy skin of other animals abound on the market. In some cases, especially when they were made by the Indians themselves, their identification as fakes is rather difficult. However, even in such specimens, we must admire the masterly skill of primitive men.

Acknowledgements
My special thanks to the late Reverend Ernesto Fischer, Jíbaro missionary for many years, and also to Professor Luis Rengel Sanchez and other Ecuadorian colleagues for the data they provided regarding headhunting.

DISEASE IN SOUTH AMERICAN MUMMIES
John W. Verano

Only a relatively small number of diseases that affect humans leave any trace of their presence in the skeleton, and some diseases affect bone in similar ways, making a confident diagnosis difficult in many cases (Ortner 1992). Diseases that affect the skeleton are most commonly long term ailments such as arthritis, chronic infections, and certain dietary deficiencies. Most illnesses that kill quickly, particularly acute infectious diseases such as influenza and pneumonia, do not leave their signature on the skeleton. Paleopathologists studying skeletal populations are therefore limited to a relatively narrow field of inquiry, although the development of new molecular techniques in recent years, as described in this chapter, holds new promise for the diagnosis of disease in ancient skeletons. Preservational conditions in such arid regions of the New World as the American Southwest and the west coast of South America provide unique opportunities for paleopathological research. Mummified human remains and well-preserved coprolites have been recovered from numerous archaeological sites in South America, some dating back as early as 9000 years BP (Muñoz *et al.*1993). The extremely dry western coast of Peru and Chile, in particular, provides an exceptional preservational environment, and spontaneous mummification of bodies is common.

Over the past 20 years, studies of these mummified remains have provided evidence of chronic infectious diseases such as tuberculosis and blastomycosis, as well as acute infectious diseases such as bronchopneumonia and lobar pneumonia. Mummy dissections and coprolite studies have provided additional insight into intestinal parasite infestation in precontact populations of the Americas.

Although the roots of paleopathological studies of South American mummies can be traced back to the beginnings of this century, the first systematic studies of pathology in South American mummies were pioneered in the early 1970s by Allison, Gerszten, and colleagues (Allison and Gerszten 1975). These studies involved the autopsies of mummies from numerous archaeological sites in coastal Peru and Chile. This work has been important not only in documenting the presence of various disease conditions in pre-Columbian populations, but also in calling attention to the exceptional research potential of South American mummies (Allison 1979).

After some years of quiescence, the past decade has seen renewed intensity in the study of South American mummies, brought about in part by the development of new laboratory techniques for paleodietary analysis and for the extraction and amplification of DNA from bone and mummified tissue. Research questions have evolved as well, reflecting the application of paleo-demographic and epidemiological models to the identification of disease in the archaeological record.

Studies of disease and general health conditions in pre-Columbian South American populations fall into two broad categories: case reports and population studies. Case reports, which document specific pathologic conditions in single specimens (Allison *et al.* 1973, 1974, 1979; Kelley and Lytle 1995), have been important in establishing the presence of particular diseases in pre-Columbian New World cultures. Population studies examine broader patterns of morbidity across space and time. Some of these focus on a single disease, such as tuberculosis or Carrión's disease, and use demographic or epidemiological models to explain the observed frequencies and characteristics of skeletal and soft tissue lesions (Schultz 1968; Buikstra and Williams 1991; Arriaza *et al.* 1995). Others look at general indicators of community health such as childhood growth, anemia, non-specific bone infection, and dental disease (Elzay *et al.*1977; Allison 1984; Ubelaker 1992; Benfer 1990; Kelley *et al.*1991). All three kinds of studies have made important contributions to the understanding of patterns of health and disease in pre-Columbian South America (Verano and Ubelaker 1991; Verano 1992).

Recent decades have witnessed the development of new analytical tools for the reconstruction of ancient diet, for the evaluation of environmental health risks such as heavy metal poisoning, and for identifying the ingestion of particular medicinal plants like coca. Elemental and stable isotope analyses of ancient human tissue have been used successfully to reconstruct diet in various prehistoric populations from Peru and Chile (Burger and van der Merwe 1990; Aufderheide and Allison 1992; Verano and DeNiro 1993). The results of such studies have provided information on the relative importance of marine and terrestrial foods in their diets (Aufderheide and Allison 1992), the adaptation of highland immigrants to coastal environments (Aufderheide 1996), the relative contribution of particular cultigens such as maize to the diet (Burger and van der Merwe 1990), and the possible population affiliation of sacrificial victims (Verano and DeNiro 1993). Combined with dietary information that can be extracted from coprolites (Holden and Nuñez 1993), such studies have made significant advances in our understanding of ancient diet in South America. In an important series of studies, Cartmell and associates (Aufderheide 1996; Cartmell *et al.* 1991) have identified cocaine metabolites (from coca chewing) in the hair of mummies from coastal Chile. Positive results first show up in a single mummy dated to approximately 1000 BC, and become common in mummies from the later phases of the Alto Ramiro culture(AD 0–350). These results correlate well with archaeological evidence of increased cultural contact with the highlands (source of coca) during this time period. Trace element analysis has also been applied to evaluating environmental hazards to health, such as chronic arsenic poisoning from local water sources (Allison 1996).

Infectious disease

Tuberculosis There has been a long debate over whether tuberculosis was present in the New World in pre-Columbian times (Buikstra 1981). The number of reported examples of lesions suggestive of tuberculosis in

FIGURE 10.9. An example of probable tuber-culosis (Pott's spine) of the lumbar spine in an adult from the site of Kuelap in the high jungle of northern Peru. Late Intermediate Period or Late Horizon (AD 1000–1500). Museo Nacional de Antropología, Arqueología y Historia, Lima. (No catalog number. Field designation: Muro Perimetral, Sector 8, Forado 6.)

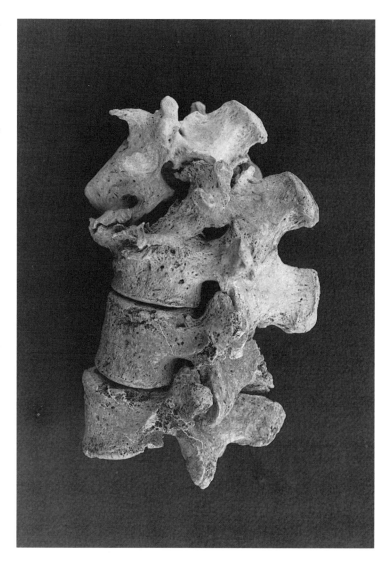

pre-Columbian skeletal remains has grown rapidly in recent decades (Figure 10.9), but confident diagnosis of many of these cases has remained elusive. Since the early 1970s, however, examination of South American mummies has provided increasingly convincing evidence that tuberculosis was indeed a pre-Columbian health problem.

In 1973, Allison, Mendoza, and Pezzia published the first diagnosis of pre-Columbian tuberculosis based on both skeletal and soft tissue evidence. The case involved the mummy of a child from a Nasca (c. AD 700) cemetery in southern coastal Peru. The mummy showed evidence of chronic bone and soft tissue disease suggestive of tuberculosis but, more important, Allison and colleagues were able to extract and identify acid-fast bacilli morphologically similar to *Mycobacterium tuberculosis*. Since this pioneering study, many additional cases of probable tuberculosis have been identified from skeletal and mummified remains from southern Peru and northern Chile (Allison *et al.* 1981; Buikstra and Williams 1991; Arriaza *et al.* 1995). Whereas differentiating bone lesions produced by tuberculosis from those by other diseases continues to present challenges (Buikstra 1981; Ortner and Putschar 1981), recent developments in ancient DNA recovery and amplification by polymerase chain reaction (PCR; see Chapter 16) have resulted in a major advance in the identification of tuberculosis in ancient tissues. Salo *et al.* (1994) recently reported the successful extraction of DNA characteristic of M. *tuberculosis* from a pre-Columbian mummy from southern Peru. Similar identifications of M. *tuberculosis* and M. *leprae* DNA in skeletal samples have been reported by other researchers, supporting the utility of PCR amplification of ancient DNA in the identification of pathogenic organisms (Spigelman and Lemma 1993; Rafi *et al.* 1994). It now appears indisputable that tuberculosis was present in the Americas before European contact.

Treponemal disease Since the late nineteenth century, there also has been debate over whether syphilis was present in pre-Columbian South America (Stewart 1950). Some suggestive cases have been illustrated by Weiss (1984), but convincing evidence of venereal or congenital syphilis in pre-Columbian skeletal remains has yet to be demonstrated. Some form of treponemal disease appears to have been present in prehistoric populations of northern Chile. Most cases consist of individuals with pronounced periosteal inflammation of the tibias, although one individual showed cranial involvement as well (Allison *et al.* 1982; Arriaza 1995). In a recent study, Rogan and Lentz (1994) report that they have successfully extracted ribosomal DNA (rDNA) characteristic of treponemal bacteria from the muscle tissue of four prehistoric individuals from El Morro, Arica and San Miguel de Azapa in northern Chile who showed characteristic tibial lesions. Thus, both skeletal and molecular evidence indicate that a treponemal disease such as yaws or endemic syphilis was present in Andean South American before European contact, although the specific nature of the disease and its mode of transmission are not fully understood.

Carrión's Disease Carrión's disease, also known as Bartonellosis, is caused by the bacterium *Bartonella bacilliformis*. Transmitted by sandflies, it is a disease that is endemic to certain highland valleys of modern-day Peru, Ecuador and Colombia. Carrión's disease manifests itself in two distinct forms – an acute form known as Oroya fever, which infects red blood cells and has a high mortality rate, and a relatively mild second stage, characterized by wart-like skin lesions, known as *verruga* (Schultz 1968; Recavarren and Lumbreras 1972).

In 1974, Allison and colleagues identified an example of the *verruga* phase of Carrión's disease in a pre-Columbian mummy dating to the Middle Horizon (AD 600–900) from the south coast of Peru (Allison *et al.* 1974). Their diagnosis was made on the basis of skin lesions containing clumps of bacilli morphologically similar to *Bartonella bacilliformis*. Interestingly, this was a mummy buried on the coast, in an area where Carrión's disease was presumably not endemic. The mummy, however, was from a cemetery showing highland (Huari) influence, and the individual may have been an immigrant from the highlands. No additional cases of Carrión's disease have been reported in mummies subsequent to this publication, although examples of ceramic vessels depicting individuals with verruga-like skin lesions are known from the Moche and Chancay cultures of central and northern coastal Peru (Moodie 1923; Schultz 1968; Weiss 1984).

Chagas' disease Chagas' Disease is caused by infection with the protozoan parasite *Trypanosoma cruzi*. The most common route of infection is through contact with the feces of reduviid bugs of the subfamily Triatominae, although other forms of transmission are known (Rothhammer *et al.* 1985). The most common species of reduviid bug found in Andean South America is *Triatoma infestans*, which frequently occupies the roofs and walls of houses in rural areas. After malaria, Chagas' disease is the most common vector-borne disease in present day Latin America (Rothhammer *et al.* 1985). Recent studies of South American mummies suggest that the disease has a long history of adaptation to human populations in the Andes. Rothhammer and colleagues (1985) reported nine possible cases of Chagas' disease in mummies from the Quebrada de Tarapacá in northern Chile approximately dated between 450 BC and AD 600. Their diagnosis was based on the presence of 'megavisceral syndromes' – enlargements of the colon, heart, or esophagus that are typical manifestations of infection with T. *cruzi*. More recently, Fornaciari and colleagues (1992) have reported a study of an Inca period mummy from Cuzco that showed similar megavisceral syndromes. Ultrastructural and immunohistochemical studies of the mummy indicated infection with T. *cruzi*.

Parasites

Recent studies of mummies and coprolites have demonstrated that some parasites previously thought to have been Old World introductions in fact plagued pre-Columbian New World populations. These include at least one species of hookworm, *Ancylostoma duodenale*, and the whipworm *Trichuris trichiura* (Allison *et al.* 1974). Research has also documented the presence of roundworms (*Ascaris lumbricoides*), marine tapeworm (*Diphyllobothrium pacificum*), pinworm (*Enterobius vermicularis*), hairworm (*Strongyloides* spp.), *Trichinella spiralis*, *Echinococcus granulosis*, and the ectoparasite *Pediculus humanus* (louse). *Entamoeba* spp. and *Moniliformis clarki*, a thorny-headed worm, were probably present as well (Confalonieri *et al.* 1991; Horne 1985; Patrucco *et al.* 1983; Reinhard 1990, 1992, Chapter 16). Coprolite samples from the central coast of Peru document the presence of tapeworm and roundworm in cultural strata dating to approximately 2800 BC, and pinworm at approximately 2300 BC. Although some parasites show great antiquity, most of the evidence has come from later agricultural populations living a sedentary village life.

Parasitism may, in part, provide a key to explaining regional variation in the frequency of porotic hyperostosis and cribra orbitalia in prehistoric Ecuador and Peru. Porotic hyperostosis and cribra orbitalia, porous lesions found on the external table of the skull vault and orbital roofs, are generally considered to represent a physiological response to iron deficiency anemia, which can be caused and exacerbated by a variety of factors, including dietary deficiencies, intestinal parasites, infectious disease, and their synergistic effects (Goodman *et al.* 1984). Hereditary anemias like sickle cell disease and thalassemia do not appear to have been present in the Americas in pre-Columbian times (Ortner and Putschar 1981). In his studies of skeletal samples from prehistoric Ecuador, Ubelaker (1992) found a significantly higher frequency of porotic hyperostosis in coastal populations. Ubelaker hypothesized that parasitism, due to hookworm and possibly other parasites that require warm and damp conditions to propagate, may have been a significant contributing factor, citing similar geographic patterning of hookworm infestation from modern clinical data in Ecuador. Hrdlička (1914) and Weiss (1961) found similar patterns in the frequency of porotic hyperostosis in prehistoric Peruvian crania from coastal and highland sites. Although parasitism is probably not the only factor that might explain these differences, Ubelaker believes it played a significant role in producing the distribution of porotic hyperostosis observed in prehistoric population samples from Peru and Ecuador.

Tumors

In a recent review of soft tissue tumors in paleopathology, Gerszten and Allison (1991) echo previous workers in noting how rarely they have been found in mummy studies. In autopsies of over 1000 mummies from Chile and Peru, they found only two examples of soft tissue tumors: a subcutaneous lipoma on the right side of the chest of an adolescent male, and a rhabdomyosarcoma on the right cheek of a male child approximately 12 to 18 months old. Tumors affecting bone, whether primary or metastatic in origin, are more common in the paleopathological literature, probably due to the much greater quantity of skeletal material available for study. Nevertheless, there is not a great number of cases noted in South American skeletal remains. One of the earliest reported and most visually impressive examples of a malignancy, probably a meningioma, was first described by MacCurdy (1923), from an Inca site near Cuzco (Figure 10.10). I found another possible example of a meningioma (Figure 10.11) while studying skeletal and mummified remains excavated by Tello at the site of Paracas on the south coast of Peru (Tello 1929), and have described several examples of tumors in skeletal remains from Pacatnamu on the north coast of Peru (Verano 1997). Merbs has described bony tumors from the Hrdlička Paleopathology Collection (Tyson and Alcauskas 1980), and Baraybar and Shimada (1993) have recently reported a probable case of metastatic carcinoma in an adult male from the site of Batán Grande on the north coast of Peru.

Population studies

In contrast to studies that focus on single diseases, some researchers have taken a broader approach and have attempted to identify general trends in human health through time in pre-Columbian South America. The focus of most of these studies is the effect of subsistence and settlement pattern changes on community health, as measured by the frequencies of skeletal and dental stress indicators such as Harris lines, enamel hypoplasias, periostitis, porotic hyperostosis, dental caries, and other indicators (Goodman *et al.* 1984). The results of these studies reveal some general patterns in health through time, and provide important baseline data with which future studies can be compared. Benfer and associates examined the early transition from migratory hunting and gathering to sedentary village life and incipient agriculture on the central coast of Peru at the site of La Paloma, which dates to between 8000 and 4500 BP (Benfer 1984, 1991). Based on the age distribution of burials in different occupational levels and the relative frequency of skeletal stress indicators, Benfer concluded that although the earliest inhabitants

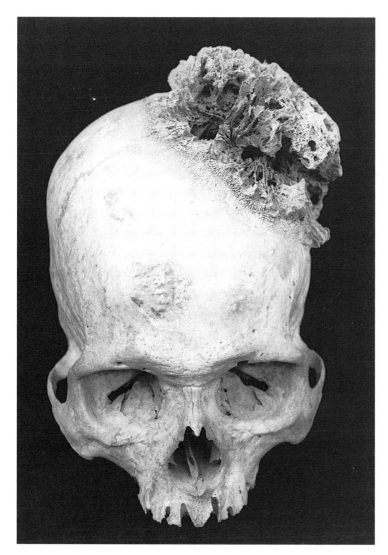

FIGURE 10.10. Cranium with probable meningioma in left parietal region. Recovered from a cave at Paucarcancha, an Inca site in the highlands northwest of Cuzco (MacCurdy 1923). Museo Nacional de Antropología, Arqueología y Historia, catalog number AF:6992.

of La Paloma were severely stressed, there was evidence of decreased infant mortality, greater adult life expectancy, and some indications of improved nutritional status with the adaptation to sedentism and incipient food production.

Based on a study of 16 populations from coastal Peru and Chile ranging in time from approximately 2000 BC to the early Colonial Period, Allison (1984) examined patterns of demography and disease through time. He found childhood mortality to be high, with nearly 50 percent of children in most samples dying before 15 years of age. No evidence of a general improvement in health was observed with the adoption of sedentism and intensification of

FIGURE 10.11. Cranium with probable meningioma from the site of Paracas on the south coast of Peru (Tello and Mejía 1979: Lámina XI D). Date: c. 500–200 BC. Museo Nacional de Antropología, Arqueología y Historia, catalog number AF:6921.

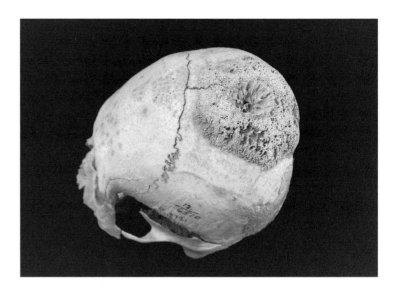

agricultural production. On the contrary, Allison interprets his data as indicating that sedentary village life was generally detrimental to health, due to crowding and sanitation problems, and that the increasing social stratification seen at some later sites resulted in health benefits only for the elite minority.

In a review of temporal trends in disease and demography in prehistoric Ecuador, Ubelaker (1992) concludes that although early populations of coastal Ecuador had low levels of infectious disease, anemia, dental caries, and various measures of nutritional stress, samples of human remains from more recent time periods show regular temporal increases in the frequencies of these problems. These frequency increases are particularly notable in coastal populations, and correlate with an increase in sedentism and a less varied diet.

Differences in the frequency of porotic hyperostosis in highland and coastal Andean skeletal samples suggest that parasite ecology, in addition to other factors such as settlement density and sanitary conditions, may have been a significant determinant of community health in prehistoric Andean populations. On the other hand, variability in the frequency of porotic hyperostosis among different coastal population samples, and between contemporary cemeteries at a single site, suggests that additional factors such as the degree of social stratification, local differences in residential pattern and settlement density, and differential access to dietary resources, also need to be considered in reconstructing the dynamics of community health at complex sites (Verano 1992).

Although Benfer's study of La Paloma suggests that there was some improvement in general health and life expectancy with the initial adaptation to sedentism and food production on the central coast of Peru, surveys of long-term temporal trends in skeletal pathology by Allison and Ubelaker point to a general deterioration in health conditions with increasing sedentism, agricultural intensification, and population growth. Studies of mummified human remains from coastal Peruvian and Chilean sites indicate that both chronic infectious diseases, such as tuberculosis, and acute pulmonary infections were significant factors in morbidity and mortality in prehistoric Andean populations. Coprolite studies have documented the presence of various intestinal parasites in Andean populations as early as 3000 BC, and some data suggest that parasite infestation may have been an important contributing factor in elevated frequencies of porotic hyperostosis seen in later prehistoric coastal Ecuadorian and Peruvian populations. Paleopathological evidence indicates that prehistoric South American populations faced significant health challenges in their adaptation to sedentism, agricultural production and population growth. With increasing population size and density came inevitable problems of sanitation, parasitism, and increase in infectious disease. Agricultural intensification and social stratification led to a less varied diet for many, exacerbating the effects of infectious disease and parasitism. It should be emphasized, however, that such problems were not unique to populations of prehistoric South America, but were challenges faced by human populations worldwide in the transition in lifestyle from mobile foragers to sedentary agriculturists (Cohen 1989).

Ancient surgery

Medical treatment in ancient times is a subject of continuing interest for paleopathologists. Although accurate knowledge of the causes and treatment of most diseases is a relatively recent development in the history of medicine, evidence of some forms of surgery is found surprisingly early in various parts of the world. Evidence of two forms of early surgery has been reported in prehistoric South American mummified and skeletal remains: trephination and amputation. In the case of amputation, only a few possible cases have been reported (Tyson and Alcauskas 1980; Merbs 1989; Anderson and Verano 1996), although artistic representations of individuals with missing limbs are well known from several north coastal Peruvian cultures (Donnan 1978; Urteaga-Ballon 1991). Evidence of trephination, in contrast, is extensive and widespread, both geographically and temporally.

Trephination (or trepanation), the surgical removal of a portion of the skull vault, is known to have been practiced in prehistoric times in many parts of the world. Andean South America stands out for having more examples of trephined skulls than all other geographic areas of the world combined. Stewart estimated that more than 1000 South American trephined skulls could be found in museums and private collections, and my own research indicates that this is a reasonable estimate (Stewart 1957; Verano 1996). Trephination is known to have been practiced widely in the region encompassed by the boundaries of modern Peru and Bolivia for over 2000 years, from circa 500 BC until the sixteenth century AD (Verano and Williams 1992; Verano 1996).

Since the late nineteenth century, when prehistoric trephined skulls were first described from Peru and Bolivia, there has been continued speculation about the motivation for the procedure. Early observers noted that trephinations were often associated with skull fracture, and suggested that the procedure might have been a practical treatment for acute head injury (MacCurdy 1923; Daland 1935; Stewart 1957). Others suggested different motivations for the practice, including the treatment of headaches, the removal of tumors, and the release of spirits (Muñiz and McGee 1897; Moodie 1929; Canalis *et al.* 1981; Weiss 1984; Mann 1991). Although some theories are more plausible than others, most arguments have been based on very small samples or even single specimens. Unfortunately, few researchers have systematically collected data on large samples of trephined skulls.

Four principal trephination techniques were practiced in Andean South America: scraping, linear cutting, circular grooving, and boring and cutting (Lisowski 1967; Merbs 1989). Scraping was the earliest technique practiced. It appeared on the south coast of Peru circa 500 BC, and continued to be a popular technique in later times. The linear cutting technique is most characteristic of the central highlands of Peru, although trephinations by both the scraping, and the boring and cutting techniques are also found in this area, as well as in the highland valleys and high jungle of northern Peru. Circular grooving appears later, and is characteristic of the southern highlands of Peru during the Inca Empire. In general, a trend can be seen towards a reduction in the size of trephination openings through time, although there is substantial variability within samples. The largest trephinations are found in the early samples from the south coast, whereas the smallest are found in the southern highlands during the Inca Empire (Verano and Williams 1992; Verano 1996). Many South American trephinations are clearly associated with skull fracture (Figure 10.12). Depressed skull fractures are common in skeletal collections from Peru, with particularly high frequencies found in areas

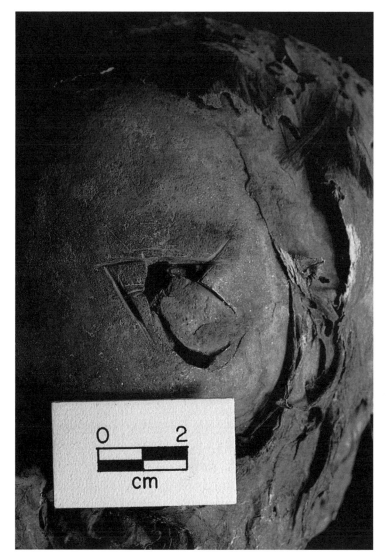

FIGURE 10.12. Incomplete trephination by the linear cutting method at the site of a depressed skull fracture (left frontal squama). Mummified head from the vicinity of Huarochiri, Peru. Dating is uncertain, but probably prehistoric (Muñiz and McGee 1897). National Museum of Natural History, Smithsonian Institution, catalog number 178482.

such as the central highlands (Verano and Williams 1992; Verano 1996). The majority of these injuries were probably produced by blows from clubs and sling stones, weapons widely used in the Andes in prehistoric times, although some fractures may have been the result of falls or other accidents. In these cases, the objective of the trephination was presumably to elevate or remove depressed bone fragments, smooth broken edges, and, possibly, evacuate epidural hematomas. Although there is no soft tissue evidence to confirm this, practitioners probably learned to avoid penetration of the dura mater, due to the high risk of infection and physical damage to the brain.

FIGURE 10.13. Inca cranium showing four well-healed trephinations by the grooving or scraping technique. Museo Arqueológico de la Universidad Nacional de San Antonio Abbad, Cuzco, catalog number 2580.

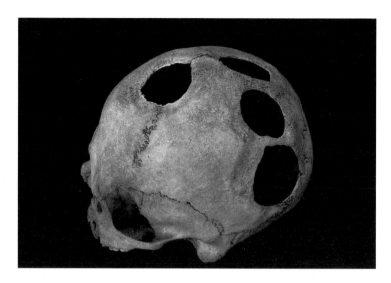

A significant percentage of South American trephinations show evidence of healing, indicating survival following the procedure (Stewart 1956, 1957; Lastres and Cabieses 1960). Healing can be classified into three general categories, based on the degree of bony reaction to the trephination: (1) none, where there is no evidence of bony reaction, suggesting that death occurred during the procedure or shortly thereafter; (2) short-term survival, where evidence of osteoclastic activity, bone necrosis, or hypervascularity is evident around the margins of the trephination opening, indicating survival perhaps for several weeks, and (3) long-term survival, where there is evidence of extensive remodeling of the margins of the defect. In general, trephinations by the scraping and by the circular grooving technique seem to show the highest success rate, whereas trephinations by straight cutting or by drilling and cutting show the lowest. This probably reflects the fact that penetration of the dura mater was more frequent with the latter two techniques. The most impressive cases of healing are found in some crania from Inca sites that show from four to seven well-healed trephinations (Figure 10.13). Overall, the Inca appear to have developed the most successful methods, as data I have collected show a long-term survival rate of over 70 percent for Inca trephinations, in contrast to a roughly 40 percent survival rate for the earliest trephinations from southern coastal Peru (Verano and Williams 1992; Verano 1996). Such statistics certainly compare favorably with the 25 percent or lower survival rate of neurosurgery patients in nineteenth and early twentieth century Europe and North America (Aufderheide 1985).

REFERENCES

Chinchorro mummies of Peru and Chile

Allison, M., Focacci, G., Arriaza, B., Standen, V., Rivera, M. and Lowenstein. J. 1984. Chinchorro momias de preparación complicada: métodos de momificación. *Chungará* **13**: 155–73.

Arriaga, P. J. [1621] 1968. *The extirpation of idolatry in Peru.* Transl. and ed. C. Keating. Reprint. Lexington: University of Kentucky Press.

Arriaza, B. T. 1994. Tipología de las momias Chinchorro y evolución de las prácticas de momificación. *Chungará* **26**(1): 11–24.

Arriaza, B. T. 1995a. Chile's Chinchorro mummies. *National Geographic* **187**(3): 68–89.

Arriaza, B. T. 1995b. *Beyond death: the Chinchorro mummies of ancient Chile.* Washington, DC: Smithsonian Institution Press.

Aufderheide, A. C. and Allison, M. J. 1992. Chemical dietary reconstruction of north Chile prehistoric populations by trace mineral analysis. In *Proceedings of the I World Congress on Mummy Studies*, vol. 2, 451–61. Santa Cruz de Tenerife:Museo Arqueológico y Etnográfico de Tenerife.

Binford, L. R. 1971. Mortuary practices. Their study and their potential. In *Approaches to the social dimensions of mortuary practices*, ed. J. A. Brown, 6–29. Washington, DC: Society for American Archaeology Memoirs.

Bittmann, B. 1982. Revisión del problema Chinchorro. *Chungará* **9**: 46–79.

Bittmann, B. and Munizaga, J. 1976. The earliest artificial mummification in the world? A study of the Chinchorro Complex in northern Chile. *Folk* **18**: 61–92.

Brown, J. A. 1981. The search for rank in prehistoric burials. In *The archaeology of death*, ed. R. Chapman, I. Kinnes, and K. Randsborg, 25–37. Cambridge: Cambridge University Press.

Chapman, R., Kinnes, I. and Randsborg, K., eds. 1981. *The archaeology of death.* Cambridge: Cambridge University Press.

Cobo, B. 1964. Historia del Nuevo Mundo [1653]. In *Obras del P. Bernabe Cobo. Vol 2. Biblioteca de autores Españoles.* ed. F. Mateos. Madrid: Ediciones Atlas.

Fox, S. 1996. The mortuary practices on children. Thesis. University of Nevada, Las Vegas.

Guillén, S. 1992. The Chinchorro culture: mummies and crania in the reconstruction of preceramic coastal adaptation in the south central Andes. Doctoral dissertation, University of Michigan, Ann Arbor.

Hapke, R. 1996. An evolution of creativity and ritual: the immortalizing craftsmanship of the Chinchorro morticians. Thesis. University of Nevada, Las Vegas. 1996.

Mostny, G. 1944. Excavaciones en Arica. *Boletín del Museo Nacional de Historia Natural* **22**:135–45.

Núñez, L. 1969. Sobre los complejos culturales Chinchorro y Faldas del Morro del norte de Chile. *Rehue* **2**:111–42.

Reinhard, K. J. and Aufderheide, A. C.1990. 'Diphyllobothriasis in pre-Columbian Chile and Peru. Adaptive radiation of a helminth species to Native American populations.' Paper presented at the VIIIth European Members Meeting of the Paleopathology Association, Cambridge, (UK), September 1990. Abstract in *Paleopathology Newsletter* **70** (supplement):18.

Rivera, M. 1991. The prehistory of northern Chile: a synthesis. *Journal of World Prehistory* **5**: 1–47.

Salomon, F. 1991. 'The beautiful grandparents: Andean ancestor shrines and mortuary ritual as seen through colonial records.' Paper presented at the conference Tombs for the living: Andean mortuary practices. Dumbarton Oaks, Washington, DC, October.

Schiappacasse, F. and Niemeyer, H., eds. 1984. *Descripción y análisis interpretativo de un sitio arcaico temprano en la Quebrada de Camarones.* Publicación ocasional, no. 41. Santiago: Museo Nacional de Historia Natural.

Standen, V. 1991. El cemeterio Morro 1: nuevas evidencias de la tradición funeraria Chinchorro (período arcaico, norte de Chile). Thesis. Universidad Católica de Lima, Perú.

Standen, V., Allison, M. and Arriaza, B. 1984. Patologías óseas de la población Morro-1, asociada al complejo Chinchorro: norte de Chile. *Chungará* **13**:175–85.

Standen, V., Allison, M. and Arriaza, B. 1985. Osteoma del conducto auditivo externo: hipótesis en torno a una posible patología laboral prehispánica. *Chungará* **15**: 197–209.

Thomson, B. 1987. *Gauguin*. London: Thames and Hudson.

Uhle, M. 1922. *Fundamentos étnicos y arqueología de Arica y Tacna*. Quito: Sociedad Ecuatoriana de Estudios Históricos.

Urioste, G. 1981. Sickness and death in preconquest Andean cosmology: the Huarochirí oral tradition. In *Health in the Andes*, ed. J. Bastien and J. Donahue, 9–18. Washington, DC: American Anthropological Association.

Wise, K. 1991. 'Complexity and variation in mortuary practices during the preceramic period in the south central Andes.' Paper presented at the Annual Meeting of the American Anthropological Association, Chicago, November.

Mummies from Colombia and other South American Areas

Anthony, R. and Rivet, P. 1908. Etude anthropologique des races précolombiennes de la République de l'Equateur. Recherches anatomiques sur les ossements (os des membres) des abris sous roches de Paltacalo. *Bulletins et Mémoires de la Société d'Antropologie de Paris* (5a série) **9**: 314–430.

Arriaza, B. T. 1995. *Beyond death: the chinchorro mummies of ancient Chile*. Washington, DC: Smithsonian Institution Press.

Beck, L. A. 1995. *Regional approaches to mortuary analysis*. New York: Plenum.

Cardale Schrimpff, M. 1986. Painted textiles from caves in the Eastern Cordillera, Colombia. In *The Junius Bird Conference in Andean Textiles*, ed. A. Rowe, 205–17. Washington DC: The Textile Museum.

Cárdenas-Arroyo, F. 1989. La momificación indígena en Colombia. *Boletín Museo del Oro* 25:120–3.

Cárdenas-Arroyo, F. 1990. La momia de Pisba, Boyacá. *Boletín Museo del Oro* 27: 3–13.

Cárdenas-Arroyo, F. 1992. Momias, santuarios y ofrendas: el contexto ritual de la momificación en el altiplano central de los Andes colombianos. In *Proceedings of the I World Congress on Mummy Studies*, 633–42. Santa Cruz de Tenerife: Museo Arqueológico y Etnográfico de Tenerife.

Cieza de León, P. 1962 [1553]. *La crónica del Perú*. Madrid: Espasa Calpe S. A.

Correal-Urrego, G. and Flórez, I. 1992. Estudio de las momias guanes de la Mesa de Los Santos, departamento de Santander (Colombia). In *Proceedings of the I World Congress on Mummy Studies*, 307–13. Santa Cruz de Tenerife: Museo Arqueológico y Etnográfico de Tenerife.

Dawson, W. R. 1928. Two mummies from Colombia. *Man* 53:73–4.

Drennan, R. D. 1995. Mortuary practices in the Alto Magdalena: the social context of the 'San Agustín Culture'. In *Tombs for the living: Andean mortuary practices*, ed. T. D. Dillehay, 79–110. Washington, DC: Dumbarton Oaks Research Library and Collection.

Fernández de Oviedo y Valdés, G. 1851 [1532]. *Historia general y natural de las Indias, islas y tierrafirme del mar océano*. Madrid: Biblioteca de Autores Españoles.

Guhl-Nanneti, F. and Cárdenas-Arroyo, F. 1992. *Paleoparasitología, paleopatología y genética prehispánica: un estudio interdisciplinario en momias arqueológicas*. Bogotá: Banco de La República.

Guzmán, E. and Gómez Garzón, J. 1988 [1595]. Santuarios indígenas en el repartimiento de Iguaque. *Revista de Antropología* **4**(2): 217–50.

Holden, T. 1989. Preliminary work on South American mummies held at the British Museum. *Paleopathology Newsletter* **65**: 5–9.

Langebaek, C. H. 1992. Competencia por prestigio político y momificación en el norte de Suramérica y el itsmo de Panamá. *Revista Colombiana de Antropología* **29**: 7–26.

Linné, S. 1929. *Darién in the past. The archaeology of Eastern Panama and Northwestern Colombia*. Handlingar Fjärde Följden, Serie A, Band 1(3). Göteborg: Göteborgs Kungl. Vetenskaps och Vitterherts Samhälles.

López, P. 1970 [1572]. *Ruta de Cartagena de Indias a Buenos Aires y sublevaciones de Pizarro, Castilla y Hernández Girón 1540–1570*. Madrid: Ediciones Atlas.

Malinowski, B. 1974. *Magia, ciencia, religión*. Barcelona: Ariel.

Mártir de Anglería, P. 1944 [1574]. *Décadas del Nuevo Mundo*. Buenos Aires: Editorial Bajel.

Monsalve, M. V., Cárdenas-Arroyo, F., Guhl, F., Delaney, AD and Devine, D. V. 1996. Phylogenetic analysis of mtDNA lineages in South American Mummies. *Annals of Human Genetics* **60**: 293–303.

Monsalve, M. V., Groot, H., Espinel, A., Correal, O. and Devine, D. V. 1994. Evidence of mitochondrial DNA diversity in South American aboriginals. *Annals of Human Genetics* **58**: 265–73.

Reichel-Dolmatoff, O. 1945. Los indios motilones. Etnografía y lingüística. *Revista del Instituto Etnológico Nacional (Bogotá)* **2**(1): 15–115.

Salazar, E. 1995. *Entre mitos y fábulas. El Ecuador aborigen.* Quito: Corporación Editora Nacional.

Salo, W., Aufderheide, A. C., Buikstra, J. and Holcomb, T. A. 1994. Identification of *Mycobacterium tuberculosis* DNA in a pre-Columbian Peruvian mummy. *Proceedings of the National Academy of Science (USA)* **91**: 2091–4.

Schottelius, J. W. 1946. Arqueología de la Mesa de Los Santos. *Boletín de Arqueología* **2**(3):213–25

Schurr, T. G., Ballinger, S. W., Gan, Y., Hodge, J. A, Merriwether, D. A., Lawrence, D. N., Knowler, W. C., Weiss, K. M. and Wallace, D. C. 1990. Amerindian mitochondrial DNAs have rare Asian mutations at high frequencies, suggesting they derived from four primary maternal lineages. *American Journal of Human Genetics* **46**: 613–23.

Stothert, K. E. 1988. *La prehistoria temprana de la península de Santa Helena, Ecuador: cultura Las Vegas.* Miscelánea Antropológica Ecuatoriana, Serie Monográfica No.10. Guayaquil: Museos del Banco Central del Ecuador.

Ubelaker, D. 1980. Human skeletal remains from site OGSE-80, a preceramic site on the Sta. Elena Peninsula, Coastal Ecuador. *Journal of the Washington Academy of Sciences* **70**(1): 3–24.

Ubelaker, D. 1981. *The Ayalán Cemetery: a Late Integration Period burial site of the south coast of Ecuador.* Smithsonian Contributions to Anthropology No.29. Washington, DC: Smithsonian Institution Press

Villalba, Marcelo. 1988. *Cotocollao: una aldea formativa del valle de Quito.* Miscelánea Antropológica Ecuatoriana, Serie Monográfica No.2. Quito: Museos del Banco Central del Ecuador.

Vreeland, J. M. and Cockburn, A. 1980. Mummies of Peru. In *Mummies, disease and ancient cultures,* ed. A. Cockburn and E. Cockburn, 135–74. New York: Cambridge University Press.

Shrunken Heads

Baudez, C. F. 1970. *Mittelamerika (Archaeologia Mundi).* München: Nagel Verlag.

Cranstone, B. A. L. 1961. *Melanesia: a short ethnography.* London: British Museum.

Gusinde, M. 1937. Schädelkult, Kopftrophäe und Skalp. *Ciba Zeitschrift* **5**(49): 1678–705.

Hansmann, L. and Kriss-Rettenbeck, L. 1966. *Amulett und Talisman.* München: Callwey Verlag.

Heine-Geldern, R. v. 1924. *Kopfjagd und Menschenopfer in Assam und Birma.* Vienna: Anthropologischen Gesellschaft.

Karsten, R. 1923. *Blood revenge, war and victory feasts among Jíbaro Indians of Eastern Ecuador.* Smithsonian Institution, bulletin 79. Washington, DC: Smithsonian Institution Press.

Kleiss, E. 1966. Tsantsas: ein Mythus wird Maskottchen. *Wiener Tierärztliche Monatsschrift* **53**: 482.

Kleiss, E. 1975. La momificación natural y artificial. *Arquivos de Anatomia e Antropología* **1**: 37–56.

Kleiss, E. 1981/82. Los albores de los conocimientos anatomicós entre los pueblos primitivos y antiquos. *Arquivos de Anatomia e Antropología* **6/7**:61–112.

Kleiss, E. 1984. Kopfjägerei und Haarzauber (Mumien 2. Teil). *Anatomisher Anzeiger (Jena)* **156**: 389–401.

Kleiss, E. 1989. Haare einmal ganz anders. *Kosmetik International* **1989** (7): 10–7.

Kleiss, E. and Simonsberger, P. 1964. *La parafinización como método morfológico.* Mérida: Universidad de los Andes.

Paredes Borja, V. 1963. *Historia de la medicina en el Ecuador.* Quito: Casa de la Cultura Ecuatoriana.

Sowada, A. (O. S. C.) 1968. New Guinea's fierce Asmat: a heritage of headhunting. In *Vanishing people of the earth.* Washington, DC: National Geographic Society.

Diseases in South American mummies

Allison, M. J. 1979. Paleopathology in Peru. *Natural History* **88**(2): 74–82.

Allison, M. J. 1984. Paleopathology in Peruvian and Chilean populations. In *Paleopathology at the origins of agriculture,* ed. M. N. Cohen and G. J. Armelagos, 531–58. Orlando, FL: Academic Press.

Allison, M. J. 1996. 'Chronic arsenic poisoning in South American Mummies.' Paper presented at the annual meeting of the International Academy of Pathology, Washington, DC, March 1996.

Allison, M. J. and Gerszten, E. 1975. *Paleopathology in South American mummies: application of modern techniques.* Richmond: Medical College of Virginia.

Allison, M. J., Focacci, G., Fouant, M. and Cebelin, M. 1982. La Sífilis. ¿Una enfermedad Americana? *Revista Chungará* **9**: 275–84.

Allison, M. J., Gerszten, E., Munizaga, J., Santoro, C. and Mendoza, D. 1981. Tuberculosis in Pre-Columbian Andean Populations. In *Prehistoric Tuberculosis in the Americas*, ed. J. Buikstra, 49–61. Evanston, IL: Northwestern University Archaeological Program.

Allison, M. J., Gerszten, E., Shadomy, H. J., Munizaga, J. and Gonzales, M. 1979. Paracoccidioidomycosis in a mummy. *Bulletin of the New York Academy of Medicine* **55**: 670–83.

Allison, M. J., Mendoza, D. and Pezzia, A. 1973. Documentation of a case of tuberculosis in Pre-Columbian America. *American Review of Respiratory Diseases* **107**: 985–91.

Allison, M. J., Pezzia, A., Gerszten, E. and Mendoza, D. 1974. A case of hookworm infestation in a Pre-Columbian American. *American Journal of Physical Anthropology* **41**: 103–5.

Anderson, L. S. and Verano, J. W. 1996. 'A possible case of amputation of the feet, with evidence of healing, in a Moche burial from the north coast of Peru.' Paper presented at the Twenty Third Annual Meeting of the Paleopathology Association, Durham, North Carolina, April, 1996. Abstract in *Paleopathology Newsletter* **94**(supplement):16.

Anderson, L. S. and Verano, J. W. 1995. *Beyond death: the chinchorro mummies of ancient Chile*. Washington, DC: Smithsonian Institution Press.

Arriaza, B. T., Salo, W., Aufderheide, A. C. and Holcomb, T. A. 1995. Pre-Columbian tuberculosis in northern Chile: molecular and skeletal evidence. *American Journal of Physical Anthropology*. **98**(1): 37–45.

Aufderheide, A. C. 1985. The enigma of ancient cranial trepanation. *Minnesota Medicine* **68**(2): 119–22.

Aufderheide, A. C. 1996. Secondary applications of bio-anthropological studies on South American Andean mummies. In *Human mummies: a global survey of their status and the techniques of conservation. Vol. 3. The man in the ice*, ed. K. Spindler, H. Wilfing, E. Rastbichler-Zissernig, D. zur Nedden, and H. Nothdurfter, 141–51. Wien: Springer Verlag.

Aufderheide, A. C. and Allison, M. J. 1992. Chemical dietary reconstruction of north Chile prehistoric populations by trace mineral analysis. In *Proceedings of the I World Congress on Mummy Studies*, vol. 2, 451–61. Santa Cruz de Tenerife:Museo Arqueológico y Etnográfico de Tenerife.

Baraybar, J. P. and Shimada, I. 1993. A possible case of metastatic carcinoma in a Middle Sican burial from Batán Grande, Perú. *International Journal of Osteoarchaeology* **3**: 129–35.

Benfer, R. A. 1984. The challenges and rewards of sedentism: The preceramic village of Paloma, Peru. In *Paleopathology at the origins of agriculture*, ed. M. N. Cohen and G. J. Armelagos, 531–58. Orlando, Fl.: Academic Press.

Benfer, R. A. 1991. The preceramic period site of Paloma, Peru: bioindications of improving adaptation to sedentism. *Latin American Antiquity* **1**(4): 284–318.

Buikstra, J. E., ed. 1981. *Prehistoric tuberculosis in the Americas*. Evanston, IL: Northwestern University Archaeological Program.

Buikstra, J. E. and Williams, S. 1991. Tuberculosis in the Americas: current perspectives. In *Human paleopathology: current syntheses and future options*, ed. D. J. Ortner and A. C. Aufderheide, 161–72. Washington, DC: Smithsonian Institution Press.

Burger, R. L. and van der Merwe, N. J. 1990. Maize and the origin of highland Chavin civilization: an isotopic perspective. *American Anthropologist* **92**: 85–95.

Canalis, R. F., Hemenway, W. G., Cabieses, F. and Aragon, R. 1981. Prehistoric trephination of the frontal sinus. *Annals of Otology, Rhinology, and Laryngology* **90**: 186–9.

Cartmell, L. W., Aufderheide, A. C., Springfield, A., Weems, C. and Arriaza, B. 1991. The frequency and antiquity of prehistoric coca-leaf-chewing practices in northern Chile: radioimmunoassay of a cocaine metabolite in Human-mummy hair. *Latin American Antiquity* **2**(3): 260–8.

Cohen, M. N. 1989. *Health and the rise of civilization*. New Haven: Yale University Press.

Confalonieri, U. E. C., Ferreira, L. F., Araújo, A. J. G., Chame, M. and Ribeiro Filho, B. M. 1991. Trends and perspectives in paleoparasitological research. In *Human paleopathology: current syntheses and future options*, ed. D. J. Ortner and A. C. Aufderheide, 76–8. Washington, DC: Smithsonian Institution Press.

Daland, J. 1935. Depressed fracture and trephining of the skull by the Incas of Peru. *Annals of Medical History* **7**: 550–8.

Donnan, C. B. 1978. *Moche art of Peru: pre-Columbian symbolic communication.* Los Angeles: Museum of Cultural History, University of California.

Elzay, R. P., Allison, M. J. and Pezzia, A. 1977. A comparative study on the dental health status of five pre-columbian Peruvian cultures. *American Journal of Physical Anthropology* **46**: 135–40.

Fornaciari, G., Castagna, M., Viacava, P., Tognetti, A., Bevilacqua, G. and Segura, E. L. 1992. Chagas' disease in a Peruvian Inca mummy. *Lancet* **339**: 128–9.

Gerszten, E. and Allison, M. J. 1991. Human soft tissue tumors in paleopathology. In *Human paleopathology: current syntheses and future options,* ed. D. J. Ortner and A. C. Aufderheide, 257–60. Washington, DC: Smithsonian Institution Press.

Goodman, A. H., Martin, D. L., Armelagos, G. J and Clark, G. 1984. Indications of stress from bone and teeth. In *Paleopathology at the Origins of agriculture,* ed. M. N. Cohen and G. J. Armelagos, 13–49. New York: Academic Press.

Holden, T. G. and Nuñez, L. 1993. An analysis of the gut contents of five well-preserved human bodies from Tarapacá, northern Chile. *Journal of Archaeological Science* **20**: 595–611.

Horne, P. D. 1985. A review of the evidence of human endoparasitism in the pre-Columbian New World through the study of coprolites. *Journal of Archaeological Science* **12**: 299–310.

Hrdlička, A. 1914. Anthropological work in Peru in 1913, with notes on the pathology of the ancient Peruvians. *Smithsonian Miscellaneous Collections* **61**(18): 57–69

Kelley, M. A. and Lytle, K. 1995. Brief communication: a possible case of melorheostosis from antiquity. *American Journal of Physical Anthropology* **98**(3): 369–74.

Kelley, M. A., Levesque, D. R. and Weidl, E. 1991. Contrasting patterns of dental disease in five early northern Chilean groups. In *Advances in dental anthropology,* ed. M. A. Kelley and C. Spencer Larsen, 203–13. New York: Wiley-Liss.

Lastres, J. B. and Cabieses, F. 1960. *La trepanación del craneo en el antiguo Peru.* Lima: Universidad Nacional Mayor de San Marcos.

Lisowski, F. P. 1967. Prehistoric and early historic trepanation. In *Diseases in antiquity,* ed. D. R. Brothwell and A. T. Sandison, 651–72. Springfield, IL: Charles C. Thomas.

MacCurdy, G. G. 1923. Human skeletal remains from the highlands of Peru. *American Journal of Physical Anthropology* **6**: 217–329.

Mann, G. 1991. Chronic ear disease as a possible reason for trephination. *International Journal of Osteoarchaeology* **1**: 165–8.

Merbs, C. F. 1989. Trauma. In *Reconstruction of life from the skeleton,* ed. M. Y. Iscan and K. A. R. Kennedy, 161–89. New York: Alan R. Liss.

Moodie, R. L. 1923. *Paleopathology, an introduction to the study of ancient evidences of disease.* Urbana: University of Illinois Press.

Moodie, R. L. 1929. Studies in paleopathology, XXIII, surgery in pre-columbian Peru. *Annals of Medical History* **1**: 698–728.

Muñiz, M. A. and McGee, W. J 1897. Primitive trephining in Peru.16th Annual Report of the Bureau of American Ethnology for 1894–95, 3–72. Washington, DC: Government Printing Office.

Muñoz, I., Arriaza, B. and Aufderheide, A., eds. 1993. *Acha-2 y los origines del poblamiento humano en Arica.* Arica, Chile: Universidad de Tarapacá.

Ortner, D. J. 1992. Skeletal paleopathology: probabilities, possibilities, and impossibilities. In *Disease and demography in the Americas,* ed. J. W. Verano and D. H. Ubelaker, 5–13. Washington, DC: Smithsonian Institution Press.

Ortner, D. J. and Putschar, W. G. J. 1981. *Identification of pathological conditions in human skeletal remains.* Washington, DC: Smithsonian Institution Press.

Patrucco, R., Tello, R. and Bonavia, D. 1983. Parasitological studies of coprolites of Pre-Hispanic Peruvian populations. *Current Anthropology* **24**(3): 393–4.

Rafi, A., Spigelman, M., Stanford, J., Lemma, E., Donoghue, H. and Zias, J. 1994. DNA of *Mycobacterium leprae* detected by PCR in ancient bone. *International Journal of Osteoarchaeology* **4**:287–90.

Recavarren, S. and Lumbreras, H. 1972. Pathogenesis of the verruga of Carrión's disease, ultrastructural studies. *American Journal of Pathology* **66**(3): 461–4.

Reinhard, K. J. 1990. Archaeoparasitology in North America. *American Journal of Physical Anthropology* **82**(2): 145–63.

Reinhard, K. J. 1992. Parasitology as an interpretive tool in archaeology. *American Antiquity* **57**(2): 231–45.

Rogan, P. and Lentz, S. 1994. Molecular evidence suggesting treponematosis in pre-Columbian Chilean mummies. *American Journal of Physical Anthropology* **18**: 171–2.

Rothhammer, F., Allison, M. J., Nuñez, L., Standen, V. and Arriaza, B. 1985. Chagas' disease in pre-Columbian South America. *American Journal of Physical Anthropology* **68**: 495–8.

Salo, W. L., Aufderheide, A. C., Buikstra, J. and Holcomb, T. 1994. Identification of *Mycobacterium tuberculosis* DNA in a pre-Columbian Peruvian mummy. *Proceedings of the National Academy of Sciences* **91**: 2091–4.

Schultz, M. G. 1968. A history of bartonellosis (Carrión's disease). *The American Journal of Tropical Medicine and Hygiene* **17**(4): 503–15.

Spigelman, M. and Lemma, E. 1993. The use of the polymerase chain reaction (PCR) to detect *Mycobacterium tuberculosis* in ancient skeletons. *International Journal of Osteoarchaeology* **3**: 137–43.

Stewart, T. D. 1950. Pathological changes in South American Indian skeletal remains. In *Handbook of South American Indians*, Vol. 6, ed. J. H. Steward, 49–52. Bureau of American Ethnology, Bulletin 143. Washington, DC: Smithsonian Institution Press.

Stewart, T. D. 1956. Significance of osteitis in ancient Peruvian trephining. *Bulletin of the History of Medicine* **30**(4): 293–320.

Stewart, T. D. 1957. Stone Age skull surgery: a general review, with emphasis on the New World. *Annual Report of the Smithsonian Institution*, 469–91. Washington, DC: Smithsonian Institution Press.

Tello, J. C. 1929. *Antiguo Perú, primera epoca*. Lima: Comisión Organizadora del Segundo Congreso Sudamericano de Turismo.

Tello, J. C. and Mejia Xesspe, T. 1979. *Paracas, segunda parte: cavernas y necrópolis*. Lima: Universidad Nacional Mayor de San Marcos, Dirección Universitaria de Biblioteca y Publicaciones.

Tyson, R. A. and Alcauskas, E. S. D. 1980. *Catalogue of the Hrdlička Collection*. San Diego: San Diego Museum of Man.

Ubelaker, D. H. 1992. Porotic hyperostosis in prehistoric Ecuador. In *Diet, demography and disease: changing perspectives on anemia*, ed. P. Stuart-Macadam and S. Kent, 201–17. New York: Aldine de Gruyter.

Urteaga-Ballon, O. 1991. Medical ceramic representation of nasal leishmaniasis and surgical amputation in ancient Peruvian civilization. In *Human paleopathology, current syntheses and future options*, ed. D. J. Ortner and A. C. Aufderheide, 95–101 Washington, DC: Smithsonian Institution Press.

Verano, J. W. 1992. Prehistoric disease and demography in the Andes. In *Disease and demography in the Americas*, ed. J. W. Verano and D. H. Ubelaker, 15–24. Washington, DC: Smithsonian Institution Press.

Verano, J. W. 1996. 'La trepanación como tratamiento terapéutico para fracturas craneales en el antiguo Peru.' Paper presented at the VIII Coloquio Internacional de Antropología Física 'Juan Comas', Mexico City, November, 1996.

Verano, J. W. 1997. Physical characteristics and skeletal biology of the Moche population at Pacatnamu. In *The Pacatnamu papers*, Vol. 2, *The Moche occupation*, ed. C. B. Donnan and G. A. Cock, 189–214. Los Angeles: Fowler Museum of Cultural History, University of California, Los Angeles.

Verano, J. W. and DeNiro, M. J. 1993. Local or foreigners? Biometric and isotopic approaches to the question of group affinity in human skeletal remains recovered from unusual archaeological context. In *Investigations of ancient human tissue: chemical analysis in anthropology*, ed. M. K. Sandford, 361–86. Amsterdam: Gordon and Breach.

Verano, J. W. and Ubelaker, D. H. 1991. Health and disease in the pre-Columbian world. In *Seeds of change, a quincentennial commemoration*, ed. H. J. Viola and C. Margolis, 209–23. Washington, DC: Smithsonian Institution Press.

Verano, J. W. and Williams, J. M. 1992. Head injury and surgical intervention in pre-Columbian Peru. Abstract in *American Journal of Physical Anthropology*, Supplement 14, 167–8.

Weiss, P. 1961. *Osteología cultural: practicas cefálicas*. Vol. 2. Lima: Universidad Nacional Mayor de San Marcos.

Weiss, P. 1984. Paleopatología Americana. *Boletín de Lima* **33**: 17–52.

PART III

Mummies of the world

11

Bog bodies of Denmark and north-western Europe

CHRISTIAN FISCHER

Bog bodies are usually considered a northwest European phenomenon reflecting specific forms of sacrifice or punishment common among the Germanic peoples around the time of the birth of Christ, but recent discoveries and information about old obscure finds from Holland and the British Isles indicate that similar practices were observed there. Dieck (1965) noted that there were more than 1400 reported bog finds worldwide, a large percentage of them only body parts, varying in date from 9000 BC to World War II, but his data are now considered unreliable. A recent, thorough study has an estimate of 122 bodies that can be accounted for (van der Sanden 1996). Apart from giving possible explanations of the legal and religious structures of society, bog bodies offer a unique chance of getting to know Iron Age Man, his life conditions, illnesses, fashions in dress and hair styles, and the awareness that Iron Age Man, had he been dressed in modern clothes, would look no different than we do today.

The occurrence of bog bodies is widespread geographically and chronologically (Lund 1976). Most of the Danish finds that have been dated by scientific methods (Tauber 1956, 1979) or by accompanying objects are, with very few exceptions, from 500 BC until the birth of Christ, a period that in Danish archaeological terminology is referred to as the pre-Roman Iron Age. The bog bodies from Holland, Germany, Great Britain and Ireland generally seem to be from the first century AD (van der Sanden 1996), but some bog bodies fall into considerably older and younger categories, as for example the Koelbjerg Woman, whose well preserved skeleton dates to 8000 BC, and the Second World War victims found in the Russian wetlands.

THE PRESERVATIVE QUALITIES OF BOGS

The preservation of bog bodies must be seen as a result of nature's influence and not as a culturally created phenomenon like the Egyptian mummies. The reason for the preservation of the bodies lies in the specific physical and bio-chemical composition of bogs. The manner in which the body was deposited is important, e.g., for fixation of the body and rapid exclusion of air. It is also important that the weather was cold enough (less than 4 °C) to prevent rapid decomposition of the body. If a body was deposited in warm weather, one may assume that the anaerobic bacteria present in the intestinal system would have destroyed the interior of the corpse before the bog water could penetrate the body. The bogs in which these bodies are found can be roughly divided into three groups: raised bogs (acid), fens (calcareous), and transitional types. The raised bogs are of special interest because the bodies found in this type of bog can be so well preserved that they are hardly different from the day they were deposited; in fens and bogs of transitional types all the soft parts have generally disappeared, and the body is found as a skeleton or adipocere.

The flora of raised bogs is scanty in species and, naturally, dominated by peat moss (*Sphagnum*), the leaves of which are of special construction. Only a small proportion of the leaf cells contain chlorophyll granules and are therefore able to carry out the process of photosynthesis. The rest of the cells, which lie among those containing chlorophyll, are dead, empty structures of cellulose with an extraordinary ability to absorb water. They do not absorb subsoil water but rather imbibe surface rain water, and the underlying peat retains it. The nutritive salts that the peat moss requires, i.e., Ca, Mg, Na and K, come from atomized seawater carried into the atmosphere; the amount of nutritive salts increases the closer one gets to the sea. Measurements have shown that the annual growth of raised bogs is some 15 mm, but pressure from the upper layers reduces the true annual growth to about 6.4 mm. This compression prevents oxygen from coming into contact with the underlying layers, thus oxygen dependent bacteria cannot destroy the peat and the organisms contained in it. Bog moss (*Sphagnum*) has a substance known as sphagnan in its cell walls. When the moss dies, the sphagnan is slowly released, dissolved into the bog water, and converted into humic acid. Sphagnan, the intermediate compounds, and the humic acid all produce two results: the bacterial growth is stopped, and the skin, hair and nails of the body are tanned (Painter 1991).

Today, there are only very few untouched raised bogs in western Europe as peat has been utilized for fuel since before the birth of Christ. Many bog bodies were placed in Iron Age peat diggings; wooden peat spades dating from the Iron Age were found next to Tollund Man and Elling Woman. Today, peat is still dug on a large scale in Ireland and in Great Britain, and this is

Bog bodies of Denmark and northwestern Europe

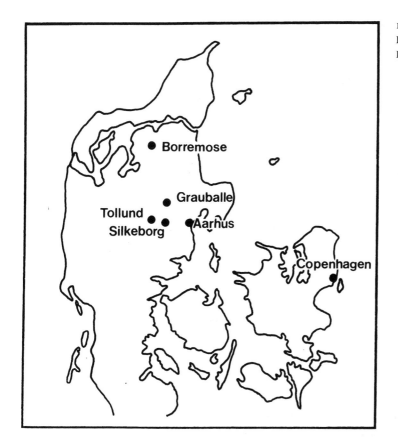

FIGURE 11.1. Locations of bog bodies in Denmark. (Map by Timothy Motz, Detroit Institute of Arts.)

where the recent finds were made: Worsley Man and the bodies from Lindow Moss were discovered near Manchester. In addition to these finds, new information has been obtained by applying modern research methods to older bodies such as Yde Girl and Weerdinge Couple from the Netherlands.

DANISH BOG BODIES

A number of the best preserved Danish bog bodies are among those that have been dated and carefully examined (Figure 11.1); they were all excavated within the first decade after World War II, a period in which peat was still being dug for fuel. During the war, peat cutting activities peaked, but as a consequence of poor communication only a few reports of finds of bog bodies reached the museums. Among those discovered and scientifically excavated and examined, special mention must be made of the three bodies from Borremose found in 1946, 1947, and 1948, Tollund Man found in 1950, and the last to be found in Denmark, Grauballe Man in 1952.

239

FIGURE 11.2. Borremose Man 1946, with the noose still around his neck. (Courtesy of the National Museum, Copenhagen.)

Borremose Man 1946 (Thorvildsen 1947) was found two meters beneath the surface of the bog in an upright, strongly flexed position (Figure 11.2), which can best be explained by assuming that the body had been placed in the bog in a sitting position; pulled by its own weight, the body had then sunk against its thighs. A birch stick had been placed above the body; this is seen fairly often with bog bodies and also considerably later, with Christian burials. The purpose is probably to prevent the dead from haunting the living. The body was that of an adult man, quite short of stature, scarcely more than 1.55 m tall. Due to the acidity of the bog, the bones had decalcified and were soft, but they were covered with skin, sinews and muscle tissue. His face, abdomen, sexual organs, and hands and feet were exceptionally well preserved. His left eye was intact; the yellowish white eyeball protruded and had a dark iris. His nose and lower part of the face were undamaged. His tongue was in a good state of preservation. A few of his teeth were preserved; they were loose. Scattered stubble six millimeters in length was found on his upper lip, cheeks and chin, indicating that his last shave had been a few days before his death. Of his inner organs, the small intestine and its contents were partly intact. The colon contained his last meal (some 40 cubic cm) consisting of approximately 65 percent spurrey (*Spergula arvensis*) and 25 percent pale willowweed (*Polygonum lapathifolium*) plus other species of minor importance. Some unknown animal tissue was found, and a few short animal hairs were present, probably mouse hair, which is often found in grains and seed (Brandt 1951). The back of his head had been crushed so the skull was open and the brain matter visible. The edge of the skull fracture was not new, and the fracture probably dated from the time of death, that is, the skull had been crushed before the body was deposited in the bog. Borremose Man's arm bones were intact, but the right thigh bone was fractured just above the knee. The shaft protruded through the skin on the underside of the thigh. The sharp edges of the fracture proved that the fracture had occurred prior to the bones being decalcified by the acid bog water. Borremose Man's hands were well preserved, narrow, and delicately shaped, giving no impression of having done heavy work; the fingernails had been dissolved. His feet were arched, his toes in normal position; the toenails were loose, and were handsomely shaped with a regular curve, and had been trimmed or cut.

A bast rope, 94 cm long and one cm thick, was tightened round his neck to the point where his neck measured only 31 cm in circumference. The rope was probably the cut-off end of the cord with which he was hanged. It could not be ascertained whether the mutilations mentioned above, the crushed skull and the broken thigh, were inflicted before or after the hanging, or whether they had been contributory death causes. The man was naked, but two almost identical skin capes were placed at his feet. They were probably his only clothing, corresponding to the style of dress that Caesar attributes to the Germanic tribes: 'They wore only short fur capes and were otherwise naked'. The pollen test conducted at the National Museum indicates that Borremose Man was buried in the bog sometime during the first centuries

AD; radiocarbon dating indicates his time of death to have occurred around 650±80 bc (calibrated to 840 BC). (Note: uncalibrated radiocarbon dates are indicated by the lower case bc.)

Borremose Body 1947 (Thorvildsen 1952) was found one kilometer from the body found in 1946. Due to its state of decomposition, it was impossible to determine its sex. The body had been placed on its stomach in an Iron Age peat dig. Boughs and heather twigs lay above the body in the peat digging. The upper part of the body was naked, but its hips and legs had been covered with a woolen blanket, a shawl and a piece of worn out cloth. Parts of the body were in a state of advanced decomposition; the stomach and part of the abdomen had dissolved completely, and some of the upper part of the body was partially dissolved. The head, the gullet, the left shoulder, arm and hand were well preserved. The back of the head was flattened, and the skull crushed so that the brain was visible. The hair, darkened by the bog water, was short, only three to five centimeters. An ornamental leather string with an amber bead and a perforated conical bronze disc was placed round the neck. The right leg was fractured ten centimeters below the knee. The fracture was not recent and dates to the time of deposit; it was not possible to establish whether it had occurred before or after death. The flattening of the skull was probably caused by pressure from the overlying peat. Close to the upper part of the body some small bones of an infant were found, which may indicate that a mother and her baby had been deposited in the bog. The cause of death could not be established. The dating of the find was established by the remains of a clay vessel of pre-Roman type, which lay in immediate contact with the body. Pollen analysis of the body dates it to the time around the birth of Christ. Borremose Body 1947 has been radiocarbon dated to 430±100 bc (calibrated to 475 BC).

The peat cutting was continued the following year and now a third body, that of Borremose Woman 1948 (Thorvildsen 1952) was found two meters under the surface of the bog; like the other two bodies, it was lying in an Iron Age peat digging. The dead person was a plump woman; she was lying on her stomach. Her left arm was bent at the elbow. Her right hand was resting against her chin. Her left hand was propped against her left shin, her left leg bent at the knee and vigorously pulled up against her abdomen. The body was surrounded by cotton-grass peat (Eriophorum). In 1977 the body was described according to forensic methods. The back of the woman's head was intact, but her face had been crushed; it was impossible to establish whether this was the cause of death or whether it had happened after death, the latter being the most probable. The damage cannot have been caused by the pressure of the peat as this would have crushed the back of the head also. Most of the scalp with the hair had been loosened from the skull and was lying above the skull in the bog. The hair seems to have been of medium length. No warding off lesions could be established by the forensic examination. The dead person had been placed on a rectangular woolen blanket measuring 1.75 x 1.15 m, otherwise the dead person was naked. The blanket may have been used as a kind of skirt. The body has been radiocarbon dated to 570±100 bc (calibrated to 770 BC). Borremose Woman lived in the transitional period between the Bronze Age and the Iron Age. Pollen analysis indicated the time of the deposition of the body to be around the birth of Christ.

Tollund Man (Thorvildsen 1951) was found in central Jutland in May 1950 when two farmers who were digging peat had reached a depth of 2.5 meters below the present surface. A displacement in the peat layers showed that he was lying in an Iron Age peat digging, along with a short, wooden spade. The police were summoned and as the officers estimated that the body was prehistoric, Silkeborg Museum was called in. Professor P. V. Glob of Aarhus University advised that the body be sent to the National Museum of Copenhagen (Figure 11.3); it was still lying in the peat block in which it had been found. The final excavation, sampling, and conservation were made at the National Museum. The body was that of an adult male, 1.60 m tall; he was lying in a normal sleeping position, resting on his right side. His body was slightly bent, his knees pulled up tightly against his body, and his arms were bent so that his left hand was close to his chin while his right hand was close to his left knee. It must be assumed that he was deliberately placed in this position, which makes him differ from most other bog bodies, who appear to have been deposited in a rather casual manner. The influence of rigor mortis means that Tollund Man must have been placed in his sleeping position either within the first eight to twelve hours after his death, or after one, two, or three days of waiting; this is the time needed for rigor mortis to end, although a high ambient temperature will shorten the period. The skin and most of the soft parts were intact; only the skin and the soft parts of the hands were gone, and the arms and legs were partially dissolved. An incipient dissolving of the skin of the upper part of the body could be observed, but the rest of the body was intact, skin and soft parts included. The sexual organs were well preserved and male. The best preserved part of the body was the head with its composed sleeping expression (Figure 11.4). Its wrinkled forehead and closed eyelids and lips were so intact that he could be mistaken for a living person fallen asleep. His hair was completely preserved, cut short with no specific style. There was a stubble of one to two millimeters on his upper

FIGURE II.3. Tollund Man during curation in 1950 at the National Museum in Copenhagen. (Courtesy of the Silkeborg Museum; photograph by Lars Bay.)

lip, chin and cheeks, which represents some two days of growth. Also his eyebrows were intact. Dissection showed that the inner organs such as heart, lungs and liver were very well preserved. Unfortunately, they were not examined further. The alimentary tract was intact with the stomach, small and large intestines. The botanist Helbæk (1951) examined the alimentary canal for evidence of the dead man's last meal. The contents of the stomach and the small intestine were modest, a mere 0.5 and 10 cubic cm, but the large intestine contained 260 cubic cm. The fact that Tollund Man's last meal was found in his large intestine indicates that it was eaten twelve to twenty four hours before death.

The body was naked except for a narrow leather belt and a pointed hood made from calf skin with the hair on the inside. The hood was held in place by a thin thong under the chin. It is possible that Tollund Man wore clothes made from vegetable fibres, as they would disappear in the acid ambience of the bog. Even while the corpse was lying *in situ*, a rope made from two braided

244

FIGURE 11.4. Tollund Man 1950 seen from the side that was downward while he was in the bog. It is the best preserved side of him. (Photograph courtesy of the Silkeborg Museum.)

leather straps was observed, the rope having been pulled tightly around the man's neck. At the nape of his neck, one end of the rope was tied in an open loop through which the other end was pulled so that it circled his neck. The free end of the rope was 1.25 meters long and had been cut sharply, so the rope had probably been longer. The rope was pulled so tightly around the neck that it had left a visible furrow in front and on the side of the throat, whereas there was no mark left on the nape of the neck where the loop was fastened. In order to establish whether death had been caused by regular hanging with injury or dislocation of the axis or by choking (the rope was unquestionably the instrument of death), the dead man's neck and head were examined radiographically by Christian Bastrup. He stated that there was no firm evidence of the dislocation of vertebrae or fracture of the axis, which would be expected had the man been hanged by a free fall with the noose around his neck. Most hangings are performed without a free fall and thus without injury to the vertebrae. Unfortunately, most of the bones and teeth were so decalcified that evaluation was difficult. As far as could be observed, the man's wisdom teeth had erupted, which indicates that he was no younger than twenty-two years. The radiographs also showed that his brain had shrunk (Figure 11.5) in a peculiar way, just as a number of his bones were strongly bent and curiously shaped as a consequence of the decalcification.

245

FIGURE 11.5. Radiograph from 1950 of the head of Tollund Man. His brain is visible as are his wisdom teeth. (Photograph courtesy of the Silkeborg Museum.)

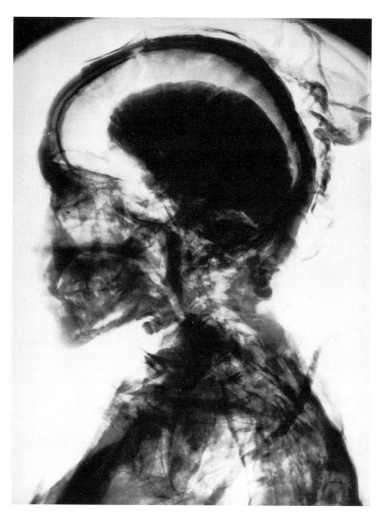

Analysis of the stomach contents showed that they consisted of a purely vegetable porridge or gruel with absolutely no trace of animal matter. According to the examining doctors, animal matter would be present if it had been eaten shortly before death, considering the excellent state of preservation of the body. The meal was a combination of grain and collected weed seeds with addition of vegetable fat from linseed (*Linum usitatissimum*) and gold of pleasure (*Camelina linicola*). The species of grain were naked and hulled barley (*Hordeum tetrastichum, var. nudum*, and *H. tetrastichum*); the most important species of weeds were pale willowweed (*Polygonum lapathifolium*) and persicaria (*P. persicaria*). Further examination showed that the water drunk with the meal must have been bog water as tiny leaves of sphagnum moss were found in the stomach contents. Furthermore, the stomach contents showed that Tollund Man suffered from the intestinal whipworm (*Trichocephalus dispar*) in quite large numbers. The composition of the meal was a clear indication of the dating of Tollund Man, as the ratio of naked and hulled barley closely corresponds to the ratio known to be used around the time of the birth of Christ; linseed and spelt, also found among the stomach contents, do not enter the Danish flora until around 400 BC. Radiocarbon dating made after the examination showed the time of death to be 210 ± 40 bc (calibrated to 220 BC).

When the detailed examination was concluded, it was unfortunately decided that conservation of the head only should be attempted. It should be mentioned that apart from the body from Rendswühren in northern Germany, which had been preserved in 1871 by being smoked, no one had any experience in preserving bog bodies at this time. The conservation of the head of Tollund Man began by replacing the bog water contained in his cells with distilled water containing formalin and acetic acid. Subsequently, this liquid was replaced by 30 percent alcohol, which was gradually concentrated to 99 percent with the addition of toluol. Finally, the head was submerged in pure toluol which was gradually saturated with paraffin. Afterwards, the paraffin was replaced with a blend of primarily bees' wax. The solution underwent various heat treatments. By using this method of conservation, all facial proportions and expressions were fully preserved, but as a whole the head shrank twelve percent; nevertheless, today it is the best preserved head of any person from prehistory. The rest of the body was left to dry, so the soft parts were partially destroyed. Tollund Man's feet were kept, one in water, the other in formalin; in 1976 both feet were preserved. The foot kept in water was dried and preserved with wax, a treatment that caused a shrinkage of some 25 percent. The foot kept in formalin was preserved by freeze drying, which caused practically no shrinkage and proved to give an excellent result initially. However, today the soft parts of the preserved foot show signs of cracking. In 1985, Silkeborg Museum decided to make a reconstruction of the unpreserved body in order to show the public what Tollund Man looked like when he was found in 1950. The actual body was conserved in a way that permits it to become an object of future scientific analyses.

Elling Woman (Fischer 1951) was found in 1938 only 60 meters from the place where Tollund Man was lying. The men who found her thought they had found a drowned ox, but when they discovered that the 'ox' was wearing a woven woolen belt around its waist, the body was transported to the National Museum for examination (Figure 11.6). The corpse was clad in a sheepskin cape and wrapped in another cape of oxhide, and it had some kind of plaited

FIGURE 11.6. The Elling Woman during curation at the National Museum in 1938. (Courtesy of the Silkeborg Museum; photograph by Lars Bay.)

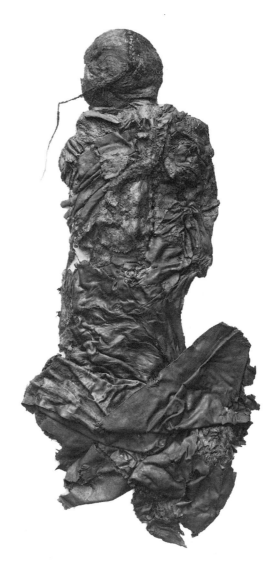

coiffure. Sex determination and dating of the corpse were impossible to perform at that time, but in 1978 the body was the object of new and thorough archaeological and medical examinations. The examinations were done by Silkeborg Museum in cooperation with forensic experts, radiologists and a forensic odontologist. It was concluded that the body was that of a woman of 25 to 30 years of age. She had been hanged. Photographs taken in 1938 showed a clear rope mark to be seen on her throat, and a leather rope fitting the mark was among the things found with the woman. The cape she wore was sewn from various pieces of sheepskin, fastened at the neck with a thin leather string; another cape of oxhide was wrapped around her hips and legs.

Bog bodies of Denmark and northwestern Europe

The hair, which was intact in spite of lack of conservation, consisted of a braid that was plaited from the top of the skull, just above the forehead, then the hair from the neck was included in the plaiting, and the braid was left to hang loose with a length of some 80 cm. At the moment of the hanging, the braid had been pulled around itself twice in a sort of bun at the back of the head. A hair length of 1.2 m is needed for a style like this.

In 1986, a reexamination was made of Huldremose Woman (Brothwell *et al.* 1990), who had been found in 1879 in the Huldremose bog in Djursland, in the eastern part of Jutland. This is probably the best preserved bog body ever found in northwestern Europe. Her clothing especially has been the object of much attention, consisting of a skirt, a woolen shawl, two capes of lambskin, one worn with the hairy side turned inside, the other one worn with the hairy side turned outside so that the capes were both warm and water repelling. The clothing has been on exhibition at the National Museum of Copenhagen, but the body has been kept in storage. A neatly shaped horn comb was tied to her belt, and a woven, woolen hairband was included in the finds. Her hair appeared to have been cut or sheared quite close to her scalp. Medical and archaeological analyses made in 1986 showed that in spite of the lack of conservation the body was still in a condition to render plenty of new information. Severe injuries to her arms and legs make it probable that she died from loss of blood as the injuries look old and seemed to have come from a sharp instrument rather than a peat spade. Recent peat cutting had left its traces on her body, but these lesions are naturally out of context when the cause of her death is considered. Two radiocarbon datings have been made, but the possibility of contamination of the samples is present. One dating made by the conventional method indicates the time of death to be 30±100 AD (Munksgaard 1973); the other dating made by the accelerator method indicates 40 AD, so the two methods are in accordance. The textile technology, however, points towards an earlier date, the time before the birth of Christ.

The last bog body to be found in Denmark is Grauballe Man (Figure 11.7) who was discovered in 1952 some 20 km east of the discovery site of Tollund Man and some 5 km north of the town of Silkeborg (Glob 1956). The body was found in a small bog where peat was being dug. The body had been placed in an Iron Age peat digging, in a slightly slanted position. It was lying on its chest with its left leg almost stretched out and its right leg and arm bent. The pressure of the peat had deformed the head slightly. Professor P. V. Glob had a crate constructed around the corpse and the surrounding peat, and the crate with its contents was taken to the museum, where further

FIGURE 11.7. Grauballe Man 1952. The long cut from ear to ear is clearly visible. He is displayed at the Moesguard Museum, Aarhus. (Photograph by Jan Friis and Torben Petersen for Illustreret Videnskab.)

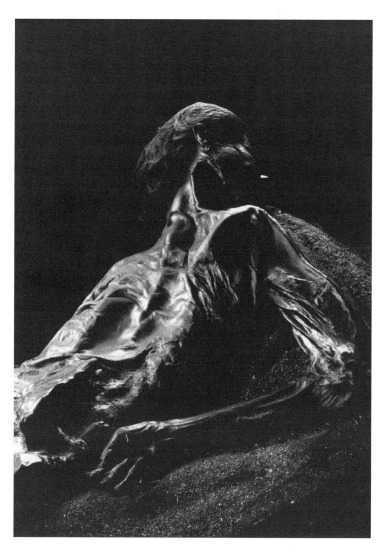

examination and conservation could be performed. A plaster cast of Grauballe Man was made to ensure later control of the body's position and possible shrinkage through preservation. Pathological, anatomical, and forensic examinations of the body were performed by Professor Willy Munck (1956), and Professor Carl Krebs and Erling Ratjen made an x-ray examination of the body (1956).

On external examination, it was seen that the head was bent slightly backward and turned a little to the right. On the left side of the forehead a slightly curved depression was found of 10 cm in diameter. The left earlobe was well preserved, but close to the ear opening some irregular defects were seen, which had probably occurred after death. The eyes were tightly shut, the eyeballs completely flattened and dried out. The colour of the iris could not be established with any certainty, but it is probable that the eyes had been quite dark; no eyebrows were present. The mouth, which was slightly open, appeared to have been quite large. In the upper jaw the teeth 4+ and 3+, 4, 5 were found; in the lower jaw, −1, 2, 3, 4, and 5. The teeth were very black and worn on the masticating surface (Glob 1965). Seven teeth were still in their proper position in the upper jaw, five in the lower jaw. There were open sockets of 14 more teeth, of which nine were found loose in various parts of the mouth. The teeth were quite small. One tooth must have been lost long before death, as the socket had healed. Some of the teeth showed periodontitis and caries, which must have caused toothache at times, and one bad tooth had caused malocclusion. No wisdom teeth were found. The tongue was shriveled, but still so preserved that its shape could be reasonably recognized, including its tip. The epiglottis could be seen. The trachea and esophagus had been severed by a deep throat wound.

The internal examination revealed the rest of his lungs, which did not appear to be fastened to the wall of the chest. In place of the liver there was found a large, soft, red mass, some 15 by 10 cm in size, covered with a capsule. The intestine with its contents could be extracted. In the scrotum, a flat body was recognized, probably a testis. Neither the stomach, spleen, pancreas, suprarenal glands, kidneys, ureters, nor bladder were recognizable. On the crown of his head some long, reddish hair was found, and a few strands of beard from about three to ten mm long were on his upper lip and chin. Microscopic analysis of the hair of the head showed it to be of medium thickness, probably dark; the present reddish colouring was due to bog water tanning. The hair of the beard was somewhat coarser than that of the head. No signs of disease were found. The examinations revealed no signs of illness apart from early arthritis in his thoracic vertebrae, an ailment indicating that Grauballe Man probably was more than 30 years old. At the upper front part of his neck there was a large wound, the upper edge of which began 5 cm below and 3 cm behind his right ear, and the wound continued upward and forward along or rather a bit above the lower jaw. The edges of the wound were quite smooth, but there was a notch at the middle of the lower edge.

The conclusions of the thorough radiographic examination were as follows. No signs of serious illness marking the bone system were found, and the fractures revealed by the examination formed two groups. One group includes a skull fracture in the right temple region and a fracture of the left shin bone. The radiographs showed that the skull was partly flattened and somewhat depressed toward the middle, and at the back of the crown there was a break of 2×1 cm, turning upward into a linear fracture. The further skull deformations were attributed to the pressure of the surrounding peat mass. The open fracture of the shin bone (tibia) was oblique, the fracture line beginning 10.5 cm under the knee on the outer side of the under part of the leg, traveling downward and inward to the inner (medial) side of the bone 14 cm from the knee. The bone ends showed no sign of callus formation. The fibula had not been fractured. Both lesions, the skull and the tibial fractures, must have been inflicted immediately before or after death. The break in the tibia without a corresponding break in the fibula suggests a direct blow to the shin. Indirect violence, a fall or similar accident would also cause the fibula to break. The other group of lesions consists of deformations or breaks which are attributed to postmortem displacements caused by the pressure of the peat. Radiographs of the thoracic part of the vertebral column showed early arthritic changes (spondylosis deformans), an ailment rarely occurring before the age of 30.

The medical examinations of Grauballe Man can be summarized as follows: the cause of death is undoubtedly the long cut from ear to ear, which was so deep that it severed the esophagus. The wound must have been inflicted by another person because its direction and appearance rules out the possibility of suicide or postmortem lesion. Whether the man was knocked unconscious before his throat was cut could not be established. The skull fracture seems to have been inflicted by a blunt instrument. Likewise, it could not be determined whether the oblique fracture of the left shin bone had been inflicted before or after death. The state of preservation of the right hand (Figure 11.8) and foot especially, was so exceptionally good that the papillae lines could be clearly observed. To find out whether these lines corresponded to those found in people living today, the technical department of the Criminal Investigation Department of the police of Aarhus made an examination of the fingerprints and footprints (Vogelius Andersen 1956). The clearest print was that of the right thumb, which could be classified immediately as a whorl pattern, a so-called twin loop pattern; the right hand middle finger had an ulnar loop pattern. The fingerprint expert concluded his examination by saying that had fingerprint card index been in use at the time of Grauballe Man, he would have been identified without any trouble. Four parts of the skin would have made the job an easy one, namely the sole of the right foot, the outer ball of the right hand (hypothenar), the ball of the right hand thumb (thenar), where moreover a clear commencement to a loop formation on the first interdigital was seen, and finally the area around the radial delta of the

Bog bodies of Denmark and northwestern Europe

FIGURE 11.8. The right hand of Grauballe Man. (Courtesy of the Moesguard Museum.)

thumb. The two characteristic fingerprint patterns occur with a frequency of 11.2 percent and 86.3 percent respectively among the present day Danish population; this means that there was nothing unusual about this fingerprint, so far the oldest ever found.

The intestine, which was extracted in connection with the internal examination, contained the remains of his last meal. The contents were of approximately 610 cubic cm, that is more than twice the amount of the 275 cubic cm found in Tollund Man's intestine. To what extent these volumes of meal remains correspond to the amount of food eaten, is impossible to calculate. Remains of food of the same characteristics were found more or less evenly distributed throughout the entire alimentary channel, from stomach to intestinal outlet, which means that Grauballe Man must have eaten shortly before he was killed. The intestinal contents consisted of millions of single components, the relative frequency of which was estimated by Hans Helbæk (1959), who had previously examined Tollund Man. In contrast to Tollund Man, Grauballe Man had ingested animal matter with the vegetable matter. The animal matter was seen as 15 tiny bits of dissolving bone. A bone specialist, conservator Ulrik Møhl, suggested that the bones were possibly from the ribs of a small pig. The soup that Grauballe Man had eaten consisted of barley

(*Hordeum tetrastichum*, var. *nudum* and H. *tetrasticum*), seeds of knotgrass
((*Polygonum lapathifolium* and *P. persicaria*), soft bromegrass (*Bromus mollis*),
and smaller quantities of emmer wheat (*Triticum dicoccum*) and oats (*Avena sativa*). Furthermore, there were seeds of more than 50 species of weeds,
some of them undoubtedly gathered on purpose, whereas the rest were prob-
ably accidentally included at the harvesting of cultivated species. Two of the
last mentioned plants grow close to the sea (Grauballe is at a distance of some
45 km from the coast), so the presence of these seeds shows that either an
exchange of foodstuff took place between the coastal areas and the inland or
Grauballe Man had been close to the seaside shortly before his death. In
Grauballe Man's intestine two small pebbles and a small piece of charcoal
were found, a sign that Grauballe Man did not chew his food very thoroughly.
Also, like Tollund Man, he had intestinal worms (*Trichuris*). Just as in the case
of Tollund Man, there was no trace of fresh fruit, vegetables, herbs, or
berries, which would be expected at the time of the year when they are
present. This points to the probable time of death of both Grauballe Man and
Tollund Man as either winter or early spring when the beneficial effects of the
cold bog water would result in the excellent preservation of both men's soft
tissues.

After the thorough examination it was fortunately decided to attempt
preservation of the entire body. Dissection had revealed that the acid bog
water had a tanning effect on Grauballe Man's skin. The conservator of the
Museum of Prehistory, G. Lange-Kornbak (1956), decided to complete the
tanning that nature had begun. The process used was a method known
among specialists as pit tanning. This lasted 18 months, during which time
the body was submerged in an oak tub filled with a tannin solution that was
gradually concentrated by the addition of larger and larger amounts of oak
bark (the process consumed about 875 kg of oak bark). After this bath the
body was treated with a solution of Turkey red oil and dried. This preservation
process had not altered the appearance or the size of Grauballe Man.
Unfortunately, the preservation has turned out to be problematic as the oils
used tend to evaporate and go rancid, thereby damaging Grauballe Man by
causing cracking, among other things. In 1996 a decision has been made to
construct an air-tight glass case filled with inactive gases, thus reducing
evaporation and oxidation considerably. Immediately after Grauballe Man
was discovered a radiocarbon dating indicated the time of death to be AD
355±100 (calibrated). In 1978, a new dating was made as the sample taken at
the time of the discovery had not been cleansed for humic acid; this dating
pointed to the time of death being 55±80 BC (calibrated). In 1996 a new

dating was made, this time by use of the accelerator method; the sample was taken from the hair of the man's head and indicates the time of death to be 265±40 BC (calibrated).

OTHER BOG BODIES OF NORTHWESTERN EUROPE

The Netherlands

The idea of making new examinations of old finds of bog bodies met with immediate interest when such new methods of research as radiocarbon dating, radiography, and CT scanning saw the light. This enabled the Drents Museum of Assen, The Netherlands, to gain new knowledge of Yde Girl (van der Sanden 1996). In 1897 the mummified body of a 16 year old girl was dredged out of the peat in a small raised bog near the village of Yde. The remains of a large and rather worn woolen cloak were found with the girl. Her vertebral column was slightly wry as she suffered from a mild scoliosis. A hairband round her neck may indicate the cause of death. In accordance with observations made on two other bog bodies, Borremose Woman 1948 and Windeby Girl from Germany, her hair had been cropped, almost shaven. A reconstruction has been made of the head of Yde Girl with the cooperation of more than 25 specialists from the Netherlands and Great Britain. Radiocarbon dating indicates the time of her death as sometime between 170 BC and AD 230.

The Weerdinge Couple represents another Dutch find, made in 1904. A couple was found, one person lying in the arm of the other one. The couple, like Yde girl scientifically examined and shown at the Drents Museum, was for many years known as 'the bridal couple'. But a new examination has proved both persons to be male. One of the men has a deep stab wound in the abdomen through which his intestine has protruded, a wound that undoubtedly caused his death. The time of death is indicated by radiocarbon dating to have been 30±70 BC.

Great Britain

In Great Britain and Ireland peat is still being dug, and the head of Worsley Man was found in 1958 during peat digging in Worsley Moss near Manchester (Turner and Scaife 1995). In spite of a thorough search made by the police, the remainder of the body was never found. The head was that of a man of 20 to 30 years of age. He had definitely not died a natural death. Violent blows had fractured his skull at the crown, and a thin cord had been drawn tightly around his neck (it can be seen between the soft tissue and the bone of his right cheek). In addition, the head had been severed at the second cervical vertebra. Worsley Man died sometime between 80 and 400 AD.

Another isolated skull (Lindow I) was found in 1983 in Lindow Moss, also near Manchester (Stead *et al.* 1986). At first, it was thought to be the skull of a woman of 30 to 50 years of age. This led the police to interrogate a man who lived near the bog and whom they suspected of having murdered and dismembered his wife. On being told of the discovery of the skull, he confessed. Shortly afterwards the skull was dated, and it proved to be 2000 years old. Nonetheless, the man was convicted of his wife's murder on the evidence of his own confession. Today the skull is not considered a female, but believed to belong to the male corpse found in 1987 (Lindow III).

The Lindow II find (Lindow Man) came to light in 1984 when a loose foot was found on a peat conveyor belt. This led to the discovery of a bog body whose lower part had been damaged by the peat digging. After the find was declared to be prehistoric, more than 50 specialists were involved in thorough examinations: radiocarbon dating experts, archaeologists, pathologists, anatomists, radiologists, palaeobotanists, odontologists, analytical chemists, microbiologists, experts in the field of facial reconstructions, and so forth (Brothwell 1987). The conclusion of their examinations proved the man to have been well built, about 1.68 m in height, and 60 or more kg in weight. No traces of disease were found, apart from intestinal worms; he was a fellow sufferer of Tollund Man and Grauballe Man. Very slight deformations of the bones caused by rheumatism were registered. His head had been rather large, with large nostrils and surprisingly small ears. His hair was dark and he had a beard. The day before he died, he had eaten a meal, possibly some flat baked cake consisting mainly of wheat and barley. The water that he drank with his meal must have been taken from a bog as it contained sphagnum. He was naked, except for a fox skin armband round his left arm. On the basis of the forensic examination his death can be described thus: standing or possibly kneeling, he received two blows on the crown of his head dealt with a small axelike weapon, and was probably dealt a simultaneous blow on his back, which broke one of his ribs. A string was tied tightly around his neck, and a twig had been fastened to the string at the nape of his neck; the twig was used for tightening the string, thus strangling him and breaking his neck. He had also been stabbed in the neck. After this violent treatment, he was flung into a pond in the bog, head first. Lindow Man II has been radiocarbon dated to AD 10 ± 25, this date representing the average of nine datings made by the Oxford laboratory.

Ireland

In 1978, when a farmer was cutting peat by hand in Meenybraddan Moss, County Donegal, he found the body of Meenybraddan Woman, who was between 25 and 35 years of age (Turner and Scaife 1995). Her age was determined by pathological and archaeological examinations conducted in 1985; until the examinations were carried out, she had been kept in a frozen condition. Her body height was measured to be about 1.50 m; no traces of violence or disease were revealed by the examinations. She had been deposited naked in the bog apart from a cape covering her body. The body was in a fine state of preservation although previous peat digging had caused some drying up of her feet. Microscopical analysis of her fingernails showed only slight wear and the experts therefore concluded that she had done light work only. Some particles of soot were found in her lungs, but there was no sign of burns. Probably the soot particles were inhaled while she was close to a hearth. Her internal organs were too dissolved to be made objects of research. Radiocarbon dating indicates the time of her death to be AD 1220±90.

Germany

The biggest collection is in the Landesmuseum, in Schleswig (van der Sanden 1996). Among other bodies on display is Rendswühren Man, who was found in 1871. He was naked apart from a piece of leather, the furry side turned inward, tied around his left ankle. His death had been caused by a triangular hole in his forehead. Two bodies from Windeby, a male and a female, were found in 1952, a mere five meters between them. Both date to the time just after the birth of Christ; whether they were deposited at the same time is impossible to prove. The female (Figure 11.9), who died at the age of about 14, was naked apart from a skin collar and a band covering her eyes; it is possible that the band originally covered her mouth instead (Gebühr 1979). The man's skin and hair of the head had been preserved, but his bones were totally dissolved. He had probably been strangled with a hazel twig found around his neck. Both bodies had been covered with branches in the bog, the girl further weighted with a stone. Damendorf Man, of whom only the skin and hair were preserved, was naked, covered with a cape and a few other garments, among those a pair of shoes. Dätgen Man and the severed skull of Osterby Man both have long hair, which is twisted and gathered in a knot; Tacitus mentions that the Germanic tribe called the Swabians wore this style, known as a 'Swabian knot' (Figure 11.10).

FIGURE 11.9. The
Windeby Girl from
Schloss Gottorf,
Northwest Germany. She
died at about age 14.
(Photograph by Jan Friis
and Torben Petersen for
Illustreret Videnskab.)

CULTURAL ASPECTS OF THE EARLY IRON AGE

The Pre-Roman Iron Age, from 500 BC until the birth of Christ, was the first period of the Iron Age in Scandinavia and northwest Germany. It is contemporaneous with the end of the Hallstatt Culture of Central Europe and the following La Tène Culture (also called Celtic culture). The pre-Roman Iron Age is followed by the early Roman Iron Age which lasts from the birth of Christ until AD 200. Apparently, only a few of the Danish bog bodies come from this period, whereas the Dutch, German, English, and Irish bog bodies seem to date from the first centuries AD. The pre-Roman society in Denmark was a peasant society, in which livestock and human beings lived under the same roof, but each in their own half of rectangular houses of about fifteen by five meters. The houses would stand isolated or, as was often the case, be grouped in small villages. The burial custom was for cremation of the body; the remains would be placed in cemeteries and in Central Jutland such a grave would be covered with a circular layer of stones. Apart from human beings, ornaments, clothing accessories, and pottery containing food were also sacrificed; rare cases of wagon sacrifices are known (Dejbjerg and Rappendam), and a unique case of a boat of 13.5 m in length with equipment for an army (Hjortspring). Although Central Europe, Great Britain and Ireland were dominated by outstanding cultures of wide geographic influ-

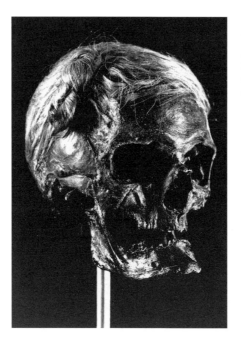

FIGURE 11.10. The Osterby Skull, showing the characteristic style of long twisted and gathered hair known as a 'Swabian knot'. Displayed at Schloss Gottorf, Northwest Germany. (Photograph by Jan Friis and Torben Petersen for Illustreret Videnskab.)

ence, these cultures do not seem to have influenced the Germanic peoples living in northwestern Europe to any great extent. In Denmark, a certain influence can be registered through the presence of a number of imported metal vessels, such as the large, richly decorated cauldron from Gundestrup, which shows a panoply of Celtic gods, religious processions, sacrificial scenes, and scenes of Greek inspiration.

Gaius Julius Caesar (100–44 BC) presumably wrote his books on the Gallic War during the winter of 52/51 BC. The first book describes the Roman army's first meeting and confrontation with the Germanic king Ariovist, who is portrayed as every inch the barbarian. During the reign of Augustus, the Romans pushed the frontier of the empire to the area between the Danube and the Rhine. The Emperor's plans to extend the frontier further north by conquering Germania were put to an abrupt end in AD 9, when the Roman commander Varus suffered total defeat to the Germanic chieftain Arminius in northern Germany, not very far from the present frontier between Germany and Denmark. After this defeat the frontier of the Rhine–Danube area remained permanent until AD 260 when it broke down at the fall of the Roman Empire. England, as far north as today's Scottish border, became a Roman province during the reign of Claudius, and Ireland remained a Celtic country.

The trading connections between Rome and the Germanic areas have given rise to various Roman chronicles of the Germanic peoples. The most important of these is probably *Germania*, written by C. Cornelius Tacitus in AD 98; it is assumed, however, that Tacitus never visited Germania. The value of the Roman sources is a matter of much debate as they are not ethnographical literature in the modern sense of the word; they were written to show the superiority of the Romans and their deeds by contrasting them with their supposed primitive Germanic neighbours.

The basis for Iron Age execution of human beings and their subsequent deposit in bogs is a matter of intense discussion. It is by no means clear whether it is a question of regular punishment, punishment and subsequent sacrifice to the god(s) of the bog, or regular sacrifice to the gods. The theory of punishment has its origin in the description given by C. Cornelius Tacitus in *Germania*, chapter 12:

At the public assembly it is possible to bring an action against somebody that can result in the death penalty. The punishment depends on the gravity of the offense: Traitors, and those who have offended their bodies (homosexuals) are drowned in swampy bogs and branches are laid over their bodies.

The theory of sacrifice also finds its origin in Tacitus (chapter 39), in his description of the Semnonians, a Germanic tribe from northern Germany:

At a set point of time all peoples of the same name and same kin represented by emissaries meet in a wood consecrated by the ancestors, surrounded by fear, sacred from the earliest times. A human sacrifice is made by those assembled to celebrate the horrible beginnings of their barbaric cult.

Professor P. V. Glob and many other scholars have interpreted the very clear papillary pattern of Tollund Man and Grauballe Man as proof that they had done superior work (i.e., not rough labour) in the society, perhaps as priests or chieftains. The papillary pattern, however, comes from the subcutis and not the epidermis, as the epidermis has been dissolved by the long stay in bog water. It has also been argued that as winter or early spring was the time of the year preferred for sacrifices of bog bodies, this was proof that the bog bodies had been sacrificed to Nerthus, goddess of the spring – but in order for a body to be preserved in the bog, it must be deposited in winter or early spring when the water is cold. We cannot rule out the possibility that sacrifices were made at other times of the year, but the warmer temperature of the bog water would have caused those corpses to dissolve and disappear.

As regards an interpretation of the Danish bog bodies, I will base my interpretation on the contexts in which thoroughly examined bog bodies have been found. In my opinion, they have not suffered a treatment more violent than was necessary for killing them. Were they criminals who had been executed, they would have been thrown into a pit like Lindow Man II from England, and not carefully laid in a sleeping position like Tollund Man, or wrapped in their clothing like Elling Woman and Borremose Woman 1948. I do subscribe to the theory of sacrifices made to a deity, but dare not guess to which. Perhaps there is a clue to the mystery. In the later half of the millennium before the birth of Christ (the time frame for the greatest concentration of bog bodies in Denmark), the bogs assumed greater importance to society. A climatic deterioration meant that peat had to be cut for fuel, and bog iron ore contained the raw material necessary for the beginning Iron Age. In primitive cultures it is customary to make sacrifices to higher beings whose lands are being usurped. Denmark's bog bodies may be offerings to divinities whose domains have been thus violated.

REFERENCES

Brandt, I. 1951. Planterester i et moselig fra Borremose. *Aarbøger for Nordisk Oldkyndighed og Historie* **1950**: 342–51. English summary.

Brothwell, D. 1987. *The bog man and the archaeology of people.* Cambridge, MA: Harvard University Press.

Brothwell, D., Liversage, D. and Gottlieb, B.1992. Radiographic and forensic aspects of the female Huldremose body. *Journal of Danish Archaeology* **1990**: 157–78.

Dieck, A. 1965. *Die europäischen Moorleichenfunde.* Neumünster: Karl Wachholtz Verlag.

Fischer, C. 1951. Moseligene fra Bjaeldskovdal. *KUML* **1979**: 7–41.

Gebühr, M. 1979. Das Kindergrab von Windeby. *Offa* **36**: 75–107.

Glob, P. V. 1956 Jernaldermanden fra Grauballe. *KUML* **1956**: 99–113.

Glob, P. V. 1965. *Mosefolket.* Copenhagen: Gyldendal. Also published in English.

Helbæk, H. 1951. Tollundmandens sidste måltid. *Aarbøger for Nordisk Oldkyndighed og Historie* **1950**: 311–41. English summary.

Helbæk, H. 1959 Grauballemandens sidste måltid *KUML* **1958**: 83–116. English summary.

Krebs, C. and Ratjen, E. 1956 Det radiologiske fund hos moseliget fra Grauballe. *KUML* **1956**: 138–50.

Lange-Kornbak, G. 1956. Konservering af en Oldtidsmand. *KUML* **1956**: 155–9. English summary.

Lund, A. A. 1976. *Moselig.* Wormianum 1976.

Munck, W. 1956. Patologisk-anatomisk og retsmedicinsk undersøgelse af Moseliget fra Grauballe *KUML* **1956**: 131–7.

Munksgaard, E. 1973. *Oldtidsdragter.* Copenhagen: Nationalmuseets. English summary.

Painter, T. J. 1991. Lindow Man, Tollund Man and other peat-bog bodies: the preservative and antimicrobial action of sphagnan, a reactive glycuronoglycan with tanning and sequestering properties. *Carbohydrate Polymers* **15**: 123–42.

Stead, I. M., Bourke, J. B. and Brothwell, D., eds.1986. *Lindow Man. The body in the bog.* Ithaca, NY: Cornell University Press.

Tacitus, C. C. 1942. [AD 98] *Germania.* New York: Modern Library.

Tauber, H. 1956. Tidsfaestelse af Grauballemanden ved kulstof-14 maling. *KUML* **1956**: 160–3.

Tauber, H. 1979 Kulstof-14 datering af moselig. *KUML* **1979**: 73–8. English summary.

Thorvildsen, E. 1952. Menneskeofringer i Oldtiden. *KUML* **1952**: 32–48. English summary.

Thorvildsen, K. 1947. Moseliget fra Borremose i Himmerland. *Nationalmuseets Arbejdsmark* **1947**: 57–67.

Thorvildsen, K. 1951. Moseliget fra Tollund. *Aarbøger for Nordisk Oldkyndighed og Historie*. **1950**: 302–9. English summary.

Turner, R. C. and Scaife, R. G. 1995. *Bog bodies*. London: British Museum Press.

van der Sanden, W. 1996. *Through nature to eternity*. Amsterdam: Batavian Lion International.

Vogelius Andersen, C. H. 1956. Forhistoriske Fingeraftryk *KUML* **1956**: 151–4. English summary.

12

Mummies from Italy, North Africa and the Canary Islands

ANTONIO ASCENZI, PAOLO BIANCO, GINO FORNACIARI
AND CONRADO RODRÍGUEZ MARTÍN

THE ROMAN MUMMY OF GROTTAROSSA
Antonio Ascenzi and Paolo Bianco

Mummification was never a Roman custom, and at present the Grottarossa mummy must be considered a unique specimen (Ascenzi *et al.* 1996).

The Grottarossa district is on the outskirts of Rome, nine miles north of the Capitol along the via Cassia; the mummy was accidentally discovered there on 5 February 1964, during digging prior to building work. The corpse was found in a rectangular sarcophagus of white marble, with a lid opening at the front, and masks on its corners. Both the sarcophagus and its lid are decorated with fine ornamental carvings. There is a deer-hunting scene on the long front side, continuing as a boar hunting scene on the short right side. According to E. Paribeni in a press conference following the discovery of the mummy, the scene is inspired by the Aeneas and Dido episode in Book IV of the *Aeneid*. A lion-hunting scene is shown on the lid opening. Africa, Venus and a fluvial divinity are displayed in symbolic form on the short left side.

The mummy was an 8 year old girl (as indicated by the height and dental development). It exhibited jewels of a type that corresponded to her youth: a pair of gold earrings, a gold necklace with sapphires, and a gold ring. The funerary items included an articulated ivory doll, a small amber shell-shaped box, a small amber pot, a little box with a handle, and a little amber die. Considering the special features of the sarcophagus and funerary items, the Grottarossa girl must have lived in the second century AD, probably under the Antonine emperors (AD 160–180), according to Bordenache Battaglia (1983).

The Grottarossa mummy looks satisfactorily preserved. The whole of the body is now wrinkled by complete dehydration. As a result its weight is only 4960 g, in spite of an overall length of 120 cm. The tough stiff skin reveals an intense brownish colour. According to the eyewitness accounts of the few

FIGURE 12.1. A precise copy of a photograph of the Grottarossa mummy taken by an amateur soon after the discovery and printed in several newspapers at that time (left). The present appearance of the mummy (right). (From Spindler *et al.*, reproduced with permission from *The man in the ice*, Springer-Verlag.)

people who were able to examine the mummy immediately after its discovery, the body was apparently well hydrated and its features resembled those of a white living subject (Figure 12.1, left), but the body very rapidly became wrinkled and discoloured (Figure 12.1, right). It is probable that the sudden exposure to air of a mummy previously kept in an air-tight setting led to rapid dehydration, which could have activated the discolouring capability of the mummifying material.

As to the mummification technique used, it should be described *sensu strictiori* as 'embalming' (i.e., treatment with balms), as revealed by the absence of any trace of sectioning or residual thin crystals to be attributed to natron on the skin or in the wrappings, the persistence of all the internal organs, and the aromatic odours exhaled from the body at the time of the discovery. Chemical analysis revealed the presence of abietic acid derivatives, giving evidence that products from *Cupressaceae*, especially *Juniperus*, were used in the embalming procedure. This technique was commonly applied in Egypt during the last period, including the Roman era when the Grottarossa girl was alive. In the case of the Grottarossa mummy the absence of bitumen in

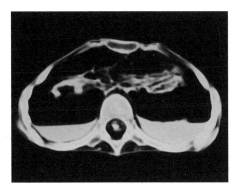

FIGURE 12.2. CT scan of the chest of the mummy: bilateral pleural effusion posteriorly and collapse of the lung by pneumothorax.

the wrappings leads one to attribute the intense brownish colour of the skin to the action of the resin.

In examining the problem of the origin of the Grottarossa mummy, reference must be made to the anthropometric data obtained from the cranium, especially its prominent brachicephaly. The geographical distribution of the cephalic index yields evidence that brachicephaly was rare among southern Mediterranean coastal populations. This is specially true of Egypt, where dolicocephaly is prominent. This makes it unlikely that the girl was born of Egyptian parents; she probably had Italic parents who came from the center or possibly the north of the peninsula, where brachicephaly is common.

As to the cause of death, there is no doubt that the main pathologic finding is a bilateral pleural effusion (Figure 12.2), with microscopic evidence of the features of a pleuritis, possibly associated with a septic pneumothorax.

The lack of funerary inscriptions makes it difficult to be specific as to where mummification took place. According to the archaeologists some of the scenes carved on the sarcophagus allude to Africa. But these scenes might simply refer to the fact that the girl was born or lived for a time in that continent. Also, the finding that the sarcophagus, jewels and funerary equipment are all typical of Roman workmanship cannot exclude the hypothesis that the girl died and was mummified in another country – Egypt, for example. According to Granger-Taylor (1982, 1982, 1987), the crucial bit of evidence that the mummy was prepared in Rome is provided by its linen wrappings. They have Z-spun yarns in both warp and weft. In Roman Italy the normal direction for spinning wool and silk was Z, while linen could be S- or Z-spun. In Egypt linen, cloths were woven of yarns that were almost invariably S-spun. Elsewhere in the Near East, wool was sometimes Z-spun, but linen thread was again virtually always S-spun. The only Mediterranean country besides Italy where there is good evidence for the Z-spinning of linen in Classical Antiquity is Greece (Beckwith 1954).

In conclusion, the wrappings offer strong indications that the site of mummification of the Grottarossa girl was Rome. The most probable reason for her Egyptian-style mummification is that she or her parents were believers in the Egyptian religion, as a result of a period of residence in Africa, or because they had become familiar with it while living in Rome. At that time foreign faiths, especially Egyptian ones, had made such inroads in Rome (Malaise 1972 a,b; Roullet 1972) that Egyptian style mummifications could have been performed there.

ITALIAN MUMMIES

Gino Fornaciari

Contrary to common belief, mummies in Italy, especially single mummies, are quite numerous (Di Colo 1910; Terribile and Corrain 1986; Fulcheri 1991; Fornaciari and Capasso 1996). According to a recent survey, there are 315 preserved bodies of saints, including at least 25 mummies (Fulcheri 1996). The mummies are distributed throughout Italy from the north (Aufderheide and Aufderheide 1991) to the south (Fornaciari and Gamba 1993), where the most important collections are found (Figure 12.3). The burials, which represent extremely precious paleopathological material, range from the medieval period, through the Renaissance, to more recent times, principally between the seventeenth and nineteenth centuries (Table 12.1). The samples vary from a small number to several thousand individuals present in the Catacombs of the Capuchins (Figure 12.4) in Palermo (Di Colo 1910).

Italian mummies can be divided into two different basic groups: natural and artificial. The natural mummies, such as the mummy of Santa Zita in Lucca, Tuscany (Fornaciari *et al.* 1989c) or of Pandolfo Malatesta, prince of Fano in central Italy (Fornaciari and Torino 1995), form the most consistent part of the Italian collections and were preserved because of favorable climatic and environmental conditions, without direct human intervention. On the other hand, the artificial mummies, such as the royal mummies of the Aragonese Mausoleum of San Domenico Maggiore in Naples (Fornaciari 1986), were exclusively special members of society, either of high social class or of great importance for the community, for example kings or saints. With regard to the first category, there is some documentary evidence of the special treatment to which the bodies were submitted, in order to facilitate the drying process and preservation. Natural mummification was facilitated by special drainage methods of the cadaveric fluids, carried out in the crypts of churches, especially in southern Italy. Up until the past century, after an important per-

Mummies from Italy, North Africa and the Canary Islands

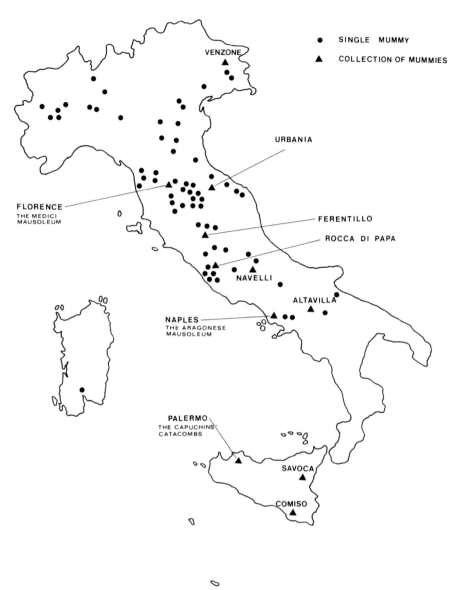

FIGURE 12.3.
Distribution of ancient mummies in Italy.

sonage died, the body was placed and left for several months in the vault of the church, probably in a seated position with the cadaveric sewage collected in large stone or pottery vases named cantarelle (Figure 12.5). Even today, in Naples, the expression 'drain off' is an omen of death that is still addressed to people (Fornaciari 1984a, 1986). After a few months, the body, still flexible but no longer draining, was laid horizontally in special tubs covered with mineral-rich volcanic soil, which completed the dehydration and mummification

Table 12.1. *Collections of mummies in Italy*

Site	N	Type	Century
Venzone (Northern Italy)	15	Natural	14th–18th
Urbania (Central Italy)	18	Natural	17th–19th
Medici Mausoleum (S.Lorenzo, Florence)	39	Natural and Artificial	16th–18th
Ferentillo (Central Italy)	16	Natural	18th–19th
Rocca di Papa (Central Italy)	Hundreds	Natural	16th–18th
Navelli (Central Italy)	Hundreds	Natural	17th–19th
Aragonese Mausoleum (S.Domenico, Naples)	31	Natural and Artificial	15th–19th
Altavilla Irpina (Southern Italy)	Hundreds	Natural	17th–19th
Savoca (Sicily)	Tens	Natural	17th–18th
Comiso (Sicily)	50	Natural	18th–19th
Capuchins Catacombs (Palermo)	Thousands	Natural	16th–20th

process. The corpse, by then completely desiccated and mummified, was dressed and positioned in its coffin (Fornaciari and Gamba 1993).

We shall now describe the mummies of the church of Santa Maria della Grazia, at Comiso, Sicily, and those of the Abbey of San Domenico Maggiore in Naples, the two series that have been studied more extensively.

The 'Chapel of the Dead', a mortuary chapel annexed to the church of Santa Maria della Grazia in Comiso at the beginning of the eighteenth century, contains 50 mummified bodies placed in niches above the entrance and in the right and lateral walls (Figure 12.6) (Fornaciari and Gamba 1993). Nearly all the bodies, which lie in an oblique position, with their faces always directed towards the inside of the church, belong to males varying in age from young to adult to old. They are Capuchin friars or laymen of the Third Order of the Capuchins. Twenty mummies are labeled with the individual's

FIGURE 12.4. Catacombs of the Capuchins (Palermo): overview of one of the main galleries (eighteenth–nineteenth century).

FIGURE 12.5. Church of Annunziata (Comiso, Sicily): vault with the typical 'cantarelle' for draining of the bodies (eighteenth century).

name and date of death, ranging between 1742 and 1838. The mummies without a label are probably more ancient, dating back to 1693 when the church was erected. All the mummies were wearing monastic clothes, except for one dressed in characteristic eighteenth century civilian clothes

FIGURE 12.6. Church of S. Maria della Grazia (Comiso, Sicily): lateral wall with the mummy niches (eighteenth–nineteenth centuries).

and placed vertically in the middle of the left wall. Examination of the bodies revealed that the mummies were natural, in the sense that none had been submitted to any type of treatment, neither evisceration nor craniotomy. Natural mummification of the bodies was probably made possible by the hot, dry climate of Comiso, which is at the same latitude as Tunis. Confirmation that the bodies in the chapel were dressed only after mummification derives from the discovery that all the monastic clothes had a posterior longitudinal cut running from the bottom to the hood, a cut that must have been made to facilitate the dressing of a dry and therefore very stiff human body.

The Provincial Bernardino del Comiso, who died in 1742 at the approximate age of 50, showed severe arteriosclerosis with calcifications of the lumbar aorta and iliac arteries. A 35 year old individual presented an enormous enlargement of the thyroid gland, histologically a colloid goiter (Fornaciari *et al.* 1997b), and another, about 45 years of age, suffered from massive splenomegaly with infarcted areas. A man aged 30–35 years showed pulmonary fibrosis with multiple, apical calcifications, and was probably affected by tuberculosis; another, who died at about 60 years of age, displayed diffuse skin acariasis, treated during life with sulphur ointments, with hyperkeratosis and abundant eggs, nymphs and mites at different stages of development still *in situ*. There was also a case of colon diverticulosis, two cases of inguino-scrotal hernia and a case of varicose veins with ulcers in the lower limbs (Fornaciari and Gamba 1993).

The Basilica of San Domenico Maggiore, which dates back to the beginning of the fourteenth century, is one of the largest and most important churches in Naples. The humanist Pontano and the philosophers Tommaso Campanella and Giordano Bruno studied in this Abbey, and Saint Thomas Aquinas taught in the annexed convent of the Dominicans. The impressive Sacristy of San Domenico Maggiore, in a suspended gateway close to the vault, contains 38 wooden coffins or 'arks', with the bodies of 10 Aragonese princes and other Neapolitan nobles who died in the fifteenth and sixteenth centuries. The coffins were initially placed in different parts of the church, but in 1594 Philip II, King of Spain, ordered that they should be gathered in the Sacristy (Miele 1977). The sarcophagi, containing bodies richly dressed in precious clothes made of silk, brocade and other material, are distributed in two rows, one above the other. The smaller coffins of the lower row are generally of anonymous individuals, whereas the larger coffins of the upper row are identified by the coats-of-arms and the names of the personages buried inside. In particular they include the Aragonese kings Alfonso I (who died in 1458), Ferrante I (1494), Ferrante II (1496), Queen Giovanna IV (1518) and the Marquis of Pescara, Ferdinando d'Avalos, who won the famous battle of Pavia against the French King François I in 1525.

A first survey showed that the bodies contained in the coffins were generally mummified and well preserved. That of Pietro of Aragon, III Duke of Montalto, who died in 1552 at the age of 12 (Fornaciari 1984b), is an example of a typical burial of Santa Maria Maggiore. It consists of a large external sarcophagus that contains a second coarse wooden coffin; there are plants, such as laurel, rosemary and boxwood, covering the body, which is richly dressed in sixteenth century style, and lying on a layer of small lime fragments, for the

Table 12.2. *Basilica of S. Domenico
Maggiore (Naples): general status*

Total no. individuals	31
Primary deposits	27 (87.1%)
Secondary deposits	4 (12.9%)
Natural mummies	12 (38.7%)
skeletonized	5 (41.7%)
Artificial mummies	15 (48.4%)
skeletonized	1 (6.7%)

drainage of cadaveric fluids. The mummy, with the hands crossed on the pubis, is in an excellent state of preservation.

The mummies of San Domenico Maggiore are unique in Italy not only for the antiquity and excellent state of preservation of the bodies, but also for the fame of the personages, whose lives and causes of death are well known. King Ferrante II, for example, died of malaria, and the Marquis of Pescara died of pulmonary tuberculosis. The possibility of comparing paleopathological with historical data provided extremely interesting results. The only mummies of this type known in Europe have been those of the Hapsburg princes in Vienna (Kleiss 1977).

The sarcophagi of San Domenico Maggiore were carefully examined from 1984 to 1987 by a team from the Institute of Pathology, Pisa University. Radiography followed by anthropological and autopsy examination on site were carried out on the mummies, and the laboratory studies were performed in Pisa. The extremely precious clothes and jewels of the buried individuals have been carefully recovered and will soon be restored by the Superintendence of Naples before going on display at the Museum of Capodimonte.

Let us now summarize the results obtained so far: of the 38 sarcophagi explored, eight were empty and one contained a double deposit. There were 27 primary deposits and four secondary deposits, all previously disturbed. Fifteen individuals (48.4 percent) had been embalmed, and twelve (38.7 percent) had not been treated (Table 12.2). Therefore, the majority had been embalmed, which is certainly not surprising, considering the high social class of the individuals buried in San Domenico. From the physician Ulisse Aldrovandi, we know that during the Renaissance European kings and great personages entrusted the embalming of their bodies to their doctors and surgeons (Aldrovandi 1602). With regard to San Domenico, there is a document

Table 12.3. *Basilica of S. Domenico Maggiore (Naples): types of evisceration in artificial mummies*

Jugulo-pubic incision	9
Xipho-pubic incision	5
Umbilical-transverse	4
(associated with the above)	

Table 12.4. *Basilica of S. Domenico Maggiore (Naples): types of craniotomy in artificial mummies*

Number of mummies	15
Horizontal craniotomy	7
Posterior craniotomy	6
Without craniotomy	2

that tells us about the embalming of the body of Antonio of Aragon, IV Duke of Montalto, who died in 1584: 'Lo corpo e in sacrestia imbalsamato' (his body was embalmed in the sacristy) (C. Vultaggio 1984, personal communication). There were six skeletonized individuals (22.2 percent), but only one from the group of embalmed individuals (Table 12.2). For partial preservation of the bodies, the embalming process was obviously very important. In this respect, nine of 14 individuals, including five children and four adults, had been eviscerated by a long anterior incision running from the base of the neck to the pubic symphysis (Table 12.3). In order to penetrate the thorax, the sternum was cut or sawn or even removed; otherwise, the ribs or costal cartilages were cut sideways with the aid of shears; in one particular case both operations were performed. The sternum was generally cut in newborn babies and sucklings, and less often in adults where, as in modern autopsies, the costal cartilages were cut on each side of the sternum and the anterior thoracic wall was removed. The other five individuals (one child and four adults) presented only an abdominal incision running from the xiphoid process of the sternum to the pubis (Table 12.3). In this case, the thorax had to be eviscerated through the diaphragm. Of the 15 cases of embalmed individuals, 13 had the brain removed by craniotomy, which was horizontal and circular in seven cases and posterior, often circular, in six. (Table 12.4). Widespread defleshing of the muscular masses was observed at the level of

Table 12.5. *Basilica of S. Domenico Maggiore (Naples): frequency of different embalming materials in artificial mummies*

Material	Numbers	Percentage
Resin	10	66.7
Wool	6	40.0
Soil or clay	6	40.0
Lime or ash	4	26.7
Leaves or twigs	3	20.0
Tow	2	13.3
Sponge	2	13.3
Mercury	2	13.3
Cotton	1	6.7

Table 12.6. *Basilica of S. Domenico Maggiore (Naples): types of wood used for inner coffins in primary depositions*

	Natural mummies	Artificial mummies	Total
Fir	5	4	9 (56.2%)
Poplar	2	2	4 (25.0%)
Chestnut	0	3	3 (18.7%)

the dorsum, the glutei, and the limbs in four cases, which included two newborn babies and two adults. The embalming material consisted principally of resinous substances, which were present in ten cases; wool or similar material, and clay or earthy substances were present in six cases; lime was found in four cases, leaves or twigs in three, whereas tow, sponges and mercury were used only twice (Table 12.5). Finally, in four cases, including two newborn babies and two adults, the body was wrapped in bandages previously soaked in resinous substances. Wood for the inner coffins was determined in 16 cases of primary deposits; there was a high incidence of pine wood, used in nine deposits, followed by poplar in four deposits and chestnut wood in three (Table 12.6). Resinous essences, which were thought to favour the preservation of the bodies, were also used in the case of the coffins. These very complex evisceration and embalming methods indicate long-practised and widespread customs but, as already said, some well preserved individuals show no apparent signs of embalming. Natural mummification of the bodies can probably be attributed to the warm and dry climate of Naples during the summer. Preservation of the bodies may have been

FIGURE 12.7. Detail of face with vesiculo-pustular exanthema typical of smallpox in a two year old child (Carbon 14 dating:1569±60).

favoured by the particular microclimatic conditions of San Domenico Maggiore, as well as by the disposition of the coffins, placed near the windows of the sacristy, 5 m above the floor. Furthermore, two large rooms, certainly devoted to dehydration of the bodies, have been discovered recently in the crypts of San Domenico. These two rooms were provided with numbered spaces for the coffins, with wide ventilation shafts, and thick sand beds for gathering the cadaveric fluids. The mummies of San Domenico were probably submitted to the previously described treatment of natural mummification practised in Naples until the last century.

We shall now describe two cases of infectious disease and two cases of neoplastic pathology, from a strictly paleopathological point of view. The mummy of an anonymous two year old boy, whose death dates back to the mid sixteenth century (radiocarbon dating is 1569± 60), presented a diffuse vesiculo-pustular exanthemous skin eruption (Figure 12.7). Macroscopic aspects and regional distribution suggested a case of smallpox. This possibility was confirmed by light microscopy and indirect immunofluorescence with anti-vaccinia virus antibody. Electron microscopy revealed, among the residual bands of collagen fibers, pyknotic nuclei, and membrane remains with rare desmosomes, many egg-shaped, dense virus-like particles (250 ×

FIGURE 12.8. Artificial mummy of Maria d'Aragona (1503–1568).

50 nm), composed of a central dense region (or core) surrounded by a low density area. Following incubation with human anti-vaccinia virus antiserum, after protein A-gold complex immunostaining, the particles were completely covered by protein A-gold. These results showed that the antigenic structure of the viral particles was well preserved and that this Neapolitan child died of a severe form of smallpox some four centuries ago (Fornaciari and Marchetti 1986a, 1986b, 1986c).

The study of a case of treponematosis in the mummy of Maria of Aragon (1503–1568), Marchesa of Vasto in southern Italy, was particularly interesting (Figure 12.8). Famous for her beauty, this noblewoman of the Italian Renaissance belonged to the intellectual and religious circles of Ischia, which also included a friend of Michelangelo's, the poetess Vittoria Colonna. An oval 15 × 10 mm cutaneous ulcer covered by a linen dressing with ivy leaves appeared on the left arm of the mummy (Figure 12.9). Indirect immunofluorescence with human anti-*Treponema pallidum* antibody identified a large number of filaments with strong yellow-green fluorescence and the morphological characteristics of fluorescent treponemes (Figure 12.10). Morphological aspects typical of the spirochetes, as for example the axial fibril, were evidenced by the ultrastructural study. Immunohistochemical and ultrastructural findings clearly demonstrated treponemal infection and the cutaneous ulcer was typical of a third-stage luetic gumma. Venereal syphilis was the most probable diagnosis (Fornaciari *et al.* 1989f, 1994). This discovery is extremely important because it dates back to the sixteenth century and can help to clarify the biology of treponema in the epidemic phase of the disease.

Another important paleopathological case is that of Ferdinando Orsini, Duke of Gravina in Apulia, who died in 1549. The mummy presents wide erosion of the upper orbital margin and the glabella, and complete destruction of the right nasal and retro-orbital bones (Figure 12.11). Histology showed solid neoplasia, with cords of spindle-shaped cells destroying compact and spongy bone and forming osseous lacunae, with no bone reaction. A widely destructive skin epithelioma seems to be the most probable diagnosis (Fornaciari *et al.* 1989d).

The artificial mummy of Ferrante I of Aragon, King of Naples, who died in 1494 at 63 years of age, was submitted to autopsy. This revealed in the pelvis a fragment of a hollow muscular organ, which reached the dimensions of 6 × 4 × 1 cm after dehydration. Histologically, neoplastic epithelial cells disposed in cords, nests and glands were disseminated in a fibrous stroma containing scattered striated muscular fibers (Figure 12.12). The cells were tall, crowded, with abundant cytoplasm and pseudo-stratified pleomorphic hyper-

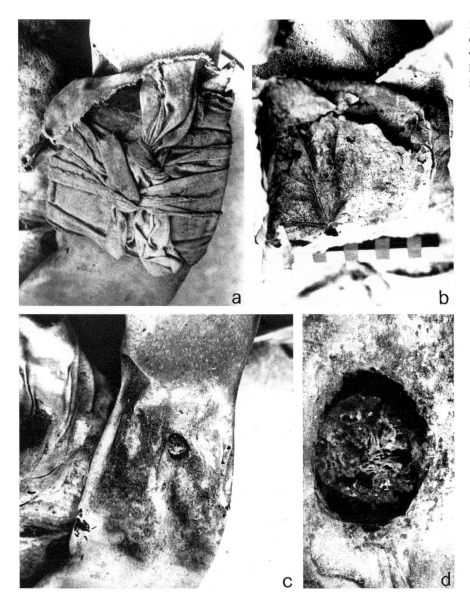

FIGURE 12.9. The left arm dressing still *in situ* (a), with ivy (*Hedera helix*) leaves (b) and the underlying cutaneous ulcer (c, d).

chromatic nuclei. The scant mucus was limited to the pseudoglandular formations, as appeared from the specific Alcian blue staining. The use of a monoclonal antibody against pancytokeratin displayed strong intracytoplasmic immunoreactivity of the tumoral cells. The ultrastructural study evidenced well preserved pleomorphic nuclei with indented membranes. These results clearly indicate a mucinous adenocarcinoma infiltrating the muscles and fibrous layers of the pelvis. The site of the primary neoplasm was at first

FIGURE 12.10. Section of the cutaneous ulcer. Intense, positive indirect immuno-fluorescence reaction with human anti-*Treponema pallidum* antibody: heaped (a, b); or isolated (d); treponemes of various size (c, e). Original magnification: a, b: 250×; c, d: 400×; e: 1000×.

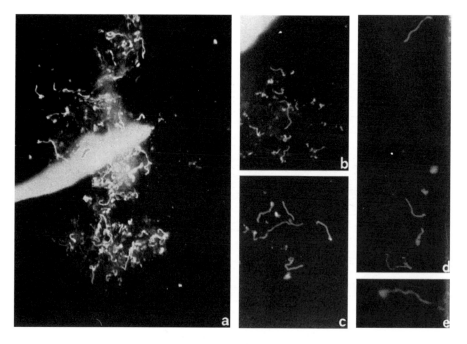

impossible to establish. The histological features only suggested prostatic adenocarcinoma or an adenocarcinoma of the digestive tract (Fornaciari *et al.* 1993). Because colorectal tumors are characterised by frequent mutations of the K-*ras* oncogene and prostatic adenocarcinomas rarely are, we decided to investigate the status of the K-*ras* gene in the DNA extracted from the mummified tumor tissue (Caligo *et al.* 1994). The samples were subjected to a nested polymerase chain reaction (PCR) protocol designed to yield a 77 base pair (bp) K-*ras* fragment encompassing codon 12, the main hotspot for mutations in colon cancer. The hybridization with 32P-labelled mutation specific oligonucleotide probes showed the presence in the tumor sample of a K-*ras* codon 12 point mutation. The normal sequence GGT (glycine) was altered to GAT (aspartic acid). These data clearly demonstrate that Ferrante I was affected by a cancer of the digestive tract, most probably a colonic adenocarcinoma (Marchetti *et al.* 1996). The observed genetic change indeed represents the most frequent mutation of the K-*ras* gene in present-day colorectal cancer and it is thought to be induced by alkylating agents (Topal 1988). Therefore we speculate that mutagens similar to those responsible for the induction of K-*ras* mutations in contemporary colon cancer could be present in the rich diet of a court of the XV century, as supported by paleonutritional studies (Fornaciari *et al.* 1989a). This is the first time an oncogene mutation has been found in an ancient tumor.

FIGURE 12.11. Malignant tumor destroying the right nasal bone and the orbit in the mummy of Ferdinando Orsini, Duke of Gravina (1549).

In conclusion, the paleopathological study of the mummies of eleven adult individuals from the Abbey of San Domenico Maggiore, with good or excellent preservation, allowed us to diagnose two cases of cancer. The number of available specimens was very limited; however, it was possible to observe an incidence of neoplastic pathology (18.8 percent), similar to the one we find nowadays.

Other miscellaneous abnormalities that we wish to point out are a mortal stab-wound, with surrounding hemorrhagic infarction, between the eighth

FIGURE 12.12. Adenocarcinoma with pseudoglandular lumina in fibrous stroma. Hematoxylin and eosin, original magnification: 200×.

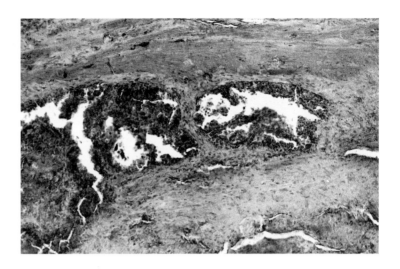

and the ninth left rib in the mummy of an anonymous gentleman who died at the age of about 27 in the second half of the sixteenth century (Fornaciari *et al.* 1989e); a case of liver cirrhosis with typical nodules; a case of acute pulmonary oedema, or pneumonia, in an individual with severe anthracosis; and an individual affected by calculosis of the gall-bladder with chronic cholecystitis (Fornaciari *et al.* 1989b). Particularly important is the recent discovery of a sequence of hepatitis E virus (HEV) in the DNA extracted from the mummy of Maria of Aragon (Marota *et al.* 1997).

Most Italian mummies have not yet been examined. For example, the recent restorations of the Basilica of San Francesco in Arezzo (Tuscany) revealed the presence of some unexpected burials, a series of nine anthropoid coffins at a depth of one meter, with a cross painted on each lid. These contained nine well preserved bodies, among them the completely dressed mummies of a prelate in his ceremonial tunic, a woman, a young girl, and a child about three years old wearing a small garland of flowers. The child was wrapped in a sudarium (a napkin or cloth to wipe the face), and the woman, still wearing valuable rings and earrings, was dressed in an elegant long dress with embroidered cuffs and a lace collar. Two other adult mummies clasp a rosary and a crucifix in their hands. Based on known architectural changes of the Basilica, the mummies could be dated between 1377 and the beginning of the seventeenth century. Identification of the individuals is not possible at present, but considering the importance of the burial site, we can assume that they were eminent members of the wealthy Renaissance class, certainly benefactors of the Franciscan Order (Fornaciari 1997).

These natural mummies have since been dated to the second half of the sixteenth century (Fornaciari *et al.* 1997a). Radiographic examination of the asymmetrically enlarged abdomen of the woman in the long dress excluded pregnancy but revealed spina bifida. Computed tomography also showed biliary and renal lithiasis, and several dilated loops of bowel, which suggested intestinal obstruction as a cause of the enlarged abdomen and the probable cause of death. Only a classical autopsy will allow us to establish the true etiology, perhaps a tumor, of this clinical picture from four centuries ago.

THE UAN MUHUGGIAG INFANT MUMMY

Antonio Ascenzi

The mountain range called Tadrart Acacus, in southern Libya (Fezzan), is situated to the east of the Ghat oasis, with a surface area of about 6000 km². Much of it was explored by F. Mori during the winter of 1958–1959 on the occasion of his fourth paleoethnological expedition (Mori 1960). Almost at the end of the mission, a deposit was discovered in the Tagzelt Valley, under a natural shelter called Uan Muhuggiag. Like the other shelters in the zone, the walls and ceiling are covered by more than 100 rock paintings, indicating that the site was actively used during the prehistoric era.

In order to examine the structure of the deposit, an excavation was made measuring 160 by 80 cm and running east and west. In this way it was determined that the deposit was about 1 m deep and rested on sandstone flags. On the western side of the excavation, fragments of long animal bones and bone tools were found. The eastern side of the excavation revealed a clear stratification caused by alternating layers of coals, ashes, and fibrous matter. Under the lowest layer of coals, the sandstone floor showed an intentional circular excavation 25 cm in diameter but only 3 cm deep. Here, under a layer of randomly distributed vegetable fibers, the mummy of a child was found (Figure 12.13), almost completely wrapped in an envelope of animal skin and bearing a necklace of little rings made from the shells of ostrich eggs (Arkell *et al.* 1961).

Dating by the radiocarbon method was carried out by Professor E. Tongiorgi at the University of Pisa using two different types of sample: the lowest coal layer of the deposit and the envelope of animal skin. The first sample was 7438±220 years old, and the second 5405±180 years old.

The body was in an unusual position, with an extreme flexion of the trunk and a forced rotation of the head to the right. The upper right arm was stretched and pulled backwards to some extent behind the trunk. The right

FIGURE 12.13. The Uan Muhuggiag infant
mummy. (Courtesy of F. Mori.)

forearm was flexed. The legs were in a squatting position near the head, but it
was not possible to deduce their exact position because a partial dislocation
had occurred. A careful examination revealed a long incision in the anterior
abdominal wall, apparently for the purpose of removing the thoracic and
abdominal viscera, of which no traces were left. An irregular, 10 cm long cone
lay between the edges of the abdominal incision. The structure consisted of a
light, porous conglomerate of black mold mixed with granules, probably
vegetable seeds. The genital organs were badly preserved, so that the sex
could not be determined.

Anthropological research (Mori and Ascenzi 1959) provided evidence that
the child had negroid characteristics, and that at the time of death it was
about 30 months old. The skull showed the following main features: pen-
tagonoid form with sharp occipital heel, protuberant forehead of infantile
type, dolichocephaly near to mesocephaly, camecephaly, and tapeinocephaly.
The face revealed an obvious prognathism, with a Camper's angle of 70°.

Micro- and macroscopic examination supports the view that, in the Uan
Muhuggiag child, mummification was obtained by drying after removing
thoracic and abdominal viscera. This conclusion emphasizes that the
spontaneous preservation of bodies in warm, dry environments probably

played a major role in suggesting to ancient populations how artificial mummification could be achieved.

THE GUANCHE MUMMIES

Conrado Rodríguez-Martín

The Canarian archipelago consists of seven major islands rising out of the Atlantic Ocean near the northwestern coast of Africa (the western Canary Islands: Tenerife, La Palma, La Gomera and El Hierro; and the eastern Canary Islands: Gran Canaria, Fuerteventura and Lanzarote). Due to the tradewinds, the northern parts of the western Canary Islands and Gran Canaria are humid with frequent rains permitting luxuriant forests. The southern slopes are separated from the north by high mountains and are dry.

The first people to colonize this archipelago arrived in the Canaries around the fifth century BC; they belonged to the Berber tribes of nearby North Africa. Recent studies indicate that they were brought here by sailors of the Phoenician–Punic area in the Mediterranean basin, to set up colonies for tuna fishing (González Antón *et al.* 1995). During the two millennia that elapsed between the first colonies and the Spanish conquest in the fifteenth century of our era, different cultures developed in the seven major islands of the archipelago. Despite the similarities existing among those cultures, the isolation from the external world and among the islands themselves made possible different cultural manifestations and practices, including the language. The raising of cattle, goats, sheep and pigs, along with primitive forms of agriculture and food gathering and some fishing, constituted the economic basis of the earlier Canarian population.

This was the scene found by Europeans when the Conquest began in 1402 in Lanzarote, progressing slowly to the other islands until 1496, the year that Tenerife, the largest island, was conquered. After a century of war, slavery, famines, plus diseases imported by the new settlers, especially the influenza that killed one third of the Guanche population of Tenerife (Rodríguez-Martín 1994), the aboriginal population decreased rapidly. By the early sixteenth century, the pre-Hispanic Canarian world was only a memory.

Guanche mummies have been famous since the Spaniards discovered them and were astonished by the superb preservation of those specimens. In the five centuries since then, the reasons for mummification, the climatic influence on the preservation of mummies, the mummification methods, social status, and the existence of specialists in that work, have all been debated. However, neither the early historians of the Canaries nor modern scientists investigated the mummies in detail and their studies were focused on earlier historical sources. The lack of direct analysis was due to the scarcity of these most valuable relics due to degenerative changes, and/or the technical difficulties in carrying out those studies. Until very recently, research in this important field of Canarian prehistory has not been as brilliant as might have been hoped (Rodríguez-Martín 1992, 1996).

Verneau (1887) and Hooton (1925) agreed that mummification was a common practice in the whole archipelago. Arco (1976) affirms that mummification has been demonstrated only in the islands of Tenerife, Gran Canaria, La Gomera and El Hierro. Here we shall discuss only the Guanche mummies of Tenerife, the best preserved and most thoroughly studied.

It seems clear that only the elite members of Guanche society were mummified. There was a 'corpus' of specialists (males or females depending on the sex of the corpse) responsible for carrying out that job, who were considered as contaminated and impure by the rest of Guanche society. In the majority of cases, an anthropogenic mummification can be demonstrated, although spontaneous mummification has been reported in many cases. Of the methods reported by the ancient chroniclers (exposing to sun and smoke, evisceration, craniotomy, external use of preservatives, introduction of preservatives through corporal cavities, and so on), only three have been observed in Guanche mummies;

1.   Evisceration: Chil (1876) observed thoracic and abdominal incisions in some mummies that could be used for visceral removal. Perhaps evisceration was used only in the individuals of the highest stratum of Guanche society.

2.   Preservatives: recent analyses demonstrate the presence of mineral substances (red lapilli, pumice stone, and soil); vegetals (needles of *Pinus canariensis*; seeds of *Visnea mocanera*; Dragon Tree blood remains; gramineous stems; and charcoal); and solidified fat (Ortega and Sánchez-Pinto 1992).

3.   Sand-stuffing: this method was not described in the ancient chronicles and was first identified by Brothwell and colleagues (1969).

Although not identifiable, sun exposure and smoking of the mummy (small burns in the mummy surface have been observed) must have played a role in the dehydration process. According to Aufderheide and associates (1992), the island's climate would have provided the appropriate conditions for the preservation of the specimens. The last step in the mummification process was wrapping in animal skins, the number used depending on the social status (*menceys*, or kings, were wrapped in 10 to 15 skins). After that,

FIGURE 12.14. Mummy MVC 1. Mummified adult male from San Andrés (Santa Cruz de Tenerife). The mummy rests on the typical *chajasco* (funerary board) in order to avoid contact with the soil. Source: Museo Arqueológico de Tenerife (OAMC).

the corpse was placed in a cave, avoiding contact with the soil by means of funerary boards (Figure 12.14), and was isolated from the external world by walls of dry stone.

Demographic profiles are different within the island. On the northern slope, the general life expectancy was around 30 years, whereas in the more arid south life expectancy was about five years less. The shortest life expectancy (under 25 years) was observed in the isolated region of Anaga, where agriculture, cattle raising, and forest gathering are very difficult and inbreeding was frequent until recently.

Dietary analysis demonstrates that vegetal fractions in the north were higher than in the south. The diet on the northern slope of Tenerife was 50 percent meat and dairy products and 40 to 45 percent vegetals, whereas on the southern slope 60 to 70 percent of the diet was based on meat and dairy products. Marine fractions were low in both regions (less than 10 percent). This reflects the different economical basis in the two areas: cattle raising, agriculture and/or forest gathering were equally distributed in the north but in the south it was mainly cattle raising.

Physical stress played an important role in Guanche daily life, beginning in adolescence and early adulthood. High frequencies of degenerative changes in joints, especially shoulder and elbow, osteochondritis dissecans, postcranial trauma, and markers of occupational stress are present on both slopes of Tenerife. Analysis of cranial trauma demonstrates high frequencies among the Guanche population, especially in the south, where some series show 10 to 20 percent of cranial fractures. Almost 90 percent of the fractures observed among the Guanches were produced by violent practices (depressed fractures caused by stone missiles and bolas, and spear and wooden sword wounds). This reflects almost constant warfare among the Guanches, and agrees with the chronicles affirming that battles were common in pre-Hispanic Tenerife due to conflicts over cattle and territory.

The high frequencies of various congenital malformations, especially spina bifida occulta and transitional vertebrae at the lumbosacral level, are indicators of inbreeding. This is more marked in some regions of the island like Daute-Teno and Anaga, where inbreeding played an important role for many years after the Conquest. Low frequencies of metabolic stress markers and iron deficiency anemia (Harris lines, enamel hypoplasia, nonspecific infections, porotic hyperostosis, and cribra orbitalia) along with well marked sexual dimorphism in most series, tall stature, and marked robusticity indices imply that the Guanches were, in general, well adapted to the island's environment.

REFERENCES

Grottarossa mummy

Ascenzi, A., Bianco, P., Nicoletti, R., Ceccarini, G., Fornaseri, M., Graziani, G., Giuliani, M. R., Rosicarello, R., Ciuffarella, L. and Granger-Taylor, H. 1996. The Roman mummy of Grottarossa. In *Human mummies: global survey of their status and the techniques of conservation*, vol. 3. *The man in the ice*, ed. K. Spindler, H. Wilfing, E. Rastbichler-Zissernig, D. zur Nedden and H. Nothdurfter, 204–17. Vienna: Springer Verlag.

Beckwith, J. 1954. Textile fragments from classical antiquity. *Illustrated London News*, Jan. 23: 114–15.

Bordenache Battaglia, G. 1983. *Corredi funerari di età imperiale e barbarica nel Museo Nazionale Romano*. Roma: Edizioni Quasat.

Granger-Taylor, H. 1982. Weaving clothes in the Ancient World: the tunic and toga of the Arringatore. *Textile History* 13: 3–25.

Granger-Taylor, H. 1983. Two Dalmatics of St. Ambrose? *CIETA Bulletin* 57: 127–63.

Granger-Taylor, H. 1987. Two silk textiles from Rome and some thoughts on the Roman silk-weaving industry. *CIETA Bulletin* 65: 13–31.

Malaise, M. 1972a. *Inventaire préliminaire des documents égyptiens découverts en Italie* Leiden: Brill.

Malaise, M. 1972b. *Les conditions de pénétration et de diffusion des cultes égyptiens en Italie*. Leiden: Brill.

Roullet, A. 1972. *The Egyptian and Egyptianizing monuments of imperial Rome*. Leiden: Brill.

Italian Mummies

Aldrovandi, U. [1602]. Cited in Gannal, J. N. 1841. *Histoire des embaumements*. Paris: Desloges.

Aufderheide, A. C. and Aufderheide, M. L. 1991. Taphonomy of spontaneous (natural) mummification with applications to the mummies of Venzone, Italy. In *Human paleopathology, current syntheses and future options*, ed. D. J. Ortner and A. C. Aufderheide, 79–86. Washington, DC: Smithsonian Institution Press.

Caligo, M. A., Cipollini G., Ghimenti C., Moretti, A., Bevilacqua G. and Fornaciari, G. 1994. Caratterizzazione degli acidi nucleici estratti dalle mummie della Basilica di S. Domenico Maggiore in Napoli. *Rivista di Antropologia* **72**: 105–10.

Capasso, L. and Di Tota, G. 1991. The human mummies of Navelli: natural mummification at new site in central Italy. *Paleopathology Newsletter* **75**: 7–8.

Di Colo, F. 1910. L'imbalsamazione umana: manuale teorico pratico. Milano: Hoepli.

Fornaciari, G. 1984a. The mummies of the Abbey of Saint Domenico Maggiore in Naples: a plan of research. *Paleopathology Newsletter* **45**: 9–10.

Fornaciari, G. 1984b. The mummies of the Abbey of Saint Domenico Maggiore in Naples. *Paleopathology Newsletter* **47**: 10–14.

Fornaciari, G. 1986. The mummies of the Abbey of Saint Domenico Maggiore in Naples: a preliminary survey. In *Proceedings of the V European Meeting of the Paleopathology Association*, ed. V. Capecchi and E. Rabino-Massa, 97–104. Siena: Siena University.

Fornaciari, G. 1997. The mummies of the Basilica of San Francesco in Arezzo (Tuscany, Central Italy). *Paleopathology Newsletter* **97**: 13–14.

Fornaciari, G. and Capasso, L. 1996. Natural and artificial mummies in Italy (13th–19th centuries). In *Human mummies: a global survey of their status and the techniques of conservation*, vol. 3, *The man in the ice*, ed. K. Spindler, H. Wilfing, E. Rastbichler-Zissernig, D. zur Nedden and H. Nothdurfter, 195–203. Vienna: Springer Verlag.

Fornaciari, G. and Gamba, S. 1993. The mummies of the church of S. Maria della Grazia in Comiso, Sicily (18th–19th century). *Paleopathology Newsletter* **81**: 7–10.

Fornaciari, G. and Marchetti, A. 1986a. Intact smallpox virus particles in an Italian mummy of sixteenth century. *Lancet* **2**(8507): 625.

Fornaciari, G. and Marchetti, A. 1986b. Intact smallpox virus particles in an Italian mummy of the XVI century: an immuno-electron microscopic study. *Paleopathology Newsletter* **56**: 7–12.

Fornaciari, G. and Marchetti, A. 1986c. Italian smallpox of the sixteenth century. *Lancet* **2**(8521): 1469–70.

Fornaciari, G. and Torino, M. 1995. Exploration of the tomb of Pandolfo III Malatesta (1370–1427), prince of Fano (Central Italy). *Paleopathology Newsletter* **92**: 7–9.

Fornaciari G., Bruno J., Corcione N., Tornaboni D. and

Castagna M. 1989d. Un cas de tumeur maligne primitive de la région naso-orbitaire dans une momie de la basilique de S. Domenico Maggiore à Naples (XVIe siècle). In *Advances in paleopathology: Proceedings of the VII European Meeting of the Paleopathology Association*, ed. L. Capasso, 65–9. Chieti, Italy: Solfanelli.

Fornaciari, G., Bruno J., Corcione, N., Tornaboni, D. and Tognetti, A. 1989e. Blessure mortelle de pointe dans une momie de sexe masculin de la basilique de S. Domenico Maggiore à Naples. In *Advances in paleopathology: Proceedings of the VII European Meeting of the Paleopathology Association*, ed. L. Capasso, 71–4. Chieti, Italy: Solfanelli.

Fornaciari, G., Castagna, M., Naccarato, A. G., Tognetti, A., Collecchi, P. and Bevilacqua, G. 1993. Adenocarcinoma in the mummy of Ferrante I of Aragon, King of Naples (1431–1494). *Paleopathology Newsletter* **82**: 7–11.

Fornaciari, G., Castagna, M., Naccarato, A. G., Viacava, P. and Bevilacqua, G. 1994. New observations on a case of treponematosis (venereal syphilis?) in an Italian mummy of the 16th century. In *L'origine de la Syphilis en Europe – Avant ou après 1493?* ed. O. Dutour, Gy. Pálfi, J. Berato and J-P. Brun, 206–10. Paris: Editions Errance-Centre Archéologique du Var.

Fornaciari, G., Castagna, M., Tognetti, A., Tornaboni, D. and Bruno, J. 1989f. Syphilis in a renaissance Italian mummy. *Lancet* **2**(8663): 614.

Fornaciari, G., Castagna, M., Tornaboni, D., and Lenziardi, M. 1997b. Thyroid goiter in a XVIII century Sicilian mummy. In *Proceedings of the Xth European Meeting of the Paleopathology Association*, ed. M. Schultz, K. Kreutz and W-R. Teegen. Espelkamp: Leidorf Verlag. In press.

Fornaciari, G., Ceccanti, B., Corcione, N. and Bruno, J. 1989a. Recherches paléonutritionelles sur un échantillon d'une classe socialement élevée de la Renaissance Italienne: la série de momies de S. Domenico Maggiore à Naples (XVe–XVIe siècles). In *Advances in paleopathology: Proceedings of the VII European Meeting of the Paleopathology Association*, ed. L. Capasso, 81–7. Chieti, Italy: Solfanelli

Fornaciari, G., Ciranni R. and Gibilisco, G. 1997a. Expansive abdominal mass in a mummy of the XVI century: 'clinical picture,' digital radiology and CT, Paper presented at the 12th International Congress of the Adriatic Society of Pathology, Ostuni (Brindisi), 27–29 June 1997.

Fornaciari, G., Pollina, L., Tornaboni, D. and Tognetti A. 1989b. Pulmonary and hepatic pathologies in the series of mummies of S. Domenico Maggiore at Naples (XVI century). In *Advances in paleopathology: Proceedings of the VII European Meeting of the Paleopathology Association*, ed. L. Capasso, 89–92. Chieti, Italy: Solfanelli

Fornaciari, G., Spremolla, G., Vergamini, P. and Benedetti, E. 1989c. Analysis of pulmonary tissue from a natural mummy of the XIII century (Saint Zita, Lucca, Tuscany, Italy) by FT-IR microspectroscopy. *Paleopathology Newsletter* **68**: 5–8.

Fulcheri, E. 1991. Il patologo di fronte al problema della perizia in corso di ricognizione sulle reliquie dei Santi. *Pathologica* **83**: 373–97.

Fulcheri, E. 1996. Mummies of saints: a particular category of Italian mummies. In *Human mummies: a global survey of their status and the techniques of conservation*, vol. 3, *The man in the ice*. ed. K. Spindler, H. Wilfing, E. Rastbichler-Zissernig, D. zur Nedden and H. Nothdurfter, 219–30. Vienna: Springer Verlag.

Kleiss, E. 1977. Some examples of natural mummies. *Paleopathology Newsletter* **20**: 5–6.

Marchetti, A., Pellegrini, S., Bevilacqua, G., and Fornaciari, G. 1996. K-ras mutation in the tumor of Ferrante I of Aragon, King of Naples (1431–1494). *Lancet* **347**: 1272.

Marota, I., Fornaciari, G. and Rollo, F. 1997. Hepatitis E virus (HEV) sequence in the DNA of a XVI century Italian mummy. *Naturwissenschaften* submitted.

Miele, M. 1977. *La Basilica di S. Domenico Maggiore in Napoli*. Napoli: Laurenziana.

Terribile, V. and Corrain, C. 1986. Pratiche imbalsamatorie in Europa. *Pathologica* **18**: 107–18.

Topal, M. D. 1988. DNA repair, oncogenes and carcinogenesis. *Carcinogenesis* **9**: 691–6.

Uan Muhuggiag mummy

Arkell, A. J., Cornwall, J. W. and Mori, F. 1961. Analisi degli anelli componenti la collana della mummia infantile di Uan Muhuggiag. *Rivista di Antropologia* **48**: 161–6.

Mori, F. 1960. Quarta missione paletnologica nell'Acacus (Sahara Fezzanese). *Ricerca Scientifica* **30**: 61–72.

Mori, P. and Ascenzi, A. 1959. La mummia infantile di Uan Muhuggiag: osservazioni antropologiche. *Rivista di Antropologia* **46**: 125–48.

Guanche mummies

Arco Aguilar, M. C. del. 1976. El enterramiento canario prehispánico. *Anuario de Estudios Atlánticos* **22**: 13–124.

Aufderheide, A. C., Rodríguez-Martín, C. and Torbenson, M. 1992. Anatomic findings in studies of Guanche mummified human remains from Tenerife. In *Proceedings of the I World Congress on Mummy Studies*, vol. 1, 33–40. Santa Cruz de Tenerife: Museo Arqueológico y Etnográfico de Tenerife.

Brothwell, D., Sandison, A. T. and Gray P. H. K. 1969. Human biological observations on a Guanche mummy with anthracosis. *American Journal of Physical Anthropology* **30**: 333–48.

Chil y Naranjo, G. 1876. Estudios históricos, climatológicos y patológicos de las Islas Canarias. Las Palmas: Miranda.

González Antón, R., Balbín Behrmann, R., Bueno Ramírez, P. and Arco Aguilar, M. C. del. 1995. *La piedra Zanata*. Santa Cruz de Tenerife: Museo Arqueológico y Etnográfico de Tenerife.

Hooton, E. A. 1925. *The ancient inhabitants of the Canary Islands*. Cambridge, MA: Harvard African Studies.

Ortega, G. and Sánchez-Pinto, L. 1992. Análisis de los materiales de relleno de las momias Guanches. In *Proceedings of the I World Congress on Mummy Studies*, vol. 1, 145–50. Santa Cruz de Tenerife: Museo Arqueológico y Etnográfico de Tenerife.

Rodríguez-Martín, C. 1992. Una historia de las momias Guanches. In *Proceedings of the I World Congress on Mummy Studies*, vol. 1, 151–62. Santa Cruz de Tenerife: Museo Arqueológico y Etnográfico de Tenerife.

Rodríguez-Martín, C. 1994. The epidemic of Modorra (1494–1495) among the Guanches of Tenerife. *Journal of Paleopathology* **6**: 5–14.

Rodríguez-Martín, C. 1996. Guanche mummies of Tenerife (Canary Islands): conservation and scientific studies in the CRONOS Project. In *Human mummies: a global survey of their status and the techniques of conservation*, vol. 3, *The man in the ice*. ed. K. Spindler, H. Wilfing, E. Rastbichler-Zissernig, D. zur Nedden and H. Nothdurfter, 183–93. Vienna: Springer Verlag.

Verneau, R. 1887. Rapport sur une mission scientifique dans l'Archipel Canarien. *Archives des Missions Scientifiques et Litteraries* **3**: 567–817.

13

Mummification in Australia and Melanesia

GRAEME L. PRETTY AND ANGELA CALDER

Any description of mummification in Australia and Melanesia is made more difficult by the irregularity of the evidence about funerary customs. There are two reasons for this. First, the accuracy of ethnographic reports has varied considerably, both spatially and temporally. Second, the variability and complexity of mortuary practices in these regions have continued to defy systematization. Mummification was considered to be only one component in a spectrum of cultural rituals associated with death and was practiced by relatively few tribal groups.

The most adequately documented area for this practice is the Torres Strait Islands. Ethnographic accounts for the entire region have proved exceptionally valuable sources of information about the techniques involved and the diverse motives for the preservation of the dead. In Australia, study of the corpse was instrumental in determining the suspect agent of death; by contrast, Melanesian customs were concerned more with maintaining the physical integrity of the deceased. Similarly, preservation techniques ranged from simple procedures involving natural desiccation by solar processes to more complex methods of smoke drying corpses.

A further problem has been created by vagueness in the definition of mummification and in the use of the word. Whereas accidental preservation of exposed bodies by desiccation occurred widely and randomly, purposeful preservation of bodies, or true mummification, was seldom recorded for Australia or Melanesia.

Despite these limitations, the evidence for mummification in this part of the world deserves serious attention. First, it refines our knowledge of mummification as a globally distributed custom. Second, this type of research also provides uncontaminated source material for biological assessments of indigenous populations in regions where hybridization has recently occurred.

FIGURE 13.1. Areas in Australia where mummification was practiced. (Map by Timothy Motz, Detroit Institute of Arts.)

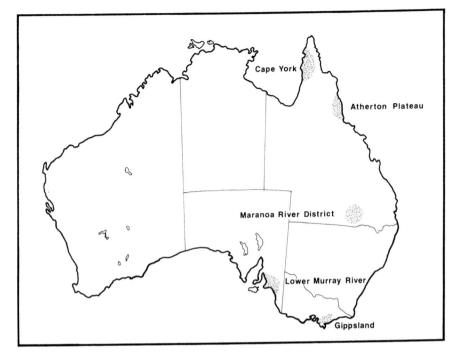

DISTRIBUTION

In Aboriginal Australia a great range of mortuary rituals was employed in the disposal of the dead. The processes involved were either simple (primary disposal) or compound (secondary disposal) (Hiatt 1969: 104). Simple disposal was characterized by the use of only one procedure, at a specific time, and was generally spread across the south of the continent. Compound disposal, of which mummification or desiccation was occasionally a part, was widespread in the northern part of Australia. Desiccated and partly decayed bodies have been randomly reported from widely scattered localities, as well as preserved parts of bodies such as hands and organs (Howitt 1904: 459–60; Mathews 1905; Dawson 1928). Although smoking and drying techniques for preserving bodily parts were widespread, deliberate mummification was restricted to five main areas (Berndt and Berndt 1964: 392–4; Figure 13.1). These were the Lower Murray River and Adelaide Plains (Angas 1847a: Flower 1879; Taplin and Meyer, in Woods 1879: 20–1; 198–200; Tolmer 1882: 273; Stirling 1893; Basedow 1925; Elkin 1954: 313); Gippsland (Howitt 1904: 459–60); the Maranoa district in southeastern Queensland (Howitt 1904: 467–8; Hamlyn-Harris 1912b; Bull 1965); the Atherton Plateau near Cairns (Roth 1907: 366–403; Hamlyn-Harris 1912b); and Cape York (McConnel 1937).

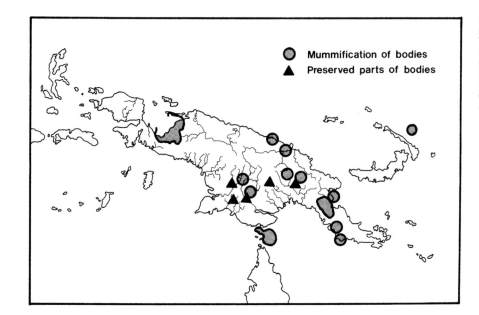

FIGURE 13.2. Areas in New Guinea where mummification was practiced. (Based on Pretty 1969; map by Timothy Motz, Detroit Institute of Arts.)

In Melanesia the preserving of fleshed and integumental parts and whole bodies appeared to be an extension of a widespread tradition of conserving relics of the dead as memorials. The best known example of this practice was the Melanesian penchant for preserving heads, usually as trophies. Deliberate mummification of whole bodies was, however, performed in several distinct localities (Pretty 1969; Figure 13.2). One area where the practice was common until very recent times was the Central Highlands in a locality inhabited by the Kukukuku tribes (Simpson 1953: 163–6; Bjerre, 1956: 85–9; Pretty 1972: 20–8). Numerous references exist to mummification in surrounding areas (Rhys 1947: 148; Le Roux 1948: 747–755) as far south as coastal Port Moresby, west as far as the the Wahgi valley, and toward the north coast where the Buang tribes smoke dried bodies (Vial 1963: 37; Girard 1957).

Another main center was in West New Guinea, where the custom extended along part of the southern shore of Geelvinck Bay and into the ranges east of Wissel Lakes (Held 1957: 177–8; J. V. de Bruijn 1963; personal communication). Closer to Torres Strait, in an area enclosed by the tract of swampy, lowlying country that extends from the lower Fly River across in Irian Jaya, there were frequent references to the preservation of sections of bodies and occasionally entire corpses (Haddon 1935: 332–3).

A third important center for mummification was the Torres Strait (Pretty 1969; Figure 13.3) There the practice was confined to the eastern islands (Pretty 1969: 35), which Haddon distinguished culturally from the western

Mummies of the world

FIGURE 13.3. Areas in
the Torres Strait where
mummification was prac-
ticed. (Based on Pretty
1969; map by Timothy
Motz, Detroit Institute of
Arts.)

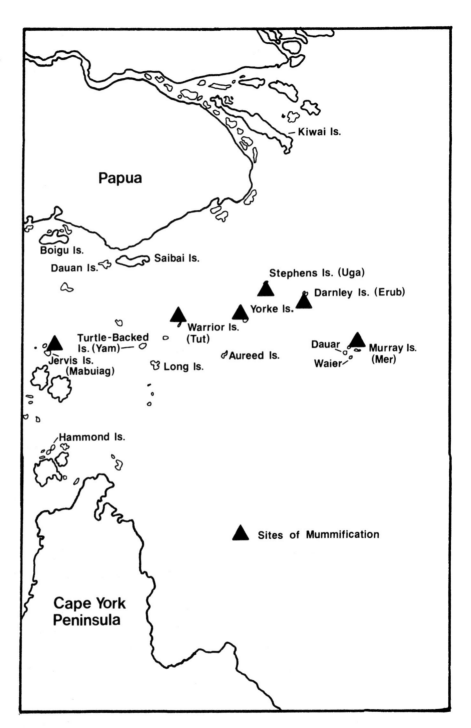

group (Haddon 1935: 322). However, most reports have concerned Darnley Island (Flower 1879; Albertis 1880; Sengstake 1892), in particular the mummy collected by Macleay (Hamlyn-Harris 1912a; Elliot Smith 1915; Dawson 1924; Fletcher 1929; Abbie 1959; Pretty 1969).

The distribution of mummification in Melanesia was not restricted exclusively to the aforementioned areas. As mummification was not an obligatory ritual for many tribes, its practice was sporadic. This behavioural flexibility was demonstrated at the 1963 Mount Hagen Agricultural Show, when a community from Laiagam, not known as practitioners of mummification, brought in attendance the preserved body of one of their fight leaders. While alive, this leader had expressed a desire to see the show, but had died two years earlier. His kinsmen had preserved his body and carried it to the show in accordance with his wishes (S. G. Moriarty, 1965; personal communication).

ORIGINS

Prehistorians consider that island Southeast Asia was the area from which Australia and Melanesia were first settled (Mulvaney 1969). This event occurred some 40 000 years ago during the last glacial epoch and at a time when the lowered sea levels resulted in an extension of the main land masses and the linkage of Tasmania and New Guinea with the Australian continent. Archaeological research has shown that since first settlement, Aboriginal societies have been adapting to changing local conditions and that much social and cultural diversity has ensued (Mulvaney and Golson 1971). Such variation has occurred within Australia and New Guinea, the latter being subjected to a greater range of outside influences owing to its proximity to both Southeast Asia and the Pacific.

Unlike other regions which also had extensive antiquities, Australia and Melanesia have no mummies of any great age. In this region, deliberate mummification was never intended to prolong the corpse's existence for more than a few years at most. Therefore, the identification of ancient mummies from prehistoric skeletal remains has proved extremely difficult.

One promising aspect, which may be linked with the origins of mummification but which has not yet been adequately examined, is the antiquity and distribution of compound funerary modes. All known specimens of historic mummies were from compound contexts. Compound burial practices in this region extended over a long period of time. However, to date there is no information to suggest that simple primary inhumations were as ancient as compound methods.

Prehistorians are presently unable to determine what funerary customs were practiced by the ancient people of Trinil, Modjokerto, and Ngandong in Java because the remains recovered have come from disturbed stratigraphical contexts. However, the finds from Niah (Howells 1973: 177) and the interral of cremated ashes at Mungo (Bowler *et al.* 1970) were indicative of compound disposal modes. Careful excavations have also distinguished secondary from primary burial at Roonka in South Australia.

There, preliminary interpretations suggest that the practice of using compound funerary methods may have been widespread throughout southern Australia during the period from 7000 to 4000 BP (Pretty 1977). The presence of compound disposal is indicative of a milieu in which mummification may have occurred, but extremely rigorous archaeological observation is necessary before such conclusions can be definitely reached.

Information about burial customs became more detailed from the late sixteenth to mid twentieth centuries, during which period European explorers, traders, administrators, missionaries, and scholars made ethnographic comments about the region. None of these reports was sufficiently comprehensive to give insight into the origins of mummification, and few provided explanations for the distinctiveness of the practice in such widely scattered localities.

Taplin was one author who sought explanations for the origins of the practice by studying the Narrinyeri, a confederation of aboriginal tribes who lived at the mouth of the Murray River (Taplin, in Woods 1879). He explained the distinctiveness of mummification to this community by relating it to a unique mythic hero, Ngurundere, from whom the tribes claimed their descent. This custom and a sense of community cohesion were reinforced by tribal sanctions that held all other tribal groups as enemies. The Narrinyeri, then, represented a people who, in a region characterized by simple disposal methods, practiced a highly complex mode of funerary disposal that incorporated mummification (Angas 1847b). Other scholars of the Narrinyeri have used this evidence for mummification as a tool for interpreting the prehistoric settlement patterns of the lower Murray River (Stirling 1911; Pretty 1977).

SOCIAL AND RELIGIOUS BELIEFS

The stimulus for preserving whole bodies, parts of bodies, or human bones in Australia and Melanesia was generally attributable to one or more of the following sentiments:

1   A simple compensatory and restorative reaction to the loss of a relative or friend and the sense of grief this caused.

2   The performance of a formally sanctioned duty to a certain class of person.

3   The fulfillment of obligations to avert mischief by the spirits of the dead.

4   The bearing of symbols of status; for example, the jawbone of her dead husband borne by a wife as a sign of womanhood.

In the majority of instances where the motives for purposeful mummification were recorded, the custom acccorded largely with the first of these sentiments – the playing out of a compensatory reaction to grief. Apparently, mummification in this region was neither a formal observance nor a mode of treatment conferred upon all members even of a certain class. The process and motives were limited by temporal considerations, for once the mourning period with its associated rites was over, the corpse was finally disposed of by procedures such as burial, cremation, or exposure to the elements.

This range of reasons for preserving the physical remains of the dead bore parallels to similar motives that governed several other aspects of mortuary practices, many of which were incorporated into mummification rites. Mourning observances often involved the demonstration of grief by self-inflicted injury or token cannibalism of the corpse. In some areas, inquests were held to divine the inflictor of death by study of the deceased's entrails, resulting frequently in long-term vendettas.

This plethora of funerary behaviors was inevitable in small-scale societies whose religious systems provided no transcendental dimensions to death. Death was a disaster that ranged in severity according to the social status of the deceased. Small children, women, and senile persons were generally of less importance than warriors or leaders. In such an emotional situation the feelings of grief and revenge felt by relatives often determined the funerary procedures. Mummification was an exceptional treatment conducted under special circumstances. It was an expensive process and placed considerable demands upon kinfolk.

The desperate and vindictive attitude to death in these societies and the consequent motives for mummification stood in marked contrast to other regions, such as ancient Egypt or Peru, where mummification was performed to celebrate beliefs about the afterlife. On the other hand, the actual mode of disposal corresponded to practices elsewhere, in that selection for mummification was based on the status of the deceased.

Although basic social and religious beliefs concerning the disposal of the dead were similar in Australia and Melanasia, there were distinguishable features in both regions. These differences were based more on a change of emphasis than on any single observable factor. In Australia the aim of

FIGURE 13.4. Mode of preparing the bodies of the warriors slain in battle among the tribes of Lake Alexandrina. After a fight is over, the corpses of the young men who have been killed are set up cross-legged on a platform, with the faces toward the rising sun. The arms are extended by means of sticks; the head is fastened back; and all the apertures of the body are sewn up. The hair is plucked off, and the fat of the body, which had previously been taken out, is mixed with red ocher and rubbed all over the corpse. Fires are then kindled underneath the platform, and the friends and mourners take up their positions around it, where they remain for about 10 days, during the whole of which time the mourners are not allowed to speak; a guard is placed on each side of the corpse, whose duty it is to keep off the flies with bunches of emu feathers or small branches of trees. The weapons of the deceased are laid across his lap, and his limbs are painted in stripes of red and white and yellow. After the body has remained several weeks on the platform, it is taken down and buried; the skull becomes the drinking cup of the nearest relation, Bodies thus preserved have the appearance of mummies; there is no sign of decay; and the wild dogs will not meddle with them, though they devour all manner of carrion. (Drawing by G. G. Angas 1847b.)

mummification was to obtain an accommodation between the dead and the living; in Melanesia the aim was generally to prolong the physical presence of a dead relative in defiance of decomposition.

TECHNIQUES

In Australia the techniques used generally involved the exposure of the corpse in a tree or on a specially constructed platform (Figure 13.4). Initially, the body was left tied into a sitting position, often with limbs flexed against the chest or abdomen. The corpse was left in the open until the tissues were desiccated by the sun, and then deposited in the branches of a tree or on a wooden platform. In some localities, preservation was accelerated by sewing all the orifices closed and smoking the body while it was on the platform. Sometimes the body cavity was opened and the intestines removed in order to refine the drying process. Putrefying fluids were often collected and used in allied rites. When dry, the epidermis was peeled off and the pale corpse was smeared with red ocher and grease or decorated by painting totemic designs on its face and chest. Body hair was either cut off or pulled out and used for making waistbands and other personal ornaments (Berndt and Berndt 1964: 392ff).

In Melanesia the methods employed varied slightly between the inland regions and the coastal and island areas. The most detailed accounts have come from Torres Strait (Haddon 1912, 1935; Hamlyn-Harris 1912a; MacFarlane, in Haddon 1935: 325–6). In Torres Strait, the dead body was set apart for a few days. It was then taken out from shore in a canoe, where the swollen outermost epidermal layer was stripped away. Viscera were removed through an incision in the side between the ribs and the hips and then thrown into the sea. The abdominal cavity was filled with pieces of palm pith and the incision sewed up. The brain was removed after screwing an arrow through the back of the neck and into the foramen magnum. The body was then returned to the shore, lashed to a rectangular wooden framework, and hung up to dry behind a grass screen. Punctures were made at the knees and elbows and in the digital clefts on the hands and feet to drain off bodily fluids. The tongue, palmar tissue, and soles of the feet were stripped off and presented to the spouse.

Months later, when the drying process was complete, the mummy was decorated. Artificial eyes of shell with pupils of black beeswax were cemented into the orbits, the earlobes were decorated with tufts of grass and seeds, and the wrists and ankles were sheathed in bands of palm fronds. The whole body was then given a coating of red ocher. The loins were covered, in the case of a woman with a petticoat, and in the case of a man occasionally with a shell pubic ornament. The decorated mummy, on its frame, was then tied to the center post of the bereaved spouse's house and when, in the course of time, it fell to pieces the head only was retained.

On mainland New Guinea, the techniques of mummification differed in several details. For example, preservation of the body was obtained largely by smoking. In Torres Strait, drying in the open was the major agent. Although a fire was kept constantly burning near the mummifying corpse, this was considered to be more for the deceased's comfort than for preservation. Additional differences in technique were found in the Tauri–Lakekamu watershed area of central New Guinea. Evisceration was not practiced here, and the body and limbs were arranged in a squatting position, except during smoking, when the hands were tied to a house beam. The origins of the technique of smoke drying are not definitely known, but the preservation of meat and game employing similar smoking processes was known by the Wahgi and Tauri (Kukukuku) tribes.

EXAMPLE OF A MELANESIAN MUMMY: TORRES STRAIT SPECIMEN IN THE MACLEAY MUSEUM, SYDNEY

The Macleay Museum in the University of Sydney contains the preserved body of a male Torres Strait islander. It was collected from Darnley Island in 1875 by the Australian zoologist Sir William Macleay. In 1914, during a session of the British Association for the Advancement of Science, it became a focus of attention when put forward by Professor Grafton Elliot Smith as a conclusive demonstration of ancient Egyptian influence on Oceanic culture. For various reasons, no comprehensive description of the mummy appeared until 1969 when Pretty published a detailed examination of the specimen and reviewed the controversy surrounding Elliot Smith's diffusionist hypothesis (Pretty 1969). The Macleay specimen is an excellent example of the Melanesian technique of mummification and Pretty's report is the basis of the description presented below.

General description

The mummy is that of an adult male, 177 cm in length with a breadth at the shoulders of 35 cm. It was lashed to a wooden frame of two verticals and eight crosspieces at the head, under the armpits, and below the knees. The body must have been dried in a vertical position, as its weight, suspended from under the shoulders, caused sagging at the breast and the head to sink into a deep cleft formed by the clavicles, which raised the shoulders to a position level with the ears. Facial features were restored and the whole body coated with red ocher. The skin, where exposed, was parchment yellow except on the back of the left hand, where some of the original melanin, dark gray in colour, was retained. The mummy's state of preservation was good, though there had been some postmortem insect attack around the jaw, mastoids, upper part of the breast, abdomen, and posterior surfaces of the legs. Loss of some of the distal phalanges of the left foot probably occurred during the mummification process, as the remaining bones were exposed and splashed with red ocher.

The head

The head was shaved and the crown painted an even black from the forehead around and behind the ears and across the lambdoid region, where the cranium lay against the topmost crosspiece of the frame. No hair was found, the only potential sample from the left cheek being identified as a vegetable fiber. Like the rest of the body, the face was thickly coated with red ocher and the features considerably restored. The shrunken orbits were filled with black mastic that had discolored the overlying red ocher to gray and had cracked the painted surface along its junction with the facial tissue. The artificial lentoid eyes were shell, and measured 4 by 1.5 cm. Emphasis was added to each eye by setting a spot of black resinous material in the center to imitate the pupil and by ringing the margins with flattened strips of the same substance to represent eyelids. The nasal septum had been pierced in life, but the hole plugged postmortem with a rod of coralline material broken off flush with the nostrils. The mouth had opened and the lips had parted, exposing teeth. Both upper central incisors were displaced after death but were located radiographically, one being lodged in the posterior pharynx and the other in the chest.

An interesting feature of the head was the double strand of rolled two-ply twine that ran across the center of the oral cavity. This was inserted to fix the jaw firmly to the head and made demands of the skill of the mummifiers as the twine was passed between lower lip and teeth, over the teeth and across the oral cavity, and joined with the other end of the string at the base of the jaw. This technique was well known and is beautifully illustrated by a decorated skull from Hammond Island, Torres Strait, which is housed in the South Australian Museum (registration number A.17907). In this specimen and in some other mummies, notably the one described by Flower (1879: 391), there was a supplementary lashing binding the ramus to the zygoma on each side. This was unnecessary in the Macleay specimen because the tissues surrounding the jaw were well preserved.

Only part of the ears was present, but sufficient remained to show that the lobes were intact at death. From them hung threaded strings of seeds broken in half and threaded through the ends. They were identified as Job's tears (*Coix lacrymi*). The brain had been removed, and examination from behind showed a vertical incision at the nape of the neck. Probing demonstrated that the cranial cavity was empty, and radiographs showed that articulation of the foramen magnum and the first cranial vertebra had been disrupted.

The techniques for keeping the head upright were complex. A vertical stance during drying would incline the head to fall forward on the chest, but this was prevented by two devices. First, a double strand of flat three-ply plaited twine was passed across the forehead again and across the other side, being finally knotted under the crosspiece. Second, the chin was probably supported by a small wooden prop, as the skin was pinched and depressed both beneath the chin and on the breast just above the sternum. This latter method was recorded by both Haddon (1912) and Hamlyn-Harris (1912a), but lashing the head to the top crosspiece was unusual.

Curious features were two punctures in the skin of the forehead at each end of the temples. The surrounding tissues had been discolored gray about the region of the eyes. The significance of the punctures remains problematical.

Thorax and abdomen

Both thorax and abdomen were painted with red ocher more thickly on the front than on the back. A curious feature of this region was the absence of lateral shrinkage of the skin, leaving no protruding outlines of ribs either ventrally or dorsally. X-rays confirmed that all the ribs were present. The navel was discernible and the penis and scrotum were complete. There was no pubic hair.

The abdomen was clothed with a dress consisting of fibrous material passed between the legs and kept in place by a waistband. The waistband had a zigzag pattern woven into it and was wound twice around the body and knotted at the front. The tie-ends were of blue calico, a reminder of the islanders' frequent contact with Europeans prior to Macleay's visit. Tucked into the waistband front and back were two lengths of teased-out or beaten fibers identified as coming from the bark of a species of fig. Each length had been doubled over, creased and drawn together to form a knob, then stuffed into waistband behind while the free ends had been carried out across the abdomen and tucked under the waistband in front. Behind and within the bark fiber was a length of twine, decorated at intervals of 6 to 8 cm with fronded insertions of plant material from a species of ginger. Darnley Island men normally went naked, but pubic coverings were known for other male mummies (Flower 1879; Hamlyn-Harris 1912a).

On the left flank was an incision 8.5 cm long, which had been sewed together with rolled two-ply twine by a running suture and finished by knotting at each end. Ethnographic accounts were explicit about an incision at this site for removal of the viscera and, for Macleay specimen, this was confirmed by x-rays that were consistent with complete removal.

The limbs

Close examination of the limbs showed that the body had been punctured at the joints to allow putrefying fluids to escape, thus confirming the observations of Haddon and Hamlyn-Harris. Also as a result of drainage and drying, shrinkage had occurred, which necessitated retying the lashings at fewer sites. Primary lashing sites, distinguished from the furrows and wrinkling they had left on the skin, were situated in positions suited to the binding of a body in a vertical position. The hands had originally been lashed to the frame across the wrists, so that they lay with the palms flat against the frame rather than facing the sides of the body. The feet were originally lashed to the double crosspiece at the base of the frame, which also served to support the feet. Shrinkage through drying had pulled both feet a few centimeters above the basal crosspiece, but their former contact with the base of the frame was shown by the presence of strips of skin which had remained across the soles of the feet. Other primary lashing sites were located underneath the knees and slightly above the present lashing sites.

Drainage was effected by making holes in the skin at the joints, and mourners further helped to expel putrefying liquid by stroking and kneading the limbs. In the Macleay specimen, drainage punctures were identified at the knees and on the back of the left hand where the skin was drawn back. Elsewhere they proved difficult to identify because of fractures and detoriation of the tissues. There were breaks in the skin of the hand between the first and second fingers and on the right foot between the hallux and the second toe. Another hole was located on the inside of the right arm at the elbow. Longitudinal wrinkling and folding of the skin at the joints, in particular at the knees, was suggestive of manual drainage.

Both fingernails and toenails were absent, consistent with ethnographic records of the removal of nails and palmar skin, which were peeled off and presented to the spouse.

The limbs were decorated at the ankles and wrists with bands of palm leaf, 4 cm wide. Each band consisted of two partly overlapping strips of leaf secured by wrapping and a small flat knot. These had been put on before the mummy was given its coating of red ocher as the skin beneath was free of paint.

Radiographic and gastroscopic examinations

An x-ray examination of the mummy unexpectedly showed a close scatter of granular opacities in the region of the lower abdomen. From a radiographical view point there was doubt about whether this represented the stuffing of the abdominal cavity substances or arose from radiopaque material in the coating of the red ocher itself. Weighed against this latter interpretation was the complete covering of the entire body with red ocher and the fact that the x-ray opacities were confined to the abdominal region. To resolve the problem, a series of tests was undertaken on samples of red ocher.

The first problem was to determine the composition of the paint that was smeared on the mummy. According to Hamlyn-Harris it was a mixture of coconut oil and ocher, but Haddon claimed the mixture to be of ocher and human grease. The first tests on the ocher were made from a mainland Australian sample and mixed with coconut oil and lard. This mixture was smeared onto tracing paper and x-rayed on a 10 cm thickness of Masonite board using an 80 milliamps per second ray with an intensity of 58 kilovolts from a distance of 80 cm. The plates were blank, showing the red ocher to be transradiant.

On specialist radiological advice the experiment was repeated, as the x-raying of a layer of red ocher on 10 cm Masonite slabs was held to be an unsatisfactory comparison with the ocher on the mummy. The contrasts achieved between a layer of ocher on 10 cm Masonite and 10cm of masonite alone were held to be so slight so as to escape detection. A similar mass of balsa, being transradiant, was considered to be a truer comparison. In the repeat test, a sample of red ocher confirmably from Saibai Island in Torres Strait was used. Three mixtures were prepared, ranging from fine powdered to medium grained and coarse granules. The radiographs were at 63 kV, exposed at 2, 4, and 6 seconds from a distance of 127 cm. The plates showed the red ocher to be transradiant except where it was in compact grains or masses, thus supporting the hypothesis that radiopacity would depend on the size of the particles and their specific gravity, but affirming the essential x-ray transparency of red ocher.

Reexamination of the coat of ocher covering the belly did not reveal any granular surface texture, but the paint had been thickly applied to this area, so the possibility that the ocher was affecting the radiographs still remained. To decide the issue and find out what the abdominal cavity contained, a gastroscope was inserted deep into the body from an insect whole near the right armpit. With it a series of 5 mm color transparencies was made of the body cavity. Their interpretation was limited by uncertainties, first about the precise locus of the photos within the cavity, and second by the absence of a scale. However, the photos revealed that the abdominal cavity was empty of viscera and contained several lengths of a vinelike plant buried in a matrix of dusty grass and granular material. The lengths of vine stem appeared to be circular in section and occasionally had thorns or stems branching out from them. The matrix was mostly organic, but was assumed to be crystalline in places, as it reflected the light from the camera flash. Among the matrix were some curious smooth-textured ovoid balls of unknown material, some of which adhered to the body wall and some of which had broken away from it. Pock-marked depressions appeared in the interior body wall where these ovoid balls had broken away. The balls were not punctured and, as they were unlikely to have been insect cocoons, their composition remained doubtful. They may have resulted from the drying of fatty materials inside the body cavity in combination with the granular material with which the cavity had been stuffed. The gastroscopic examination demonstrated, without destroying any tissues, that the body had been emptied of viscera through an incision in the side and the cavity packed with lengths of a light vegetable stem and some earthy debris.

Paleopathology

The most striking radiographic finding was the irregular thickening of many of the long bones. Changes were observed in the left radius, left humerus, right clavicle, right ulna, both femora, both tibiae, and the right fibula. In general the changes consisted of an irregular thickening of the cortex involving the shafts of the long bones and containing irregular areas of erosion that were of both a sclerotic and a destructive type, as seen by the formation of cloacae. The ends of the long bones were normal in appearance, as were the joints. The changes in the right tibia and fibula were especially interesting in that the lesions, which extended over several centimeters, occurred at the same level in both bones. The left radius and tibia were severely affected, whereas the left ulna and fibula were spared. These osteological changes are consistent with the diagnosis of yaws but no complementary skin lesions were detected on the mummy's external surface.

No evidence of any bony defects or fractures within the skull or facial bones was detected, nor was there any indication of degenerative arthritis in the skeleton as a whole.

EXAMPLES OF AUSTRALIAN MUMMIES

Although several Aboriginal mummies have been recorded, none has been described as thoroughly as the Macleay Museum specimen. Preserved bodies and organs were collected from early Colonial times onward. That recovered from Adelaide by Sir George Grey and presented to the Royal College of Surgeons (London) in 1845 was one of the earliest known. Flower briefly described this specimen as an adult male bound in a sitting position (Flower 1879: 393–4). The legs were flexed in line with the sides of the thorax and abdomen and the forearms were crossed, with each hand resting on the opposite foot. All orifices were sewed with a running suture, but the viscera had not been removed. The body had been decorated with ocher and the mouth stuffed with emu feathers. Ironically, Flower directed the body be unfleshed and the skeleton preserved so that the specimen would be more instructive! Unfortunately, even this has since been destroyed when the college was damaged during World War II.

A more detailed account of another South Australian mummy found at Rapid Bay near Cape Jervis was given by Tindale and Mountford (1936: 487–502). The specimen was excavated from Kongarati Cave and was found in association with a wide range of molluscs, some wooden fire-making implements, a bone point, fragments of netting, and a kangaroo-skin cloak. The mummy was that of an elderly female, buried in a slate-lined cist grave (specially prepared burial pit) in a flexed position. The right side had been oriented in a northerly direction. In view of the charred nature of the spine and hips and the presence of fatty matter on the right side, the authors concluded that the body had been smoke-dried. A proportionate amount of decomposition had ensued to parts of the right side, and the chest was well distorted as if the lateral walls of the thorax had been crushed. This was explained by the local custom of forcing out the dying breaths of an individual by jumping on the thorax.

A third notable South Australian mummy was located in cliffs above the Murray River at Fromm's Landing (Sheard et al. 1927: 173–6). The preserved corpse of an infant about two years of age was found lying on a net bag filled with long grasses. The body had been placed on its left side in a crouched position and was covered with a further layer of loose grasses and a wallaby hide. Hackett's examination of the body indicated that a depression on the right parietal was probably caused by a fracture, but this had not been sufficiently serious to cause death as there were osteological signs of healing. Both this specimen and that found in Kongarati Cave are housed in the South Australian Museum.

Other equally interesting mummies have been found elsewhere in Australia. Klaatsch (1907) has described his ruthless acquisition of the body of Ngatja; its present whereabouts are uncertain. An Aboriginal mummy from Morphett Vale is stated to be in the ethnographic collection of the Berlin Museum (Tindale 1974: 55), and several specimens are housed at the Queensland Museum in Brisbane. The latter were all found in Queensland and have never been adequately examined, although Hamlyn-Harris gave a cursory account of them in his 1912 paper (1912b).

CONCLUSION

The nature of mummification techniques in New Guinea, Torres Strait, and Australia was such that the duration of a preserved body was only temporary. Concern expressed for a dead relative would not continue much beyond one or two generations, which eliminated the necessity of seeking more durable preserving methods. Consequently, as the practice of mummification lapsed with intensified European contacts, and with the introduction of Christianity in particular, the number of mummified specimens available to science declined. For this reason, scholars have had to rely more upon ethnographic and historical sources for details about funerary modes in Australia and Melanesia. One important advantage in such reports is their status as first-hand accounts of the rationale for mummification. The motives recorded and techniques described were as varied as the cultures in which mummification was practiced, a fact that runs contrary to the original diffusionist hypothesis proposed by Elliot Smith (Pretty 1969).

Ethnographic and historical records, however, are rarely sufficiently complete to enable prehistorians to reconstruct ancient mummification practices in detail, and further investigations of the few surviving specimens using modern scientific and medical acumen are required. More research about the disposal of the dead is especially necessary for clarifying traditional Australian Aboriginal thought.

It is clear that a great deal of uncertainty still remains about mummification in this region. There exists, moreover, important undescribed material whose study is long overdue and whose description will help dispel some of these obscurities. Similarly, the contribution from such specimens is of immense value to human biological and paleopathological research. The contribution of mummified material to research about indigenous peoples prior to recent hybridization will be extremely important. The authors have attempted to present a comprehensive survey of Australian and Melanesian mummification with a view to indicating appropriate directions for future research.

REFERENCES

Abbie, A. A. 1959. Sir Grafton Elliot Smith. *Bulletin of the Postgraduate Committee on Medicine, University of Sydney* **15**(3): 101–50.

Albertis, L. M. 1880. *New Guinea : what I did and what I saw there*. London: Sampson Low, Marston, Searle and Rivington.

Angas, G. F. 1847a. *Savage life and scenes in Australia and New Zealand*. London: Smith, Elder.

Angas, G. F. 1847b. *South Australia illustrated*. London: Thomas McLean.

Basedow, H. 1925. *The Australian aboriginal*. Adelaide: F. W. Preece.

Berndt, R. M. and Berndt, C. H. 1964. *The world of the first Australians*. Sydney: Ure Smith.

Bjerre, J. 1956. *The last cannibals*. London: Michael Joseph.

Bowler, J. M., Jones, R., Allen, M. and Thorne, A. G. 1970. Pleistocene human remains from Australia, a living site and human cremation from Lake Mungo, Western New South Wales. *World Archaeology* **2**(1): 39–60.

Bull, J. 1965. The sleepers in the ranges. *People* **16**(11): 12–13.

Dawson, W. R. 1924. A mummy from Torres Straits. *Annals of Archaeology and Anthropology* **11**: 87–96.

Dawson, W. R. 1928. Mummification in Australia and America. *Journal of the Royal Anthropological Institute* **58**: 115–38.

Elkin, A. P. 1954. *The Australian aborigines: how to understand them*. Sydney: Angus & Robertson.

Elliot Smith, G. 1915. On the significance of the geographical distribution of the practice of mummification: a study of the migrations of peoples and the spread of certain customs and beliefs. *Memoirs and Proceedings of the Manchester Literary and Philosophical Society* **59**: 1–143.

Fletcher, J. J. 1929. The society's heritage from the Macleays: part 2. *Proceedings of the Linnaean Society of New South Wales* **54**(3): 185–272.

Flower, W. H. 1879. Illustrations of the mode of preserving the dead in Darnley Island and in South Australia. *Journal of the Anthropological Institute* **8**: 389–95.

Girard, F. 1957. Les peintures rupestres Buang, district de Morobé, Nouvelle Guinée. *Journal de la société des océanistes* **13**: 4–49.

Haddon, A. C. 1908. Sociology, magic and religion of the eastern islanders. In *Reports of the Cambridge Anthropological Expedition to Torres Straits*, vol. 6. Cambridge University Press.

Haddon, A. C. 1912. Arts and crafts. In *Reports of the Cambridge Anthropological Expedition to Torres Straits*, vol. 4. Cambridge: Cambridge University Press.

Haddon, A. C. 1935. General ethnography. In *Reports of the Cambridge Anthropological Expedition to Torres Straits*, vol. 1. Cambridge: Cambridge University Press.

Hamlyn-Harris, R. 1912a. Papuan mummification, as practiced in the Torres Straits islands, and exemplified by specimens in the Queensland Museum collections. *Memoirs of the Queensland Museum* **1**: 1–6.

Hamlyn-Harris, R. 1912b. Mummification. *Memoirs of the Queensland Museum* **1**: 7–22.

Held, G. J. 1957. *The Papuas of Waropen*. The Hague: Nijhoff.

Hiatt, B. 1969. Cremation in Aboriginal Australia. *Mankind* **7**(2): 104–14.

Howells, W. 1973. *The Pacific Islanders*. Wellington: Reed.

Howitt, A. W. 1904. *The native tribes of South-East Australia*. London: Macmillan.

Klaatsch, H. 1907. Some notes on scientific travel amongst the black population of tropical Australia in 1904, 1905, 1906. *Report of the Eleventh Meeting of the Australasian Association for the Advancement of Science*, 1907, pp. 577–92. Adelaide: The Association.

Le Roux, C. C. F. M. 1948. *De bergpapoea's van Nieuw-Guinea en hun woongebied*. Leiden: Brill.

Mathews, R. H. 1905. *Ethnological notes on the Aboriginal tribes of New South Wales and Victoria*. Sydney: White.

McConnel, U. H. 1937. Mourning ritual tribes of Cape York Peninsula. *Oceania* **7**(3): 346–71.

Mulvaney, D. J. 1969. *The prehistory of Australia*. London: Thames & Hudson.

Mulvaney, D. J. and Golson, J. eds. 1971. *Aboriginal man and environment in Australia*. Canberra: Australian National University Press.

Pretty, G. L. 1969. The Macleay Museum mummy from Torres Straits: a postscript to Elliot Smith and the diffusion controversy. *Man* **4**(1): 24–43.

Pretty, G. L. 1972. Report of an inspection of certain archaeological sites and field monuments in the territory of Papua and New Guinea. Typescript. South Australian Museum.

Pretty, G. L. 1977. The chronology of the Roonka Flat: a preliminary consideration. In *Stone tools as cultural markers: change, evolution, and complexity*, ed. R. V. S. Wright, pp. 288–331. Canberra: Australian Institute of Aboriginal Studies.

Rhys, L. 1947. *Jungle Pimpernel: the story of a district officer in central Netherlands New Guinea*. London: Hodder & Stoughton.

Roth, W. E. 1907. Burial ceremonies and disposal of the dead, North Queensland. *Records of the Australian Museum* **6**(5): 365–403.

Sengstake, F. 1892. Die Leichenbestattung aus Darnley Island. *Globus* **61**(16): 248–9.

Sheard, H. L. Mountford, C. P. and Hackett, C. J. 1927. An unusual disposal of an aboriginal child's remains from the Lower Murray, South Australia. *Transactions and proceedings of the Royal Society of South Australia* **5**: 173–6.

Simpson, C. 1953. *Adam with arrows: inside New Guinea*. Sydney: Angus & Robertson.

Stirling, E. C. 1893. Report on inspection of Aboriginal mummy chambers at two localities on the Coorong, South Australia, 1893. Field notes in department of Anthropology research file, South Australian Museum.

Stirling, E. C. 1911. Preliminary report on the discovery of native remains at Swanport, River Murray, with an inquiry into the alleged occurrence of a pandemic among the Australian aboriginals. *Transactions of the Royal Society of South Australia* **35**: 4–46.

Tindale, N. B. 1974. *Aboriginal tribes of Australia, their terrain, environmental controls, distribution, limits and proper names*. Berkeley: University of California Press.

Tindale, N B. and Mountford, C. P. 1936. Results of the excavations of Kongarati Cave, near Second Valley, South Australia. *Records of the South Australian Museum* **5**(4): 487–502.

Tolmer, A. 1882. *Reminiscences of an adventurous and chequered career at home and at the Antipodes*. London: Sampson Low, Marston, Searle and Rivington.

Vial, L. G. 1936. Disposal of the dead among the Buang. *Oceania* **7**(1): 63–8.

Woods, J. D. 1879. *The native tribes of South Australia*. Adelaide: Wigg.

14

Mummies from Japan and China

KIYOHIKO SAKURAI, TAMOTSU OGATA, IWATARO MORIMOTO,
PENG LONG-XIANG AND WU ZHONG-BI

JAPAN: A RESEARCH AND CULTURAL HISTORY

Kiyohiko Sakurai (translated by R. Freeman)

In a country of high humidity, such as Japan, the belief that mummification could not, and did not, exist would not be altogether unfounded, but rather more a matter of common sense. However, through our investigations we have been able to establish that mummification was in fact a very old custom in our country and one that was practiced right until the early part of the twentieth century.

It is recorded that the great priest Kûkai (Kôbô-daishi. AD 774–835), who is famous not only for the studies of esoteric Buddhism he made while in China, but also for founding the Shingon sect of Japanese Buddhism, became mummified upon his death at Mount Kôya (a sacred mountain of the sect). In addition, during the eleventh and twelfth centuries there were many priests who voluntarily attempted self-mummification.

In existence today are the twelfth century mummies of the Fujiwara family, a powerful clan of northern Japan, and, dating from the seventeenth to the twentieth centuries, the mummies of numerous priests. Apart from those of the Fujiwara family, all Japanese mummies are those of priests who voluntarily sought self-mummification.

The Japanese idea of mummification, practiced in accordance with Buddhist principles, was subject to a strong Chinese influence. In China, Buddhists had long been practicing mummification of the dead; these mummies were known as *nikushin* (of the body or flesh). The act of self-immolation in order to become a mummy was termed *nyûjô* (entering into Nirvâna). Priests who became mummies were given the title of *nikushin-butsu* (a Buddha of the body) or *nyûjô-butsu* (a Buddha of Nirvâna) and were worshipped and respected in the same way as the Buddhist statuary. In this regard, there was a great difference between the principles of mummification in China and Japan and those practiced in Egypt and South America.

This section describes mummies unique to Japan under the headings: (1) mummies as recorded in literature, (2) existing mummies, and (3) the principles of mummification.

Mummies as recorded in literature

The number of mummies mentioned in Japanese literature is quite large. I should like here to introduce only a few examples.

In the *Genkô-shakusho* (completed in 1322) – a history of Japanese Buddhism and collection of priests' biographies covering a period of more than 700 years up to 1273 – it is recorded that in AD 1003 the priest Zôga attained nyûjô at the age of 87. In compliance with his will, his body was placed in a large barrel, buried for three years and then exhumed. At that time he was found to be in a state of perfect preservation. This procedure of placing the body in a large barrel or earthenware urn and burying it for three years followed by exhumation was a method of mummification that had been practiced in China from the fifth to sixth centuries up until modern times. The *Genkô-shakusho* indicates that the practice was brought to Japan during the eleventh century. Whether or not the mummy of priest Zôga ever became the object of worship cannot be ascertained.

The *Genkô-shakusho* also contains an account of the priest Rinken who attained nyûjô in 1150. It is recorded that upon mummification he was duly enshrined at Mount Kôya. Thus it can be seen that by the middle of the twelfth century the practice of worshipping mummies of those who attained nyûjô had become established in Japan.

Existing mummies

In Japan there are 19 mummies in existence (Andô and Sakurai 1969). Figure 14.1 shows their geographical distribution. The following paragraphs describe several of the mummies in detail. These include the mummies of the Fujiwara family preserved at the Chûson-ji Temple, Hiraizumi City, Iwate prefecture. The four mummies (Table 14.1) are enshrined in the *Konjiki-dô* (the Golden Hall) of Chûson-ji Temple. Whether these four examples became mummified through natural processes or by embalming is difficult to judge, for their internal organs have been devoured by rats. However, there is general agreement that some form of embalming must have been carried out.

The Fujiwara family, a powerful clan of northeast Japan, created in this remote region a culture comparable to that of the capital of those days. It was undoubtedly to ensure the permanent preservation of the remains of the leaders of this powerful family that mummification was carried out.

FIGURE 14.1. Locations of
mummies found in Japan.
(Map by Timothy Motz,
Detroit Institute of Arts,
modified by I. Morimoto.)

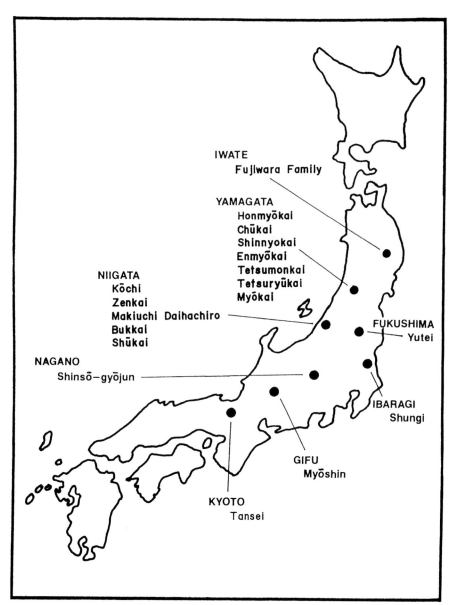

IWATE
Fujiwara Family

YAMAGATA
Honmyōkai
Chūkai
Shinnyokai
Enmyōkai
Tetsumonkai
Tetsuryūkai
Myōkai

NIIGATA
Kōchi
Zenkai
Makiuchi Daihachiro
Bukkai
Shūkai

FUKUSHIMA
Yutei

NAGANO
Shinsō–gyōjun

IBARAGI
Shungi

GIFU
Myōshin

KYOTO
Tansei

The mummy of priest Kôchi is preserved at the Saishô-ji Temple,
Teradomari City, Niigata prefecture. Born in Shimo-osa (the modern Chiba
prefecture), Kôchi became a priest at Renge-ji Temple in the village of Ôura,
which is in his native district. Later he departed on a pilgrimage to various
provinces. His journeys took him to the northernmost parts of Honshû
before he traveled to, and settled at, the temple of Saishô-ji in Echigo (the

Table 14.1. *Mummies of the Fujiwara family*

Relationship	Name	Date of mummification	Age at death (yr)
Grandfather	Fujiwara Kiyohira	1128	73
Father	Fujiwara Motohira	1157	Unknown
Son	Fujiwara Hidehira	1187	66
Grandson	Fujiwara Yasuhira	1189	23

modern Niigata prefecture). There he attained nyûjô in AD 1363. His mummy soon became an object of faith and is displayed annually on 2 October, when it is worshipped by numerous believers.

The head of this mummy is yellowish brown in color. Its soft tissues have dried and adhered, although those of the face have almost completely fallen away, exposing the bone. The skin and tissues covering the areas from the head down to the small of the back have been well preserved, but there are large cavities made by rats in the stomach and chest. In literature of the nineteenth century, this mummy is recorded as being in a state of perfect preservation. It is believed that the deterioration advanced rapidly following the Meiji restoration and the subsequent neglect of their traditional practices by the Japanese.

The mummy of priest Tetsumonkai is preserved at Chûren-ji Temple, Asahi Village, Yamagata prefecture. This is a comparatively well preserved example (Figure 14.2). Tetsumonkai was an ordinary day laborer who, in his youth, killed a samurai in a fight over a woman and subsequently fled to the sanctuary of Chûren-ji Temple on the slopes of Mount Yudono, a sacred mountain of the Shingon sect. Upon becoming a priest, he built roads and constructed bridges for the benefit of local inhabitants and visited various provinces in order to engage actively in the propagation of Buddhism. In his final years he settled at Chûren-ji Temple where, for a period of three years, he abstained from the five cereals (rice, barley, corn, millet, and beans). Upon his attainment of nyûjô in 1829, priests surrounded his body with numerous candles, drying it out by means of the candles' heat.

The mummy of priest Tetsuryûkai is preserved at the Nangaku-ji Temple, Tsuruoka City, Yamagata prefecture. He was a disciple of Tetsumonkai and attained nyûjô in 1868 (Figure 14.3). Although it was his wish to attain a state of mummification, he became sick and died during the course of his ascetics. Other priests buried him in an underground stone chamber (cist) beneath the temple, but later exhumed and embalmed him so that, unlike other

FIGURE 14.2. Mummy of priest
Tetsumonkai.

mummies, his internal organs have been removed. To do this, an incision about 18 cm in length was made across his lower abdomen and then sewn up with linen thread. X-ray examination shows that the abdominal cavity had been packed with lime, indicating that this mummy owes its preservation entirely to embalming rather than to natural processes.

The mummy of priest Bukkai is preserved at the Kannon-ji Temple, Murakami City, Niigata prefecture. This, the most recent of Japanese mummies, is that of a priest who practiced asceticism at Mount Yudono before attaining nyûjô in 1903. In accordance with his will, priests constructed an underground chamber and enshrined his body. After three years, they were supposed to exhume and mummify it. But in Japan at that time, exhumation became forbidden by law so Bukkai remained buried just as he was.

In 1961 we excavated his tomb. At about 1 m beneath the stone slab covering the grave, there was a skillfully constructed chamber of hewn stone, measuring 1.25 m along the sides by 2 m in depth. Near the floor of this chamber

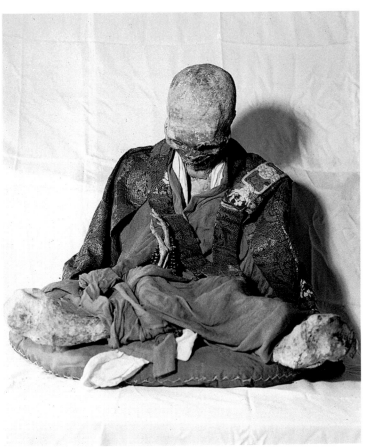

FIGURE 14.3. Mummy of priest Tetsuryûkai.

was a shelf of iron bars upon which the strong wooden coffin had been placed. As the body had been in the earth for a long time, although parts of it had mummified, the remainder had become a skeleton.

Principles of mummification

With the exception of those of the Fujiwara family, all Japanese mummies are of priests who achieved mummification through their own volition, even though other priests had to assist the process of transformation. What was it that inspired them to undertake this? It was a principle that developed from the Maitreya faith – faith in Maitreya-bodhisattva, the Buddha of the future.

They believed that 5 670 000 000 years following Šâkyamuni's (Buddha's) attainment of Nirvâna, Maitreya will appear in this world for the salvation of all sentient beings. As priests, they wanted to assist Maitreya when the time arrived. They believed that in order to do this, they should await his coming in their earthly form – that is, as mummies. This was the principle, and although there arose many legends (starting with Kûkai) of famous priests who attained mummification, quite a large number did in fact achieve this condition. For both the mummies described in literature and those that are in existence today, the principle behind their mummification was tied to the Maitreya faith.

Following the seventeenth century, as the Maitreya faith became combined with the Shûgendô or mountain asceticism of Sangaku-sûhai (a primitive form of mountain worship), many of the priests of the lower orders, living in the strict feudal society of the Tokugawa era, turned to mummification as a form of self-assertion.

Conclusion

In this section, I have endeavored to explain something about Japanese mummies. The method by which mummification was achieved is not yet clearly understood. However, from records and from tradition, the following process may be deduced:

1   By gradually reducing the body's intake of nutrition over a long period, the body's constitution was altered to one that was strongly resistant to decomposition. Abstaining from the five cereals was for this purpose.

2   After death the body was interred for three years in an underground stone chamber (cist); it was then exhumed and dried.

As explained previously, the mummies of the Fujiwara family appear to have undergone some form of embalming. Where did knowledge of this art of mummification come from? In the book *Kitaezo-zusetsu* (*An Illustrated Book of North Ezo*), compiled by the early nineteenth century explorer, Mâmiya Rinzô, there is an account of a custom among the Ainu of Sakhalin of mummifying their chieftains. Also, Aleut mummies have been discovered on Kagamil Island in the Aleutian chain. Although the practice of mummification cannot be found among the Ainu of Hokkaidô, the fact that many of the mummies that exist today come from the northern part of Japan suggests that mummification as it developed in these northern regions is an influence that must be taken into consideration.

JAPAN: SCIENTIFIC RESEARCH

Tamotsu Ogata

Books and articles on Japanese mummies have been published in great numbers (Andô 1961). We, the members of the Group for Research on

Japanese Mummies, have been doing extensive research, primarily on the mummies of people who devoted themselves to Buddhism. The following discussion is restricted to mummies whose general examination was completed between 1959 and 1969.

To the author, the most interesting question is whether these remains were artificially mummified. The investigating commission has carried out a great deal of research on the famous Fujiwara clan. Their efforts to decide whether the mummification was artificial or natural produced two opposing points of view (Furuhata 1950; Hasebe 1950; Suzuki 1950). The mummies we examined are quite different from those of the Fujiwaras; many of them show obvious traces of treatment. An investigation of these mummies therefore will suggest the solutions regarding the question of artificial mummification in Japan.

Research materials and methods of investigation

The nine mummies discussed here are all Japanese males who devoted themselves to Buddhism. The dates of their deaths range from the period of the Northern and Southern Dynasties to the Meiji era – that is, from 1363 to 1903. Their deaths were caused by starvation as a result of asceticism and by illness after asceticism. The remains show various stages of mummification, and one is almost a skeleton. Osteology, craniology, and somatology were applied according to the mummies' conditions. X-ray examination was also used on occasion. The reconstructed statures are calculated by Pearson's formulas. Fingerprint studies were done sometimes by using alginate impression material to make a plaster model and sometimes by the naked eye at autopsy. Blood groups were determined by an absorption test against anti-A, anti-B and anti-O agglutinin sera, using skin and/or muscle tissue. A lightweight portable x-ray machine was used.

Results

All mummies but one were considerably damaged by rats and insects.

Kôchi Hôin Most of the remaining skin is well preserved, but almost no viscera remain, and there is no evidence that the brain and viscera had been removed. It is therefore impossible to decide whether artificial methods of mummification had been used. The mummy is in a sitting position. It weighs 4.7 kg and is 159.9 cm in height. Many of the teeth had fallen out in his lifetime. It is reported that he died at the age of 82. X-ray examination shows the closure of the principal sutures of the skull is not complete. The bones of the lower limbs are more developed than those of the upper limbs. The vertebral column is highly kyphotic. Several sparrow sized shadows, the origins of which are unknown, are observed in the internal surface of the right parietal bone. Cervical spondylosis and osteophytes are seen on the anterior walls of the bodies of the second and fifth lumbar vertebrae; the intervertebral disc spaces are narrowed. The blood group is AB.

Shungi Shônin The skin is relatively well preserved and there are remains of hair. Although there are no viscera, there is no evidence that the brain or viscera were removed. The mummy weighs 4.1 kg and is 157.2 cm in height. It looks rather like a turtle, because it bent forward when put into the cavity of a seated stone image of *Amida-Nyorai* (Amitabha Buddha). Its hands are clasped in prayer. The cervical vertebrae show luxation. The alveolar process of the mandible and the alveolar process of the maxillary bone are highly atrophied. All teeth were lost in his lifetime. It is impossible to measure the orbit because both upper and lower eyelids are mummified in the closed state. X-ray examination shows that the closure of the principal sutures of the skull is moderately complete. The vertebral column is highly kyphotic. It is reported that Shungi Shônin died at the age of 78. The bones of the upper and lower limbs are particularly well developed. The right thumb shows a radial loop fingerprint; the blood group is O. The bodies of the sixth and seventh cervical vertebrae show spondylosis with osteophytes.

Zenkai Shônin (Figure 14.4) Most of the skin is well preserved, and the hair, penis and scrotum remain. Most of the surface is brittle, and the color of the body is yellowish brown. Although there is no evidence that the brain or viscera were extracted, only the penis and scrotum can be found. Zenkai wears the same clothes and a pair of tabi as at the time of his death. His hands are clasped, and the wrists are tied together with string. A straight deep furrow is seen from the right to the left lumbar region through the umbilical region at a right angle to the axis of the body. It seems to be a ligature mark that was made when the body was tied with string to a prop on its back to make it assume the desired posture for mummification, thus maintaining an exceedingly good sitting position. The soft parts may have decomposed at one time, but are well preserved. The lower legs are relatively short. The body weighs 7.0 kg and is 160.3 cm in height. The blood group is O. The upper and lower eyelids of both eyes are closed. In spite of its good posture, the vertebral column is highly kyphotic. Most of the molars of the maxillary bone fell out in his lifetime, and the bone has become highly atrophied. X-ray examination

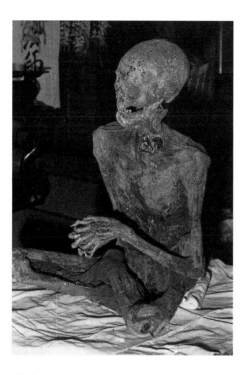

FIGURE 14.4. Mummy of Zenkai Shônin.

shows that the closure of the principal sutures of the skull is almost complete. It is reported that he died at the age of 85. X-rays reveal many fairly large oval shadows around the right internal surface of the occipital bone, the right orbit, both maxillary sinuses, and the vertebral column, but their origin is uncertain.

Chûkai Shônin (Figure 14.5) The skin is well preserved, but soft parts of the lower body have largely disintegrated. There is no evidence that the brain and viscera were extracted. The mummy is 159.1 cm in height, weighs 6.0 kg and has blood group A. It is in a sitting position. Several ligature marks can be seen in the cervical region, on the right frontal chest wall, and from the right lumbar region to the left through the umbilical region at a right angle to the axis of the body. Old pieces of cloth are found attached to the impressions caused by the rope. This suggests that Chûkai's clothed body had been tied with string to prevent it from falling forward in the mummification process. The upper and lower lids of both eyes are closed, and most of the soft parts under the headgear are decomposed. The facial part below the headgear is painted with something black (presumably Chinese ink), and most of the upper lip and some of the lower lip are shaped and mended with some black substance. A board is tied to the back of the mummy to keep it in a good

FIGURE 14.5. Mummy of Chûkai Shônin.

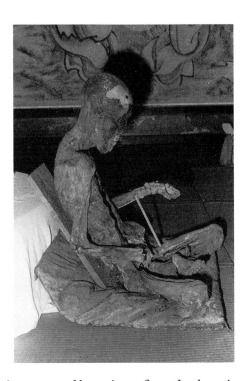

sitting position, and the left forearm is supported by a piece of wood to keep it forward and holding a bamboo stick. The mending of the face and the attempts to maintain the mummy's posture were performed after the second stage of treatment and will not, therefore, be discussed here. X-rays showed the closure of the principal sutures of the skull to be moderately complete. Dental attrition is light, and the alveolar process of the maxillary bone and the alveolar part of the mandible are not much atrophied. According to the temple records, Chûkai died at the age of 58. The lower parts of the legs are relatively short, and the whole body is of slender frame. On x-rays, spondylosis can be seen in the bodies of the fifth and sixth cervical vertebrae and the thoracic vertebrae. There are obvious osteophytes and osteosclerosis caused by osteoarthritis on the margin of the acetabulum. There is slight kyphosis of the vertebral column. The temple records say that Chûkai's corpse was smoke dried, which probably explains its black brown color.

Shinnyokai Shônin The skin is relatively well preserved but looks black brown, possibly because the body was smoke dried during mummification. The skin surface is covered with innumerable white spots. The body weighs 6.0 kg and measures 156.9 cm in height. The blood group is AB. The inferior aperture of the pelvis is wide open, and part of the diaphragm and urinary

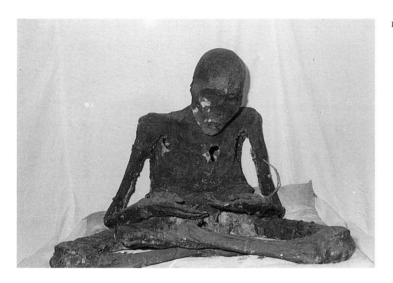

FIGURE 14.6. Mummy of Enmyôkai Shônin.

bladder remain, but there is no evidence that the brain and viscera were extracted. The mummy is in a crooked sitting posture, almost falling backward. The vertebral column is remarkably kyphotic, and a deep furrow is seen from the right lumbar region to the left through the umbilical region at a right angle to the axis of the body. A shallow furrow is also seen in the fifth intercostal space of the right side of the chest wall parallel to the ribs. These furrows may have been formed when the body was tied to a prop on its back at the time it was mummified. X-rays show the closure of the principal sutures of the skull to be moderately complete. All the teeth had dropped out in his lifetime. The alveolar process of the maxillary bone and the alveolar part of the mandible are atrophied. Shinnyokai is reported to have died at the age of 96. The skeleton is delicate. The lower parts of the legs are relatively short. X-rays show five oval shadows on the left scapula, but their origin is uncertain. Spondylosis can be seen in the lower thoracic vertebrae, and the body of the twelfth thoracic vertebra has been deformed into a wedge shape. In front of it, a new bone with a sharp margin is observed. It is not known whether the new bone was formed as the result of a compression fracture during his lifetime or because of spondylosis. There is a postmortem fracture in the second lumbar vertebra. The bodies of the third, fourth and especially the fifth lumbar vertebrae have been deformed into a wedge shape. The acetabulum protrudes slightly into the pelvis.

Enmyôkai Shônin (Figures 14.6 and 14.7) The body parts are brittle but thicker than those of the other mummies. This body has also kept its original

FIGURE 14.7. Radiograph of the mummy of Enmyôkai Shônin.

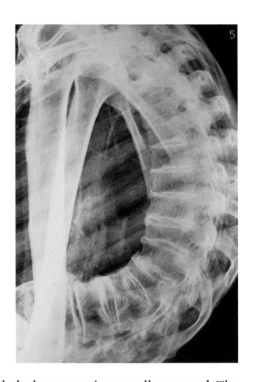

shape better than the others, though the lower part is not well preserved. The skin is atrophied, and there is no sign that the brain or viscera were extracted. The area from the right cheek to the upper lower lips has been mended, and the surface is painted brown, as is the rest of the body. The upper and lower limbs were painted black–brown (presumably with persimmon tannin) after being tied with twine in several places at a right angle to the axes. As the body had possibly been smoke dried first, it was undoubtedly painted during the second treatment. X-rays show the closure of the principal sutures of the skull to be almost complete. There is slight dental attrition. Enmyôkai is said to have died at age 55. The vertebral column is highly kyphotic and has the shape of a bow. The body is 164.7 cm tall and weighs 6.8 kg. X-ray examination shows spondylosis in the thoracic and lumbar vertebrae. Both the 12th thoracic and the first lumbar vertebrae, constituting the apex of kyphosis, have been deformed into a wedge shape. In the hip joints, osteoarthritis is seen, but there is no sign of osteoporosis. Because of its corpulence it is believed that the body became mummified after it had decomposed.

Tetsumonkai Shônin This mummy has suffered serious damage. The remaining skin is black brown and hair also remains. There is no evidence that the brain and viscera were extracted. Part of the diaphragm and the left lung remain. Temple records report that the body was smoke dried using big candles immediately after death. This suggests that the color of the skin may possibly be attributable to soot. A distinctive feature of this mummy is that the soft part of the face, from the frontal to the mandible part, has disintegrated and seems to have been mended with something black. It was painted over with yellow paint, then probably with black Japanese lacquer. Dental attrition is fairly advanced and in x-rays the closure of the principal sutures of the skull is nearly complete. It is said that Tetsumonkai died at the age of 62. Long symmetrical ligature marks can be seen on both sides of the chest. They are like those of a cord used to tuck up kimono sleeves. They were probably left when the upper part of his body was tied to a prop on his back to make it assume a sitting position during the first stage of mummification. It is said that Tetsumonkai extracted his left eyeball and cut off his external genital organs himself. A soft part, which may have been his scrotum, was preserved separately. Tetsumonkai's blood group is B, and this was also the blood group of the scrotum. It may be assumed, therefore, that this scrotum belonged to him. The mummy is 162.1 cm tall and weighs 5.0 kg. The bones of the lower limbs are well developed. The vertebral column, especially the lower lumbar vertebrae, is highly kyphotic. The left thumbprint, and possibly the right, show an ulnar loop. In x-rays, many oval shadows, origin unknown, are observed in the nasal cavity and in the right and left maxillary sinuses. Spondylosis can be seen from the eighth to the eleventh thoracic vertebrae. In the body of the twelfth thoracic vertebra, a compression fracture, possibly postmortem, can be clearly seen.

Tetsuryûkai Shônin This mummy is very well preserved because it was treated by a special method. The skin, especially of the face and head, is black because the body was dried over fire. A curved incision approximately 18 cm long runs from the right to the left iliac region through the hypogastric region. The thoracic, abdominal and pelvic cavities are filled with lime powder and some has spilled from the inferior aperture of the pelvis. The incision is continuously sutured. The forearms are relatively long. The body, 159.2 cm tall, is in a sitting position. The vertebral column is highly kyphotic. Slight dental attrition can be seen in x-rays; the closure of the principal sutures of the skull is almost complete. It is said that Tetsuryûkai died at the age of 62. The mummy weighs 15.0 kg, heavier than the other mummies, but this is because of the weight of the lime powder. The left thumbprint shows an ulnar loop; the index finger a whorl; and the middle finger possibly a whorl. The right thumbprint possibly shows an arch and the middle finger possibly an ulnar loop. The blood group is A. Osteoporosis is observed in the vertebrae. Osteophytes are found on the upper margins of each acetabulum, and osteoarthritis is also seen. Periostitis can be seen on the medial side of the upper part of the left femur. There is slight osteoarthritis in the left patellofemoral joint. The cortices of the medial sides of both tibial shafts have become rough. It is uncertain whether this is attributable to the post-traumatic periosteal reaction.

Bukkai Shônin Immediately after his death in 1903, Bukkai was put in a wooden coffin and was placed in a stone room with special devices; we excavated his body in 1961. Many bones were separated at the joints. The soft parts had decomposed and were attached to the bones like dirt, but some skin of his back was mummified. There was no evidence that the brain and viscera were extracted. The body was probably in a sitting position when it was placed in the coffin, but it was not so at the time of our excavation. Four teeth were left in the mandible. The alveolar part of the mandible was atrophied, and the roots of the teeth were exposed. X-rays show the closure of the principal sutures of the skull to be moderately complete. Bukkai's age at death is said to be 76. The body is 158.2 cm in height and weighs 7.2 kg. The lower leg bones are sturdy. Linea aspera of the femur is well developed; the tibia is nearly platycnemic; and the fibula is thick. These facts suggest that Bukkai made ample use of his lower limbs. In x-rays, all the vertebrae, from the second cervical down to the fourth lumbar vertebrae, show various deformations attributable to ankylosing spondylitis, which results in a bamboo spine. An abnormal finding is that the right fifth rib and left fourth rib are bifurcated where they touch the cartilage. In addition, bulging or spinous cortical thickening is seen in the interosseous crest of the right radius and ulna and the head of the left fibula.

Living organisms found inside and outside the bodies

All mummies except Bukkai, who was buried in the ground, had been damaged by rats, although the extent of the damage varies. In particular, the viscera were eaten, and the destruction was accelerated by rat excreta. Flies generally got into the bodies during the period of decomposition with moisture. They laid eggs in the remains either at the time of death or during mummification. The season of death and the condition of the mummies when they were placed on the ground can be deduced from the pupal sloughs of the flies that remain in the bodies. It should be noted that the lunar calendar was used before the fifth year of the Meiji era (1872) and the solar calendar after that. Among those who were mummified on the ground and in the cold season, flies were observed in Zenkai and Kôchi, although the records say that the priests' deaths occurred in January and October when such flies as *Lucilia*, *Sarcophaga* and *Calliphora* were not likely to be active. It seems, therefore, that either the viscera were kept damp until spring or the dates of death were recorded incorrectly. It is recorded that Shungi died on 15 February, was placed in a hermetic place after 17 days, and then was taken out. However, the finding of pupal sloughs of *Sarcophaga* suggests that this body had been placed in a spot where there were many flies or that it was taken out of the hermetic place with wet viscera. It is recorded that Chûkai died on 21 May and was taken from the ground after having been buried. Pupal sloughs of *Lucilia* found in the remains indicate that the viscera were still moist either when he died or when he was taken out of the ground. Pupal sloughs of *Fannia canicularis* adhered to Shinnyokai (the date of his death is uncertain) and those of *Lucilia* to Enmyôkai, who died on 8 May. This implies that these priests' viscera were still damp when the bodies were placed on the ground. If the record of the temple of Enmyôkai is correct, the priest's viscera must have been in a condition that allowed flies to adhere to them immediately after the priest died. As these examples show, pupal sloughs of flies can be a valid and important clue in determining whether the dates of death shown in records correspond to dates suggested by the condition of the body, as well as in understanding the whole process of mummification.

Discussion

The mummies discussed in this section were not natural mummies, nor were they found by accident. Their mummified conditions can be seen with the naked eye. They were made and enshrined in temples by people who believed in the religious ideas of Buddhism. It can be said, therefore, that all were mummified intentionally. Unlike the Egyptian mummies, the viscera had not been extracted, except for the mummy of Tetsuryûkai in 1879 or 1880 in the Meiji era. This was treated by making an incision, filling the cavity of the body with lime powder, and applying a continuous suture. Most of the viscera of the seven mummies other than those of Tetsuryûkai and Bukkai were eaten by rats, but some viscera obviously remain in two of them. There is no evidence that brains were extracted.

The most important stage of mummification is the first one, because it is then that the dead body is made into a mummy. In many cases, mummies were treated several times, but the later forms of treatment are not discussed here. According to the records, some bodies were smoke dried in the first treatment, and indeed, black soot could be observed on their skin. The most notable feature of these mummies is their posture, which is related to the tenets of Buddhism. Many were mummified with the lower and upper eyelids closed. The position of the lower limb is different in each mummy. In some, the joints were broken and the bones separated so that the original position remains uncertain, though it was probably a sitting position. In many mummies, the heads were bent forward and in some their palms were pressed together in prayer, as in the case of Zenkai, whose wrist joints were tied with string. However, the original forms were destroyed as time passed and the upper limbs are now in various attitudes.

Unlike the Egyptian method, neither oil nor resin was applied during the first stage of mummification, although in Tetsuryûkai's case, filling the body cavity with lime powder helped good preservation. Modern medical techniques had presumably been introduced by the time this work was performed. People capable of applying a continuous suture must have been exceedingly skillful.

Fingerprints could be investigated in only three cases. This had nothing to do with the period of the mummies, but was the result of damage by rats and insects and of corrosion. Blood groups were determined for all except Enmyôkai and Bukkai. Blood grouping was not possible in Enmyôkai's case because of decomposition and in Bukkai's case because of corrosion of almost all soft parts.

The mummies are enshrined as objects of religious worship at their respective temples, which were far removed from cities. It was therefore necessary to take x-rays with a lightweight portable machine. In addition, in the case of mummies with soft parts remaining on the bones, special devices were used to emphasize the bones. Senile spondylosis was found in almost all. Bukkai exhibited ankylosing spondylitis. Some remains had osteoarthritis in the hips and knees. Some had periostitis or periosteal thickness of the cortex. In some cases, fracture of the vertebral bodies was reported, but this may have been posthumous modification. Many oval shadows were found in the skulls and on the scapulas and vertebral column, but the origin of these is uncertain.

As is obvious from this discussion, these nine mummies were in the process of rapid deterioration. From the beginning of the examination, the author, together with Sôjirô Maruyama, has aimed at achieving a better state of preservation for the mummies. Preventive measures against microorganisms, insects and rats were taken, and decomposing parts were tied together with twine and fixed with glue.

Conclusion

This investigation of nine Japanese mummies dating from medieval times (1363) to the present (1903) has shown that many were mummified by artificial means.

Acknowledgments

The cultural history presented in the second part of this chapter is derived from the following sources: *Mummies in Japan* (1961) by the late Professor Kôsei Andô, the previous head of our group, and 'Research by cultural history' by the late Professor Andô and by Professor Kiyohiko Sakurai in *Research of Japanese mummies* (1969).

As reported in the second section of this chapter, its author took part in anatomical and anthropological studies of the mummies. The following staff at Niigata University School of Medicine contributed information in their professional fields: the late Professor Emeritus Dr Shungo Yamanouchi and Professor Rokurô Shigeno for medicolegal studies, Professor Emeritus Dr Shûei Nozaki for review of x-rays of mummies and Professor Emeritus Dr Sachû Kôno for observations on alterations of bone seen in x-rays. Together with Dr Ryûhei Homma, the author dealt with living organisms found in and around mummies.

The author wishes to thank Mr. Arika Matsumoto, lecturer at Nihon University, for his help during this investigation. The author would like to express his gratitude also to the following people for their help: the staff of Shônai Hospital, Tsuruoka City, Yamagata prefecture, for radiographic studies; Professor Dr Susumu Saitô, Mr. Yoshinobu Ikegami, and the late Dr Hiromasa Muraki for identifying species of living organisms; and Mr. Sôjirô Maruyama for helping mend the mummies.

Gratitude must also be expressed for the encouragement and assistance of the priests of the respective temples.

JAPAN: RECENT DEVELOPMENTS

Iwataro Morimoto

Valuable information has recently been obtained from studies on the mummies of priests Myôkai and Shûkai (Matsumoto 1991, 1993a, 1993b; Matsumoto *et al.* 1993; Morimoto 1993; Morimoto and Hirata 1993) as well as the Fujiwara family (Hanihara 1996).

The mummy of priest Myôkai is kept at Myôju-in Temple, Yonezawa, Yamagata Prefecture, on the premises of S. Matsumoto, a descendant of priest Myôkai. This is the sole Sokushin-butsu ('Becoming a Buddha in this body') mummy at the eastern foot of Mt Yudono. Priest Myôkai was of low birth and lost his sight in boyhood. After the severest asceticism at Dainichi-ji Temple, he achieved high rank from Ninna-ji Temple, Kyoto, against established custom. He died at the age of 44 in 1863 and was mummified by the same method used in making other Sokushin-butsu at the western foot of the same mountain. From the socioeconomic point of view, this mummy would bring prosperity to the temples located at the eastern foot of Mt. Yudono, because a priest's mummy attracted worshippers.

The mummy of priest Shûkai is kept at Shinju-in Temple, Kashiwazaki, Niigata Prefecture. Unlike those lower class priests (isse-gyônin) who were made into Sokushin-butsu, priest Shûkai was highly trained at Hase-dera Temple, Nara Prefecture, during his younger days, and took up his duties as the head priest of the Shinju-in later. On March 21, 1780, at the age of 62, he died of starvation caused by his intentional fasting; he was the same age and died the same date as the great priest Kûkai. His death occurred while he was practicing A-Syllable Visualization (ajikan) for 21 days inside a stone chamber attached to the wooden hut built on a hill behind his temple. This hut was copied from the Northern Pure Land of Maitreya. A meditation scroll with a Sanskrit A-Syllable in the Taizo form of Shingon Buddhism was painted on the anterior wall of the stone chamber (Figure 14.8). A bronze altar set of five-pronged vajra (goko-sho), vajra bell (kongo-rei) and pitcher (not only for his water supply, but also as a symbol of Maitreya) was laid on the floor of the chamber in front of the mummy. The terminal phalanx of his right index finger was put in the prong of the vajra, as if he grasped it tightly at the moment of his death. The Taizo means literally 'womb repository', and often indicates Maitreya. Moreover, the A-Syllable is originally unborn, ungraspable void (hon-pushô); it embraces the truth of all Buddhas everywhere. There seems no point in saying whether priest Shûkai wished to convert himself into a mummy or not, because by practicing A-Syllable Visualization, he had disregarded the peril to his life. It is recorded that his body was still completely mummified in the sixtieth year after his death, although it has now decayed into a skeleton.

Medical observations on the skeleton of priest Shûkai (Morimoto and Hirata 1993) revealed that the synostosis was complete in the hyoid bone and that the degree of calcification was normal for the priest's age at the time of death. The teeth showed moderate wear but no antemortem tooth loss. He was estimated to be 150 cm in stature but with robust long bones. There was flattening of the tibiae and femora, suggesting undernourishment during his younger years. Varying degrees of osteoarthritic lipping were present in

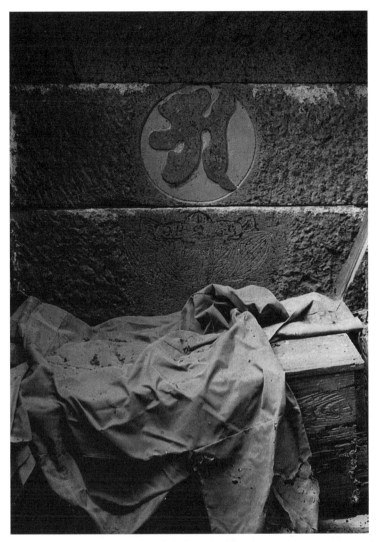

FIGURE 14.8. A meditation scroll painted on the anterior wall of the stone burial chamber of priest Shûkai. A Sanskrit A-Syllable (*aji*) superimposed upon a moon disc above a lotus flower implies the Taizo form in Shingon Buddhism. The wooden coffin in which the skeleton of Shûkai was placed can be seen in front, partially covered by a priest's robe. (From Morimoto 1993. Courtesy of the Japanese Association of Anatomists.)

lumbar vertebrae and the elbow and knee joints bilaterally, probably a result of his severe ascetic practices.

Hanihara (1996) mentioned that the Fujiwaras were descended from an aristocrat in Kyoto, not from the Ainu; their remains were mummified under natural conditions with a simple treatment for desiccation.

These discoveries require a new classification of Japanese mummies (Table 14.2). The Sokushin-butsu of type A given in this table are mummies of the priests who practiced the Shingon thought 'Becoming a Buddha in this body' (*Sokushin-jôbutsu*), which is not relevant to the Maitreya faith. The Sokushin-butsu are the only artificial ones among the mummies of Japan.

Table 14.2. *Classification of Japanese mummies based on their ideological background*

Type	Ideological background = name of priest (see text)
A	Sokushin-butsu (mummies) in Shingon Buddhism
	1. At the front foot of Mt. Yudono
	a. Dainichi-bo group = Zenkai and Shinnyokai
	b. Chûren-ji group = Hommyôkai, Chûkai, Enmyôkai, Tetsumonkai, Tetsuryûkai and Bukkai.
	2. At the rear foot of Mt. Yudono
	c. Dainichi-ji group = Myôkai
B	Mummy of priest practicing A-Syllable Visualization in Taizo form of Shingon Buddhism = Shûkai
C	Nyûjô-mummy of Maitreya faith = Kôchi
D	Mummies of Amitabha faith = Fujiwaras, Shungi, and Tansei
E	Mummies of Yakushi faith = Yûtei
F	Others.
	1. Mummy in Zen Buddhism plus something = Shinsô-Gyôjun
	2 Mummy in Mt. Fuji worship = Myôshin

Source: Modified and enlarged from Matsumoto (1991).

The mummies of types A and B are based on Shingon Buddhism, whereas those of types C, D and E are attributable to the Maitreya, Amitabha and Yakushi (Healing Buddha) faiths, respectively. It is said that Japanese Buddhists used to seek salvation through faith in one of the following: Amitabha presiding over the Western Pure Land, Maitreya over the Northern, Yakushi over the Eastern, and Kannon (Buddha of Mercy) over the Southern. No mummy of Kannon faith has been found in Japan. The mummies of type F, on the other hand, were founded on a variety of ideological backgrounds, but their common point is that they are the mummies of the priests who volunteered and prepared themselves for mummification.

CHINA: THE MAWANGTUI-TYPE CADAVERS IN CHINA
Peng Long-xiang and Wu Zhong-bi

Different types of ancient preserved cadavers such as natural and artificial mummies, adipoceres and peat-tanned cadavers have been studied and reported in the Chinese medical literature since 1949. At present there are numerous natural mummies in Xinjiang Autonomous Region, and many

Buddhist mummies in Tibet Autonomous Region, Jiu Hua Mountain of Anhui Province, and the Genuine Body Statue of Hui Neng in the Nan Hua Temple, Qujiang County, Guangdong Province. China abounds in archaeological and paleopathological resources.

In the past, the Chinese people had a traditional concept: one's skin, hair and the whole body come from one's parents. One has to return the entire body to either heaven or earth when one dies. No one should damage the body. They have found that the best way to preserve the corpse is to put it into the coffin, seal it air-tight, and then bury the coffin under the earth. The expense, fashion, and dimension of the sepulture depend upon their social position and personal property.

In 1972, the well-preserved body of an old female and over 1500 valuable relics were unearthed from a tomb at Mawangtui, Changsha City, Hunan Province (Hunan Medical College 1980). Tomb documents identified her as the wife of Litsang, Chancellor of the Kingdom of Changsha and the Marquis of Tai of the Western Han Dynasty. Relics were radiocarbon dated, which showed that this tomb had been buried for over 2100 years. It was buried 20 meters deep under the earth with a set of three wooden coffins of different sizes tightly fitted one within the other. The cadaver was sealed inside the innermost coffin. Many layers of silk and linen shrouds enveloped the cadaver, which was half immersed in a brown-yellowish coffin fluid. She was 154 cm tall and weighed 34.3 kg. The body appeared humid, the soft tissues still maintained a certain elasticity, and the joints were partially movable. It was not a mummified corpse and differed from all types of preserved cadavers reported in the past. We named this peculiar type of perfectly preserved body 'the Mawangtui-type cadaver'.

Another well-preserved ancient corpse (but male) was unearthed in 1975 from Phoenix Hill at Jiangling, Hubei Province (Wu 1982; Peng 1995). The dead man was an official of the *Wutafu* rank (equivalent to a county magistrate) before his death and was buried in the thirteenth year of the reign of Emperor Wen of the Western Han Dynasty (167 BC). The tomb was a rectangular vertical pit, about 10 meters deep. The burial containers of one outer coffin and two inner coffins were all made of wood. The coffins were tightly sealed up with raw Chinese lacquer and linen. In the inner coffin, there were about 100 liters of dark red coffin fluid in which the corpse was immersed. The dead man was about 60 years old, 167.8 cm tall and 52.5 kg in weight. The skin all over his body was soft and tough, the soft tissues remained elastic, and the joints were still movable. This ancient corpse was of the same type as the female unearthed at Mawangtui.

FIGURE 14.9. Electron micrograph of the collagen fiber of a Mawangtui-type cadaver revealed the intact ultrastructure with clear periodic cross banding.

In March 1994, an ancient corpse was excavated from robbed Tomb No.1 at Guojiagang in Jingmen City, Hubei Province (Wu *et al.* 1995). It was confirmed that this corpse was buried more than 2300 years ago, namely during the middle stage of the Warring States Period, and is the same type as the Mawangtui ancient cadaver mentioned above.

Multidisciplinary and comprehensive studies were made on these ancient cadavers to determine the method and level of preservation, the pathological changes, and the cause of death. Autopsies were performed on all three. The head, neck, trunk, and four limbs of each were preserved in a comparatively intact state. All internal organs, though collapsed and thinned to various degrees, were preserved in good condition and in normal position. Even the arteries of the appendix and cecum, and the neuroplexus of the vagus nerves on the lung were clearly visible in the Mawangtui corpse. The brain of the Jiangling body was turgid and occupied more than three-fourths of the cranial cavity, which was invested by dura mater. X-ray films showed that the whole skeleton was complete in these bodies.

Light and electron microscopic observations revealed that different tissues were preserved to varying degrees. The connective tissues, including bone and cartilage, especially the extracellular components, were by far the best preserved. Under the electron microscope, the collagen fibers possessed not only distinct margins but also intact ultrastructure with clear periodic cross banding and normal arrangement of collagen macromolecules (Figure 14.9). Each period was approximately 630 nm in width, within which more than 10 tiny striations could be detected. A considerable number of chondrocytes with relatively intact nuclei and cell membranes could still be observed (Figure 14.10). Muscular tissues ranked next in the degree of preservation. Most of the skeletal muscle fibers retained distinct contours and cross striations. Cardiac muscle, however, was not so well preserved and smooth muscle was even less so. The nervous and epithelial tissues were mostly auto-

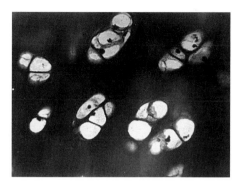

FIGURE 14.10. The section of the costal cartilage of a Mawangtui-type cadaver showed the chondrocytes with relatively intact nuclei and cell membranes within the lacunae.

lyzed, but the brain of the Jiangling corpse was preserved much better than that of the Mawangtui corpse; in the former the myelin sheath of the nerve fibers of the brain strikingly maintained its typical concentric lamellar ultra-structure. As mentioned above, bones, cartilage, striated muscles, and especially collagenous connective tissues were the essential support materials for the well preserved gross morphology of the corpse and its organ systems.

The structure and properties of some important biomacromolecules were preserved to a remarkable degree. Histochemical examination and biochemical isolation demonstrated the existence of macromolecular ribonucleic acids and deoxyribonucleic acids in the liver, muscle, and cartilage of the Mawangtui and the Jiangling corpses. Tropomyosin had almost the same iso-electric point (around 5.0) and molecular weight (37 000 daltons) as that of a contemporary corpse. The collagen presents a typical x-ray diffraction pattern, indicating that its molecular structure was preserved intact. X-ray diffraction studies revealed that hair keratin still retained its alpha configuration. An immunological study showed that various tissues of these ancient bodies still maintained their antigenicity. It means that not only tissue proteins but also their spatial structure were retained. Analyses of the lipids of the brain, liver, skin, and the surroundings of the kidney indicated that quite a lot of cholesterol and free fatty acids persisted in these tissues.

Using immunological methods to examine the blood group substance in the muscle, bone and hair of the Mawangtui corpse showed that her blood group was Group A. The blood group of both the Jiangling corpse and the Jingmen corpse was Group AB.

The preservation technique for the Mawangtui cadavers and the level of preservation of these corpses were far better than that of mummified, adipoceratous, and peat-tanned cadavers, so that pathological changes could still be recognized. As a result, we were able to diagnose with certainty the diseases the dead person contracted and the causes of death. It has been

proved by pathomorphologic and other examinations that the Mawangtui cadaver was affected by the following: (1) general atherosclerosis, (2) Coronary artery atherosclerosis, (3) multiple cholelithiasis, (4) schistosomiasis japonica, (5) chronic accumulation of lead and mercury, (6) fracture of the distal end of the right ulna and radius, with malunion, (7) enterobiasis and trichuriasis, (8) the presence of 138.5 muskmelon seeds in the esophagus, stomach, small and large intestines.

Electron micrograph of cardiac muscle showed the appearance of the minifocal scar, a large amount of dense collagen fibers. The arterial specimen was taken from the beginning segment of the left coronary. The section showed the atherosclerotic plaques of the coronary artery. (Figure 14.11). The sclerotic part of the plaques was made up of a large amount of dense collagen fibres, and the lumen of the artery was almost completely blocked. It means that she had severe coronary heart disease, and that therefore cardiovascular disease in China has a more than 2000 year history.

Several muskmelon seeds were found on the mucous membrane of the stomach, showing that the woman had died shortly after eating. Some food remained in the stomach and had not passed into the intestine. A gallstone about the size of a broad bean was lodged inside the common bile duct, and another as big as a soybean blocked the hepatic duct. The woman probably died suddenly of a myocardial infarction, or she might have died of serious arrhythmia due to a heart attack caused by biliary colic. On the other hand, throughout the systemic autopsy studies, no signs of any chronic wasting diseases, tumor growths, or any wounds suggesting a violent death were noted.

The lateral spine, the characteristic structure of eggs of *Schistosoma japonicum*, was quite clear after digesting and separating the liver tissue of this corpse. A liver section revealed a nodule containing three schistosome eggs (Figure 14.12). Blood fluke eggs enclosed in fibrous connective tissue in

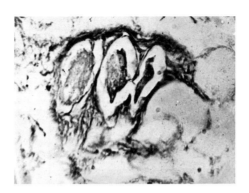

FIGURE 14.12 The liver section of the Mawangtui cadaver showed a nodule containing three schistosome eggs.

the liver and the walls of the rectum showed that she had schistosomiasis japonica.

The following pathological changes were identified in the Jiangling ancient corpse: (1) chronic gastric ulcer in the lesser curvature complicated by acute perforation, (2) extensive bleeding in pleural and peritoneal cavities, omental sac, and most of the tissues and organs, (3) clonorchiasis, (4) schistosomiasis japonica, (5) parasitic cirrhosis of the liver (due to clonorchiasis and schistosomiasis japonica), (6) chronic cholecystitis with cholelithiasis, (7) atherosclerosis, (8) diaphragmatic pseudohernia of the gastric fundus, and (9) tapeworm and whipworm infection.

Regarding the cause of death in the ancient cadaver, as Aidan Cockburn frequently pointed out, it is rare for the cause of death to be diagnosed in an ancient body, apart from accident or violence. Nevertheless, of the above-mentioned diseases, chronic gastric ulcer complicated by acute perforation was the main one, and the acute peritonitis complicated by extensive bleeding all over the body was the direct cause of death. The extensive bleeding was associated with septic shock caused by diffuse peritonitis due to perforation of a gastric ulcer. Moreover, cirrhosis of the liver might have been contributory to the coagulopathy of the blood, enhancing the bleeding and hastening death. These findings were made possible by the excellent condition of the body .

The most interesting subject is the cause of this preservation. The conditions contributing to the preservation of these ancient tombs and the cadavers, apart from the social background, are the combined effects of extrinsic and intrinsic factors. The preservation of the ancient tomb and its cadaver was related to certain external conditions (such as temperature, humidity, pressure, air, sun rays and pH value). All external conditions that helped prevent substances from being destroyed physically or chemically and that were unfavorable to the growth of putrefactive bacteria, were necessary factors in preserving the ancient tomb and its cadaver.

According to the funeral rites, following the death of a feudal nobleman, the corpse was to be bathed with perfumed water and sacrificial wine, clothed in many layers and wrapped tightly in shrouds. Prior to putting the corpse into the coffin, ice or cold water should be placed under its bed in order to 'cool the corpse'. Such burial ceremonies and measures would have had some effect on slowing down the process of early putrefaction in the corpse. After putting the body into the coffin, they would not put any fluid into the coffin next to it. In addition, the main method of preserving the corpse was to seal the coffin airtight before burial. The decomposition of the fat and protein of the corpse and of the silk protein from the shrouds would produce a large amount of organic acids, turning the environment within the coffin acidic.

Nobody could know in advance that there would be an ancient cadaver in the innermost coffin, and therefore design a device to collect gas specimens for research work, so it was very difficult for anyone to get direct data about the microenvironment inside the coffin. But it has been possible for the researchers to get certain evidence related to the microenvironment inside the coffin after studying the ancient corpse itself.

During the autopsy of the Mawangtui corpse, there were some signs of early postmortem putrefaction, such as prolapse of eyeballs, opening of the mouth, slight protrusion of the tongue, and prolapse of the rectum, but cultures for micro-organisms and other studies indicated that the process of putrefaction had stopped long ago.

In the study of the Jingmen ancient corpse, many circular or elliptical structures of 2.0–1.3 µm size, wrapped with high electron density envelope and having a dense core in the center, were observed in the section of various tissues. These structures were identified as spores of the putrefactive bacteria, strongly suggesting that the microenvironment within the coffin gradually turned unfavorable to the growth of putrefactive bacteria and they became spores in an attempt to preserve themselves. As a result, the corpses were also preserved. Bacteria with spores were found in the Mawangtui and the Jiangling corpses as well.

A study of the adipose tissue of these corpses showed that the types and quantities of lipoid substance were roughly the same as those in a modern corpse. It contained a large amount of unsaturated fatty acid. It is understood that the unsaturated fatty acids are unstable, easy to oxidize and catabolize. The presence of so much unsaturated fatty acid was evidence that these ancient corpses had stayed in an oxygen poor environment.

The stability of the molecular structure of certain tissues in the body has to be considered as a major intrinsic factor in the preservation of the bodies. For instance, the collagen fibers of the connective tissues were widely distributed in the body as the framework of various organs and tissues. Under ordinary conditions these fibers were not easily disintegrated because of the solidity and stability of their molecular structure. Thus, they helped retain the gross morphology of the corpse and provided the biological high molecular weight substances with a firm support by which the body could be preserved.

REFERENCES

Japan: scientific research

Andô, K. 1961. *Mummies in Japan.* Tokyo: Mainichi Newspapers. (In Japanese.)

Andô, K. 1969. Preparation of Nyûjô mummies. In *Research of Japanese mummies,* ed. Group for Research of Japanese Mummies, 83–95. Tokyo: Heibonsha. (In Japanese.)

Andô, K. and Sakurai, K. 1969. Research by cultural history: extant Japanese mummies. In *Research of Japanese mummies,* ed. Group for Research of Japanese Mummies, 21–82. Tokyo: Heibonsha. (In Japanese.)

Furuhata, T. 1950. Blood groups, fingerprints and teeth of four generations of the Fujiwara clan. In *The Chûson-ji Temple and four generations of the Fujiwara clan,* 45–66. Tokyo: Asahi Shimbun. (In Japanese.)

Hasebe, K. 1950. Various questions on the remains. In *Chûson-ji Temple and four generations of the Fujiwara clan,* 7–22. Tokyo: Asahi Shimbun. (In Japanese.)

Suzuki, H. 1950. Anthropological observations on the remains. In *Chûson-ji Temple and four generations of the Fujiwara clan,* 23–44. Tokyo: Asahi Shimbun. (In Japanese.)

Japan: recent developments

Hanihara, K. 1996. An additional study on the mummies of the Fujiwaras in the medieval age. *Bulletin of the International Research Center for Japanese Studies* **13**: 11–33. (In Japanese.)

Matsumoto, A. 1991. Ideological backgrounds of Japanese mummies. *Journal of the Anthropological Society of Nippon* **99**: 185.

Matsumoto, A. 1993a. Japanese nyûjô mummies. In *Worship of mummies in Japan and China,* ed. Group for Research of Japanese Mummies, 17–97. Tokyo: Heibonsha. (In Japanese.)

Matsumoto, A. 1993b. *Japanese mummies of Buddhists.* Kyoto: Rinsen. (In Japanese.)

Matsumoto, A., Araki, K. and Shibanuma, K., 1993. An example of an Ajikan Nirvâna mummy. In *Worship of mummies in Japan and China,* ed. Group for Research of Japanese Mummies, 99–131, Tokyo: Heibonsha. (In Japanese.)

Morimoto, I. 1993. Buddhist mummies in Japan. *Acta Anatomica Nipponica* **8**: 381–98. (In Japanese.)

Morimoto, I. and Hirata, K. 1993. Medical observations on the remains of the Shûkai mummy. In *Worship of mummies in Japan and China,* ed. Group for Research of Japanese Mummies, 133–44. Tokyo: Heibonsha. (In Japanese.)

Mawangtui Mummies of China

Hunan Medical College, ed. 1980. *Study of an ancient cadaver in Mawangtui Tomb No. 1 of the Han Dynasty.* Beijing: Cultural Relics Publishing House.

Peng, L. 1995 Study of an ancient cadaver excavated from a Han Dynasty (207 BC – AD 220) tomb in Hunan Province. In *Proceedings of the I World Congress on Mummy Studies,* vol. 2, 853–6. Santa Cruz de Tenerife: Museo Arqueológico y Etnográfico de Tenerife.

Wu, Z., ed. 1982. *Studies of an ancient corpse of the Western Han Dynasty unearthed from Tomb No.168 on the Phoenix Hill at Jiangling.* Beijing: Cultural Relics Publishing House.

Wu, Z., Guan, Y. and Zhou, Z. 1995. Study of an ancient corpse of the Warring States Period unearthed from Tomb No.1 at Guojiagang in Jingmen City. *Journal of the Chinese Electron Microscopy Society* **14**(4): 312–16.

15

Bodies from cold regions

J. P. HART HANSEN

The frigid regions of the World are comprised of the circumpolar part of the Northern Hemisphere (Alaska, Greenland and parts of Canada, Scandinavia, European Russia and Siberia), the circumpolar part of the Southern Hemisphere, and the high altitude mountainous areas (e.g., the Alps, the Andes and the Himalayas). In these regions, low temperatures and high winds with low humidity prevail, special climatic conditions that favor the preservation of organic material. These frigid regions are sparsely populated, particularly the Antarctic and the high altitude areas. The Arctic, the SubArctic and the vast Asian regions of permafrost have been populated for millennia, however sparsely, and have witnessed extensive migrations with temporary and permanent settlements. Investigations of ancient mummified human remains from these regions, along with garments and equipment, have provided information of decisive importance for the knowledge and understanding of local culture and history.

The low temperatures and low air humidity favour the preservation of deceased animal and human bodies (Hart Hansen 1989). The complicated chemical processes of decomposition and putrefaction normally start immediately after death. Water is necessary for the growth of bacteria and fungal organisms, and if it is removed by freezing or evaporation, bacterial growth and therefore putrefaction are prevented. Alternating periods of freezing and thawing have a particularly desiccating effect, and together can delay or stop the process of decay and the disappearance of the soft tissues. Most preserved ancient human bodies are the result of natural mummification, although artificial mummification has been carried out on the Aleutian Islands and in Siberia (Zimmerman et al.1971, 1981; Rolle 1992).

Although mummified human remains have been found in the Arctic area and from the high altitude mountainous regions, they are rare, with relatively few bodies discovered; a safe burial was often impossible and the body disappeared due to exposure to animals and the weather. In these zones, three different types of postmortem change are encountered. Bodies may be found frozen, mummified or with adipocere changes, sometimes with all three types in the same body; only persons who have died recently will be found in a purely frozen state. Some desiccation will take place over time with the disappearance of water, and the formation of adipocere or grave-wax (the postmortem change of body fat to a greyish-white waxy substance when in humid and anaerobic surroundings) is characteristic of bodies found in glaciers (Bereuter *et al.* 1996). Every year climbers, hikers and skiers disappear in mountains like the Alps, either falling in glacier crevasses or being buried by avalanches, and every year such bodies are released from the ice with adipocere changes, sometimes many years after their disappearance (Ambach *et al.* 1992).

Due to their age and excellent preservation, world-wide interest has been aroused by some of the more recent finds of mummified human remains from the cold regions. This has been particularly true of the 1991 discovery of the 5200 year old Ice Man in the Austrian/Italian Alps (Spindler 1994; Spindler *et al.* 1996), but other finds have also generated much interest: Scythian and other bodies in Siberia (Rudenko 1970; Rolle 1992; Polosmak 1994); the buried sailors from the Franklin expedition in northern Canada (Beattie and Geiger 1987), the Eskimo mummies from Qilakitsoq in Greenland (Hart Hansen and Gulløv 1989; Hart Hansen *et al.* 1991) and Inca bodies sacrificed in the Andes mountains (Schobinger 1966, 1991; Horne 1996; Reinhard 1996). This chapter will describe these discoveries; mummies from the Aleutian Islands and Alaska are described in chapter 8. The Antarctic has seen human activity of any importance only in this century, has no indigenous population, and no finds of mummified human remains are on record there.

Siberia and the Arctic and SubArctic part of North America (Greenland is geographically part of North America) have been populated by different ethnic population groups through millennia, though sparsely. Comprehensive multidisciplinary research projects have been initiated in connection with some of the recent, more spectacular finds in the cold regions, e.g., the Ice Man in the Alps and the Qilakitsoq mummies in Greenland (Spindler 1994; Hansen and Gulløv 1989). Scientific investigation of ancient human remains has provided invaluable information on ancient cultures and life styles as well as diseases and environmental conditions in those communities. Such investigations are particularly important when no written history is available for the region and period in question. Except for the most recent centuries, this is true of Greenland.

In Siberia and Alaska, frozen and mummified mammoths have been discovered, some more than 35 000–45 000 years old (Guthrie 1990; Zimmerman 1996). In these regions, mummified bison, moose, caribou, horses, lynx and rabbits and small mammals like ground squirrels and mice have been found. In the Antarctic, mummified seals that died some 2000 years ago have been found and studied (Marini et al. 1967), and at the border zones of the Greenland ice cap, frozen and mummified swans, reindeer and musk oxen 700 to 2000 years old have been discovered.

SIBERIA

Between 1929 and 1949 Rudenko excavated several graves in Pazyryk in the Altai mountains on the border between Siberia and Outer Mongolia, dating from the fifth to the third century BC (Artamanov 1965; Rudenko 1970; Rolle 1992). Large tribes of nomads roamed the steppes of Eurasia in ancient times and inhabited the vast treeless territories extending from Europe to China and north of Greece, Persia and India. The term Scytho-Siberian is used to cover the cultures of all these peoples. They were seminomadic pastoral herders and horsemen, and their culture was centered around the horse. It was the custom to bury horses with their riders.

Ancient sources called some tribes Scythian, among them Herodotus who described the culture and the special form of Scythian embalming. The technique resembled the Egyptian embalming method, but without the use of natron. The internal organs were removed, the skull opened and the brain removed, and the muscles often scraped away. The remains were embalmed with an aromatic mixture and the skin sewn up. The excavated tombs below earth were covered by stone, and a cover of ice had been created below the stones, thus turning the grave chambers into refrigerators. Although many graves had been looted, some were intact with rich stores of well preserved artifacts due to the low temperature. The bodies were carefully embalmed, and obviously people of high social status. After the removal of the internal organs and the brain, the bodies had been stuffed with grass. The heads were shaved but burial hair had been artificially attached to the heads of the females and beards to the faces of the males. On the skin elaborate tattoos of animals or mythical creatures could be seen.

Nearly 44 years after Rudenko's last find in the region, an unlooted 2400 year old tomb was discovered in 1993 on the Ukok plateau (c. 2500 m) in the autonomous republic of Altai (Polosmak 1994, 1996). A log coffin covered by solid ice held a woman about 25 years old. The tomb, which must have been flooded by rain or melting snow and frozen while still new, had remained ice-bound until its recent discovery. The woman was mummified and well preserved, and no trace of violence could be detected. The body showed tattoos on the shoulders, wrists and thumb. The tattoos consisted of lines of mythical creatures in a style similar to that on the skin of Scythian bodies found previously. Her robe was still soft and pliant, and with her was a cache of her possessions that included clothes of silk and wool, a hair and felt headdress and a hand mirror. Around the burial chamber six elaborately harnessed horses lay sacrificed.

This woman belonged to the ancient Pazyryk people. The Pazyryk Lady, as she is called, was taken to Novosibirsk and Moscow for investigations and restoration. DNA analysis has been carried out successfully. The permanent future location of the body has not been decided. The bodies from the excavations by Rudenko are in St Petersburg, but local authorities in the Altai Republic have laid claim to have the body of the Pazyryk Lady repatriated.

GREENLAND: ESKIMO REMAINS

Greenland is part of the Danish realm and attained home rule in 1979. Eighty percent of the population (approximately 55 000) are of Eskimo (Inuit) origin. About 85 percent of the country is covered by ice and the climate is Arctic. Three important finds of mummified Eskimo bodies have been made in this century. In 1929, an American anthropologist removed about 15 mummified bodies from a cave in Southwest Greenland (Hooton 1930). A few of these bodies are still preserved in the Peabody Museum at Harvard University in Boston, USA. In 1934 the site was revisited and the disturbed remains of stone graves were found. Only one grave with three infants was intact (Mathiassen 1936). These bodies are from the sixteenth or seventeenth century AD and are kept in Copenhagen, as are the bodies from the same period of three adults and seven infants and children found with equally well preserved garments in the Pisissarfik mountains of West Greenland and investigated in 1945 and 1952 (Meldgaard 1953).

The most comprehensive and closely investigated find was made in 1972. Two graves with mummified Eskimo bodies were located in a rock crevice near the abandoned settlement of Qilakitsoq in Northwestern Greenland. The graves were opened in 1978. Eight bodies were found, six adult women aged approximately 20, 25, 30, 45, 50 and 50 years respectively, and two children, a boy of 3 to 4 years and an infant aged about six months (Figure 15.1). Natural mummification was due to favourable local conditions with year-round low

FIGURE 15.1. The mummified body of a six month old Eskimo child from Qilakitsoq, Greenland. (Photograph by J. Lee, National Museum, Copenhagen, with permission of the Greenland National Museum.)

temperatures, low air humidity, the sheltered position of the graves against animals, snow, rain and direct sun, and some ventilation around the bodies. According to radiocarbon dating, the find was from AD 1475, thus being the oldest well preserved people and garments from the Thule culture, immediate predecessors of the present Eskimo population of Canada and Greenland.

An extensive, multidisciplinary program of scientific investigations applying the methods of modern archaeology, ethnography, natural science, and medicine was carried out (Hansen and Gulløv 1989; Hansen *et al.* 1991), including radiological, biological–anthropological, chemical, pathological, and forensic examinations. In the process, new scientific methods were developed; these include an indirect method of tissue typing mummified tissue (Hansen and Gürtler 1983), a biochemical method for species identification of animal skin pieces (Ammitzbøll *et al.* 1989), and a photographic method for disclosing tattooing (Figure 15.2) in mummified skin (Kromann *et al.* 1989). One of the most important results of the investigations is that 500 year old reference data have been obtained for the evaluation of present day and future environmental conditions in the Arctic (Hansen *et al.* 1989; Grandjean 1989).

Bodies from cold regions

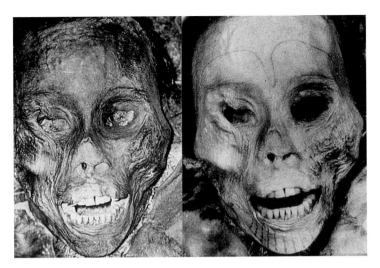

FIGURE 15.2. An ordinary (left) and an infrared photograph (right) revealing tattoos on the face of an approximately 30 year old mummified woman from Qilakitsoq, Greenland. (Photographs by E. L. Rosenløv, Gentofte Hospital, Copenhagen, with permission of the Greenland National Museum.)

The people wore garments made of seal, reindeer, and bird skins and were buried with many loose jackets, trousers, and skins. Examination gave insight into the clothing techniques of the Thule culture. The Eskimo garments of the fifteenth century were fully developed for life in the cold arid environment, similar to modern clothing standards. The ability of the Arctic people to survive in the harsh climate was due to their skillful use of animal skins for protection from the elements. No grave gifts were encountered. Most of the people were healthy, although one of the older women had an extensive cancer of the nasopharynx. A kidney stone, a few fractures, and parasites were found. The oldest child suffered from a disorder of the hip, probably Legg–Calvé–Perthes' disease, and probably also Down's syndrome. It was only possible to speculate about the cause of death for several others, partly due to the fact that internal investigation was not permitted in the best preserved mummies and probable causes could not be put to the test. In some cases, however, there were clear indications.

The smallest child did not show any sign of disease or violence. The position in the grave indicated that the child may have been buried alive, a procedure not unusual in ancient Greenland. It is well known that children and sick and disabled adults were sometimes done away with due to restricted resources in the small communities, either violently by strangulation or drowning, or by exposure. This practice was not regarded as an evil act but rather as an act of compassion. This is analogous to the behaviour of many old and disabled persons who, particularly during periods of hunger, left their homes and settlements on their own initiative and sought death, in order not to be a burden to their relatives (Hansen 1989). Human sacrifices are not known from Greenland. It was not possible in every case to determine whether the bodies had been interred simultaneously or with an interval of perhaps several years. Tissue typing indicated that the persons may have been closely related, representing three generations of the same family. DNA analysis was carried out on one person (Thuesen and Engberg 1990; Nielsen *et al.* 1993).

Investigations showed that the food was primarily of marine origin. Bone samples, teeth, and human and animal hair were analysed for heavy metals that today are related to industrial pollution (mercury, cadmium and lead), and for micronutrients like copper and selenium. Mercury and cadmium are about three times greater in present day Greenlanders than in the mummies, and lead about eight times greater. The content of these metals in present-day animals is also greater, although not to the same degree. Selenium is less in present-day humans but not in animals. These results indicate that global pollution due to industrial activities and changes in the traditional lifestyle may influence health today in the Arctic. Thus, the study of the people from Qilakitsoq, continues to give us insight into the ancient culture as compared with present day conditions in the Arctic.

Norse Greenlanders and Others

Around AD 1475, when the Qilakitsoq mummies lived and died, the last Norse descendants of Erik the Red and his followers from Iceland and Norway still inhabited parts of southwest Greenland (Hansen *et al.* 1991). The fate of the Norse who vanished from Greenland around AD 1500 after a period of colonization of approximately 500 years is unclear and remains one of the big riddles of North European history. During this period the Norse reached the shores of Labrador and Newfoundland. Was their disappearance from Greenland caused by conflicts with the Eskimos, diseases, pirates, climatic changes or starvation? Or did they just return to Iceland?

Remains of the Norse have been excavated from their Christian cemeteries but mostly skeletal remains have been recovered. Of great general importance were the extremely well preserved everyday garments of common European medieval type found in 1921 in the cemetery at Herjolfsnes (Nørlund 1924). Such garments had not been preserved in Europe proper. Some of the questions relating to the daily life of the Norse society in Greenland and its disappearance may be answered by excavating the cemetery at the Norse church ruin of Anavik, which has permafrost and which represents a broad span of years up to the late fifteenth century, plans for which are in preparation. During such work it must be kept in mind that dormant ancient microorganisms may be reactivated. In recent decades, smallpox has been eradicated but evidence of infection with smallpox has been recorded in ancient material. Although there seems to be no risk for archaeologists and others working with such material in temperate and warm regions, exhumation of bodies buried in permafrost should be carried out taking all precautions (Lewin 1985)

Finally, we must not omit the American explorer Charles Francis Hall (1821–1871), who is buried at Thank God Harbour in North Greenland, far north of the present Thule Air Base. He died in 1871 under mysterious circumstances while commanding the *Polaris* in an ill-fated attempt to reach the North Pole. It was rumoured that Hall was poisoned with arsenic by the physician of the expedition. In 1968 a small American group received permission to open the grave and perform an autopsy at the grave site (Loomis 1971). The body was well preserved and partly covered by ice, but it could not be moved and only a superficial examination was carried out. Hair and nail specimens were analysed and showed a relatively high content of arsenic. The soil near the grave also contained high arsenic levels and therefore no firm conclusions could be drawn. No other analyses were carried out.

CANADA

From the same period as Charles Francis Hall we also have three sailors from the British Franklin Expedition that was searching for the Northwest passage (1845–1848). They were exhumed on Beechey Islands in the Canadian Arctic archipelago in 1984 and 1986 and submitted to autopsies on the site (Beattie and Geiger 1987; Notman and Beattie 1996). The bodies were frozen in blocks of ice and extremely well preserved with only slight desiccation and without the formation of adipocere. Investigation showed that the men had been exposed to lead during the expedition and isotope analysis pointed to tinned foods as the primary source.

The Franklin Expedition was a major disaster. All 129 participants perished. Investigations of the three sailors and fragmentary skeletal remains from a small number of other participants support the assumption that the disaster probably was caused by the compounding effects of lead poisoning, scurvy and starvation. Lead poisoning may have contributed to the ill fate of many of the Polar expeditions in the early days of the canning industry in the nineteenth century. The investigation of the three sailors also showed that two of them suffered from tuberculous spondylitis and that viable bacteria (*Clostridium*) could be recovered from two of the bodies; contamination was regarded unlikely. Three of six strains appeared resistant to modern antibiotics. During the examination, extensive use was made of portable radiological equipment (Notman and Beattie 1996).

SVALBARD

The Svalbard archipelago lies approximately midway between northern Norway and the North Pole. Spitsbergen is the largest of the islands. Svalbard was discovered in 1596 by Wilhelm Barents in one of the unsuccessful efforts to find the North East passage, the route to India and China north of Russia. In 1611 whaling was started by Basque, British, Dutch and Danish companies, and permanent land stations were established (Albrethsen 1989). Since 1920 Norway has held sovereignty over Svalbard, but nationals of countries adhering to the Spitsbergen Treaty have equal rights to exploit living and non-living resources. The islands have no indigenous population. Many graves of whalers from the sixteenth and seventeenth century have been located on Svalbard. Some graves have been opened by archaeologists (Maat 1984, Hacquebord and Vroom 1988; Albrethsen 1989). In several cases, coffins and their contents have been well preserved, including both clothing and bodies. Except for old healed fractures, serious physical changes have not been recorded. Many bodies showed characteristic dental traces of clay pipe smoking.

THE ALPS

The recovery of human bodies and remains from the glaciers in the Alps is not unusual. Some of them are people who disappeared many years ago, in a few cases centuries ago. In September 1991 two mountain walkers discovered the apparently naked body of a man partly frozen in ice at 3210 m at Hauslabjoch in the Ötztal Alps, close to the border between Austria and Italy (Spindler 1994). Only his head and shoulders were free of the ice. The Austrian police took action as the location was believed to be in Austria. At first the body was thought to be the remains of a professor of music from Verona who had disappeared in the vicinity in 1938, and it was several days before the body could be taken down from the mountains by the forensic pathologist, who brought the body to his institution in Innsbruck. The police had used compressor drilling to remove the body from the ice and it was slightly harmed. The true nature of the body was not even imagined at that time. Archaeologist Konrad Spindler was consulted the next day. Among other things, the presence of a copper axe led him to believe that the body was approximately 4000 years old.

FIGURE 15.3. The Ice Man before recovery from the ice, September 1991. (Photograph by Anton Koler, University of Innsbruck.)

Radiocarbon dating at several different laboratories showed later that it was about 5200 years old. The body was named the Ice Man, *Homo tyrolensis* or Ötzi, a word formed by combining Ötztal and yeti (Figure 15.3).

The man was about 40 to 50 years of age and approximately 160 cm tall. The body was mummified with no signs of adipocere. The body must have been covered by a thin layer of snow immediately after death; mummification had taken place under the snow and was completed before total immersion in ice in the small local mountain crevasse where he rested. There were no traces of attacks from animals or birds.

The mummy is stored under simulated glacial conditions at the Institute of Anatomy, University of Innsbruck (−6 degrees Celsius, 96–99 % relative humidity around the body, sterile, and in darkness). A comprehensive program of investigations has been initiated comprising many scientific disciplines, e.g., paleopathology, anatomy, anthropology, mycology, photogrammetry, roentgenology, muscle function, odontology, parasitology, tattoo markings, cranial reconstruction and morphology, DNA analyses, and trace element analysis (Höpfel *et al.* 1992; Spindler *et al.* 1996). By stereolithography, a copy of the cranium at the natural size has been produced (zur Nedden and Wicke 1992).

345

By comparison with DNA from living persons inside and outside Europe, it appears that the Ice Man clearly was within the European gene pool, probably deriving from middle or northern Europe (Handt *et al.* 1994). On the back and on the extremities many tattoos were discovered, consisting of asymmetric groups of lines and small crosses. These tattoos have been interpreted as a kind of medical treatment against painful local disorders (Sjøvold *et al.* 1995). Similar tattoos have been demonstrated on Scythian bodies beside the drawings of animal figures (Rolle 1992). On the left side five healed rib fractures could be seen, on the right side four recent fractures without any signs of healing. Postmortem fractures cannot be entirely ruled out. All available evidence makes it more likely that the Ice Man suffered an accident shortly before death (Spindler 1994). Analyses showed a very low content of lead in his hair.

Several examinations of the discovery site brought various artifacts to light and his clothing could be reconstructed (Egg *et al.* 1992; Spindler 1994). The man was dressed in a loincloth, wore a pair of hose or leggings fastened to a leather belt, a fur robe made in a fairly symmetric pattern by alternating stripes of fur from deer and goat, and a cloak of grass. No sleeves for his robe have been demonstrated. He wore leather shoes and a bearskin cap with chin strap was found. Weapons found were a bow with string of bast cord, a quiver containing arrows, and an axe with copper blade. Other implements were a bone awl, a dagger with scabbard, three flint tools, a tinder tool, and a stag antler spike. He had a backpack with frame and two birch bark vessels, including one used as an ember carrier. As replacement materials he brought raw sinews, leather thongs and stag antler chips. He had a tassel with a marble bead and had brought some meat, probably from ibex, and sloe as food. Some of the items carried by the Ice Man were unfinished; others had been severely damaged prior to his death. This supports the theory of a personal disaster or violence suffered shortly before death. The various artifacts from the site have been restored at the Roman Germanic Central Museum in Mainz and transferred to Innsbruck for scientific studies. Archaeological field work in the upper Ötz Valley has revealed a stone age hunting station or shepherd camp which confirms the presence of human beings in the region in prehistoric times. In the course of a systematic search of the terrain, the Neolithic flint mine from which the tools came was discovered.

A later survey showed that the discovery site was located in Italy (South Tyrol) 93 m from the frontier and not in Austria. Italy claimed the body but an agreement was reached so that the body remains at the University of Innsbruck for scientific investigations. It may later be transferred to an institution in the Italian South Tyrol region.

This is the oldest human body naturally preserved by freezing ever found. The complete collection of everyday garments, weapons and other equipment has provided an unprecedented opportunity to obtain knowledge about the European Stone Age and its human inhabitants. The large scale interdisciplinary investigational program will not be completed for years to come.

THE ANDES

Before the establishment of the Inca empire the peoples of the high Andean regions in present day Argentina, Chile, Bolivia, and Peru venerated mountains as sacred places, centers of spiritual power or seats of deities. The Incas probably elaborated these customs and integrated them into their imperial sun worship (Schobinger 1991). On or close to many of the highest summits, sanctuaries with stone constructions and altars have been found dating from the period of the Inca empire between c. AD 1430 and AD 1536 when the Spaniards arrived (Reinhard 1992). The sanctuaries sometimes contain artifacts and the mummified remains of young people who most probably were sacrificed. Some have been killed by blunt force to the head or strangled, others poisoned or drugged before being buried or left to die by exposure. To be sacrificed was regarded as a great honour.

The first high altitude human mummy that was probably the victim of sacrifice to the Inca god of the sun was discovered in 1905. Since then, many ceremonial places and bodies have been discovered at altitudes higher than 5200 m (Guillén, personal communication 1996) The more important and most thoroughly investigated finds are from Cerro el Plomo in Chile (Schobinger 1966), Cerro El Toro between Argentina and Chile, Cerro Aconcagua in Argentina (Schobinger 1991) and Mount Ampato in Peru (Reinhard 1996).

In 1954 the undisturbed tomb of an eight or nine year old child was found above the permafrost line at 5400 m on Cerro el Plomo, east of present day Santiago, Chile (Schobinger 1966). The body, fully clothed and hunched in the fetal position in a deep pit covered by a capstone, was exquisitely preserved by low temperatures and the dry environment. The structure was part of a ceremonial complex with grave goods. No signs of violence could be discovered. After initial study, the body and the grave goods have been placed in a specially designed glass front freezer in the National Museum of Natural History in Santiago. Electron microscopy of a wart from a hand revealed papilloma virus (Horne and Kawasaki 1984; Horne 1996).

In 1985 a sanctuary was discovered under the summit of Cerro Aconcagua at the altitude of approximately 5700 m (Schobinger 1991). Beside artifacts,

FIGURE 15.4. The frozen body of a young girl found on Mt. Ampato, Peru, in 1995. (Photograph by S. E. Guillén, Peru.)

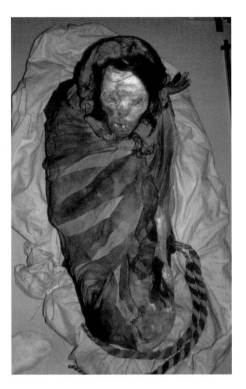

the mummified body of a boy about seven years of age was found. Like other Andean burials, he was in a flexed position and wore rich garments.

In late 1995, the well preserved frozen body of a 12 to 14 year old girl ('Juanita', Figure 15.4) was found on Mount Ampato in Southern Peru, dating back about 500 years (Reinhard 1996). The activity of a nearby volcano had melted the snowcap of Mount Ampato and caused the ground to shift, collapsing a ceremonial platform. The site had never been looted and gold and silver statues festooned with feathers were found as part of a traditional offering to the gods. Another offering was a feather covered bag holding coca leaves. The remains of two other children were found with the girl. A scientific report is not yet available.

REFERENCES

Albrethsen, S. E. 1989. Archaeological investigations of 17th century whaling on Svalbard. *Acta Borelia* 1: 43–51.

Ambach, W., Ambach, E., Tributsch, W., Henn, R. and Unterdorfer, H. 1992. Corpses released from glacier ice: glaciological and forensic aspects. *Journal of Wilderness Medicine* 3: 372–6

Ammitzboll T., Møller R., Møller G. Kobayasi T., Hino H., Asboe-Hansen G. and Hansen, J. P. H. 1989. Collagen and glycosaminoglycans in mummified skin. *Meddelelser øm Grønland; Man and Society* 12: 93–9.

Artamanov, M. I. 1965. Frozen tombs of the Scythians. *Scientific American* 212: 101–9.

Beattie, O. and Geiger, J. 1987. *Frozen in time*. Saskatoon, Saskatchewan: Western Producer Prairie Books.

Bereuter, T. L., Lorbeer, E., Reiter, C., Seidler, H. and Unterdorfer, H. 1996. Postmortem alterations of human lipids – part I: evaluation of adipocere formation and mummification by desiccation. In *Human mummies: a global survey of their status and the techniques of conservation, vol.3, The man in the ice*, ed. K. Spindler, H Wilfing, E. Rastbichler-Zissernig, D. zur Nedden and H. Nothdurfter, 265–73. Vienna: Springer Verlag.

Egg, M., Goedecker-Ciolek, R., Groenman-van Waateringe, W. and Spindler, K. 1992. Die Gletschermumie vom Ende der Steinzeit aus den ötztaler Alpen. *Jahrbuch des Römisch-Germanischen Zentralmuseums* **39**: 1–128.

Grandjean, P. 1989. Bone analysis: Silent testimony of lead exposures in the past. *Meddelelser om Grønland: Man and Society* **12**: 156–60.

Guthrie, R. D. 1990. *Frozen fauna of the mammoth steppe*. Chicago: University of Chicago Press.

Hacquebord, L. and Vroom, W., eds. 1988. *Walvisvaart in den Gouden Eeuw. Opgravning op Spitsbergen*. Amsterdam: De Bataafsche Leeuw

Handt, O., Richards, M., Trommsdorff, M., Kilger, C., Simanainen, J., Georgiev, O., Bauer, K., Stone, A., Hedges, R., Schaffner, W., Utermann, G., Sykes, B. and Pääbo, S. 1994. Molecular genetic analyses of the Tyrolean ice man. *Science* **264**: 1775–8.

Hart Hansen J. P. 1989. The mummies from Qilakitsoq – paleopathological aspects. *Meddelelser om Grønland; Man and Society*. **12**: 69–82.

Hart Hansen, J. P. and Gulløv, H. C., eds. 1989. The mummies from Qilakitsoq – Eskimos in the 15th century. *Meddelelser om Grønland; Man and Society* **12**: 1–199.

Hart Hansen, J. P. and Gürtler, H. 1983. HLA types of mummified Eskimo bodies from the 15th century. *American Journal of Physical Anthropology* **61**: 447–53

Hart Hansen, J. P., Toribara, T. Y. and Muhs, A. G. 1989. Trace metals in human and animal hair from the 15th century graves in Qilakitsoq compared with recent samples. *Meddelelser om Grønland; Man and Society* **12**: 161–7.

Hart Hansen, J. P., Meldgaard, J. and Nordqvist, J., eds. 1991. *The Greenland mummies*. London: British Museum Press.

Hooton, E. A. 1930. Finns, Lapps, Eskimos, and Martin Luther. *Harvard Alumni Bulletin* **1930**: 545–53.

Höpfel, F., Platzer, W. and Spindler K., eds. 1992 . *Der Man im Eis*. Band 1. Veröffentlichungen der Universität Innsbruck 187.

Horne, P. D. 1996. The Prince of El Plomo: a frozen treasure. In *Human mummies: a global survey of their status and the techniques of conservation, vol 3, The man in the ice*, ed. K. Spindler, H. Wilfing, E. Rastbichler-Zissernig, D. zur Nedden and H. Nothdurfter, 153–7. Vienna: Springer Verlag.

Horne, P. D. and Kawasaki, S. Q. 1984. The prince of El Plomo: a paleopathological study. *Bulletin of the New York Academy of Medicine* **60**: 925–31.

Kromann, N. P., Kapel, H., Løytved, E. R. and Hart Hansen, J. P. 1989. The tatooings of the Qilakitsoq mummies. *Meddelelser om Grønland; Man and Society* **12**: 168–71.

Lewin, P. K. 1985. Mummified, frozen smallpox: is it a threat ? *Journal of the American Medical Association* **253**: 3095.

Loomis, C. C. 1971. *Weird and tragic shores*. New York: Alfred A. Knopf.

Maat, G. J. R. 1984. Een terugblik op de vordringen van het physisch antropolisch onderzoek voortvloeiend uit de Spitsbergenexpeditie (A retrospection on the physical anthropological investigations in progress proceeding from the Spitsbergen expedition). In *Smeerenburg: Het verblijf van Nederlandse walvisvaarders op de westkust van Spitsbergen in de 17e eeuw*, ed. L. Hacquebord, 301–11. Groningen: Arctic Centre.

Marini, M. A., Orr, M. F. and Coe, E. L. 1967. Surviving macromolecules in Antarctic seal mummies. *Antarctic Journal* **2**: 190–1.

Mathiassen, T. 1936. The Eskimo archaeology of Julianehaab district V. The mummy caves at Qerrortut. *Meddelelser Grønland* **118**: 103–13

Meldgaard, J. 1953. Fra en grønlandsk mumiehule (From a Greenlandic mummy cave). *Nationalmuseets arbejdsmark* **1953**: 14–20.

zur Nedden, D. and Wicke, K. 1992. Der Eismann aus der Sicht der radiologischen und computertomographischen Daten. In *Der Man im Eis, Band 1*, ed. F. Höpfel, W. Platzer, and K. Spindler, 131–48. Veröffentlichungen der Universität Innsbruck 187.

Nielsen, H., Engberg, J. and Thuesen, I. 1993. Frozen samples: DNA from Arctic human burials. In *Ancient DNA*, ed. B. Herrmann and S. Hummel, 119–37. New York: Springer Verlag.

Nørlund, P. 1924. Buried norsemen at Herjolfsnes. An archaeological and historical study. *Meddelelser Grønland* **67**: 1–270.

Notman D. and Beattie, O. 1996. The palaeoimaging and forensic anthropology of frozen sailors from the Franklin Arctic expedition mass disaster (1845–1848): a detailed presentation of two radiological surveys. In *Human mummies: a global survey of their status and the techniques of conservation, vol 3, The man in the ice*, ed. K. Spindler, H. Wilfing, E. Rastbichler-Zissernig, D. zur Nedden and H Nothdurfter, 93–106. Vienna: Springer Verlag.

Polosmak, N. 1994. A mummy unearthed from the pastures of heaven. *National Geographic Magazine* **186**: 80–103.

Polosmak, N. 1996. La prêtresse altaïque. *Archéologie* **212**: 28.

Reinhard, J. 1992. Sacred peaks of the Andes. *National Geographic Magazine* **181**: 84–111.

Reinhard, J. 1996. Peru's ice maidens. *National Geographic Magazine* **189**: 62–81.

Rolle, R. 1992. Die skythenzeitlichen Mumienfunde von Pazyryk. Frost Konservierte Gräver aus dem Altaigebirge. In *Der Man im Eis, Band 1*, ed. F. Höpfel, W. Platzer and K. Spindler, 313–32. Veröffentlichungen der Universität Innsbruck 187.

Rudenko, S. I. 1970. *Frozen tombs of Siberia. The Pazyryk burials of Iron Age horsemen*. Los Angeles: University of California Press.

Schobinger, J. 1966. La 'momia' del Cerro El Toro. *Suplemento al Tomo XXI de Annales de Arqueología y Etnología*. Mendoza, Argentina.

Schobinger, J. 1991. Sacrifices of the High Andes. *Natural History* **4**: 63–8.

Sjøvold, T., Bernhard, W., Gaber, O., Künzel, K-H., Platzer, W., and Unterdorfer, H. 1995. Verteilung und Grösse der Tätowierungen am Eisman vom Haus-labjoch. *Der Mann im Eis. Neue Funde und Ergebnisse*. ed. K. Spindler, E. Rastbichler-Zissernig, H. Wilfing, D. zur Nedden and H. Nothdurfter, 279–86. Vienna: Springer Verlag.

Spindler, K. 1994. *The man in the ice*. London: Weidenfeld and Nicolson.

Spindler, K., Wilfing, H., Rastbichler-Zissernig, E., zur Nedden, D. and Nothdurfter, H., eds. 1996. *Human mummies: a global survey of their status and the techniques of conservation, vol. 3, The man in the ice*. Vienna: Springer Verlag.

Thuesen, I. and Engberg, J. 1990. Recovery and analysis of human genetic material from mummified tissue and bone. *Journal of Archaeological Science* **17**: 679–89.

Zimmerman, M. R. 1996. Mummies of the Arctic regions. In *Human mummies: a global survey of their status and the techniques of conservation, vol. 3, The man in the ice*, ed. K. Spindler, H. Wilfing, E. Rastbichler-Zissernig, D. zur Nedden and H. Nothdurfter, 83–92. Vienna: Springer Verlag.

Zimmerman, M. R., Trinkaus, E., LeMay, M., Aufderheide, A. C., Reyman, T. A., Marrocco, G. R., Ortel, R. W., Benitez, J. T., Laughlin, W. S., Horne, P. D., Schultes, R. E. and Coughlin, E. A. 1981. The paleopathology of an Aleutian mummy. *Archives of Pathology and Laboratory Medicine* **105**: 638–41.

Zimmerman, M. R., Yeatman, G. W. and Sprinz, H. 1971. Examination of an Aleutian Mummy. *Bulletin of the New York Academy of Medicine* **47**: 80–103.

PART IV

Mummies and technology

16

New investigative techniques

THEODORE A. REYMAN, HENRIK NIELSEN, INGOLF
THUESEN, DEREK N. H. NOTMAN, KARL J. REINHARD,
EDMUND TAPP AND TONY WALDRON

INTRODUCTION

Theodore A. Reyman

As neophyte paleopathologists, five of us in Detroit (Aidan and Eve
Cockburn, Robin Barraco, William Peck and Theodore Reyman) were
involved in the autopsy of two mummies, DIA I (Detroit Institute of Arts) in
1970 and PUM I (Pennsylvania University Museum) in 1971. The findings
from the examination of these two bodies were minimal. Both mummies
were poorly preserved and without personal data or provenance. Although
we were able to learn little from the gross and microscopic examination, we
did establish one thing – we didn't know much about identifying and testing
ancient tissues.

Aidan Cockburn was interested in extracting gamma globulin from
mummified organs, theorizing that if this were possible, we could use
modern testing techniques on this material in order to survey disease patterns in ancient times. With these data, we would then be able to track infectious diseases from antiquity to the present time and perhaps determine
whether alterations in life cycle, virulence and other epidemiological parameters had changed over the years. We were able to extract and identify small
amounts of serum albumin and globulin, although the reactivity in modern
tests for infectious diseases never came to fruition. We learned that many
proteins, carbohydrates, and lipids were present in mummified tissue but
generally in very fragmentary form (Barraco 1980).

Chemical elemental analysis told us whether the mummy had been treated
with natron and how the heavy metal content of ancient tissues correlated
with modern equivalents (Barraco *et al.* 1977). These analyses helped in
reconstructing ancient diets (Williams 1993) and also in separating embalming and postmortem artifacts from disease (Waldron 1981).

Histological examination by light and electron microscopy posed an additional problem. To cut the thin microscopic sections, water had to be put back into the tissue. This was accomplished using Ruffer's solution of formalin and alcohol (Ruffer 1910). With rehydration, it remained only to apply standardized histological techniques, with a few caveats (Reyman and Dowd 1980). Light and transmission electron microscopic patterns (Horne and Lewin 1977) often revealed quite adequate and occasionally excellent preservation, particularly the connective tissue elements. Epithelial and parenchymatous tissues did not fare so well, generally being degenerated and causing problems of interpretation. Those difficulties notwithstanding, the scanning and transmission electron microscopy as evidenced by Riddle's (Riddle 1980) exquisite displays of structure and form attest to the relative ease of handling and interpreting most mummified tissues.

Radiographic examination was less difficult than microscopy, although interpretation was still problematic at times (Kristen and Reyman 1980). Standardized radiographic techniques including tomography revealed much about a fully wrapped mummy that could not be discerned by external examination alone. Xerographic studies, first performed by Wolfe on PUM II (Cockburn et al. 1975), provided finer details in some cases. Computerized tomography (CT) scans added far greater information (Lewin and Harwood-Nash 1977; Lewin et al. 1990). This type of study could became a radiographic gross examination, eliminating the need for extended dissection of some mummies. These CT scans would be particularly valuable in those cases where no dissection of any kind could be performed. More sophisticated techniques such as magnetic resonance imaging (MRI) scans have the disadvantage that tissue fluids are necessary for optimum results and therefore have not given as good results with mummified bodies as with living or rehydrated tissues.

For a variety of reasons, mummified bodies have become less available for complete study. National, ethnic, and aesthetic considerations limit not only access but often prohibit the full autopsy dissection that was performed on PUM II. Therefore, CT scans, endoscopic examinations and core needle biopsies appear to be viable solutions to many of these prohibitions if present.

We were excited when reports of blood typing on mummies were published, hopefully providing a valuable demographic tool in our studies of ancient humans (Hart et al. 1977). Even more, we were amazed when studies of HLA (human lymphocyte antigen) tissue typing of mummified bodies came forth (Henry 1980). What has engendered the most scientific excitement, however, has been the successful extraction and identification of DNA from these long preserved bodies. In this chapter, we shall see how the amplification of minute amounts of genetic material by the polymerase chain reaction (PCR) has enabled researchers to identify both native and infectious DNA in these bodies. The use of amplified bacterial and viral DNA may turn out to be Aidan Cockburn's 'magic bullet' for solving some of the mysteries of infectious disorders in ancient populations. In the same fashion, native DNA may give us clues to a variety of genetic abnormalities that existed in those distant times.

These newer techniques will be the focus of the revised technical section in this second edition. The standardized chemical, histological, radiographic and serologic techniques can be reviewed in the technical section of the first edition or in other references from the scientific literature. These new test methods do not replace the older ones, but complement them. Both are necessary. The future will provide other methods, introduced by the ingenuity of our scientific colleagues in many disciplines. Only time will tell how many.

PALEOGENETICS
Henrik Nielsen and Ingolf Thuesen

Paleogenetics is a research discipline that applies methods from molecular biology to the genetic material recovered from ancient remains. The genetic material is referred to as ancient DNA (aDNA). The literature in this field amounts to fewer than a hundred full research papers. It has nevertheless been reviewed several times from different perspectives (Brown and Brown 1992, 1994). Special issues of journals and books have been published on the subject (Hauswirth 1994; Herrmann and Hummel 1993), not to mention an almost endless number of commentaries and popular papers.

The first attempts to characterize DNA from ancient remains was reported from a Chinese group in 1981 followed by the first generally accepted demonstration of ancient DNA published in 1984 by Allan Wilson's group in Berkeley (Higuchi *et al.* 1984). The latter cloned and sequenced a fragment of DNA isolated from the 140 year old museum specimen, the skin of the quagga, an extinct member of the horse family, in order to classify this animal into a phylogenetic tree of the horse. This was followed by Pääbo's cloning of a 3.4 kilobase (kb) fragment of DNA from a 2400 year old Egyptian mummy (Pääbo 1985). These two early reports signaled the two main courses that studies of aDNA have taken, each with its own set of perspectives and problems. One line of research has dealt with the classification of extinct organisms. In these studies, a DNA sequence is the goal. Every position in the sequence must be determined with certainty, as the sequence eventually will be aligned and compared to homologous sequences from contemporary sources. In principle, contamination with contemporaneous DNA is less of a problem, because no source of identical DNA exists. The other line of research deals with aDNA in archaeological remains in order to obtain a more precise understanding of cultural history. Typically, the analysis of the aDNA is aimed at discriminating between already known versions of the sequence in question that are characteristic of one or another trait. Contamination with contemporary DNA is in this case a significant problem, especially if the DNA is of human origin. The onset of aDNA research in the mid 1980s may seem late in view of the fact that the molecular biology revolution started more than a decade earlier. The reason was probably the general consensus that the DNA content of an organism would degrade rapidly after death. This indeed proved to be the case. In spite of the astounding preservation of, for example, the frozen Siberian mammoths or of many mummies, the DNA content has in all cases proved to be degraded into short fragments of a few hundred base pairs (bp) at most. Furthermore, the DNA has been found to be chemically modified in such a way that the readout of its genetic information is compromised. The decay of DNA has been described by Lindahl (1993), and some of the modifications in aDNA have been analysed by Pääbo (1989) and Höss and colleagues (1996). The poor state of preservation of the DNA is perhaps surprising in view of the fact that seeds and spores have been found to retain their ability to germinate for hundreds of years, and in some cases even a few thousand. In these cases, however, the DNA is preserved in the context of a living cell, in which DNA repair enzymes maintain the integrity of the DNA. These enzymes no longer operate after the cessation of life processes and the DNA will eventually become degraded, mainly by hydrolytic and oxidative processes. Based on laboratory experiments, Lindahl (1993) has estimated that as a rule of thumb, DNA will maximally survive between 20 000 and 40 000 years in a condition that allows analysis using the current methodology for aDNA. This poses a serious problem for many studies of taxonomical problems. On the other hand, most mummies are safely within this age limit. Lindahl's view has been challenged by the finding of much older DNA under special circumstances, e.g., encapsulated in amber (Brown and Brown 1994; Poinar et al. 1996). The real breakthrough in aDNA studies came in the late 1980s when the polymerase chain reaction (PCR) became generally known after the discovery of a thermostable DNA polymerase (Taq DNA polymerase). In PCR, a segment of the DNA defined by two synthetic oligonucleotide primers is amplified through repeated cycles of denaturation of the DNA, annealing of the oligonucleotide primers, and synthesis of new DNA strands. The application of the thermostable polymerase made it possible to automate the process and thus to make it generally applicable. By use of PCR, enough material could be generated from templates in aDNA to allow analysis of the sequence information by standard molecular biology techniques. PCR has therefore become a prerequisite for aDNA analysis.

Basic methodology

Because of its near universal role as the genetic material, DNA is an ideal substance to test for in excavated material. The methods that are applied to recover the DNA and subsequently to analyse its sequence information are basically the same, no matter whether the aim is to determine the gender or ethnicity of human remains according to biological parameters, to diagnose a disease or to make a species identification of plant or animal remains in a mummy's stomach contents. Due to the chemical instability of DNA, ancient remains invariably contain only very small amounts, generally in a poor state of preservation. Thus, all methods must be applied in such a way that further loss or degradation is minimised, and even more important, contamination with contemporaneous DNA must be avoided. The reason for this is that in most cases, it is necessary to amplify the aDNA in a test tube by the PCR method in order to obtain sufficient material for analysis. The PCR method is sensitive enough to detect even the tiny amounts of DNA present in skin, saliva or dandruff shed by the excavator. Because the contemporaneous DNA consists of intact template molecules, it will be copied with a much higher efficiency during the PCR process than the fragmented and damaged aDNA templates.

Sampling

Sampling for aDNA analysis should be an integrated part of the excavation strategy. Through careful planning, it is possible to ensure that the relevant specimens are kept in their context until the excavator is prepared to take samples for aDNA analysis. This involves wearing protective gloves and, if possible, a face mask and a hairnet. The tools and protective wear required are inexpensive and many ordinary household products can be used. The importance of avoiding contamination during handling of the specimens became apparent when an aDNA analysis from the Tyrolean ice man, Ötze, was reported (Handt *et al.* 1994b). This 5000 year old mummified human body was contaminated by DNA from several individuals, probably during handling and retrieval. Only a careful analysis made it possible to identify sequences representing the authentic aDNA. In our experience from excavations in the Middle East, Denmark and Greenland, sampling for aDNA analysis can be integrated into normal excavation routines without significant problems. In addition to minimising exposure and contamination, one further issue is conservation of the sample. In burials with poorly conserved bones, we have carried out the first steps of DNA extraction in the field and found this to yield somewhat better results compared with extractions initiated at a later stage. In most cases, several grams of remains are required for an aDNA analysis. Removal of this amount of soft tissue is usually not in conflict with other types of analyses or interests. With respect to bones, the lower ribs, which are of less importance to the anthropologists, can be used. Hitherto, most studies of aDNA from bones have used samples from the femur. A nondestructive way to take samples from this bone is to perfuse the bone marrow cavity with extraction buffer through a drilled hole (Tuross 1994). Sufficient amounts of dentin can be drilled out of a tooth without disturbing the overall morphology of the tooth or the masticating surface that is of prime importance to the dental anthropologist.

Extraction and purification of aDNA

Prior to extraction of the DNA, the tissue sample is fragmented into small pieces in order to allow efficient soaking of the tissue in the extraction buffer. Soft tissues are usually cut into small pieces using disposable surgical blades. Hard tissue samples, such as bones or teeth, are drilled into a fine powder or ground in a mill, preferably under liquid nitrogen. Early extraction protocols for aDNA were not very different from protocols used to extract DNA from contemporary sources. Proteinase K was used to digest away most of the protein content of the sample, after which a phenol extraction and ethanol precipitation was used to isolate the nucleic acids. Decalcification and removal of hydroxyapatite from hard tissue samples was achieved by treatment with high concentrations of EDTA. Many of the early studies were plagued with low molecular weight substances that copurified with the DNA and inhibited the Taq DNA polymerase used in the subsequent analysis of the aDNA. Some of these substances have now been identified and more recent protocols depend on a more suitable extraction principle or use postextraction clean-up procedures to get rid of the inhibitors. Protocols using silica or glass particles seem to be the most successful (Höss and Pääbo 1993; Tuross 1994). In the presence of a chaotropic reagent (e.g., a guanidinium salt) the DNA binds to the silica particles. This allows extensive washing to be performed prior to the elution of the DNA from the particles (Tuross 1994). In hard tissue samples, DNA is apparently bound to the mineral phase in addition to in the cellular remains. Taking this into consideration, some protocols are based on elution of DNA from hydroxyapatite using high phosphate concentration and elevated temperatures. We have found DNA of a better quality using this procedure, compared to the old standard protocols used in studies of bone samples from a Qilakitsoq mummy (Nielsen *et al.* 1994). This observation makes sense in view of the fact that adsorption of DNA to hydroxyapatite results in a twofold decrease in the rate of depurination (Lindahl 1993), one of the major degradation pathways of aDNA.

There is at present no meaningful way of determining the yield of aDNA from an extraction procedure. This is mainly because most of the extracted DNA is usually of microbial origin, whether ancient or contemporary. This conclusion is based on hybridization analyses of aDNA to DNA from various sources and from microscopical examinations of DNA stained sections of samples. The way to evaluate the success of a given extraction protocol is in terms of success in amplifying a given target sequence. The amount of a specific target sequence in the aDNA could in principle be determined by a method known as Quantitative Competition PCR, but this has not been frequently used. Recently, it has been shown that the extent of amino acid racemization in extracts is a good indicator of the presence of aDNA (Poinar *et al.* 1996). This method requires only milligrams of material and could prove useful as a primary screening method for aDNA work.

Analysis of aDNA

The methods used in analysis of aDNA are essentially a subset of those used in a standard molecular biology laboratory, although several important precautions against contamination must be added to the standard procedures. The sparse amounts of aDNA normally available preclude direct examination of the aDNA by hybridization analysis. DNA cloning procedures are difficult to apply because of the heterogeneous ends found in the aDNA. More important, a DNA clone is started from a single molecule. Thus, any error originating from the copying of the damaged aDNA template in the cloning host will appear in the resulting clone. Moreover, it will be impossible to detect these errors unless a large number of independent clones is examined. Ancient DNA studies are therefore dependent on the PCR method. Even this method has its specific problems when applied to aDNA. Some of the chemical modifications found in aDNA block the polymerase reaction (Höss *et al.* 1996). In cases where more than one template in the sample is amplified (e.g., two alleles), the short length of the aDNA template fragments will result in template switching by the polymerase, leading to PCR products that are the result of an artifactual recombination event. Finally, errors are introduced into the PCR product as a result of lesions in the template as well as by the error-prone copying process by the polymerase. The latter are introduced at random. Provided that this is also the case with the errors due to the aDNA lesions, these errors will constitute only 'background noise' in the final sequencing of the PCR product.

In spite of the potential of the PCR method to amplify from as little as a single template molecule, aDNA analysis has hitherto been limited to sequences that are found as multiple copies within the cell. Most popular are studies of the mitochondrial DNA that is found in thousands of copies in a typical cell. Sequence information from the mitochondria is used in genealogy and studies of biological ethnicity. A nuclear repeat sequence, the Alu-sequence, which is found in 300 000 copies in the genome, has been demonstrated in aDNA by molecular cloning (Pääbo 1985) and direct hybridization (Thuesen and Engberg 1990). These sequences contain little information of interest. Another type of nuclear repeat sequence exists in chromosome specific subtypes and has been used in sex determination in a number of studies (Nielsen et al. 1994). Analysis of single copy genes in aDNA is presently not feasible. An important exception to this is an analysis of population structure based on the characterization of class I Major Histocompatibility Complex alleles in aDNA from a mummified brain from the Windover site (8000–7000 BP) (Lawlor et al. 1991).

Validation

Because of the inherent difficulty in recognizing contamination from contemporary human DNA, certain standards must be met in order to validate the authenticity of the aDNA under scrutiny (for a detailed discussion, see Handt et al. 1994a). At least two extracts should be analysed from each sample. Mock extractions and PCR controls should be performed in parallel with the experimental samples. Preparation of the aDNA for PCR analysis and the subsequent analysis of the PCR products should be physically separated (i.e., carried out in different rooms). The laboratory should adopt high cleaning standards and only dedicated solutions, utensils, and materials should be used for the aDNA work. Unfortunately, it is impossible to demonstrate the authenticity of an aDNA sample by dating methods. Radiocarbon dating is not feasible because the aDNA is found as a mixture with ancient as well as more recent microbial DNA. The extent of amino acid racemization in ancient extracts apparently does not correlate with age (Poinar et al. 1996). It is not known whether any of the DNA lesions correlate with age. One simple criterion in assessing the authenticity of the aDNA put forward by Handt and associates (1994a) is that an inverse correlation should exist between length and amplification efficiency. In the end, the ultimate way to validate results will be to have independent analyses carried out in different laboratories.

Application to mummy studies

So far, no general correlation has been found between successful recovery of aDNA and age or state of preservation of the remains. There is a tendency towards more successful results with samples from cold environments than from hot environments and there is an upper limit in terms of age from which one can expect to find aDNA under normal conditions. Strongly alkaline or acidic conditions such as those known from bogs in Northern Europe are not compatible with the survival of DNA. In accordance with this, early work on extraction of DNA from the very well preserved Tollund Man was unsuccessful (J. Engberg, personal communication). The Egyptian mummification procedures involving preservation of the bodies by dehydration in large quantities of natron are similarly destructive to the DNA. Apart from these special cases, the prospects of finding DNA in mummies are in general good. The DNA content of some museum specimens has been destroyed in the interest of preserving the mummies for display or other types of studies. Most of the Greenland Qilakitsoq mummies have received large doses (2–2.5 megarad) of gamma irradiation and are therefore probably useless for aDNA studies.

Historically, mummy studies have played an important role in the aDNA field. The first characterization of aDNA from a human source was Pääbo's cloning of a 3.4 kb fragment of DNA from a 2400 year old Egyptian mummy of a one year old boy (Pääbo 1985). This finding is still an exception. The mummy had been dehydrated by embedding in natron, the sample was taken from superficial tissues, and the fragment cloned was of nuclear origin. Similar results have not been reported elsewhere in the literature. The results are all the more surprising in view of recent claims by the same author that it is unlikely one would find fragments of aDNA of more than hundreds of base pairs in a few thousand year old sample from dry regions such as Egypt (Poinar *et al.* 1996). The first applications of PCR to aDNA were more important. In these studies, PCR was used to amplify aDNA from a mummified brain from the Windover peat bog in Florida (Pääbo *et al.* 1988; Lawlor *et al.* 1991). The first reports of successful extraction of aDNA from bones also included a mummy study, namely the recovery of authentic DNA from the Greenland Qilakitsoq mummies (Thuesen and Engberg 1990).

Two articles by Powledge and Rose (1996a, 1996b) recently described the most popular types of aDNA research in archaeology. These are not very different from those that apply to mummies:

1   *Peopling studies* These studies are based mostly on analyses of mitochondrial DNA in contemporary populations. However, DNA from ancient remains is important in confirming or refuting interpretations based on modern DNA. As an example, the analyses of mummified tissues from Windover (Lawlor *et al.* 1991) have played an important role in studies of the peopling of the Americas.

2   *Genealogy* Family relationships can be established based on the maternally inherited mitochondrial genome. Recently, it was shown by aDNA analysis that nine skeletons from a grave in Ekatarinburg, Russia were the remains of the family of the last tsar (Gill *et al.* 1994). In the mummy field, the royal mummies of the New Kingdom in Egypt are being studied to allow proper identification and to establish genealogical relationships.

3   *Social structures* By correlating burial types with genetic traits, it is hoped to decide whether the elite or ruling class of a given society is genetically based.

4   *Disease studies* In some cases, aDNA studies are of importance in confirmation of a diagnosis based on other criteria. One example is the identification of DNA from the tuberculosis bacterium in a 1000 year old Peruvian mummy (Salo *et al.*1994). This finding confirmed that skeletal lesions in New World mummies could indeed be the result of M. *tuberculosis* infection.

5   *Associated ecofacts* One area in which mummies are likely to be an important source of information is in the study of associated ecofacts. This is particularly the case in studies of the domestication of plants and animals based on ancient remains.

Perspectives

The future looks bright for those who wish to analyse aDNA from mummies. The reason is mainly that results from other research communities with access to enormous resources will boost the field in the next few years. Large scale DNA sequencing projects will result in determination of the complete sequence of the human genome in less than a decade. This will increase tremendously the number of sequences and traits that can be analysed. The ease of automated sequencing will also result in large scale analyses of genetic variation in human populations. These studies will be invaluable as a contemporary reference source for mummy studies. Pathologists will learn much more about the molecular basis of disease, and botanists and zoologists will be able to identify species from DNA in remains. Forensic scientists will probably improve the methods for recovery of DNA from difficult sources and molecular biologists will develop new enzymatic tools for aDNA analysis. A large number of new thermostable DNA polymerases are now available as alternatives to the Taq DNA polymerase and their enzymatic properties are being characterized. The genes encoding DNA repair enzymes are being cloned at a high rate from various sources. Combined with a thorough understanding of the chemical lesions in aDNA, it is possible that these enzymes can, in the near future be applied in repair of DNA.

What is then left to do for those primarily interested in studies of mummies? Probably the most important thing is to keep their feet on the ground. The questions asked of the mummy material should be clear and concise, and the experiments designed in such a way that they can meet the normal criteria of reproducibility as discussed. It is important to develop standard procedures for field work, in particular for sampling and conservation. Systematic work on large collections of mummies is required in order to optimize the current procedures for extraction of DNA. Finally, in the interpretation of the results, it is important to keep in mind that the relationship between results based on biological parameters and those based on cultural history is not always simple

PALEOIMAGING

Derek N. H. Notman

X-rays have played an important role in the study of human mummies for 100 years; the first examination took place early in 1896, only a few months after Roentgen's discovery. Since then, the specialty of Diagnostic Radiology has revolutionized modern medical diagnosis and treatment with its remarkable assortment of imaging equipment and techniques, data acquisition, and image transmission. As the field continued to advance, these new technologies were quickly applied to ancient remains, so that the emergence of paleoimaging soon followed a parallel course. This history has been well documented in numerous publications since 1896, although the term paleoradiology, and subsequently paleoimaging, was not introduced until 1986 (Notman *et al.* 1986). The focus of this section will be to emphasize briefly those technical developments that have come into medical practice since the

publication of the first edition of this text in 1980 and their relevance to the
future of paleoimaging.

Computed imaging (CT and MRI)

The single most important breakthrough was the development of computed
tomography (CT) by Hounsfield in 1972, for which he won the Nobel Prize in
Physics. The unique concept of computerized image reconstruction from
cross-sectional x-ray scanning created a sensation in the medical world.
From that early prototype several generations of tremendously powerful CT
scanners have evolved, and computed tomography now forms a cornerstone
in modern medicine. The first CT scan of an Egyptian mummy was performed by Harwood-Nash in Toronto in 1977 (Harwood-Nash 1979), and
since then fewer than 100 Egyptian mummies have been scanned worldwide,
or only about 10 percent of the extant collections. Several CT scanning projects have been published in Europe and North America, beginning with the
Manchester Museum Mummy Project in 1979. Interestingly, the major collections of the Cairo and British Museums still await formal scanning.

Computed imaging also encompasses Magnetic Resonance Imaging
(MRI) and Digital Radiography (DR), which includes digital fluoroscopy.
Although MRI uses electrical pulse sequences in a magnetic field instead of
ionizing radiation to generate images, it is traditionally listed along with its x-
ray counterpart, CT, in radiology's pantheon of diagnostic modalities. DR
more closely resembles conventional plain film or flat plate radiography,
except that the images are first digitized by a computer for storage or laser
printing. The first MRI examination of an Egyptian mummy was performed
by the author at the Mayo clinic (Notman 1983). Because MRI relies on the
presence of free water in the soft tissues to generate an image, its application
to desiccated tissues has, not surprisingly, proved to be disappointing. MRI
does work well, however, with hydrated soft tissues (i.e., recently postmortem) or rehydrated mummified remains (Figure 16.1), and would also
apply to frozen tissues that have thawed (Notman and Aufderheide 1995).

Plain radiography

Conventional flat plate radiographic technology still possesses an important
adjunct status in studying mummified and osteological materials. It is easy
for today's students to forget that before the computer age only plain radiography, standard tomography, and rudimentary scintigraphy (employing a
radioactive source) were available to the investigator. Carefully constructed
projects will use plain x-rays first to survey the study samples, screening for

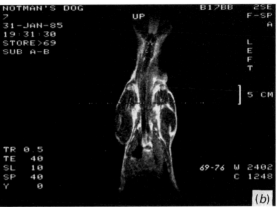

FIGURE 16.1. (a) Autopsy of a dog, six months post-mortem; (b) coronal MR scan of a mummified dog, immediately postmortem.

features of additional interest that may indicate pathology or associated archaeological effects. If there is convenient access to a CT unit, then advanced scanning of selected findings or pertinent three-dimensional (3-D) CT reconstructions may greatly enhance a project. Many studies must rely solely upon basic x-ray equipment, especially portable, if work is contemplated in the field. Diagnostic studies can still be obtained under adverse conditions in remote regions (Figure 16.2); such projects are logistically more complex but can be rewarding to the researcher (Notman 1987).

Advantages of computed imaging

Paleoimaging studies the past not only for evidence of ancient disease but also for evidence of cultural influences on the everyday life and health of the individual. Fascinating paleoepidemiological questions often arise directly from the process of correlating newly discovered pathology with established historical background, just as a physician obtains a good history from the

Mummies and technology

FIGURE 16.2. (a) William Braine (1812–1846), Royal Marine, Franklin Expedition, buried on Beechey Island, Northwest Territory, (b) antero-posterior radiography of William Braine's chest and thoracic spine.

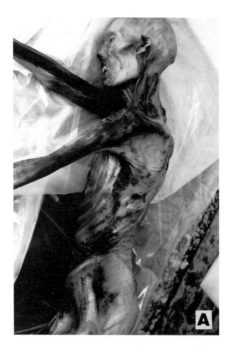
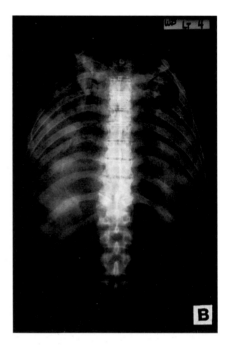

patient and correlates it with a thorough physical examination. Unfortunately, the amount of osseous paleopathology discovered by radiology has been relatively small, often limited to minor arthritic, infectious, or posttraumatic changes. Soft tissue changes are rare. Even computed tomography has not improved the detection rate significantly. This is not the fault of the technology; it merely reflects the scant pathological record. For this reason, increasing emphasis should be placed on archaeological imaging, for which the CT scanner is well adapted. With its cross-sectional display and superb high spatial and contrast resolution, CT continues to be the best modality for examining mummies. Although CT lacks MRI's direct multiplanar viewing capability, 3-D CT reconstruction software creates almost lifelike images from contiguous two-dimensional scans (Figure 16.3). This technique is particularly important for facial reconstructions (Figure 16.4).

CT permits better visualization of the body, its wrappings, internal contents, and associated artifacts by eliminating the superimposition of materials that often obscure details on plain x-ray films. CT can reveal underlying structures that would never be visible by conventional radiography (Figure 16.5). CT is also non-invasive and helps to minimize the actual handling of human remains. Because the scanning data are computer generated, images can be stored in digital format or converted to analog hard copy films. The original scans may undergo additional processing and manipulation,

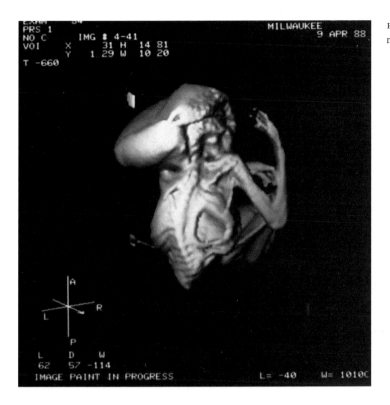

FIGURE 16.3. 3-D CT reconstruction of mummy fetus.

depending upon the software packages employed. The mummy needs to be scanned only once. Numerous direct measurements and densitometry readings can be obtained instantly and precisely from the scans, including standard craniometric planes that are used by both craniofacial surgeons and physical anthropologists for planning surgery or, for example, comparing facial features in kinship analysis.

Imaging parameters may be adjusted to answer specific questions about the mummification process itself. These may refer to textile wrappings, packing materials and resins, and visceral bundles placed in the thorax or abdomen. Subtle differences in the style of mummification may facilitate more accurate dating of the individual. Associated artifacts, such as the cartonnage, wood coffin, funerary masks, and Canopic vessels, can also be scanned. Wood is especially suitable for scanning (Notman 1995).

Separate treasures, like the priceless gold mask of Tutankhamun, may be scanned and analyzed for structural weakness or damage. A 3-D CT reconstruction of the mask could yield information about the actual assembly and composition of its internal architecture. Statuary, jewelry, pottery, or ritual burial bundles can be similarly reconstructed. Conservators could use

FIGURE 16.4. 3-D CT facial reconstruction of Egyptian mummy head (Milwaukee Public Museum collection).

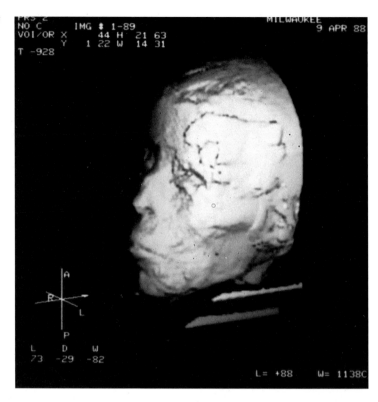

such a computer model for assessing the roadworthiness of potential traveling exhibits or for repairing the items themselves.

Electronic conservation and digital archiving

As computer software continues to improve, previously inconceivable images have become a scanning reality. Smoothing and shading algorithms, morphing techniques, and color animation can combine to produce a virtual duplicate of the human body. The 'Visible Human' project at the University of Colorado represents such an undertaking, in which an entire human cadaver was scanned with CT and MR and then microsectioned into thin contiguous slices for direct anatomical correlation. The imaging data and autopsy photographs are all stored on compact disks (CD). This computer generated wizardry offers the most exciting possibilities in diagnostic radiology and paleoimaging today and for the future.

The preceeding discussion indicates that there are other important contributions that CT can make, more in terms of preservation and not simply of detection. When the relative paucity of ancient pathological material is considered, well planned scanning can eliminate the need for costly and

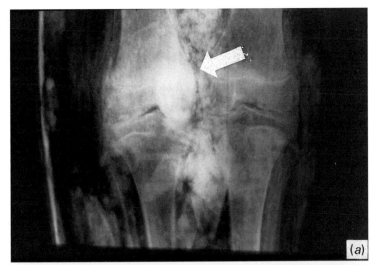

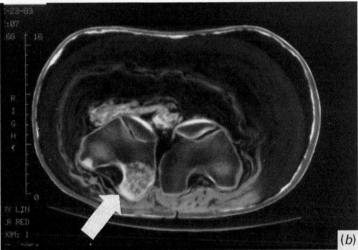

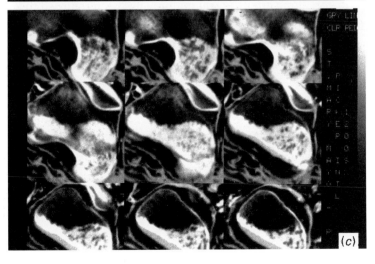

FIGURE 16.5. (a) Anteroposterior radiography of Lady Tashat's knees, with pseudotumor obscured by overlying densities (Minneapolis Institute of Arts); (b) Axial CT scan of Lady Tashat's knees. Note pseudotumor in right femoral condyle; (c) Multiple contiguous CT slices of distal femoral pseudotumor.

time-consuming reexaminations at some later date. It is important, however, to realize that computed tomography stands on the threshold of an extraordinary era in image acquisition and transmission, and its great flexibility will help to implement the new concepts of electronic conservation and digital archiving. CD-ROM technology has undergone rapid development in recent years. It is now possible to store eight individual CT images (using 2:1 compression) per megabyte of memory. One compact disk holds approximately 640 megabytes, or 5120 CT 'slices' per disk. The scan of an entire human body with detailed image reconstruction can be stored on a single CD. Scanning can be monitored at multiple sites simultaneously. With cable or satellite transmission, the procedure itself can be observed by scholars in other countries or even broadcast live on interactive educational television.

The possibilities are limitless once the data are digitized. The enormous amount of information from each mummy can then be stored in a huge archival database, creating a computerized reference center and library. These digital archives would be readily accessible to researchers all over the world. CT scans could be down-loaded from the Internet, or compact disks could be purchased directly from a catalog of archival materials. Non-invasive CT generated digital archiving will establish a model of electronic conservation, which will help to eliminate or greatly reduce the need for further handling of the mummies or other remains. This is an important concept at a time when various reburial movements are coming forward to claim their ancestors and sacred relics. There is an urgent need to document this material respectfully and in as much detail as possible before it is gone.

Researchers of the future will be able to enter the 'Visible Mummy Archives' for extensive virtual interaction with the scanning data. In this manner, a mummy can be repeatedly unwrapped and dissected (Figure 16.6) by remote investigators, long after the real mummy has been returned to its resting place. Holograms of mummies or other particularly fragile treasures may actually replace the originals on exhibit, so that they will not be disturbed except when absolutely necessary. Real-time animation techniques could profoundly enhance the archival CT data by creating a 'Living Pharaoh' CD-ROM documentary program, which would portray the kings and queens of ancient Egypt as moving, speaking individuals, recounting the history of their dynasties on the TV monitor of a home computer.

Summary

By scanning human remains and archaeological relics for archival purposes, it is possible to contribute directly to their conservation. CT libraries all over

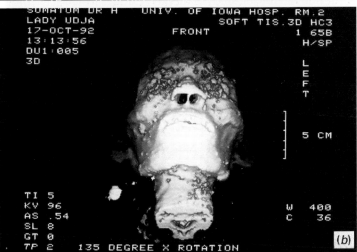

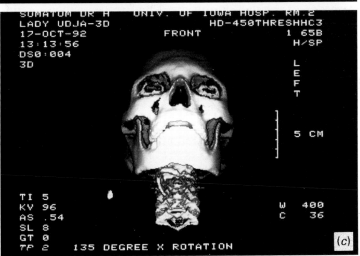

FIGURE 16.6. (a) Axial 3-D CT reconstruction of Egyptian mummy, with head 'removed' by computer (Field Museum of Natural History Collection); (b) 3-D CT reconstruction of mummy head before removal of overlying facial materials by computer; (c) Using CT window/level thresholding, orbits are cleared of packing debris.

the world will hold vast archival resources, based upon whole-body mummy scans compressed onto compact disks for future reference, so that the fragile materials will not have to be disturbed when new questions arise. Many people, students and scholars alike, will benefit from this research. So will the past.

MUMMY STUDIES AND PALEONUTRITION

Karl J. Reinhard

The study of ancient diet, paleonutrition, is a field of intense interest among archaeologists. Three goals of paleonutrition defined by Armelagos (1994) are the range of foods available (general menu), which foods were eaten (diet), and whether or not the diet was physiologically sound (nutrition). Techniques have developed for the study of dietary residues from archaeological sites such as feces, pollen, animal bone, seeds, mollusk shell, and so on. (Gilbert and Mielke 1985). In addition, bioarchaeologists have developed a wide array of techniques to identify dietary signals in human bone and hair, including stable isotopes of nitrogen and carbon and also by trace elemental analysis, usually barium and strontium (Labert and Grupe 1993; Sandford 1993). They also examine bone for pathological and developmental indicators of dietary sufficiency. All of these techniques can be transferred directly to the study of mummies.

Mummies have an extremely important role in diet studies. The tombs often contain food offerings that provide an idea of the 'menu' of ancient cultures and the ritual/social importance of different foods. Analyses of intestinal contents (coprolites) reveal exactly what foods and medicines were eaten immediately before death. Trace elemental and stable isotopic analyses provide a general idea of the diet during life. Comparative isotopic ratios between soft tissue and bone indicate whether or not starvation was a problem immediately before death. Pathological indicators of stress can be found in the skeletons of mummies. They and their burials provide for a detailed reconstruction of ancient diet.

Analysis of burial offerings

Food offerings are very common in tombs all over the world. Unfortunately, food offerings are often left unstudied by traditional archaeologists, but are of vital importance to paleonutritionists and are becoming the focus of serious, detailed study. Burial offerings provide an idea of the menu of ancient societies, but religious/social considerations may make them a poor

372

indicator of diet, as those plants that have special social importance are often over represented. Maize is a very common grave offering in Peruvian sites, but chemical studies of bone show that it was rarely eaten in some villages.

Analysis of intestinal contents

This type of analysis involves the examination of feces (coprolites) removed from the colons of mummies and provides the greatest detail of plant and animal remains. Physical evidence of plants includes pollen grains, starch grains, leaf fragments, epidermis, fiber, conductive tissue, seeds, bark, and rhizomes. The species of food plants (paleobotany) can be identified from these remains, and what parts of the plants were eaten can be determined (such as fruits, buds, roots, or vegetative tissue). Scanning electron microscopic study shows how the plants were prepared and cooked.

Invertebrate and vertebrate food animals can be found in intestinal contents. Mollusk shells from snails and clams, and spines from squids can be identified. Echinoderms such as sea urchins can be identified from the remains of calcareous spines and plates. Vertebrates can easily be identified based on the presence of bone and scale in coprolites. For larger animals, protein residue analysis can be performed to identify the full range of vertebrates available to prehistoric peoples (Sutton and Reinhard 1995).

The analysis of coprolites originated in mummy studies (Reinhard and Bryant 1992a, b) due, perhaps, to the fact that feces are dehydrated in the colon and are therefore resistant to decay (Reinhard *et al.* 1992). The first human coprolite analyses were done by Wood Jones (1910) and Netolitsky (1911, 1912), who analyzed coprolites from Nubian and Egyptian mummies respectively. Analysis of preserved coprolites from an English Bronze Age skeleton was done by Warren in 1911. Wakefield and Dellinger (1936) were the first researchers in North America to examine coprolites in mummies from Arkansas, including chemical and microscopic analyses. Also, this was the first study that evaluated skeletal pathology in the light of dietary data. In South America, Callen and Cameron (1960) were the first to publish dietary studies from coprolites recovered from a cave in Huaca Prieta, Peru, some from a partly mummified body. Since then, numerous studies have been accomplished with mummified remains.

Extensive analysis of intestinal contents from mummies was done with bog bodies from Europe. Because these mummies were sacrifices, the plants found represent those consumed in a ritual context. Both the Grauballe and Tollund mummies had eaten a mixture of wild and cultivated plant seeds immediately before death. Helbaek (1951, 1959) found a diversity of plant seeds in the Grauballe mummy; over 50 species were present. The Grauballe mummy also contained animal bone, possibly from a pig.

Intestinal contents from formal burials provide data regarding both diet and medicine. The diet of ailing individuals may be profoundly different from that of healthy people. The colon contents from a partially mummified body from New Mexico (Shafer *et al.* 1989) showed more finely ground maize seeds than any previously recovered from the Southwestern United States. Pollen present in the coprolites included an abundance of willow pollen, probably from making tea from willow bark and foliage (willow tea is an analgesic). Pollen from a plant in the mustard family was also abundant. As mustard seeds were not present in the coprolites, it is likely that the pollen was also derived from a tea, possibly used as an emetic. Coprolites from mummies can also reveal plant foods that were not recorded ethnographically. Analyses of a mummy from Ventana Cave, for example, showed that buds from the saguaro or organ pipe cactus were eaten (Haury 1950), although only fruits from these cacti are eaten by Indians today.

Chemical analysis

The chemical analysis of mummies is based on the theory that 'you are what you eat', and certain foods leave chemical signals in the body (Sandford 1993; Labert and Grupe 1993). The chronic consumption of certain foods leads to the accumulation of chemicals in the soft and hard tissues of mummies. The main focus of chemical analysis has been the determination of the quantity of meat consumed in the diet relative to plants, and the identification of how much of certain types of food were consumed.

The stable isotopes of carbon (^{12}C and ^{13}C) and nitrogen (^{14}N and ^{15}N) have been widely applied in dietary studies of mummies. Because of different physical and chemical properties of the isotopes, they are incorporated differently in biological processes. For example, there are two main photosynthetic pathways (C_3 and C_4) in different classes of plants and each utilizes these isotopes differently. Thus, it is important to know all of the isotopic signals of potential animal and plant foods in the environment under study.

One important issue that helps resolve this problem is the determination of how much meat is eaten relative to plants. This can be determined by looking at the carbon stable isotope values between apatite and collagen in bone. The stable isotopes of nitrogen are also important indicators of meat in the diet. Data from natural settings show that increasing trophic levels are enriched in [15]nitrogen. The nitrogen isotopes can reflect weaning patterns as well because mother's milk is enriched in [15]N. Nursing children, therefore, also have a high ^{15}N signal.

Strontium is one trace element that is used to determine the contribution of plants in the general diet, usually expressed as strontium to calcium ratios. High strontium levels are typical of marine foods. Strontium is also useful in identifying weaning practices as human milk contains little strontium relative to other foods. After weaning, the strontium level increases as children eat other food. To determine whether strontium has a marine or terrestrial origin, strontium isotope ratios are used because one isotope is more common in the marine environment.

The application of both types of chemical analysis has elucidated the change in diet in northern Chile over a span of several thousand years. The study showed that the earliest cultures from 3000 BC to AD 1500 had values that could be derived only from a marine ecosystem (Tieszen *et al.* 1992). Later cultures had either a mixed diet of maize and sea food or terrestrial resources (Tieszen and Chapman 1992). Strontium analysis confirmed the nitrogen and carbon data.

Multidisciplinary reconstruction of diet

The analysis of intestinal remains from the earliest cultural group, the Chinchorro, conflicted with the chemical analysis. These studies of Chilean diet highlighted one important point. For the accurate reconstruction of diet from mummies, one must use several data sources to overcome the biases inherent in each type of analysis. Currently, this is being attempted with mummies excavated by Buikstra from the Moquegua River Valley of southern Peru. Analyses have been completed of the grave goods, intestinal contents, and bone chemistry for one site, Chiribaya Alta, which was inhabited around AD 1000. The integration of these analyses allows the reconstruction of menu, diet and dietary adequacy.

Analysis of tomb contents by J. Dendy shows the menu for Chiribaya Alta. The most common grave goods were maize and coca, and in descending order of frequency, lucuma, pacay, manioc, molle, sweet potatoes, achira, guava, beans, chiles, and wild potatoes. These tomb contents provided an idea of the spectrum of foods eaten, suggesting that the inhabitants of Chiribaya Alta were largely dependent on agriculture.

Stable carbon and nitrogen isotopic study of 68 mummies and skeletons from sites throughout the Moquegua Valley by Sandness (1992) shows that there was substantial variation in Chiribaya diet in different parts of the valley. The sites closest to the sea were dependent on marine foods, and the diet of the coast was high in meat compared with that of the upper valley. Therefore, the isotopic reconstructions showed that the actual diet of Chiribaya Alta deviated from that indicated by tomb contents. Agricultural products were certainly an important part of the diet, but the people were not maize dependent. Trace elemental analysis of the mummies by Ghazi confirmed the isotopic data. He also looked at the change in strontium to calcium ratios in 40 Chiribaya Alta children to determine the weaning period. This analysis indicated that most children were weaned between 1.5 and 2 years of age.

Analysis of the intestinal contents indicated what items were most commonly eaten. Coprolites from 21 mummies and coprolites from the villages provided more insight into the diet. Ten coprolites from mummies contained a mix of marine meat (fish and /or shellfish) and agricultural plants. Nine contained only plants and two contained only marine meat. These results are consistent with 20 coprolites excavated from trash deposits in Chiribaya villages. Five samples contained maize kernels and four contained manioc tubers. Therefore, in comparison with the grave goods, which indicated a heavy reliance on maize, maize and manioc appeared to have had roughly the same importance in the diet.

In summary, four different lines of analysis provided four different perspectives on diet. The abundance of maize in the tomb offerings shows the social significance of this food to the Chiribaya Alta people. This social significance outweighed its actual importance in the diet. Coprolite analyses showed that manioc was equally important to maize in Chiribaya diet as was fish and shellfish. However, the greatest diversity of foods was found in the tomb offerings, which demonstrates the range of foods people had available to them. The nitrogen and carbon isotopic data and trace elemental data emphasized the importance of marine foods in the protein component of the diet. The coprolite data highlighted the mixed nature of Chiribaya diet with contributions from agricultural products and marine animals. It also demonstrated the wide use of non-maize plants, especially of tubers. Thus, the interdisciplinary study of diet has the greatest promise for complete paleonutrition studies.

The most important aspect of the study of paleonutrition utilizing mummies is that several lines of investigation can be pursued in the reconstruction of diet. One unanswered question relates to the adequacy of the diet, what Armelagos (1994) calls 'nutrition'. This is an issue that will be addressed in future mummy studies as nutrition-related pathology is evaluated in the context of menu and diet, an area in which mummy studies have the greatest paleonutritional potential.

MUMMY STUDIES AND ARCHAEOPARASITOLOGY

Karl J. Reinhard

Archaeoparasitology, the study of ancient human parasitism, increasingly focuses on mummy studies. Parasite remains have been studied in an archaeological context for 85 years, but the field has matured only during the past two decades with the development of its theoretical and methodological foundations. It evolved independently and simultaneously in laboratories on three continents in the 1970s and 1980s (Reinhard 1992), with well defined research goals: Ferreira, Araújo, and Confalonieri at the Fundação Oswaldo Cruz in Brazil, Reinhard in the United States, and Andrew Jones in England. All were working with both coprolites and mummies.

As indicated by the historical trends among these researchers, archaeoparasitology has an increasing focus on mummy studies. This is due to the fact that mummies offer different research potentials from those inherent in fecal debris such as coprolites and latrine soils. First, there is a greater diversity of parasites in mummies, as research on fecal debris is limited to the study of parasites that distribute their eggs in feces or urine. For example, blood fluke ova are rarely found in coprolites or latrine contents (Bouchet and Paicheler 1995), but analysis of mummies from areas where blood flukes are endemic provides ample evidence of larval and adult forms from internal organs as well as ova (Ascenzi *et al.* 1980; Millet *et al.* 1980; Ruffer 1910; Deelder *et al.* 1990). Second, there is often doubt as to whether coprolites are derived from humans, and the human origin of parasites is therefore ambiguous. This is not the case with mummies, which provide definitive and direct evidence of human parasitism. Third, definitive diagnosis is stronger with mummies. Identification in clinical laboratories is sometimes dependent on the examination of adult parasites, but coprolites and latrine soils contain only the eggs and larvae of parasites and therefore morphological description may not always provide a secure source of diagnosis. Adult parasites, however, are recoverable from mummies and provide a certain basis for diagnosis, as can be seen in hookworm research. Two species of hookworm in two different genera are the most common found in humans: *Necator americanus* and *Ancylostoma duodenale*. Hookworm larvae and eggs cannot be identified to either species, but Allison and associates (1974) were able to recover adult hookworms from a prehistoric Peruvian mummy and

377

demonstrate from examination of the buccal cavity and tooth morphology that *Ancylostoma duodenale* was the infective organism. Fourth, the analysis of mummies leads to the discovery of pathology that has a parasitological base. Lesions of flukes in liver tissue (David and David 1995), roundworms in muscle tissue and intestinal walls, enlarged hollow viscera from trypanosome infection, and muconasal destruction from South American leishmaniasis have all been observed in mummies. Thus, not only are the parasites recovered, but the pathology caused by them is evident in mummies, providing critical data regarding the illnesses caused by these organisms. Fifth, there are more mummies available for study now than ten years ago. This is due to increased excavation activity in countries where mummies are preserved and also to the development of mildly invasive techniques for the study of mummies in museum collections by archaeoparasitologists. Sixth, DNA studies hold great promise in the analysis of parasite remains. The first DNA identification of a parasite infection was recently accomplished (A. C. Aufderheide, personal communication), and the use of DNA signatures can be used with mummies to identify parasite species. There is great potential in DNA analysis of defining genetic variability within a species through time and this may permit us to define the genetic changes that occurred in parasites inhabiting different human populations in different parts of the world.

One issue at the heart of the archaeoparasitology debate in the Americas is the question of when various parasite species were introduced into the New World. These include the human specific beef and pork tapeworms, the giant intestinal round worm, hookworm, whipworm, and pinworm. The conventional wisdom has been that nearly all these parasites, except perhaps pinworm, were introduced into the New World after European contact (Desowitz 1981). During the 1980s, a significant body of data was recovered from coprolites showing that hookworm, whipworm and giant intestinal roundworm infected humans prehistorically. By 1990 all of these parasites had been found in mummies and provided irrefutable proof of the wide range of prehistoric human specific parasites (Reinhard 1991).

A second aspect of American archaeoparasitology has been the study of adaptation to immigrant humans by parasite species that infected indigenous animals. This adaptation was discussed by Cockburn (1971) as being critical in defining parasite diversity in humans. New World archaeology provides an ideal laboratory in which the adaption of zoonotic parasites can be assessed. A corpus of data from coprolites excavated from North America showed that thorny-headed worms commonly infected archaic human populations (Moore *et al.* 1969), evidence that was accepted with some reticence because it was derived from coprolite examination only. In South America, similar studies were undertaken through the examination of intestinal contents of mummies. The analysis of these South American coprolites demonstrated that prehistoric coastal populations in Chile and Peru were infected by a tapeworm species that normally cycles between sea lions and fish (Callen and Cameron 1960), sea lions being the definitive hosts and fish intermediate hosts. In preagricultural fisher populations of Chile, I have found 21 percent of the mummies examined to be positive for the eggs. The study of prehistoric North American parasite ecology (Reinhard 1988; 1996) has defined aspects of diet, sanitation, hygiene, and house construction that determine the diversity and prevalence of parasites.

Currently, I am applying this type of analysis for three prehistoric villages in the Moquegua Valley of Peru, studying trypanosomiasis and leishmaniasis using mummies as the study medium (Reinhard 1996). One aspect of parasitism that differed dramatically among villages was louse infestation. Of 164 individuals from three sites, 146 were examined for louse nits, and 34 were positive. By measuring the density of nits at the scalp and on hair shafts away from the scalp, it was possible to measure how many people were controlling louse infestations at the time of death (more nits on hair shafts than at scalp) and how many people had an increasing louse problem at death (more nits on the scalp than on the shafts). Twenty individuals had fewer nits on the hair in comparison with the scalp, eleven showed more nits on the hair than on the scalp. Therefore, most people showed increased infestation around the time of death. The fact that eleven individuals showed a decrease of lice from the scalp indicates that the people had some medicinal practices effective in the control of lice for infested individuals.

An inter-site louse comparison was made among the villages. Two were located close to the ocean and one was in the distant Andes highlands. Of the coastal villages, one site had seven mummies, five of which were infested with lice. The other site had 69 mummies with 25 (36%) infested. From the highland village 22 mummies were studied and four (18%) were positive for louse nits. The differences may reflect a less urban lifestyle at the highland village that had limited louse infestation. Sex was also a variable; 38% of women were infested in contrast to 56% of men.

Other aspects of parasitism found at these villages were trypanosomiasis, and leishmaniasis. Trypanosome infection is related to house construction, which promoted infestation of the houses with the insect vectors of the parasite. Leishmaniasis was contracted by collecting rushes in the still, moist river valley near the sites, thus exposing people to the vectors of disease. These cases demonstrate conclusively that opportunistic parasites indigenous to the New World were able to colonize humans.

Analysis of mummies from the Old World demonstrates the diversity of parasites that infected humans in ancient times (Millet *et al.* 1983; Sandison 1983; El Mahdy 1989). In Egypt especially, a wide range of parasite species has been recovered. Several fluke species have been identified including *Schistosoma haematobium*, possibly *Schistosoma mansoni*, and pathology resultant from liver flukes, possibly *Fasciola hepatica*. Tapeworms of the genus *Taenia*, which includes the beef and pork tapeworms, have also been found. Many roundworm species have been found including the guinea worm, *Dracunculus medinensis*, the whipworm, *Trichuris trichiura*, the mawworm (or giant intestinal roundworm), *Ascaris lumbricoides*, *Trichinella spiralis*, which causes trichinosis, and the wireworm *Strongyloides stercoralis*. The greater diversity of parasites found in Egyptian mummies may reflect the fact that many parasites have an African evolutionary homeland and also the diverse activities of ancient Egyptians. Schistosomes were probably related to canal building. Liver fluke infection and *Taenia* infections came from animal domestication, and Egyptian cuisine included poorly cooked meat, which resulted in *Taenia* and *Trichinella* infections. The guinea worm is transferred by drinking water that contains copepoda (tiny crustaceans). Finally, fecal borne disease in the form of *T. trichiura*, *A. lumbricoides*, and *S. stercoralis* was a problem for Egyptians.

The future of archaeoparasitology

We shall always be looking for the origins of parasite species and defining the history of expansion of parasites, but we shall also be looking in the future at the mechanisms by which parasites colonized humans, and at the genetic diversity of parasites as they dispersed across the world with human migrations. The future of archaeoparasitology is tied to two things: development of new techniques and availability of mummies. As mentioned, mummies both from the field and from museums are becoming more available for gross and microscopic study. Technological developments in molecular DNA biology should enhance the future assessment of parasite genetic diversity. There are serious technical problems from contaminating microorganisms that need to be overcome but these difficulties are being addressed successfully today, as represented by the recent find of *Trypanosoma cruzi* DNA in Peruvian mummies. I believe that this success foreshadows a rich future in the study of parasites from mummies.

ENDOSCOPY OF MUMMIES

Edmund Tapp

Endoscopes have been used for many years in medical practice, enabling doctors to see and biopsy areas suspected of harbouring disease that otherwise would be inaccessible. More recently they have also been used widely in industry, allowing (for instance) engineers to inspect the inside of an aircraft engine without dismantling it. About 15 years ago the author had experimented with various nondestructive methods of obtaining tissue from inside Egyptian mummies, but had limited success with conventional medical techniques such as needle biopsies. It was decided, therefore, to explore the use of endoscopes (Tapp 1984). The latest instruments are not only extremely sophisticated but also mobile, which allows them to be used both in museums and at excavation sites where the findings may be observed on a video monitor attached directly to the instrument.

Clearly, the usual orifices through which endoscopes are introduced into the body are often blocked by either bandages or debris, but occasionally entry by these routes has been possible in Egyptian mummies. In the Leeds mummy (Tapp and Wildsmith 1992), after the debris had been sucked out of the mouth and pharynx, an excellent view of the larynx and trachea could be obtained (Figure 16.7). It was also possible to examine the lower rectum of the Muisca mummies by the normal route. Examination of the interior of the nose and mouth has also been possible in several instances. Fortunately, the Ancient Egyptians helped the modern endoscopist by breaking the cribriform plate at the top of the nose when they were removing the brain, and in doing so, provided a passage through which the endoscope may be passed into the cranial cavity (Tapp *et al.* 1984). A clear view can often be obtained by this route of the various bones protruding into the cavity; in one instance the posterior clinoid process, which projects upwards behind the pituitary gland, was observed to be embedded in residual brain tissue at the back of the cavity. It would appear that this bone had been broken off by the Egyptian embalmers as they were attempting to remove the brain (Figure 16.8). As one might anticipate, not all the brain was removed by the embalmers and useful biopsies have been obtained from this residual cerebral tissue. Not only do these biopsies show the degree of preservation of the brain, but also reveal postmortem changes such as adipocere formation (Thompson *et al.* 1986). Moreover, parts of the walls of hydatid cysts have been seen in biopsies from the brain removed with the endoscope from two different Egyptian mummies, indicating the presence of the dog tapeworm in Ancient Egypt.

FIGURE 16.7. View through a rigid endoscope passed down the back of the throat of
the Leeds mummy. The tracheal rings can be
seen on the right of the photograph.

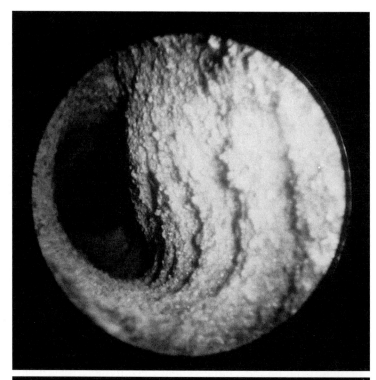

FIGURE 16.8. View through flexible endoscope passed through the nose showing posterior clinoid process (curved bone)
embedded in residual brain tissue.

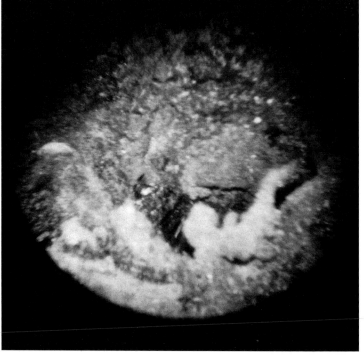

FIGURE 16.9. View through rigid endoscope passed through chest wall. Residual lung tissue is seen together with the ribs on the opposite side of the chest. cavity.

Resin is sometimes found within the skull and often may be seen radiologically as a fluid level. This may be confused with residual brain tissue that has become liquefied and biopsy of this material can resolve this problem (Stanworth *et al.* 1986). If the nasal route into the skull is not available, access may be obtained by a simple burr hole of the type used by neurosurgeons when operating on the head; in fact, evidence for one of the cases of hydatid disease was obtained by this method (Stanworth *et al.* 1986).

The use of endoscopes to view the interior of the chest and abdomen is again assisted by the ancient Egyptian embalmers who often removed the stomach, intestines, liver and lungs, leaving spaces into which an endoscope can be introduced. This has been of particular value in the examination of the chest where radiography has shown residual tissue to be present (Figure 16.9). In addition to viewing the contents of the chest, valuable biopsies have been obtained which have shown sand pneumoconiosis to be present in some degree in practically every mummy that has been biopsied. This is a condition that was originally described in lung from a canopic jar, but these techniques have demonstrated its widespread distribution (Tapp *et al.* 1975; Tapp and Wildsmith 1992). Endoscopy of the thorax and abdominal cavity has also allowed one to view the packages containing organs that have been dried, wrapped and then placed back into the cavity by the ancient Egyptian embalmers. If these cannot be removed the endoscope enables biopsies to be taken from them.

To summarise: endoscopes have allowed tissue to be obtained from a wide range of mummified remains without destroying the integrity of the body. Although museum authorities and curators at excavation sites are naturally reluctant for exhibits to be damaged in any way, they will often give permission for the small apertures to be made, which are all that is necessary for endoscopic examination and biopsy. Given these circumstances, it is clearly a valuable additional technique in our quest for information about life and death in ancient cultures – and due to the peculiarities of the methods used by ancient Egyptian embalmers, it has been of particular value in this field.

POPULATION STUDIES
Tony Waldron

The study of disease in mummies has a long history but there has generally been more concern merely to demonstrate its presence than to make any estimate of its frequency. There are at least two reasons for this; one is to do with the relatively small numbers of subjects for study, the other is that epidemiology has come lately to paleopathology. If there is to be any sense of the relative frequency with which diseases appeared in antiquity, or how their frequency may have changed over the centuries, there is no recourse other than to epidemiology. This chapter will briefly outline some of the methods used to measure the frequency of disease and point out some of the pitfalls in applying epidemiology to past populations, especially those that may be as small as the population of mummies.

Measures of disease frequency
The two measures in most common use in contemporary epidemiology are incidence and prevalence (Rothman 1986). The incidence of a disease is the rate of occurrence of new cases in a population at risk and is expressed to some time base, a week, a month or a year, for example, depending on the nature of the disease. This measure cannot be used in paleopathology because the number at risk can never be known. The word 'incidence' should, therefore, never be used to describe the frequency of disease in a paleopathological population, although it is frequently used for this purpose. The correct measure to use in paleopathology is prevalence (Waldron 1994).

Prevalence
The prevalence of a disease is simply the proportion of individuals with a particular disease in a defined population Although it is often referred to as a prevalence rate, it is not a true rate as it has no time base. It should be noted that

no rates can be calculated for paleopathological purposes. Those who report still births, neonatal mortality or infant mortality rates, for example, are deluding themselves and misleading their readers. All such rates are proportions and bear no relation at all to the true rates reported by modern epidemiologists. It is customary, however, to distinguish between point prevalence, which is prevalence at a particular point in time, and period prevalence, which is calculated over a week, a month or a year, again depending on the nature of the disease. It will be obvious that in paleopathology, only period prevalence can be determined and that the period involved may be very long indeed.

The formula for calculating prevalence is: $P = n/N$ where P = prevalence, n = number of cases of the disease, and N = total study population. Also: $P \approx I \times D$, where P = prevalence, I = incidence, and D = duration of the disease. The prevalence will approximate the incidence when dealing with diseases of very short duration (common infectious diseases, for example); with diseases of long duration (such as osteoarthritis), the prevalence may be many times greater than the incidence.

The prevalence of a disease is determined using a cross-sectional study, in which the population is defined by some criterion – it may be all the mummies from a particular site – and the number of those having the disease under study is determined, preferably using agreed criteria consistently applied; the prevalence is calculated as shown in the first equation above. In modern epidemiology, a cross-sectional study may be visualized as having a sharp cutoff point. But this is not the case in a paleopathological cross-sectional study where the interval between the death of the subjects and their being observed will be variable and usually long (Waldron 1996). When calculating prevalence in such a study, there may be some confusion about which denominator to use. It is unlikely, in most cases, to be the total number of individuals in the group, but rather the total number of some anatomical element. For example, suppose that we wished to calculate the prevalence of fracture of the radius in a group of 40 mummies. If two had such a fracture, then intuitively one might suppose that the prevalence would be 2/40 = 5 percent. From our observations (or the records from which we were working), however, it is apparent that the arms are missing from seven of the mummies and so our observations must relate only to the 33 mummies in which they are present and the prevalence of fractured radius in them is, therefore, 2/33 = 6.1 percent.

Comparing prevalences

A prevalence that uses the whole population as the denominator is called a crude prevalence, and it is not a very useful statistic with which to make

Table 16.1. *Age specific prevalences of disease in two populations*

Age group	A			B		
(years)	N	n	Prev/10³	N	n	Prev/10³
	(1)	(2)	(3)	(4)	(5)	(6)
25–34	32	2	62.5	49	3	61.2
35–44	42	12	266.7	61	20	327.9
45–54	58	27	465.5	30	16	533.3
55+	65	36	553.8	32	20	635.0
Total	197	77	390.9	172	59	343.0

Note:
N=total number in each age group; n=total number affected; Prev=prevalence.

comparisons between groups; for this purpose it is better to calculate age and sex specific prevalences. The data in Table 16.1 show that comparisons that do not allow for differences in age may give an entirely misleading impression of the frequency of a disease in two populations. In this table, the age specific and crude prevalences for a disease are shown for two hypothetical populations, A and B. The crude prevalence for A is $390.9/10^3$ and for B, $343.0/10^3$ suggesting that the disease is more common in A than in B. This difference is often expressed as a rate ratio, which in this case is $390.9/343.0=1.14$ in favour of A This conclusion seems anomalous, however, for if we consider the age specific rates in columns 3 and 6 of the table, in almost every case they are higher in B than in A. The problem lies in the age structure of the two populations. There are considerably more older individuals in A than in B, whereas the converse is true for younger individuals. A satisfactory comparison can be made using the age and sex specific prevalences but this is a rather cumbersome method and it is better to use one which gives a single summary statistic. The best for paleopathological work is the odds ratio.

The odds ratio

Suppose that we have two populations P and Q, with age specific prevalences p_1 and $q_1, \ldots, p_n$ and q_n, we can compare each age group by calculating the odds ratio (OR) as follows (Clayton and Hills 1993):

$$p_1/1-p_1 \div q_1/1-q_1 \ldots p_n/1-p_n \div q_n/1-q_n$$

The OR for each age stratum can be summed to give an overall, or common OR which relates the age specific prevalences in two populations to a single figure. The data in the table are easy to analyze as the prevalences are the same for each age group. Thus for the 25–34 year old group

$$62.5/1000 - 62.5 \div 61.2/1000 - 61.2 = 1.03$$

For the succeeding strata, the ORs are: for age 35–44, 0.75; for 45–54, 0.76; and for 55+, 0.74. The common odds ratio is obtained by summing the individual rates which comes down eventually to:

$$\frac{(62.5 \times 938.8) + (266.7 \times 672.1) + (465.5 \times 466.7) + (533.8 \times 375.0)}{(61.2 \times 937.5) + (327.9 \times 733.3) + (534.5 \times 533.3) + (466.2 \times 625.0)} = 0.75$$

From this result it is clear that prevalence in A is actually substantially lower than in B which is what we would expect from studying the age specific prevalences. The 95 percent confidence intervals can be calculated to give a measure of the significance of the common odds ratio; in this case they are 0.68–0.83. However, given the small number of mummies with which one usually has to deal, it must be remembered that these calculations and any conclusions drawn from very small samples may be misleading as may comparisons based solely on crude prevalences.

Proportional morbidity and morbidity odds ratios

Two other methods of comparing disease in populations which do not depend on having denominator data are the proportional morbidity ratio (PMR) and the morbidity odds ratio (MOR). The PMR is very simple in concept; the disease under study is expressed simply as a proportion of all diseases in the first population and then compared with its proportion in the second. If the proportion in the first population is, say, 15 percent and in the second 5 percent, then the PMR is 15/5 = 3.0, showing that it is much more common in the first than in the second.

Proportional morbidity ratios are seldom calculated in contemporary epidemiology largely because of the difficulty in obtaining morbidity data but proportional mortality ratios are, death being something about which there can be little argument. There are some theoretical problems with proportional mortality ratios and Miettinen and Wang (1981) suggested that it should be replaced with something that they call the mortality odds ratio. It is not possible to use this statistic in paleoepidemiology, but it can be adapted to obtain a morbidity odds ratio (MOR).

Table 16.2. *Spondylolysis in two skeletal populations*

Number with	Group A	Group B
Spondylosis	10 (a)	13 (b)
All other conditions	466 (c)	231 (d)

Source: From Waldron (1991).

The results of a study on the frequency of spondylolysis in two skeletal populations are set out in Table 16.2 (Waldron 1991). From these data the MOR can be obtained by the formula:

$$MOR = ad/bc$$

Substituting the figures in Table 2 shows that the MOR is 0.38; the PMR is 0.40 and it is often the case that there is not much difference between the MOR and the PMR.

Calculating either the PMR or the MOR is simple but some thought has to be given to deciding exactly what constitutes a 'disease' or 'condition'. Is a minute osteophyte or a tiny trace of periostitis, or a cyst in a carpal bone pathological or not? In practice the differentiation between normality and abnormality is somewhat arbitrary and will probably differ between one observer and the next. However, so long as the criteria for abnormality are decided beforehand and applied rigorously to all the material, the final calculation should provide a valid comparison between the two groups in question and for the particular observer or observers.

Missing data

Missing data are the bane of any epidemiological study and many techniques have been developed for dealing with them in statistical analyses (Armitage and Berry 1987). In paleoepidemiology, missing data especially affect the denominator. In the example of the fractured radius given above, mummies with missing arms were excluded from the denominator and the rule is that denominators must be appropriate to the case in hand if the sums are to give the right answers. This seems obvious but problems can (and do) arise. For example, let us suppose that we wish to determine the frequency of tuberculosis in a mummy population. This is a disease that may affect almost any joint or any bone, albeit it has a special predilection for some sites, most notably the spine. If we found one spine affected and one further case in which another joint (say the wrist) was affected, then in our hypothetical group of 40 mummies, what is the prevalence of tuberculosis? One thing it almost certainly will not be is 5 percent (2/40) because we cannot guarantee that we have complete spines present in each case, or that all the mummies have wrist joints or other joints or bones likely to be affected. We may either have to restrict our calculation to only those mummies that are sufficiently complete for us to be certain that no element likely to have been affected by tuberculosis is missing, or we may have to calculate the prevalence of the disease for different anatomical sites separately.

The reason to hammer home this point is simply that it affects the way in which data are to be collected. It is never sufficient to know merely that so many mummies were in the study group; their state of preservation must also be recorded and which anatomical elements were (and were not) present. It is incumbent on the investigator to think carefully about which data will be needed for all calculations and thus ensure that they are collected. In the interests of future generations of paleopathologists who may never get their hands on human remains, data collection should be as comprehensive as possible so that further work can be undertaken at some later date. I realise this is a counsel of perfection; most people have enough trouble thinking about their own studies, let alone trying to foresee what might conceivably be needed in the future. Be assured, however, that one of the cardinal rules of epidemiology is that the one piece of information which you do not record will be the one you eventually need!

Operational definitions

One frequently stated aim of paleoepidemiology is to compare the frequency of disease in the past with that in modern populations to see what changes there may have been over time, but I doubt if this is ever likely to be realized for the majority of diseases. The reason for this is that diagnostic procedures in clinical practice and in paleopathology differ so greatly. Take osteoarthritis as an example. This is the most common disease found in human remains but its paleopathological diagnosis depends upon different criteria from the clinical diagnosis. Clinically, osteoarthritis depends upon the radiological demonstration of joint space narrowing, marginal osteophytes and sclerosis of subchondral bone. When the radiological and paleopathological diagnoses of osteoarthritis were compared in a series of skeletal knee joints, there were profound differences between the two, the paleopathologist recording the presence of osteoarthritis much more frequently than the radiologist (Rogers *et al.* 1990).

What may reasonably be achieved, however, is for comparisons to be made of the frequency of disease in different groups of human remains, although here another problem arises from the fact that there are no established and universally agreed upon criteria for diagnosing disease in human remains. The standard way of achieving uniformity of effort in epidemiology is through the use of operational definitions, and it seems to me that this is a matter to which some urgent attention needs to be given. We have made some suggestions for an operational definition of osteoarthritis in human remains; that is, the disease is diagnosed when eburnation is present on the joint surface (this is pathognomonic of osteoarthritis in the skeleton) or, in the absence of eburnation, if two of the following are present: marginal osteophytes, new bone on the joint surface, pitting on the joint surface, or deformation of the joint contour (Rogers and Waldron 1995). In practice, if the diagnosis is restricted solely to joints showing eburnation, this should cause the least confusion and the greatest agreement between different observers and I would now advocate this approach. To prepare operational definitions for the most commonly found conditions in human remains is a difficult (not to mention tedious) task but unless some agreement can be made on diagnostic features of a disease, paleoepidemiological studies will have very limited value.

In the case of mummies, the situation may be slightly less pessimistic than I have outlined above because there is a much greater possibility of using clinical criteria for diagnosis since anatomical relationships are better preserved and soft tissue is present, which will permit the carrying out of a number of diagnostic tests, including histological examination of tissues and an increasing range of immunological tests now that the polymerase chain reaction (PCR) and other techniques are becoming more widely available.

REFERENCES

Introduction

Barraco, R. A. 1980. Paleobiochemistry. In *Mummies, disease, and ancient cultures*, ed. A. and E. Cockburn, 312–26. New York: Cambridge University Press.

Barraco, R. A., Cockburn, T. A. and Reyman, T. A. 1977. Paleobiochemical analysis of an Egyptian mummy. *Journal of Human Evolution* 6: 533–46.

Cockburn, T. A., Barraco, R. A., Peck, W. H. and Reyman, T. A. 1975. Autopsy of an Egyptian mummy. *Science* 187: 1155–60.

Hart, G. D., Kvas, I. and Soots, M. L. 1977. Blood group testing: autopsy of an Egyptian mummy. *Canadian Medical Association Journal* 117: 461–73.

Henry, R. L. 1980. Paleoserology. In *Mummies, disease, and ancient cultures*, ed. A. and E. Cockburn, 327–34. New York: Cambridge University Press.

Horne, P. D. and Lewin P. K. 1977. Electron microscopy of mummified tissue: autopsy of an Egyptian mummy. *Canadian Medical Association Journal* 117: 461–73.

Kristen, K. T. and Reyman, T. A. 1980. Radiographic examination of mummies with autopsy correlation.

In *Mummies, disease, and ancient cultures*, ed. A. and E. Cockburn, 287–300. New York: Cambridge University Press.

Lewin, P. K. and Harwood-Nash, D. C. 1977. X-ray computed axial tomography of an ancient Egyptian brain. *International Research Communication System* **5**: 78.

Lewin, P. K., Trodagis, J. E. and Stevens, J. K. 1990. Three-dimensional reconstructions from serial x-ray tomography of an Egyptian mummified head. *Clinical Anatomy* **3**: 215–18.

Reyman, T. A. and Dowd, A. M. 1980. Processing of mummified tissue for histological examination. In *Mummies, disease, and ancient cultures*, ed. A. and E. Cockburn, 258–73. New York: Cambridge University Press.

Riddle, J. M. 1980. A survey of ancient specimens by electron microscopy. In *Mummies, disease, and ancient cultures*, ed. A. and E. Cockburn, 274–86. New York: Cambridge University Press.

Ruffer, M. A. 1910. Note on the presence of *Bilharzia haematobia* in Egyptian mummies of the Twentieth Dynasty (1250–1000 BC). *British Medical Journal* **1**: 16.

Waldron, H. A. 1981. Postmortem absorption of lead by the skeleton. *American Journal of Physical Anthropology* **55**: 395–8.

Williams, J. A. 1993. Benefits and obstacles of routine elemental isotopic analysis in bioarchaeological research contracts. In *Investigations of ancient human tissue: chemical analyses in anthropology*, vol. 10, ed. M. K. Sandford, 387–412. Amsterdam: Gordon and Breach.

Paleogenetics

Brown, T. A. and Brown, K. A. 1992. Ancient DNA and the archaeologist. *Antiquity* **66**: 10–23.

Brown, T. A. and Brown, K. A. 1994. Ancient DNA: using molecular biology to explore the past. *BioEssays* **16**: 719–26.

Gill, P., Ivanov, P. L., Kimpton, C., Piercy, R., Benson, N., Tully, G., Evett, I., Hagelberg, E. and Sullivan, K. 1994. Identification of the remains of the Romanov family by DNA analysis. *Nature Genetics* **6**: 130–5

Handt, O., Höss, M., Krings, M. and Pääbo, S. 1994a. Ancient DNA: methodological challenges. *Experientia* **50**: 524–9.

Handt, O., Richards, M., Trommsdorff, M., Kilger, C., Simanainen, J., Georgiev, O., Bauer, K., Stone, A., Hedges, R., Schaffner, W., Utermann, G., Sykes, B. and Pääbo, S. 1994b. Molecular genetic analysis of the Tyrolean Ice Man. *Science* **264**: 1775–8.

Hauswirth, W. W. 1994. Ancient DNA: an introduction. *Experientia* **50**: 521–3.

Herrmann, B. and Hummel, S., eds. 1993. *Ancient DNA*. New York: Springer Verlag

Higuchi, R., Bowman, B., Freiberger, M., Ryder, O. A. and Wilson, A. C. 1984. DNA Sequences from the quagga, an extinct member of the horse family. *Nature* **312**: 282–4.

Höss, M. and Pääbo, S. 1993. DNA extraction from Pleistocene bones by a silica-based method. *Nucleic Acid Research* **21**: 3913–14.

Höss, M., Jaruga, P., Zasatawny, T. H., Dizdaroglu, M. and Pääbo, S. 1996. DNA damage and DNA sequence retrieval from ancient tissues. *Nucleic Acid Research* **24**: 1304–7.

Lawlor, D. A., Dickel, C. D., Hauswirth, W. W. and Parham, P. 1991. Ancient HLA genes from 7,500 year old archaeological remains. *Nature* **349**: 785–8.

Lindahl, T. 1993. Instability and decay of the primary structure of DNA. *Nature* **362**: 709–15.

Nielsen, H., Engberg, J. and Thuesen, I. 1994. DNA from arctic human burials. In *Ancient DNA*, ed. B. Herrmann and S. Hummel, 122–40. New York: Springer Verlag.

Pääbo, S. 1985. Molecular cloning of ancient Egyptian mummy DNA. *Nature* **314**: 644–5.

Pääbo, S. 1989. Ancient DNA: extraction, characterization, molecular cloning and enzymatic amplification. *Proceedings of the National Academy of Sciences (USA)* **86**: 1939–43.

Pääbo, S., Gifford, J. A. and Wilson, A. C. 1988. Mitochondrial DNA sequences from a 7,000 year old brain. *Nucleic Acid Research* **16**: 9775–87.

Poinar, H. N., Höss, M., Bada, J. L. and Pääbo, S. 1996. Amino acid racemization and the preservation of ancient DNA. *Science* **272**: 864–6.

Powledge, T. A. and Rose, M. 1996a. The great DNA hunt. Genetic archaeology zeroes in on the origins of modern human. *Archaeology* **49**(5): 36–47.

Powledge, T. A. and Rose, M. 1996b. The great DNA hunt, part II. Colonizing the Americas. *Archaeology* **49**(6): 58–66.

Salo, W. L., Aufderheide, A. C., Buikstra, J. and Holcomb, T. 1994. Identification of *Mycobacterium tuberculosis* DNA in a pre-Columbian Peruvian mummy. *Proceedings of the National Academy of Sciences* **91**: 2091–4.

Thuesen, I. and Engberg, J. 1990. Recovery and analysis of human genetic material from mummified tissue and bone. *Journal of Archaeological Science* **17**: 679–89.

Tuross, N. 1994. The biochemistry of ancient DNA in bone. *Experientia* **50**: 530–5.

Paleoimaging

Harwood-Nash, D., 1979. Computed tomography of ancient mummies. *Journal of Computer Assisted Tomography* **3**(6): 768–73.

Notman, D. N. H. 1983. Nuclear magnetic resonance imaging of an Egyptian mummy. *Paleopathology Newsletter* **43**: 9.

Notman, D. N. H. 1987. Arctic paleoradiology: portable radiographic examination of two frozen sailors from the Franklin Expedition (1845–1848). *American Journal of Roentgenology* **149**: 347–50.

Notman, D. N. H. 1995. 'CT Densitometry of Wood.' Paper presented at the 2nd World Congress on Mummy Studies. Cartagena, Colombia. February 1995.

Notman, D. N. H. and Aufderheide, A. C. 1995. Experimental mummification and computed imaging. In *Proceedings of the I World Congress on Mummy Studies*. vol. 2, 821–8. Santa Cruz de Tenerife: Museo Arqueológico y Etnográfico de Tenerife.

Notman, D. N. H., Tashijian, J., Aufderheide, A. C., Cass, O. W., Shane, O. C. III, Berquist, T. H., Gray, J. E. and Gedgaudas, E. 1986. Modern imaging and endoscopic biopsy techniques in Egyptian mummies. *American Journal of Roentgenology* **146**: 93–6.

Mummy studies and paleonutrition

Armelagos, G. J. 1994. You are what you eat. In *Paleonutrition: the diet and health of prehistoric Americans*, ed. K. D. Sobolik, 235–44. Carbondale. IL: Center for Archaeological Investigations, Southern Illinois University at Carbondale.

Callen, E. O. and Cameron, T. W. M. 1960. A prehistoric diet revealed in coprolites. *The New Scientist* **90**: 35–40.

Gilbert, R. I., Jr. and Mielke J. H. 1985. *The analysis of prehistoric diets.* New York: Academic Press.

Haury, E. W. 1950. *The stratigraphy and archaeology of Ventana Cave, Arizona.* Tucson, AZ: University of Arizona Press.

Helbaek, H. 1951. Tollundmandens sidste måltid. *Aarbøger for Nordisk Oldkyndighed og Historie* **1950**: 311–41.

Helbaek, H. 1959. Grauballemandens sidste måltid. *KUML* **1958**: 83–116.

Labert, J. B. and Grupe G. 1993 *Prehistoric human bone-archaeology at the molecular level.* Berlin: Springer Verlag.

Netolitsky, F. 1911. Nahrungs- und Heilmittel der Urägypter. *Die Umschau* **46**: 953–6.

Netolitsky, F. 1912. Hirse und Cyperus aus dem prähistorischen Agypten. *Beihefte zum Botanischen Centralblatt* **29**: 1–11.

Reinhard, K. J. and Bryant, Jr., V. M. 1992a Coprolite analysis: a biological perspective on prehistory. In *Advances in Archaeological Method and Theory*, No.14, ed. M. B. Schiffer, 403–8. New York: Academic Press.

Reinhard, K. J. and Bryant, Jr., 1992b. Investigating mummified intestinal contents: reconstructing diet and parasitic disease. In *Proceedings of the I World Congress on Mummy Studies*, vol.1, 403–8. Santa Cruz de Tenerife: Museo Arqueológico y Etnográfico de Tenerife.

Reinhard, K. J., Geib, P. R., Callahan, M. M. and Hevly, R. H. 1992. Discovery of colon contents in a skeletonized burial: soil sampling for dietary remains. *Journal of Archaeological Science* **19**: 697–705.

Sandford, M. K., ed. 1993. *Investigations of ancient human tissue: chemical analyses in anthropology.* Langhorne, PA: Gordon and Breach.

Sandness, K. L. 1992. Temporal and spatial dietary variability in the prehistoric lower and middle Osmore drainage; the carbon and nitrogen isotope evidence. Master's thesis, Department of Anthropology, University of Nebraska, Lincoln.

Shafer, H. J., Marek, M. K. and Reinhard K. J. 1989. A Mimbres burial with associated colon remains from Nan Ranch, New Mexico. *Journal of Field Archaeology* **16**: 17–30.

Sutton, M. Q. and Reinhard K. J. 1995. Cluster analysis of the coprolites from Antelope House: implications for Anasazi diet and cuisine. *Journal of Archaeological Science* **22**: 741–50.

Tieszen, L. L. and Chapman, M. 1992. Carbon and nitrogen isotopic status of the major marine and terrestrial resources in the Atacama Desert of northern Chile. In *Proceedings of the I World Congress on Mummy Studies*, vol. 1, 409–25. Santa Cruz de Tenerife: Museo Arqueológico y Etnográfico de Tenerife.

Tieszen, L. L., Iverson, E. and Matzner, S. 1992. Dietary reconstruction based on carbon, nitrogen, and sulfur stable isotopes in the Atacama Desert of northern Chile. In *Proceedings of the I World Congress on Mummy Studies*, vol. 1, 427–41. Santa Cruz de Tenerife: Museo Arqueológico y Etnográfico de Tenerife.

Wakefield, E. F. and Dellinger, S. C. 1936. Diet of the bluff dwellers of the Ozark Mountains and its skeletal effects. *Annals of Internal Medicine* 9:1412–8.

Wood Jones, F. 1910 Mode of burial and treatment of the body. In *Archaeological survey of Nubia report for 1907–1908*, vol. 2, *Report on human remains*, ed. G. Elliot Smith and F. Wood Jones. Cairo: National Printing Department.

Mummy studies and archaeoparasitology

Allison, M. J., Pezzia, A., Hasigawa. I. and Gerszten, E. 1974. A case of hookworm infection in a pre-Columbian American. *American Journal of Physical Anthropology* 41: 103–6.

Ascenzi, A., Cockburn, A. and Kleiss, E. 1980. Miscellaneous mummies. In *Mummies, disease, and ancient cultures*, ed. A. and E. Cockburn, 224–38. New York: Cambridge University Press.

Bouchet, F. and Paicheler, J. 1995. Paléoparasitologie: présomption d'un cas de bilharziose au XVe siècle à Montbéliard (Doubs, France). *C. R Academy of Science (Paris)* 319: 147–51.

Callen, E. O. and Cameron, T. W. M. 1960. A prehistoric diet revealed in coprolites. *The New Scientist* 90: 35–40.

Cockburn, T. A. 1971. Infectious disease in ancient populations. *Current Anthropology* 12: 45–62.

David, A. R. and David, A. E. 1995. Preservation of human mummified specimens. In *The care and conservation of paleontological material*, ed. C. Collins 73–89. Oxford: Butterworth-Heinemann.

Deelder, A. M., Miller, R. L., de Jonge, N. and Krijger, F. W. 1990. Detection of schistosome antigen in mummies. *Lancet* 335: 724.

Desowitz, R. S. 1981. *New Guinea tapeworms and Jewish grandmothers: tales of parasites and people.* London: W. W. Norton.

El Mahdy, C. 1989. *Mummies, myth, and magic.* London: Thames and Hudson.

Millet, N. B., Hart, G., Reyman, T. A., Zimmerman, M. R. and Lewin, P. K. 1980. ROM I: mummification for the common people. In *Mummies, disease, and ancient cultures*, ed. A. and E. Cockburn, 71–84. New York: Cambridge University Press.

Moore, J. G., Fry, G. F. and Englert, E. 1969. Thorny-headed worm infection in North American prehistoric man. *Science* 163: 1324–5.

Reinhard, K. J. 1988. The cultural ecology of prehistoric parasitism on the Colorado Plateau as evidenced by coprology. *American Journal of Physical Anthropology* 77: 355–66.

Reinhard, K. J. 1991. Recent contributions to New World archaeoparasitology. *Parasitology Today* 7: 81–82.

Reinhard, K. J. 1992. Parasitology as an interpretive tool in archaeology. *American Antiquity* 57: 231–245.

Reinhard, K. J. 1996. Parasite ecology of two Anasazi villages. In *Case studies in environmental archaeology*, ed. E. J. Reitz, L. A. Newson and S. J. Scudder, 175–89. New York: Plenum Press.

Ruffer, M. A. 1910. Note on the presence of *Bilharzia haematobia* in Egyptian mummies of the Twentieth Dynasty (1250–1000 BC) *British Medical Journal* I: 16.

Sandison, A. T. 1983. Diseases in ancient Egypt. In *Mummies, disease, and ancient cultures*, ed. A. and E. Cockburn, 29–44. New York: Cambridge University Press.

Endoscopy of Mummies

Stanworth, P. A., Wildsmith, K. and Tapp, E. 1986. A neurosurgical look inside the Manchester Mummy heads. In *Science in Egyptology*, ed. A. R. David, 371–3. Manchester: Manchester University Press.

Tapp, E. 1984. Disease in the Manchester Mummies – the pathologist's role. In *Evidence embalmed*, ed. A. R. David and E. Tapp, 78–95. Manchester: Manchester University Press.

Tapp, E. and Wildsmith, K. 1992. The autopsy and endoscopy of the Leeds mummy. In *The Mummy's tale*, ed. A. R. David and E. Tapp, 132–53. London: Michael O'Mara.

Tapp, E., Curry, A. and Anfield, C. 1975. Sand pneumoconiosis in an Egyptian mummy. *British Medical Journal* 2: 276.

Tapp, E., Stanworth, P. and Wildsmith, K. 1984. The endoscope in mummy research. In *Evidence embalmed*, ed. A. R. David and E. Tapp, 65–77. Manchester: Manchester University Press.

Thompson, P., Lynch, P. G. and Tapp, E. 1986. Neuropathological studies on the Manchester Mummies. In *Science in Egyptology*, ed. A. R. David, 375–8. Manchester: Manchester University Press.

Population studies

Armitage, P. and Berry, O. 1987. *Statistical methods in medical research*, 2nd edn. Oxford: Blackwell.

Clayton, D. and Hills, M. 1993. *Statistical methods in epidemiology*. Oxford: Oxford University Press.

Miettinen, O. S. and Wang, J-D. 1981. An alternative to the proportionate mortality ratio. *American Journal of Epidemiology* 114: 144–8.

Rogers, J. and Waldron, T. 1995. *A field guide to joint disease in archaeology*. Chichester: J. Wiley and Sons.

Rogers, J., Watt, I. and Dieppe, P. 1990. Comparison of visual and radiographic detection of bony changes at the knee joint. *British Medical Journal.* **300**: 367–8.

Rothman, K. J. 1986. *Modern epidemiology*. Boston: Little Brown.

Waldron, T. 1991. Variations in the rate of spondylolysis in early populations. *International Journal of Osteoarchaeology* 1: 63–5.

Waldron, T. 1994. *Counting the dead: the epidemiology of skeletal populations*. Chichester: J. Wiley & Sons.

Waldron, T. 1996. Prevalence studies in skeletal populations: a reply. *International Journal of Osteoarchaeology* **6**: 320–2.

Index

Index

Index

Index

Index